THE ACCOUNTABILITY AND AUDIT
OF GOVERNMENTS

for

VAL

who helped

THE ACCOUNTABILITY AND AUDIT OF GOVERNMENTS

A Comparative Study

by

E. L. NORMANTON

MANCHESTER UNIVERSITY PRESS

FREDERICK A. PRAEGER, NEW YORK

Published by the University of Manchester at
THE UNIVERSITY PRESS
316–324 Oxford Road
Manchester, 13

U.S.A.
Published in the United States of America in 1966
by Frederick A. Praeger, Inc., Publishers
111, Fourth Avenue, New York 3, N.Y.

Library of Congress Catalog Card Number: 66–12160

Printed in Great Britain by Butler & Tanner Ltd, Frome and London

Contents

Foreword

ONE of the hardest problems about this book has been to choose a title. 'Audit' is a tough subject; therefore, let us have a tough title, which plays fair with the reader. But (on the other hand) the public—even the sophisticated political public—has little idea what state audit entails. Their interest is occasionally awakened by cases such as that of Ferranti and the Bloodhound contract; but it soon flags, because it is not based on direct experience of the work and function of public auditors. Hence (it was said) we need a dramatic title, which will draw readers in unawares.

The result has been a compromise. Like most big subjects in the modern world, the problem of public audit is in its essence hard, dry and technical. Nothing useful can be done except by grinding hard work, of a meticulous, even pedantic kind. Yet, the subject is explosive. Without audit, no accountability; without accountability no control; and if there is no control, where is the seat of power? Hence the trade of the auditor, private or public, covers a continuous spectrum; at the one end, routine checks of 'regularity' in the presentation of vouchers, at the other extreme a check upon the effectiveness of an instrument in relation to the job for which it has been designed. The humble process of 'tick and turnover' has little meaning except as the basis for a wider assessment of the honesty and efficiency of government agencies; that continuing assessment is one of the things we mean by public accountability, under any form of government. Yet great issues often come to light only because of scrupulous verification of details.

Probably all this is accepted everywhere as a principle of government, in the U.S.S.R. as in the U.S.A., in China or India as in Britain. Yet it is easier to look up in a library the practices of audit in ancient Athens or medieval England than to find a convenient account of contemporary institutions. This book is a new look at a very big and ancient subject, and Mr Normanton is entitled to some indulgence as a pioneer. His qualifications are however exceptional.

He entered the Exchequer and Audit Department straight from school (the usual practice of the Department) in 1939. After war service he returned to the Department, enrolled as a part-time student at Birkbeck College and obtained one of the best London University Firsts in History of his year. He had acquired incidentally a working knowledge of three European languages, and was a natural choice as a member of the audit staff of NATO, a job which set him to work in close contact with the audit departments of every country in the Western Alliance. In 1960 his Department released him to work for a period as a Simon Fellow in the University of Manchester; hence this book.

It is important that it should be judged first as a work of scholarship. Mr Normanton is extremely learned in a subject for which he feels professional enthusiasm, but doubtless he is sometimes in error, by omission or commission; and such cases deserve amplification and judgment, as much as if this were a treatise about the medieval Barons of the Exchequer, and their analogues elsewhere in feudal Europe. But, as will appear from the references, there are far fewer books about modern public audit than there are about audit in the Middle Ages, and Mr Normanton has been his own master in the difficult job of organizing a great quantity of factual material and of presenting it in a comparative form.

It was not Mr Normanton's business, as a serving civil servant, to prescribe reforms in British institutions. But probably, even if he had been free from that limitation, it would have been wrong for him to shape this book prescriptively. We have an audit system which is—within its limits—very good indeed. But it was designed in the 1860's and everyone who reflects at all about financial control in the 1960's comes quickly to the conclusion that difference of scale entails a qualitative difference, that our problems are not those of Mr Gladstone and the very competent Parliamentarians and officials with whom he worked. This is easy: but it is hard to recommend immediately practicable improvements. The debate is already in progress, and perhaps the most useful task for the academic writer at this stage is to produce not proposals, but food for thought. I hope most readers will agree that Mr Normanton's account of audit arrangements elsewhere casts a good deal of light on our own situation.

What has struck me most, in recent public discussion, is that there has been so much talk about audit and so little about auditors. Two aspects have been discussed very fully both by academics and by participants. Much has been said and written about what might be called the supervisory committees of the House of Commons, the Public Accounts Committee, the Estimates Committee, and the Committee on Nationalized Industries, and there is no doubt that the debate will go on (and may even lead to decisions) in the House of Commons. Similarly the Plowden Report on the control of Public Expenditure (Cmnd. 1432, 1961)—what may be called 'Plowden I'—has taken a vigorous view about the future character of the Treasury as a managerial department in the modern industrial style; and one characteristic of big modern organizations is that they plan for continuous 'feed-back' from executive agencies to the central control, so that the turn-out of decisions is quickly measurable in terms of cash and other resources employed.

Yet very little has been said so far of the auditors, the effective agents of the House of Commons and of the Treasury. One can perhaps sum up the lessons of international comparison, somewhat crudely, as follows:

1. In France and Germany, the equivalent of an audit office recruits partly by taking in young entrants from the University by tests which confer high intellectual and social prestige. To these it adds at a later stage men of recognized ability and experience in the public service. The body constituted from these two sources is a self-sustaining 'college' of distinguished public servants, and the highest appointments in the audit service go to people who have grown up within it. But the service is not isolated from the main currents of government and business administration, partly because of recruitment in the middle levels, partly because its men are in demand for other jobs, and may venture out from their base in audit and return to it.

This model is over-simplified—there are very substantial differences in practice between France and Germany; and it is not valid for all European countries, some of which have audit bodies which rank much lower in the hierarchy of prestige. But it offers a scheme for an audit body which is in the tradition of the generally educated public servant, yet maintains an independent character of its own.

2. In the U.S.A., the office of the Comptroller General is on the whole staffed by the same sort of people as serve as auditors and accountants in business. The job is done within a professional atmosphere which is common to all big American organizations; and it is quickly responsive to developments of professional opinion and technique. Mr Normanton could not be expected to say how good accountants in the American public service are as

compared with their colleagues in business; nor to give the rate of turnover in public jobs. These matters are important to the working of the system, but are not of its essence, which is to regard financial control, public and private, as a single professional job.

3. Contrast the British organization. The office derives intellectual and social prestige mainly from its head, who is a Permanent Secretary (generally a Treasury man) of long experience, holding this as his last office in the public service. There are a few posts in the Civil Service which rank higher as objects of ambition; nevertheless, he is one of the great men of Westminster and Whitehall.

He reigns, it seems, somewhat in isolation from his office, which is manned by what is in effect a special branch of the Executive Class. The main body are direct entrants from grammar schools to the Executive Class at VIth form level; there are a substantial number of promotions from the Clerical Class, a few additions from outside.

In normal conditions, this is a self-contained body, with its own internal seniority and promotions procedure. During the war, it served to some extent as a reservoir from which able people were drawn to expand the Administrative Class (they came also from Inland Revenue and from Customs & Excise), but nothing of this sort happens in the present period of promotion block, and promoted auditors never return to their old Department. Some members of the office obtain external qualifications, in accountancy or through degree courses, but they cannot readily obtain experience outside the office. Their office experience covers all government departments and is thus in one sense wide; but it covers virtually nothing not subject to Treasury control and to the traditional form of public accounts.[1]

An office thus constituted was in Victorian times a formidable instrument. Very able lower middle class boys were available at 16 or 18. The organization of the office gave them great independence, and this had social force behind it. These officials were not the same sort of person as generals or admirals, or Clubland civil servants, or government contractors. The Commons lent them power and prestige, and they were not reluctant to use them

[1] In general, audit of the accounts of public corporations is carried out by private firms of commercial accountants, but their role has always been very narrowly construed.

independently. A job still to be done is to write a centenary history of the office; without this, one can only guess, but I should guess that much of the system was built by able men of this type, who were not University men nor yet in the modern sense professional men. They established 'regularity', a great achievement in its day, as those concerned with administration in developing countries know.

The Civil Service Commission report that in recent years the field of recruitment to the Executive Class has been relatively satisfactory, and there is certainly no immediate crisis about the staffing of the Department so far as recruitment is concerned. But it is reasonable to take a fairly long perspective. Assume that the Robbins Report on higher education works out more or less as written; can we expect that in the 1980's the Executive Class will draw, from those who miss full-time higher education, entrants with the talent and self-confidence needed in audit work above a routine level? The probability that the answer is 'no' is so high that forethought is needed lest a historic office slip gradually into desuetude; and forethought should be taken long before the event, because it is a rule of the game that the prospects of present officers must be preserved. It is characteristic of organizations based on a formal career structure that they cannot be changed quickly, except in great emergency; the role of the independent observer is to criticize and make proposals, but within the limits of realism. Here are some suggestions for debate:

1. It will be remembered that 'Plowden I' proposed and secured quite radical changes in the form of the Estimates, but held up its (metaphorical) hands in horror at the form of the Accounts and passed by on the other side. So long as the present form of Accounts is maintained, there must be audit based on it, and every now and then points of major importance will emerge from audit directed primarily to 'regularity'. The traditional office will not find itself out of a job in the immediate future. But it may be bypassed if it cannot rise to a larger opportunity.

2. The front benchers on both sides of the House are reluctant to strengthen the collective power of the House of Commons against the government. But there have been during the 1950's a number of well-known cases in which internal financial control in government and public enterprise has broken down. Surely the point has been reached at which it would be tactically wise for the front

benches to share their responsibility with the House of Commons? This means in practice that in the 1964 Parliament front-benchers and back-benchers should take a hard look at the supervisory committees of the House of Commons—Public Accounts, Estimates, and Nationalized Industries. This can be done without raising also the much more difficult question of 'subject committees' for Foreign Affairs, Defence, Social Services and so on. It will be a difficult enough job to organize the talents of M.P.'s to work on the supervisory committees, especially if there is to be added a committee on grievances, to be served by some sort of Ombudsman.

3. There is general agreement that the Commons are constitutionally entitled and bound to supervise, and that success depends partly on their own organization but largely on adequate staff. It seems natural that the office of the Comptroller and Auditor General should be modified, perhaps by adding three senior assistants, so as to serve all three supervisory committees. It would clearly be essential that in the formal audit of accounts he should be backed by his existing Department. What more is needed? Surely Mr Normanton's book indicates that this is not enough? There is a function of financial scrutiny which goes beyond the scope of the existing office. How to handle this task should be explored undogmatically in the light of existing institutions and the availability of talent. For this exploration, it might be best to create a new unit, staffed partly by 'Treasury young men' and partly by experienced business accountants. This would not be an audit unit but an investigating team or teams; it would have no routine obligation to cover all the Accounts, and it would not be an 'enclosed' unit—there would be free movement in and out.

During 1963 and 1964 Treasury organization was being reforged on the anvil of 'Plowden I'. It was unusually flexible, even diffident, and too much should not be assumed from evidence given in 1964. Nevertheless what is written above could be fitted well into Treasury organization as it was then explained to the Estimates Committee (*Treasury Control of Establishments*, H.C.228, 1964).

The Plowden reorganization was essentially functional; one result of it was to bring together in one Division three different sorts of Treasury 'hunting-dog': the Staff Inspectors, the O. & M. men, and the automatic data processing men. These are all experienced Executive Class people, like the staff of the Audit Office. To them has been added a new and more speculative organization, the Management (General) Division, a small section, mainly drawn from the Administrative Class, which has terms of reference as wide and vague as possible. It has to find its own game, then chase it.

It is odd that both Lord Bridges[1] and the Estimates Committee forgot all about the Audit Office in this context: but there are the elements of a central team, which could be a tremendous force if organized for combined action, tactfully directed, and strengthened by support from the Commons.

4. To whom should such a unit be responsible? The Treasury would certainly wish to claim this as one of its own functions, and would be reluctant to see a relatively large staff (I am thinking in terms of perhaps twenty-five first line staff, with their assistants) established separately in the House of Commons. Need there be difficulty and dispute over this? The great strength of the Gladstonian system lay in the close alliance formed between the Treasury and the backbenchers in matters of financial control, and the object of reform should be above all to maintain and strengthen this alliance. Could not a self-contained unit within the Treasury serve the Comptroller and Auditor General in these new forms of financial control, and so serve also the House of Commons? 'Plowden I' implies some sharp comments on the ineffectiveness of the Commons as financial controllers: but in Whitehall every man's hand is against the Treasury, and the Treasury will not be effective as controller unless it can educate back-bench opinion and harness this political driving force.

5. How would such a unit be related to the existing Audit Department? In the first place a new Investigating Unit could not function at all without the present Department: they would be mutually dependent. Secondly, it is to be hoped that promising young men could be seconded from the Department to the Unit, both for what they could give and for what they would learn. Thirdly (and here we can only peer dimly into the future), it seems certain that, if 'Robbins' works, there will have to be a shake-up in the system of Executive Class entry within the next fifteen years, at the most. There is already quite a substantial intake of graduates into the Special Departmental Classes and into the Executive Class

[1] *The Treasury*, New Whitehall Series, Allen & Unwin, 1964.

generally. These are good average graduates, not exceptionally distinguished graduates: and they tend to be socially provincial in the sense that most of them are not much attracted by the idea of working in London and making their way in 'the corridors of power'. But there is much latent driving force to be found among them (most obviously expressed at present in the Income Tax Inspectorate), and if they come to dominate the Exchequer and Audit Department it will be a very different place. In fact, the time may in the end come when the Department and the Unit can merge, and at the same distant day we may have reached an accounting system designed and staffed for the control of effectiveness, not merely of regularity. One would then have a system of continuous control based on an alliance between Treasury and back-benchers and served by a strong Audit and Investigation Department manned by men of various talents and training, independent in function, but not isolated from wider experience.

'Gladstonian institutions' were not built in a day: they were hammered out step by step, over a period of at least twenty years, during which the educational system was also re-modelled. In 1840 the Civil Service was still in a sort of heroic age; there were giants in the land, but no system. By 1870, the pattern of modern administration had been sketched, though not filled in. It is realistic to assume that we cannot make the future more quickly. But the 1950's (as did the 1840's) have given ample warning of what the new problems are; the Parliament of 1964 has not much time to waste if it is to take a historic place as moulder of institutions.

W. J. M. Mackenzie

September, 1964

Preface

THE existing machinery of public accounting in Great Britain, under the sovereignty of Parliament and the management of the Treasury, is almost a hundred years old. It was established as a coherent system by Mr Gladstone's Exchequer and Audit Departments Act of 1866. So also was the post of Comptroller and Auditor General, chief public auditor of the realm, together with his staff in the Exchequer and Audit Department. Indeed, it seems that the ideas embodied in the Act were developed several years before 1866, the measure being retarded by the longevity of the Comptroller of the Exchequer, Lord Monteagle. In a sense, therefore, the British system of government accounts and audit is already a centenarian.

Accordingly, when Professors W. J. M. Mackenzie, Ely Devons and T. E. Chester asked me at Manchester University in 1957 to attempt a comparative study of the national audit systems of the United Kingdom and other Western countries, my first reflection was that a comparison of a historical and descriptive kind would be timely, especially as no such thing yet exists in the English language. Closer acquaintance with the sources and the facts led me to favour a rather different approach.

This was because I became aware of the existence of some impressive new institutions and procedures in certain countries of the West. Progress had also been made in Britain, despite the rigidities of mid-Victorian statute, which had scarcely been relaxed. It seemed, however, that the most important new developments were taking place outside this country. Prominent among these were the deliberate creation in France and Germany of an audit of administrative efficiency, and the ingenious arrangements for public audit of state enterprises in the United States and France. Countries beyond the Iron Curtain, and even a few this side of it, were also learning to use state audit as an auxiliary of economic planning. In these and other ways, solutions were being found for major problems of public accountability which had largely been shelved in Great Britain.

I therefore concluded that what was most needed was a study with emphasis upon the present and future. This was indeed appropriate, since most of the work was to be done under a Simon

Research Fellowship (1960–2) at Manchester, and the intention of Lord Simon of Wythenshawe when he endowed these Fellowships was to provide for work which might have a practical value. The historical side has not been abandoned altogether, but this study does not claim to cast new light upon the dark places (and they are many) of British administrative history in the nineteenth century.

The present work has two main subjects, and the first of these is state, or national audit, which is an activity *sui generis*, not merely a part of the financial control system but an important element of the constitution itself. It is also one of the most ancient devices of government; no state with the slightest pretensions to civilization has ever been without it. At present, since everyone is spending more and more public money, its techniques are in course of rapid evolution, an advance not expressed by an increase in numbers of staff, but by a greater sophistication in the application of audit to the whole process of government. My endeavour has been to describe this development, in law and practice, at home and abroad.

It is, however, impossible to consider state audit without examining the broad and controversial subject of public accountability, for without accountability there can be no independent audit, and (as will be maintained later in this book) without such an audit there is no genuine accountability. This, therefore, with its important political, administrative and financial repercussions, is a second but by no means a secondary object of concern in what follows.

* * * *

My subjects are not very familiar ones, and some account of what I have tried to do may assist the reader. In the first two chapters I have indulged in the luxury of theorizing about the meaning of two widely used but not always clearly understood terms, namely 'public accountability' and 'financial control', and about the part played by state audit in them. Chapter III introduces the state audit bodies of the principal Western countries and of several smaller ones. In the following three chapters, I have described the traditional function of state auditors, which is solely to confirm the formal correctness, the 'regularity'—as distinct from irregularity—of government accounts. As Chapter VI shows, however, state auditors have everywhere advanced beyond the narrow limitations of this ancient activity, often in an instinctive response to the new problems posed by government finance upon a revolutionary scale. They seek out waste and extravagance and assess the conduct of transactions according to the vital if elusive criteria of 'efficiency'. The traditional duties continue, but they have, in practice if not in theory, become a sideline.

This development is accepted in the present work as being greatly in the public interest, and the second half of the book amounts to an account and an assessment of its potentialities for public administration as a whole. Since it inclines towards new ideas and the future, this second part is on the whole more significant and topical (and perhaps therefore also more readable) than the first part. Chapters VII and VIII consist of an analysis of the published state audit reports of Britain, France, the U.S.A. and Germany. In the next chapter I have considered the modern phenomenon of the 'efficiency audit'. In Chapter X the work, status and qualifications of state auditors are examined. Chapter XI deals with the advances made by several countries in a highly controversial field, the public accountability of nationalized industries. Chapter XII contains thoughts upon the constitutional relationship between state audit on the one hand and government administrations and elected assemblies on the other.

The final chapter contains a brief survey of the most obvious lessons to be learned from earlier chapters, with emphasis upon such possibilities as they may suggest for administrative innovation in Great Britain.

The book makes no claim to contribute to the knowledge of auditing as the word is conventionally and professionally understood; it aims rather to show that in modern circumstances the word has a totally new meaning. I do not refer, except incidentally, to the audit of local authority expenditures. Neither do I deal comprehensively with the parliamentary machinery for financial control, such as the Public Accounts Committee and the Estimates Committee; this is a subject which has already been exhaustively covered, and in a book of distinction.[1] In one sense, what I present here is the essential background to the parliamentary control of finance—the work of the back-room boys.

I have preferred not to compile a bibliography, since such a thing would inevitably be more pretentious than valuable. The fact is that we are upon something like virgin academic territory. There are very few general works of substance upon those aspects

[1] Basil Chubb, *The Control of Public Expenditure*, Oxford, 1952.

of public accountability and audit which concern us herein, at any rate in Western languages. The state audit bodies have mostly been silent services, and if they have produced any published works outside the line of official duty, these have tended to be legalistic portrayals of themselves alone. A few of these are nevertheless good, and I have been fortunate enough to come across a considerable number of widely dispersed essays, lectures and miscellaneous articles, including some of high quality. All these, together with a variety of incidental sources, are listed in my footnotes. The lack of standard works has also had the consequence of obliging me to adopt a modest amount of technical phraseology of my own; where I have used words in a specialized sense I have explained this in text or footnotes. I have sometimes felt that we should ultimately replace the very word 'audit', which inhibits progress by the associations of its hum-drum past.

Every state has a magnificent façade, but, as with other façades, what matters is what goes on behind. That is where administration really lives, and there the state auditor, a privileged interloper, is in his element. Perhaps the description of his work may at the same time convey an occasional glimpse of the apparatus of the state itself, as it appears from behind the scenes. Here is an aspect of government which touches closely upon the mechanics of central power.

* * * *

My thanks are due to many persons and organizations. The state audit bodies of France, Western Germany, the Netherlands, Belgium, Denmark, Norway and the United Kingdom answered a questionnaire in considerable detail. I received help from various members of the International Board of Auditors for Infrastructure Accounts of N.A.T.O., for whom I worked between 1957 and 1960, and in particular from Mr Morris Chase (U.S.A.), Ambassador Arne Sunde (Norway), Monsieur P. Escoube (France), and Dr K. Reineck (W. Germany). Another member of the N.A.T.O. Board, Monsieur F. Vrancken (Premier Président of the Belgian Cour des Comptes), kindly provided me with the valuable papers of the Congress of Supreme Audit Institutions which took place at Brussels in 1956. I also received assistance from former colleagues in N.A.T.O., notably Mr Arne Johansen (Denmark), Messieurs F. Quaetaert and P. Tossijn (Belgium), T. Challa (Netherlands) and I. Erdogan (Turkey). My friend Monsieur Pierre Viot, Conseiller référendaire at the French Cour des Comptes, placed his wide knowledge of international financial control methods at my disposal.

For information and documents about American state audit, my thanks are due to the staff of the European Headquarters of the United States General Accounting Office in Paris, and especially to Mr R. Drakert.

During visits to the French Cour des Comptes, I was fortunate enough to be able to discuss state audit problems with many persons, including the Premier Président, Monsieur Roger Léonard, and the author of a learned work on French audit and financial control, Monsieur Pomme de Mirimonde, Président de Chambre. The librarian, M. Riberette, was an exceptionally helpful guide to the large library of the Cour.

For much help received at the Bundesrechnungshof in Frankfurt I am grateful to the late President, Dr Guido Hertel, and to his former Private Secretary, Regierungsrat Herbert König, who answered innumerable questions, both on the spot and by correspondence. Many other persons also devoted time to my enquiries; not least the interpreter, Herr W. Spahn, who initiated me into the complexities of German official terminology.

In London, I received valuable assistance from the O. & M. Division of the Treasury.

At the University of Manchester, my thanks are due to the Warden and Tutors of Woolton Hall for help and hospitality. Mr Gordon Neal of the Classics Department aided me with Greek and Latin translations. Several members of the Department of Government assisted me in various ways. My debt to my principal sponsor, Professor W. J. M. Mackenzie, for patient understanding and shrewd criticism is inexpressibly great.

The staff of Manchester University Press dealt assiduously with a cumbersome and detailed manuscript. Miss Jennifer Smith and others kindly gave up their leisure to help me with proof reading.

Finally, I acknowledge the benevolent attitude of my parent office in the home Civil Service, the Exchequer and Audit Department, which made this study possible through the grant and extension of sabbatical leave. I am also indebted to the ideas suggested to me by many colleagues, who must, by tradition, remain anonymous.

The text in no way represents any official standpoint but is purely a personal view, and the errors which may exist are the author's own responsibility.

In attempting to write about administration as I have seen it in N.A.T.O. countries as well as the United Kingdom, I have tried to bear in mind the warning recorded by a French civil servant, Gilbert Devaux, in the preface to his stimulating book, *La Comptabilité Publique*. He believes that a 'neutral' and legalistic way of writing may create 'a static and deformed image of administration', which is 'not a collection of uncomprehending cog-wheels in the service of immanent laws, but a living being.'

E. L. N.

London, 1964

CHAPTER I

Public Accountability

> 'To protect the treasury from being defrauded, let all public money be issued openly in front of the whole city, and let copies of the accounts be deposited in the various wards . . .'
>
> —Aristotle, *The Politics*

> 'Responsibility is null when nobody knows who is responsible'—John Stuart Mill, *Representative Government*

WHEN an official is holding or deciding upon the disposal of wealth which is not his own, opinion is likely to insist that he shall be fully accountable, in theory and practice. But there may be doubts about how, and to whom, he must render account. There is popular uncertainty about the meaning of the word accountability. In one limited sense, it means to give a formal statement of money dealings; the Company Acts in 'capitalist' countries provide for this kind of accountability in the relationships of directors towards shareholders. The idea that accountability means no more than this is widely held, yet hard to sustain.

To be accountable means, as any dictionary will confirm, to give reasons for and explanations of what one does. But a certified financial account rarely provides explanations, and it never gives reasons. It does not as a rule even contain much detail of what actually has been done. A final account must be technically correct and is therefore a device essential to the prevention of fraud. It is not, however, an adequate public record of policy and transactions during the period concerned. A financial account on any large scale hides far more than it reveals. The law provides that it may not conceal criminal sins, but any other kind of sin can and normally will be lost without trace among the headings and totals.

This is important because bodies exist which receive and spend public funds but which do not explain their annual accounts. They have them certified as the law demands, but the accounts are not subjected to a detailed independent scrutiny. They present a financial façade which in the present state of the law is impenetrable. Such bodies are not really accountable for the moneys which they receive. In the sense of a discharge of public responsibility, accounts without the possibility of explanations are to all intents and purposes worthless. They leave to the body concerned the administrative liberty to do almost anything, and then cover up afterwards. It would perhaps be less misleading to render no accounts at all.

I therefore wish, for the purpose of this study, to define public accountability as consisting in a statutory obligation to provide, for independent and impartial observers holding the right of reporting their findings at the highest levels in the state, any available information about financial administration which they may request. The *mystique* of formal accounts is a hindrance, not a help, to public accountability in this sense. The accounts themselves are no more than the basic guide for the investigation, the outline map of the whole financial territory. The outline must be filled in by systematic exploration; by obtaining explanations and documentation about all unusual features encountered.

This operation is public audit, as distinct from professional or private audit. The latter undertakes certification of accounts and it must ensure their technical correctness and the absence of fraud. Any other services which it may provide are private and confidential to the management from which it draws its remuneration. In consequence, no country has ever employed it for public audit, which demands complete independence of status and remuneration.

Public audit, or, on the national level, state audit, is a special device for making public accountability a reality. The state auditor acts on behalf of at least one public power deemed sovereign in matters of finance, whether that be an individual, a group, an assembly, or an abstraction called 'the people'. As far as the person or organization rendering account is concerned, the auditor is wholly independent and his voice cannot therefore be coerced or bought. The law requires that he be shown everything he wishes to see and told everything that he wants to know (where the law does not require this there is no accountability). His basic concern is with the proper conduct of financial transactions. But, as we shall see, his audit may invoke much wider responsibilities; the duty to act with reasonable prudence and wisdom, and even the duty to be reasonably efficient. There are of course other ways of securing accountability to the state, as by the political responsibility of ministers.[1] But the avenue of communication through state audit is a very important if sometimes neglected one, and it is this which concerns us here.

The idea of accountability is perhaps as old as organized government. It was highly developed in classical Athens and was a matter of pride and principle. 'I claim,' declared Demosthenes, 'that throughout my career I have been subject to public audit in all the posts I have held.'[2] 'In our great and ancient city-state,' said Aeschines, 'no holder of any public office whatsoever is exempt from audit.'[3]

But accountability is not the same thing in all ages; it depends upon the nature of the state itself.

The most primitive organization of government is a small unit under a tribal chieftain or king. When any kind of coherent local administration arises in such a realm there must be accountability. The provincial representative of the monarch must render account to his master for his acts, his receipts and his expenditures. A simple pattern of accountability develops (though it may not be simple in operation); it is that of a servant to his lord. We find such a pattern very clearly in medieval history, becoming more complex when the servant is no longer able to render account to the king in person but must deal with the royal auditors appointed to act for him. The principle, however, is not altered thereby; the state is a hierarchy and all accountability is to the head. We find that the same remains true under the absolute monarchies of the Renaissance and the Baroque Age. It is true once again whenever a tyrant, be he Emperor or Dictator, re-establishes the hierarchical state. All such accountability is consistent with secrecy. The ruler must learn what his servants have been doing, so that he can promote or punish; private persons need know nothing of the secrets and the errors of administration, and within unitary states they are rarely allowed to do so. Government is an authoritarian mystery. There is a historical connection between administrative secrecy and the hierarchical state.

It is not the nature of civilized and property-owning man to

[1] For the formal pattern of accountability in Britain see *The Accountability of Government Departments*, a course of studies paper published by the Administrative Staff College, 1955.

[2] *Speeches*, 18, 111.

[3] Ibid., 3, 17.

live contentedly in hierarchies. The broadest trend of state development from the seventeenth until the twentieth centuries was to break them down and distribute power more widely. A very important part of this movement was to distinguish a law-making function from an executive or state-managing function, and to confide them to different elements of the body politic. This was the idea of the separation of powers, which was not invented but merely codified by Montesquieu. It evolved before his time in the revolutionary England of the Stuarts. The result was the constitutional state, which for present purposes we may define as one in which an assembly, reposing upon at least a minimum of popular election, managed to secure a monopoly of the power to make, if not to initiate, laws. Such power could be Whiggish and conservative or Jacobin and radical, but in either case it was closely interested in finance. When the law-making power was dissociated from the managing power in financial matters, the old hierarchical pattern of accountability was upset. The managing power became itself accountable to the power which made the law in matters of receipt and expenditure.

The change was fundamental. Kings found that they had been down-graded to headship of the executive,[1] and that they could no longer make or easily sponsor new law. As the status of the law-giving assemblies rose, Kings became answerable to them for the financial sinews of power, at first for provision of the sinews and later also for their employment. If Kings could be made accountable, so much the more easily could ministers and officials. Finance was the yoke with which the executive was bound in service.

Meanwhile the separation movement, originally the device of an aristocracy anxious to share power and protect its interests, was extended in meaning. The earliest financial demand was for legislative control of taxation; the control of expenditure gradually followed, and with it the requirement of proper accounts. These had to be public documents, so that the ancient spirit of secrecy in financial administration needed to be broken. The idea of finance as a private dynastic secret was incompatible with the

[1] The term 'the executive' has several usages (e.g. in the U.S.A. it can refer to the President or a State Governor personally). In the present work it is taken to mean the sum total of 'the government' (the political headship of the executive) plus 'the administration' (the civil service, or that large part of it which is under the direct orders of the government).

constitutional state. The United States Constitution was specific that:

No Money shall be drawn from the Treasury but in Consequence of Appropriations made by Law; and a regular Statement and Account of Receipts and Expenditures of all public Money shall be published from time to time.[1]

The French Revolution went much further and proclaimed a doctrine of popular sovereignty over finance:

All citizens have the right to ascertain, either in person or through their representatives, the necessity for public taxation, to consent freely thereto, to observe its expenditure, and to determine its apportionment, its assessment, its collection and its duration.[2]

The pattern of accountability was now that of the executive towards the people, or at least the 'active', property-owning citizens. In practice 'the people' meant the legislature.

A wholly new dimension of financial control had been created by the separation of powers. The principle of legislative supremacy in finance was established, although at first only in a few advanced countries.

It remained to translate the principle into an effective mechanism of control. This was a tremendous exercise in administrative ingenuity. Financial accountability cannot be created by proclamation, as the French revolutionary assemblies discovered. It demands an appropriate structure of financial planning, accounting, banking and auditing institutions, with a regular routine for them all.

Some sort of forward planning in finance had always been a necessity for any kind of systematic government. But the preparation of a comprehensive advance list of estimated receipts, expenditures and liabilities, for a full year and for all the central activities of the state, was a concept and a task on a very different scale. The practical difficulties of compilation were formidable,

[1] Article I, Section 9.

[2] *Declaration of the Rights of Man and Citizen*, 1791, Article 14. (This is the first of many quotations in the present work from official and unofficial sources in modern languages other than English. These quotations are almost invariably given in translation, and an attempt has been made to render them literally enough to give some idea of the flavour of the originals. The French, the Germans and the Italians, like the British, each have their own special official languages, each with its own peculiarities.)

and yet such a list was essential as the basis of the financial law by which the legislature would establish its control.

This law came to be called the national budget, a truly revolutionary instrument of government. In Great Britain the word budget has come to refer specifically to the Chancellor of the Exchequer's annual statement to Parliament on budget day. In the present study, however, the wider meaning of the word is everywhere intended. A typical definition is that of the French Commission on Budgetary Reform, which began work in 1948:

> The State Budget is the law or the sum total of the laws initiated by the government, which accord prior authority each year to the government to make the expenditures and collect the receipts which are estimated or fixed by the same laws.[1]

This definition implies clearly that the executive can only initiate and execute the laws and that there must therefore be another constitutional element, a legislature, in order actually to make them. The modern budget was in fact a product of the separation of powers; in absolutist states the executive not only formulates and executes the law but also makes it. It was not, however, a development contemporary with the earliest manifestations of the constitutional state. It had to await improvements in general administrative standards. The development of adequate state budgeting, through trial and error, was one of the most durable, and by no means one of the simplest achievements of the nineteenth century. In many countries it was not adopted until the twentieth.

The importance of the budget for accountability was that it provided quite precise standards by which to judge the annual accounts. The whole sequence of events from the preparation of the budgetary estimates to the rendering and audit of annual accounts came to be known as the budget cycle, encompassing the entire life of national finance for a period of time. Accountability became a comparison of the accounts submitted at the end of the cycle with the budget laws made at the beginning, a check of performance against legislative authorization. It therefore amounted to supervision of the managing power, which executed the laws, on behalf of the legislature which made them. Accountability worked between the separate powers and through the budget.

[1] A. Le Henaff, in *La Réforme Budgétaire*, vol. 1, Paris, Les Editions de l'Epargne, 1954.

Of course, in practice few legislatures and executives were as 'separate' as those of the American Union;[1] in most cases they were able to influence each other in direct as well as indirect ways. In particular the executive retained strong powers of leadership within most legislatures. This did not invalidate the significance of the separation of powers for financial control and accountability. As long as the members of the legislature were not the simple nominees of the executive, as long as their corporate will was expressed with some degree of independence and was the sole source of law, there was a separation of powers. Legislative control of finance may sometimes have been a fiction, but it was a fiction so widely believed as to have the effects of a reality. And within the framework of the legislative budget cycle, a high degree of accountability was attained in Britain, France and elsewhere before the end of the nineteenth century. It was, as we shall show, accountability of a limited and mechanical kind, but its coverage was coterminous with the whole of the activities of the central governments. Everyone who handled the funds of the state was held accountable.

The legislature had an absolutely prime interest in effective accountability. This was not simply a matter of preventing financial scandals which could be politically embarrassing. Far more was it a question of power itself. There was little point in proclaiming the exclusive right to vote taxation if the executive proceeded to collect such levies and duties as it saw fit. It would have been a mockery solemnly to appropriate the revenues to chosen objects if the government then spent them with impunity upon other things. Firm restriction of the executive to the financial limits set by law was the vital key to legislative influence

[1] The Constitution of the United States included a much more extreme form of separation than Montesquieu, influenced as he was by Whig example, had ever envisaged. The British Parliament and its imitators are a special form of legislature, which is taken in the present work to be a generic term which includes them. For purposes of direct departmental administration the differences between the American and the British versions of separation are, of course, very great. But in matters of financial accountability and state audit they are in practice quite unimportant. Both the House of Commons and the House of Representatives faced, and still face, the same problem: how to make a large administration genuinely accountable in matters of finance to a numerous assembly of elected persons. In consequence the strict theoretical difference between 'parliaments' on the one hand and 'legislatures' of the American kind on the other may not always be emphasized in what follows.

over policy, as well as over the cost of everyday administration. The citizen believed that legislative control was his guarantee that he would not be arbitrarily or excessively taxed. In the decades before the First World War this firm control was achieved, and legislative power enjoyed a sort of golden age.

It was partly a matter of scale. Government was by present-day standards a modest form of activity and its proportions were manageable in terms of the 'classical', or Gladstonian, budgetary system. Economic doctrine as well as sectional interest favoured a low level of government spending. The state was envisaged as a mere consumer, that is to say a destroyer, of wealth; money could only 'fructify' in private hands. 'Economy', wrote J. S. Mill, 'equally preserves the existing stock of national wealth and furthers the creation of more'[1]—and he meant economy on the part of the state. National expenditure was an evil to be accepted only in so far as it provided essential services unobtainable from other sources, in particular the forces of defence and internal order. 'The avarice of the State', says Professor Maurice Duverger, 'is at the root of classical public finance.'[2]

Since 1914, if not indeed earlier, all this has changed. It is a truism that public spending has vastly increased; the experience is universal. Governments, their muscles exercised by the organization of gigantic wars, have entered the fields of public welfare and economic control and proved that they are not mere clumsy destroyers of wealth. They have in many countries acquired a large sector of industry and transport, formerly in private hands; although as we shall note in a later chapter, they have not yet learned to handle this with confidence. Governments engage in every kind of activity; they are the largest owners of productive power and incomparably the largest employers of labour.

Figures of national expenditures give some idea of the change of scale. The amount spent upon United Kingdom supply services, as recorded in the Public Income and Expenditure Accounts, was £39 millions in the financial year 1866–7, when the budgetary cycle had just been established in its refined form by the Exchequer and Audit Departments Act of 1866. By 1938–9 the

[1] J. S. Mill, *Representative Government.*

[2] Maurice Duverger, *Institutions Financières*, p. 27, Paris, Presses Universitaires de France, 1956.

equivalent expenditure was £775 millions. In 1955–6 it was £4,017 millions.[1] In 1961, expenditure by all public authorities combined had grown to £9,161 millions, or some 38½ per cent of the gross national product. Payments by the central government were about £7,720 millions, including £870 millions in the form of grants to local authorities.[2] In the United States, expenditures by federal, state and local governments rose from a total of about $1·5 thousand millions in 1900 to some $60 thousand millions by 1950. Even in terms of a dollar of constant purchasing power, this represents a thirteen-fold increase and it is a three-fold augmentation of the percentage of national income devoted to government.[3] American federal expenditure alone amounted to $517 millions in 1903, compared with $92,537 millions estimated for 1963.[4] In France the expenditures of the state totalled 5 thousand million francs in 1913 and 4,120 thousand millions in 1955; in terms of a constant franc this was a five-fold increase, and as a percentage of total national income, more than three-fold.[5] The statistical history of almost any aspect of government—for example the number of state employees[6]—tends to show the same sort of growth.[7]

This immense increase in the scope and cost of public services is the phenomenon which has been called 'big government'. The stresses and strains which this has created within the 'classical' budgetary framework are very great. Arrangements which were made at a time when governments spent money principally to maintain armies and navies of moderate size and to service the

[1] Quoted by the late Sir Frank Tribe, Comptroller and Auditor General, in an article entitled, 'The Exchequer and Audit Department'.

[2] Quoted from the current *Blue Book on National Income and Expenditure*, by *The Accountant*, 29 September 1962.

[3] Quoted by John D. Millett, *Government and Public Administration*, p. 9, New York, McGraw-Hill, 1959.

[4] Paper read by L. H. Noble, U.S. Deputy Assistant Postmaster-General, to the 8th International Congress of Accountants, New York (*The Accountant*, 6 October 1962).

[5] Maurice Duverger, op. cit., pp. 61, 65.

[6] See, e.g., the figures for various civil services quoted by Herman Finer, *The Theory and Practice of Modern Government*, p. 710, London, Methuen, 1954.

[7] For a systematic analysis of public spending in relation to the national economy, see Alan T. Peacock and Jack Wiseman, *The Growth of Public Expenditure in the United Kingdom*, Princeton University Press and Oxford University Press, 1961.

public debt, have been used without fundamental change to encompass major sections of national life. There has at the same time been a formidable growth in the complexity of social and technical problems which have constant repercussions upon public spending.

The administrative result has been a general malaise, particularly serious in the domain of finance. The imposition of vast operations upon a limited machine has had two clear results. There has been *a crisis of planning* and *a crisis of accountability*. It is the latter which is our principal concern, but the two crises are interrelated aspects of the same fundamental problem. They amount to *a crisis of the whole system of financial control*; this has been experienced in all the advanced countries, although not simultaneously.

The nineteenth century achieved a compromise between effective control and effective administration. But the small scale of government was what made the compromise workable. 'The whole Gladstonian system,' says Professor Chubb, '. . . was devised in and for a period of small expenditure.'[1] Since then administrative progress has been far less rapid than economic and social development. Weighty and serious questions must therefore now be asked. Has the balance of compromise been totally and permanently upset? Can its principles be adapted to comprehend the vast scale of modern administration and of the financial activity which it involves? Will those who work the old institutions be prepared to accept the adaptations and modifications necessary to the new scale of action? Or must we return to the restraints of the hierarchical state (as many countries have in fact done) in order to attain administrative coherence in the age of 'big government'? These are questions which vitally concern state audit, which in most Western countries is one of the institutions closely associated with the 'classical' budgetary system. They cannot all be answered here, but they must be considered, especially where they touch upon the issues of public accountability.

The crisis of accountability is not usually presented as a problem under this particular name. It is in fact the sum total of a number of questions, which are commonly dealt with separately. The most familiar of them are often discussed under such titles as 'the

[1] B. Chubb, op. cit.

decline of parliamentary control',[1] 'the control of nationalized industries',[2] and the matter of 'bureaucracy'.[3]

More ink has been used upon 'bureaucracy' in the twentieth century than upon any other question of public administration. The civil services of the world have been made the scapegoats for the problems of scale in government which we have outlined.

The subordination of administrative bodies to the traditional political powers did indeed become more and more difficult to achieve as the civil servants grew in numbers, and as the problems which they handled grew in complexity. A doctrine of political neutrality and obedience has been a help but not a solution. Academic debates about 'bureaucracy' have gone on in all western countries (and indeed in Communist countries too) for many years. There have been two fairly clear lines of argument. There has been a 'political' line, accusing 'bureaucracy' of non-cooperation, undemocratic tendencies, mushroom growth, narrow departmentalism and many other things. The conclusion drawn has been the need for more 'control'. The opposing 'official' line (and it has been an effective one), has been to represent politicians as ignorant amateurs and demagogues, interfering with the professionals for the wrong reasons. This argument implies that decisions should increasingly be taken within an official world which alone possesses the necessary knowledge. But others, including some civil servants, have hinted that amateurishness and lack of information may be characteristics even of that world.

This interminable argument is a symptom of the malaise arising from the conduct of 'big government' by forces designed

[1] See e.g. Dr Paul Einzig, *The Control of the Purse*, London, Secker and Warburg, 1959. Dr Einzig considers that Parliament's control of finance, as perfected under the Gladstonian system, is declining and should be restored. It is significant that he favours 'the spirit of retrenchment', as Gladstone himself did.

[2] See e.g. William A. Robson, *Nationalised Industry and Public Ownership*, London, Allen and Unwin, second edition, 1962. Also A. H. Hanson, *Parliament and Public Ownership*, London, Cassell, for the Hansard Society, 1961.

[3] The word 'bureaucracy' has three alternative meanings at least: Firstly, large-scale hierarchical and specialized organization in many kinds of activities, private as well as governmental. The classic analysis of this was that of Max Weber; secondly, the exercise of political power by officials, either by usurpation or as a recognized form of government; thirdly, as a term of derision for the real or imagined faults of official bodies, such as 'red tape', delay, over-caution, indecision and fear of change.

for operations on a small scale. For there has been little adaptation of the form of established administrative institutions in the twentieth century, and even less experiment with new ones. The commonest reaction to 'big government' has been merely to expand old public bodies. But the expansion has often upset the arrangements for accountability. New branches and auxiliaries of old institutions have tended to become increasingly autonomous in finance. At the same time, more and more public money has been granted to outside bodies for expenditure wholly beyond the traditional limits of accountability. Entire sections of national budgets, which formerly laid down a pattern for administrators, have been degraded to the condition of mere distribution lists.

The nationalization of industry, social security, and other elements of economic life has, of course, involved the creation of new institutions. But although public ownership was perhaps a bold political innovation it was not an administrative one. Insufficient thought was given to the problems of integration, and huge new public corporations have remained largely un-coordinated with the legislative, budgetary and auditing apparatus created in the 'classical' era. This has aggravated the crisis of accountability.

The separation of powers has in recent centuries been fostered deliberately in order to disintegrate government, in the interests of liberty. The danger in the age of 'big government' is that disintegration may have gone too far and become incoherence. Many institutions expect to be provided for in the budget although they are neither subordinated nor accountable.

A fresh conception of accountability is, nevertheless, evolving. It implies not merely the possibility of imposing budgetary discipline upon the accountable bodies, or of criticizing their errors, but also of contributing towards understanding of the general administrative process. The institutions concerned with accountability therefore need fresh consideration. The chief among these, if we exclude the legislatures themselves, is state audit. Our principal theme, accordingly, is the background and present characteristics of state audit in the principal Western countries, leading to an examination of its potentialities for the future. This necessarily gives rise to thoughts about the extent of public accountability itself; what organizations should be within its confines, and in which ways they should be accountable.

CHAPTER II

State Audit and Financial Control

'Some officials handle large sums of public money; it is therefore necessary to have other officials to receive and examine the accounts. These inspectors must administer no funds themselves. Different cities call them examiners, auditors, scrutineers and public advocates.'—Aristotle, *The Politics*

SPECIALIZED procedures for verifying income and expenditure were a very early historical manifestation of organized rule. The state auditor, professional or elected, was one of the first of all administrative technicians; in the Nile kingdoms, in Athens as one of the *Logistai*, or in Rome as one of the *Quaestores*.

Similarly, in the new civilizations of our European middle ages, we meet again with this inevitable official, ensuring that the state receives its due from its creditors and that its debts are being measured and met with exactitude. Henceforward, the development of audit follows the same phases as that of accountability.

For the proper governance of extensive realms, medieval kingship depended upon local magnates. The King's feudal rights in the provinces were largely a matter of finance, and the loyal administration of these rights required a regime of strict accountability for the royal representatives. The hard facts of geography, slow communications and the penury of banking facilities meant that such officials were simultaneously collectors of revenue, treasurers and paying officers. From time to time they were summoned to deliver up to the central government the balance of revenues which they held after paying the king's debts in their districts. In Plantaganet England these men were the Sheriffs of the counties and they were held accountable in the Exchequer. Richard Fitz Nigel, Bishop of London and Treasurer of England, in his celebrated *Dialogue of the Exchequer* (circa 1178–9),[1] explains with great clarity how the Sheriffs handed over King Henry II's

[1] The most recent edition of the *Dialogus de Scaccario*, is that of Charles Johnson. London, Nelson & Sons, 1950.

revenues from the counties, less the sums which they had been ordered by Writs to expend in the King's name, and how these balances were audited by the great nobles sitting in the Exchequer. Chances were not taken, and the silver pennies were even tested for quality by melting, before the Sheriff received his discharge and his account in the King's roll was cleared by the entry, 'Et quietus est', 'And he is quit'. If all was not well, the roll was marked, 'Et debet . . . ', 'And he owes . . . '.

The characteristic of medieval accountability was the direct responsibility of the individual servant to his King. The members of the Exchequer were the King's commissioners for the enforcement of that accountability. And since the King's Sheriffs were often magnates in their own right, the members of the Exchequer were, for their intimidation, the greatest magnates in the land.

The Exchequer, moreover, was a court of law. Its audit was a judicial audit, a form of procedure which has long passed out of English usage, but which still survives in France and elsewhere. In judicial audit the person held accountable appears as a defendant and must satisfy the court as to his conduct of finance in order to obtain acquittal. It is a system which can only be used effectively when the pattern of accountability is individual. Corporate bodies can be held accountable collectively, but not in a court of law.

In the Exchequer, says Bishop Richard, 'some come to sit and judge, some to pay and be judged'. How the system worked is described by a student of the Exchequer as it still was in the eighteenth century, in principle almost unchanged:

> The hub about which all else revolved was judicial audit of account by the Barons—the Trial of an Accountant. . . . In these audit proceedings the charge, so to speak, against the accountant was that of having king's money in his hands. The nature of his receipts, and the amount they ought to be, were proved by record in the court; and beyond this the accountant was on oath to disclose any other receipts. All this constituted the substance of the prosecution. The accountant then had to exonerate himself of the obligation to have collected any revenue which he could prove to be incapable of levy; he had to prove that he had neither disbursed, nor retained in his hands, any money otherwise than under sufficient legal authority; and he had to prove that he had delivered the balance to the king in his Exchequer. . . . If he cleared himself on these counts, the court acquitted him of the charge.[1]

[1] J. E. D. Binney, *British Public Finance and Administration 1774–92*, pp.238–239, Oxford, 1959.

A formal organization not unlike the Exchequer (and indeed probably influenced by the Exchequer of Normandy, which was attached to the French crown in 1202) was in existence in Paris by the reign of Saint Louis. In 1262 this great King ordered certain officials by decree to come to his Court and render account before the *gens de comptes*.[1] A decree of Philippe V in 1319 gave some precise form to the Chambre des Comptes of Paris, which was to have a president, seven maîtres des comptes and eleven clerks. From this foundation the present French state audit body traces an almost direct descent—interrupted, like that of all other corporate institutions, by the great Revolution.

The Normans, who seem to have had a special talent for this form of state organization, maintained a judicial audit, the Great Court of the Masters of Accounts (*Magna curia dei maestri razionali*) in the Kingdom of Naples in the twelfth century. In the following century, officials and ambassadors of the Venetian Republic were obliged to render account to the *Superstantes Rationum* (Controllers of Accounts). By 1320, Genoese public officers were held accountable by six *Visitatores*, wealthy men holding temporary office as auditors of state.[2] Many mercantile cities in more northerly parts of Europe had permanent auditing institutions—among them Basle, Lille, Nuremberg and Brussels. The Italian Court of Accounts traces its origin to medieval Chambers of Accounts in Turin and Savoy, mentioned in the Statutes of Amadeus IV in 1351.[3] Similarly, the Algemene Rekenkamer (General Chamber of Accounts) of the Netherlands claims ancestry dating from a foundation of Philip the Good of Burgundy, in the fifteenth century.[4]

No general history of these significant medieval institutions exists, although they arose at a very early date and played an important part in general administration. Audit was their common function, but they had a variety of supplementary duties. Many of them, like the English Exchequer, were also custodians of the treasury. Some of them were also regulators of the currency,

[1] Catalogue of the exhibition on the 150th anniversary of the *Cour des Comptes*, Paris, Archives Nationales, 1957.

[2] Onorato Sepe, *La Corte dei Conti*, Milan, Guiffre, 1956.

[3] Salvatore Sica, *Introduzione allo Studio delle Fonti relative al Controllo Sulla Pubblica Finanza*, Rome, Istituto Poligrafico dello Stato, 1957.

[4] L. Van der Tempel, 'Overzicht der Geschiedenis van het beheer en de controle der Openbare geldmiddelen in Nederland', (unpublished monograph at the Algemene Rekenkamer).

judges for various pleas, supervisors of usury, registrars of royal marriage contracts, treaties and other vital state papers, guardians of crown jewels and crown lands. The systematic control of finance and royal resources in the middle ages was chiefly entrusted to the judicial audit institutions. It was control based upon accountability.

In the sixteenth century the powerful audit bodies of the high middle ages entered a period of decline. This was due to the rise of new administrative and judicial bodies, for example the Cour des Aides and the Cour des Monnaies in France, and the Courts of Augmentations and First Fruits, which exploited the resources confiscated by King Henry VIII from the Church. This was also an era when royal councils gained greatly in importance. The new division of administrative labour was partly at the expense of the judicial audit institutions, which lost many of their interesting and valuable miscellaneous duties.

The medieval audit bodies had by now acquired set routines and a reputation for slow and cumbrous procedure. Rabelais made merry at the expense of the Chambre des Comptes of Paris; Pantagruel found its eating and drinking habits extravagant, and Panurge laughed at its technical jargon and the exaggerated secrecy of its deliberations. The office of Premier Président in the Chambre became the hereditary monopoly of the single family of de Nicolai, and this continued from generation to generation until the French Revolution, which made an end of the Chambre and guillotined the last de Nicolai. The English Exchequer was by the eighteenth century in equally low repute, and Lord North, no reforming genius himself, described its procedures as 'old and obstinate'.[1]

> Like the laws of the Medes and the Persians, the Exchequer's practices changed not, and it required an Act of Parliament to tamper with its organization, or even with so trivial a matter as superseding its traditional form of acquittance for money received, the anachronistic and preposterous wooden tally.... The Exchequer was hamstrung by the force of its non-statute law, and could not bring itself up to date even if it had wished to do so—which it is very evident that its permanent officials did not wish.[2]

There was in the later eighteenth century widespread awareness of a crisis of accountability, though one different and simpler in

[1] Quoted by Binney, op. cit., p. 237.

[2] Ibid., pp. 4–5.

form than that of the present day. In England, the public became conscious of the existence of administrative anomalies, corruption, highly remunerative sinecure offices, and large expenditures which were not accounted for. The novelty was not in the abuses themselves, which were ancient, but in a new kind of public opinion about them. This was the movement for Economical Reform, associated with the name of Edmund Burke. It brought about an important measure of administrative reform two generations before political reform became possible. In the process, the old Exchequer lost its constitutional monopoly of audit. In 1780, six Commissioners were appointed by Act of Parliament, with powers to recommend improvements in the system of issuing and accounting for public funds.[1] In 1785, an 'Act for the better examining and auditing of the Public Accounts of this Kingdom',[2] was passed. This vested the powers and duties of two important Exchequer officials, the joint Auditors of the Imprests,[3] in five Commissioners for Auditing the Public Accounts, holding office during good behaviour. The Commissioners were less independent of the Treasury than the old Exchequer audit had been, and they did not yet conduct an audit on behalf of Parliament. But their office organization was a little more modern and much less costly than that of the Auditors of the Imprests, and it survived, whereas the remains of the Exchequer fell away and by 1834 had ceased to exist as part of the machinery of public finance. Judicial audit was quite soon a thing of the past.

In France the eighteenth-century crisis of accountability was so grave as to form one of the most important causes of the Revolution. The ruin of the Royal finances and the chaotic state of the accounts form a well-known story. Several attempts were made by the revolutionaries to improve the situation by the creation of new auditing organizations after the suppression of the Chambres des Comptes[4] in 1791. The enthusiasts of that year proclaimed the

[1] 20 Geo. III, c. 54. The Commission was renewed annually by Acts until 1787, by which time it had submitted 15 reports containing proposals for improving the public services. Its powers then lapsed.

[2] 25 Geo. III, c. 52.

[3] The Auditors of the Imprests were in fact themselves sinecurists and the value of their emoluments is revealed by the level of compensation granted to them when they vacated their offices—no less than £7,000 a year each for life (Binney, op. cit., p. 204).

[4] There had been a dozen independent Chambres des Comptes in the French provinces, in addition to the Chambre des Comptes of Paris.

principle that 'the National Legislative Assembly will itself examine and finally verify the accounts of the Nation'. A *bureau de comptabilité* was established to help,[1] but the operation was not a success. The Cour des Comptes was created in 1807[2] by the great Napoleon, and charged with a judicial audit of the old type.[3] It was, however, responsible for audit throughout France; the old provincial Chambres were not re-established.

The budget cycle under legislative control was an idea already current in the eighteenth century, but it was not achieved until well into the nineteenth. The French revolutionaries failed to develop the necessary administrative technique. The British Parliament had long asserted its claim to vote taxation and had frequently intervened in finance in various other ways. But a permanent control through budget and audit was not yet in existence in the year of Waterloo.

Progress in the new direction was at first more rapid in France than Britain, even though the Cour des Comptes was not intended by its creator to serve as the agent of an elected assembly. Its primary duties were to judge the accounts rendered by public accountants (*comptables publics*)[4] in all parts of France, and to submit a confidential report to the Emperor. After the Bourbon Restoration, however, a system of parliamentary control of finance grew up with surprising rapidity;[5] the Bourbons were aware of the part which financial chaos had played in the events leading up to 1789. But if Parliament was to obtain the assistance of the Cour des Comptes, serious practical difficulties had to be faced.

[1] Decree of 17–29 September 1791.

[2] Law of 16 September 1807.

[3] The idea expressed by Binney (op. cit., pp. 256–7) that the creation of a judicial audit in 1807 was a 'reform' of the Chambre des Comptes, 'carried out with an eye to the proved English system', is quite wrong. The Chambres des Comptes had in fact conducted a judicial audit for many centuries. They were not 'reformed' in 1807, since they had been abolished sixteen years previously. There is no evidence of any English influence behind the foundation of the Cour des Comptes. The influence of the Exchequer on French institutions was felt in the thirteenth not the nineteenth century (by which time it was scarcely in a fit state to influence anybody).

[4] The term *comptable public* means quite simply a public accountant, but the French *comptable* is a characteristic national phenomenon, a member of a fiscal service which has no real counterpart elsewhere and which is represented even in small villages. I have therefore preferred to retain this official's French title throughout the present work.

[5] *Ordonnances* of 14 September 1822, 10 December 1823 and 9 July 1826.

These arose partly from the development of ministries, great hierarchical groupings which had scarcely existed in a recognizable form in the eighteenth century. It was they, rather than individual officials, which were to set the problems of accountability for the future. They could not be subjected to judicial audit. By the eighteen-twenties, French ministers were producing their own set of central accounts, although the actual payments were made on their behalf by the *comptables publics*, who were subject to the audit jurisdiction of the Cour des Comptes. In order to verify the ministerial accounts for Parliament, the Cour evolved a complicated and ingenious system of reconciling them with the accounts of the *comptables*, which dealt with the same moneys but presented them in quite a different form. The *comptables* themselves were made strictly responsible for verifying the legal validity of payment orders received by them from the ministries. They had also to confirm, before complying with the orders, that credits legally voted were available and unspent. Thus the *comptables* became a check upon the ministries, and if they failed in this duty they were answerable in person to the Cour.

In 1832, when the Orleanist monarchy had replaced the Bourbons, the annual report of the Cour des Comptes was for the first time submitted to the Chambers, and by that year the state audit body performed several regular services in support of the legislative control of the budget. This was the greatest advance in the techniques of the Cour until the thirties of the twentieth century.[1] But the new procedures were slow in operation and at best a compromise. The Cour des Comptes was never to become a parliamentary audit in a full sense. In the nineteenth century it inclined towards the elected assembly rather than towards the executive, and it gained in influence as a result. Its essential characteristic, however, was a proud judicial independence, dedicated to a task of financial control, as the servant only of 'the nation'.

Immediately after the achievement of Belgian independence in 1830, the Brussels parliament created a Cour des Comptes designed specifically to sustain its own control of finance rather than to copy the independent magnificence of the Napoleonic Cour. The budgetary system of Belgium established in the

[1] The French 'classical' system of budgetary control, accounting and audit was codified in a long decree dated 31 May 1862, some of whose articles are still in force.

mid-nineteenth century[1] was an extreme example of the new type of financial control based upon the separation of powers.

Everything pointed to a similar development in Great Britain. As from 1832 a system grew up under which departmental accounts covering the expenditure of voted moneys ('appropriation accounts') were audited and compared with the estimates by the Commissioners for Auditing the Public Accounts, who reported the result to the House of Commons.[2] The basic elements of the 'classical' budgetary system were already in existence before the establishment of the Public Accounts Committee in 1861 and the office of Comptroller and Auditor General in 1866. The Exchequer and Audit Departments Act of the latter year was, nevertheless, the greatest achievement of the classical budget movement. The Comptroller and Auditor General was an independent officer combining the old duties of the Comptroller General of the Exchequer with those of the Commissioners for Auditing, and his audit was to be 'on behalf of the House of Commons'.[3] Many details of his audit, however, continued to be associated with the Treasury, and the British state audit was less exclusively the instrument of Parliament than has sometimes been supposed.

As a general system, supervision of the legislative budget by state audit had several advantages. There was the obvious one of upholding the financial supremacy of the legislature through the budgetary laws. Enforcement of these vital acts was a special problem, outside the competence of the police and the ordinary law-courts. Budgetary offences were not crimes unless they also involved fraud. Their traces were hidden in the immense paper records which are the inevitable monuments of administrative action. Legislatures had therefore turned to the state auditors for enforcement services.

Another advantage was that by serving representative assemblies the state auditors themselves became more independent of the executive and therefore more courageous as critics.

Moreover, the whole arrangement was satisfactory for the audit of ministries, which were impervious to the old judicial

[1] Loi sur la Comptabilité de l'Etat, dated 15 May 1846, as expanded and clarified by a Royal Order dated 10 December 1868 (Règlement Général sur la Comptabilité de l'Etat).

[2] The innovation was made by the Navy Accounts Act, 1832. It was adopted for War Office and Ordnance Office Accounts in 1846, the Office of Woods and Works in 1851 and the Revenue Departments in 1861.

[3] E. & A. Depts. Act, 1866, Sections 5 and 27.

methods. The growth of ministerial departments in the nineteenth century was not the least among the factors which gave rise to classical budgeting; without it the problem of their collective accountability would have been a very serious one. The state no longer needed to work through magnates in remote provinces. New railways, new Morse telegraphs, new banks and new accounting techniques had abolished the independent remoteness of dispersed officialdom and created a taut new administrative world in which fraud faced new difficulties and risks. Ministries had taken the local money-handling officers in hand and made them part of a pyramidal structure of departmental chiefs. They had become underlings, appropriately supervised and inspected. The problem of the legislative power, and so the main problem of state audit in the new constitutional landscape, was ultimately how to control the ministries themselves.

This was also a problem for the leadership of the executive power; some great ministries were given to the insubordination of the over-mighty. The budget cycle was not only a device which kept the executive as a whole in its place, but also one which harnessed the ministries in the service of the heads of the executive who framed and initiated the budgets. The fact that these documents were given due form of law by the parliaments gave them much greater weight than if they had merely been direct instructions to the ministries.[1] And the whole cunningly contrived system depended for its effectiveness upon the surveillance provided by state audit.

In all its essentials the system still survives. It was not adopted in the United States of America until 1921,[2] nor in Germany until 1922.[3] By that time it had become widely generalized in the West and was supported by a body of academic theory.[4] It is the strain

[1] In Britain, the Treasury as well as Parliament gained greatly in power and influence as the result of the budgetary system of 1866, which translated vague prerogatives into effective authority. The budget cycle everywhere tended to exalt the authority of the Ministries of Finance, although in some countries this was kept in check by the resolute jealousy of rival Departments.

[2] Budget and Accounting Act, 1921.

[3] Reichshaushaltsordnung (Reich Budgetary Law), 1922, in implementation of an intention expressed in the Constitution of the Weimar Republic, 1919, which adopted the principle of the legislative budget cycle in Articles 85, 86 and 87.

[4] Perhaps the best known theorist of the classical budget period was

placed upon this classical system by 'big government' which creates the crisis of accountability today. There are problems of *scope* and *quality*. We have seen how well the classical system serves for the control of ministries; it will not, however, serve as well in the case of nationalized industries.[1] For them, as also for miscellaneous grant-aided and semi-autonomous bodies, it has in a number of countries conspicuously failed as a framework of accountability. This does not mean that failure is inevitable. It means that the bonds of the budgetary cycle need to be freely adjusted where at present they do not fit at all. The budget is a device of absolutely basic administrative importance and its supersession by an alternative is at present scarcely thinkable. But the budget cycle is too rigid, and those public services which do not fit readily within it tend to escape accountability altogether. This is the problem of *scope*.

The other problem is that the *quality* of accountability achieved in the classical age is inadequate by modern standards. The purpose in the nineteenth century was to permit the application of a strictly limited set of disciplinary rules to the departments which rendered accounts. They were not to spend money for illegal or unauthorized purposes. They were to observe common regulations for accounting and financial procedure. They were to keep accounts correctly and honestly. Above all they were to comply with the budget and spend within its limits. These standards, which we summarize here under the general term of 'regularity', are still necessary to sustain the budgetary system.[2] They are nevertheless merely negative standards. An audit which concerns itself with nothing but 'regularity' is a narrow routine, totally un-

---

Gaston Jèze whose *Théorie générale du budget* was written before the First World War. Other notable works included, in England, Durell and Harris, *The Principles and Practice of the System of Control over Parliamentary Grants*, 1917, and in Germany, F. Neumark, *Der Reichshaushaltsplan*, Jena, 1929.

[1] The orientation of the classical system towards the control of ministries is demonstrated by the widespread assumption that if nationalized enterprises are to become accountable they must abandon the structure of public corporations and adopt an organization similar to that of traditional administrative departments. But, as we shall see in a later chapter, this does not necessarily follow; compromise is possible.

[2] Although exemptions from some of the rules of budgetary regularity (notably those of strict compliance with the budget and with common regulations) are possible, and indeed necessary, if we are to bring bodies of an exceptional character, such as nationalized corporations, within the scope of accountability at all. Of this there will be more said in later chapters.

helpful to the operations of government in any constructive sense. It does not provide the information and lessons about administrative operations which should be by far the most vital product of accountability. It does not concern itself with such valuable notions as the merit and economy of transactions, or the efficiency of administrative organizations. These criteria provide the basis of a vastly improved *quality* of accountability, which is the new concern of all the major state audit bodies in the age of 'big government'. It is also a major theme in our later chapters.

Before we proceed to those chapters, some examination of terminology is necessary. In particular we need to understand more of what is meant by the vague notion of 'financial control', and the part which state audit plays in it.

Our concern is with the 'control' of administrative activity. 'Control' is a word of elusive definition, and it is enough here to say that persons engaged upon it are not usually charged with direct and positive administrative duties and that they have some powers of guidance, restraint or criticism over those who are. 'Control' exists '*internally*', within the executive: for example in the form of 'internal' audit services inside public departments. Control by Finance Ministries is 'internal' in terms of the executive as a whole. But legislatures and state audit bodies are not part of the executive, and their control is therefore '*external*'. By extension, public opinion is also a sort of external control. The characteristics of internal and external control are necessarily different. The former is a confidential service to the administrative and political heads of departments. The latter is independent and critical.[1]

Financial control is a very important special kind of control. But the term, in its governmental application, has been loosely used, and in consequence misunderstood. It has been popularly taken to mean 'the financial prerogative of the legislature', or alternatively 'the duties of the Ministry of Finance'. In some countries it is used as synonymous with the activity of the state audit body. In fact, of course, financial control is not a private function but a complex series of combined operations, involving legislature, Finance Ministry, state auditors and other groups as

[1] We are speaking always of countries with a separation of powers. In hierarchical states the distinction between internal and external control would have little or no meaning.

well. It is the sum total of the work which guides, directs and interprets the budget cycle.

Financial control is capable of analysis on the basis of the chronology of budgetary operations. For purposes of this analysis the decisive moment in the life history of any single transaction is that in which it results in a payment[1] from public funds. All the activity of control before that moment was *a priori control*, and all after it is *a posteriori control*.

These terms can be translated into more meaningful language by saying that financial control passes through *a planning phase* before the time of payment and through *an accountability phase* thereafter. The planning phase, during which the nature of future transactions is decided, sets the framework for accountability. After payment there will be a general investigation and a comparison of actual performance with the planned framework; this is the accountability phase.[2] In a well-ordered and modern system the findings of the second phase contribute substantially towards the pattern of future planning phases. For financial control, like the budgetary system, is a continuous series of recurring cycles. The old idea that a critical examination of completed transactions is 'sterile' does not take into account the cyclical nature of financial control. Just as accountability follows planning, so also it precedes future planning. The machinery of government has not always been designed to take advantage of this; accountability has been conceived in terms of an historical operation. The end of the accountability phase remains the weakest point, or even a real gap, in the financial control cycle. The planning phase is conducted by separate authorities which do not seek the views of those who have learned the lessons of accountability. Valuable experience is wasted.

In general, every transaction requires at least a double authorization during the planning phase. It is not sufficient for a payment

[1] Or a receipt of income. Financial control works both ways, but is perhaps more readily understood on the expenditure side.

[2] The accountability phase is, historically speaking, the senior phase of financial control, which was not always a cyclical operation. For example, there was scarcely any planning phase in twelfth century England, as the *Dialogus* shows. Most of the Sheriffs' business was a perpetual administration of the King's feudal rights, although they received occasional Writs instructing them to transact individual items of business. Financial control on behalf of the King consisted almost wholly in the accountability of the Sheriffs to the royal Exchequer.

to be covered by budgetary authority only. It should also fall within the scope of general policy legislation,[1] the financial elements of which are incorporated annually into budgets. There may, in addition, be prior approval, by decree or letter, of individual policies, commitments or activities within the broad boundaries of legislation; this is the most important single element of traditional 'Treasury control' in the United Kingdom.[2] There may, finally, be a last-minute control before payment, either by a public *comptable*, as in France, or by state audit in Italy and Belgium. The responsible department will in any case make its own check internally.

The planning phase, whether in the authorization of financial policies or the preparation of budget estimates, is an 'internal' control operation of the executive. The actual legislative process for both policy laws and money bills is, however, an 'external' control, and therefore subject to publicity.

Accountability is mainly a matter of external control. The record of a new payment or receipt will usually, however, come first to the notice of internal audit within the department concerned.[3]

Thereafter, the transaction comes under the scrutiny of state audit and thus of external control. In the age of the classical budgetary system, its duty was the enforcement of 'regularity', and little else.

It is a curious paradox that the classical age was also the period of lowest prestige for the functions of state audit.[4] It was the planning phase of financial control which gained enormously in importance from the evolution of the budgetary system. This system was conceived by the planning authorities in both execu-

[1] Transactions (for example, the payment of pensions) may of course be based upon policy legislation which is many years old. In this sense, the planning phase of financial control is a long-term process—much longer than the budget cycle. The same is true if—as in countries with planned economies—each annual budget amounts to a fragment of a general plan covering a number of years.

[2] According to Professor Samuel H. Beer, *Treasury Control*, p. 36, Oxford, 1957.

[3] Internal audit is chiefly a twentieth-century phenomenon. In the Gladstonian age it was primitive, where it existed at all.

[4] Distinction must be made here between the prestige of function, conceived in terms of the actual work of the auditing staff, and the great constitutional prestige accorded, for example, to the person of the Comptroller and Auditor General.

tive and legislature to be so automatic and infallible that accountability seemed necessary only to enforce their own decisions within it. It was not recognized that accountability and audit might have a positive role to play in financial control. The cyclical nature of such control was scarcely perceived. The auditor was essentially a mere policeman, not a contributor of constructive ideas.[1] 'Big government' requires a more balanced type of financial control, in which the consequences of planning decisions may be understood through the findings of the accountability phase. This demands a restoration of due dignity to the tasks of state audit. Yet according to the law in a number of countries, its concern is still confined to 'regularity'.

Here we have a starting point for our further study. For the law in such countries has lost touch with the facts. It is still living in the classical age, whereas the state audit bodies are perforce confronted with the problems of 'big government'. We shall find that they have been compelled to adapt their activities and move onwards from the limitations of regularity in spite of the law. It is precisely in the countries which first developed the classical system that the statutes of audit are furthest from modern realities—which is perhaps natural enough. We shall see that countries such as the United States which adopted the budget cycle in the twentieth century have audit statutes of a very much broader kind, covering the ideas of merit, economy and efficiency in financial business.

The continued existence of outdated statutes is a hindrance to the state audit departments which are theoretically governed by them, even though in practice they have been able to advance far beyond a mere control of 'regularity'. For their status continues to be thought of in terms, not of what they actually do but what the law supposes them to do—which is something far simpler and narrower than the reality. This in turn complicates the issue when new requirements arise which demand the attention of state audit. Such requirements, which derive from 'big government', have been the audit of nationalized industries and the control of administrative efficiency in public departments. We shall have to see how the various state audit bodies have confronted these new

[1] The development of commercial audit, which was contemporary with that of the Gladstonian budget, no doubt also influenced thinking about the role of state audit. In early private audit the only criterion, apart from profit or loss, was that of regularity.

issues, and some lesser ones. We must also examine how these bodies have adapted themselves and their personnel to the modern financial age. For the adjustment of state audit and its functions to the age of 'big government' is a prerequisite for solving the crisis of accountability. It is not the whole solution but an important contribution to it.

Nothing written here should be taken to belittle the achievements of the state audit institutions as they now exist. On the contrary, their achievements are all the more remarkable in that the statutes have often been a handicap rather than a help. The most valuable activities being carried on daily by some audit bodies are without sanction in law.

CHAPTER III

State Audit in Various Countries

'Who will correct the great?'
—François Villon

ONE may learn a good deal about state audit bodies, and perhaps a little about their countries also, from the buildings which they occupy in various capital cities.

The Exchequer and Audit Department

State audit in the United Kingdom is not directed from that traditional amphitheatre of officialdom which is Whitehall, where the ministries are set in ever-increasing circles around the stage at No. 10 Downing Street, and where nearness to the stage bears some relation to ministerial influence and power. The audit is housed far away, on the Victoria Embankment near Blackfriars Bridge, which is a quarter of London long associated with the law and the press, but never with the public service. Audit House is not very far from Somerset House, where the auditors were once located, but it is remote not only from the executive in Whitehall but from the House of Commons which the audit serves.

Audit House, built at the turn of the century, is a red brick building without pretensions to architectural distinction. The front rooms have an agreeable view over the Thames. The other rooms face inwards upon a well faced with a glazed yellow brick unrestful to the eye. Most of the interiors have a little of that old-world atmosphere of amiable disorder which is still one characteristic of British public authorities. Some of the desks are of venerable mahogany and on top of them are black 'round rulers', shaped like a stick of rock, which were official issue to a former generation and with which it is impossible to draw a straight line.

Before 1890, we learn from the old Office Rules, the public service was not over-strenuous. Officers of the then Directing Branch could choose whether they attended from 10 until 4 o'clock or from 11 until 5 o'clock and their annual holidays were at least 45 days. We also read that Registers were to be kept of both Black Ink Letters and Red Ink Letters and that, 'The several

Porters will wash the steps of the Office front entrance by turns, for one week at a time.' The spirit of Dickens, which then presided over life in English offices, is not even yet entirely banished.

This building is a headquarters first of all. The state audit in the United Kingdom is dispersed among the ministries and departments; this is one of its particular virtues. It speeds the task, obviates endless forwarding of documents, and above all greatly increases the possibilities of familiarity with the records and policies of the authority under examination. Wherever there are important contingents of the central administration—and some of these have been in the provinces since 1939 and 1940—there also are representatives of the Comptroller and Auditor General, members of the staff of his office, the Exchequer and Audit Department.

In 1960 this Department consisted, in addition to the Comptroller and Auditor General himself, of 430 persons engaged upon audit duties (including the Secretary, the Deputy Secretary, nine Directors of Audit and sixteen Deputy Directors), plus 79 persons with clerical duties and 26 messengers, cleaners, etc. The audit staff are organized into a conventional hierarchy of eight Divisions, each headed by a Director and dealing with a particular group of ministerial and departmental accounts, and an extra Division for internal administration. Audit observations are submitted through the hierarchical channels to the Director and thence, in the most important cases, onwards to the Comptroller and Auditor General.

This high officer of state has full personal powers of decision in matters of office business. The Exchequer and Audit Department is not a collegiate body like many state audit organizations on the continent of Europe. Significantly, Audit House has no conference room; procedure is based upon the British tradition of written minutes on the official files, rather than upon meeting and debate. Most of the Directors are housed at headquarters, which is the assembly point for major observations submitted by the audit sections all over London and the provinces. It is there that the most important matters are collated, in accordance with the C. & A.G.'s instructions, to form the annual Reports which are laid before Parliament together with the accounts to which they relate. The accounts are themselves certified by the C. & A.G., and when they come up for consideration by the Committee of Public Accounts each year he, or in his absence the Secretary, attends in an advisory role, to explain and amplify the observations made in his Report. The Committee and the successive C.&A.G.s have achieved almost a century of highly fruitful co-operation.

The French Cour des Comptes

The original home of audit in Paris was the oldest seat of royal power, the palace on the Ile de la Cité. At the close of the Middle Ages the Chambre des Comptes became occupant of a graceful late gothic building whose entrance stairway merged with that of its immediate neighbour, the Sainte-Chapelle.[1] This splendid office, which is familiar in many old prints, was burned down in 1737. Not until 1842 did the state audit, by then refounded as Napoleon's Cour des Comptes, find another permanent home, a great new colonnaded palace overlooking the Seine from the Quai d'Orsay. This home, which was shared with the Conseil d'Etat, was burnt by the revolutionary Commune of Paris in its death struggle in May 1871, together with the Tuileries, the Palais Royal and other famous buildings associated with conventional state power.

The present home of the Cour was built early in the present century and occupies a new site in Rue Cambon, in the midst of the patrician First Arrondissement, between the Rue de Rivoli and the Rue du Faubourg St Honoré, with its back against the Hôtel Talleyrand, which has housed in turn the German Navy and the United States Foreign Service. The large new office, built by the architect Moyaux and opened by Armand Fallières, President of the Republic, in 1912, has the prestige and solidity of a Grand Opera House, but perhaps less of elegance than either of the former buildings which were lost by fire.

It is here that the state audit of France is centralized; this is the address to which the accounts of *comptables* are ultimately delivered. They lie in heaps along the corridors of the upper floors, where the conseiller-référendaires and the auditeurs have their offices, with windows set too high in the walls to permit the distraction of a view outside. On the first floor, the carpeted *piano nobile*, and the second floor, are offices of a more diplomatic solemnity. There is a Grand' Chambre where the Cour meets in Solemn Session, the Premier Président and the Présidents de Chambre in ermine robes, the conseillers in black robes and white

[1] The Chambre des Comptes of Paris was given the administration of the Sainte-Chapelle, the private chapel of the medieval monarchy, by Charles VII in 1438.

lace. It is in Solemn Session, usually in the presence of leading personalities of the government,[1] that new members of the Cour bow to the four corners of the hall and take oath faithfully to fulfil their functions, to maintain the secrecy of deliberations and in all things to conduct themselves as worthy and loyal magistrates.[2] It is here that persons appointed to high office in the Cour exchange orations with the Premier Président. It was in the Grand' Chambre on 28 May 1957, that the Cour met in Solemn Session in the company of President René Coty, the Presidents of the Assemblies of Parliament, Paul Ramadier and Paul Reynaud, respectively Minister of Finance and President of the Finance Commission of the National Assembly, of three other Ministers and twelve Secretaries of State, of nineteen Ambassadors and three Ambassadorial representatives, of delegates from twenty-two state audit bodies in foreign countries[3] and of various leaders of the official and the academic life of France. On this day was commemorated the hundred-and-fiftieth anniversary of the foundation of the Cour des Comptes by Napoleon.

This stately ceremonial symbolizes several things. It represents pride in a tradition which, although directly descended only from 1807, draws its deeper inspiration from the *ancien régime*. It represents a survival of that blending of administrative functions with courts of law which seemed perfectly normal in earlier centuries. There is a note of the *noblesse de robe* about this *grand corps*, and its oath of secrecy is a conspicuous survival. After picturing the ceremonial, we read without surprise that:

> The *grands corps de l'Etat*, whose role is one of counsel and jurisdiction, are readily associated with similar institutions of the *ancien régime*. From them they derive nobility and prestige. Fundamentally their tasks are similar. To enlighten the sovereign, to state the law, to judge the accounts, these duties imply permanent conditions of independence, learning and serenity.
>
> To resolve immediate difficulties, to decide, to compel and to govern; these are the daily and thankless tasks of the active administration. . . .[4]

---

[1] In 1960 General de Gaulle attended and addressed the Cour.

[2] It is interesting to note that before the collapse of the Second Empire in September 1870, and again under the Government of Vichy, an oath of political fidelity was also required.

[3] The audit bodies of Great Britain and the United States were represented. So also were those of India and Australia.

[4] Albert Louvel, 'Grand Corps et Grand Commis: Les Administrations

We should not be wrong in inferring from the ceremonial a certain social solidarity of the French ruling classes. Since the Revolution this has been harder to observe and document than before, and more difficult than in countries with uninterrupted aristocratic continuity. In 1955, however, the results of a study of the social origins of civil servants in selected departments were published. In this the population was divided into six categories, *haute*, *moyenne* and *petite bourgeoisie*, peasantry, *classe ouvrière*, and proletariat. Remarkable findings were shown. In three ministries, National Defence (War), P.T.T., and Labour, there were no representatives of the *haute bourgeoisie*, even at the highest administrative levels. The Post Office (P.T.T.), with a staff of 191,000, had not even any *moyen bourgeois*; the entire personnel was descended from *petit bourgeois*, worker and peasant families. The directing grades, though not the lower ranks, in some other ministries were rather higher in the scale, with 5 per cent *haute bourgeoisie* at Agriculture, 10 per cent at Industry and Commerce, 8 per cent at France d'Outre-Mer, 4 per cent at Justice (which includes the law-courts) and 10 per cent in the Ministry of Finance central administration. Even the corps of prefects had only 10 per cent from the highest social group. But the two *grands corps* which were examined, the Inspection des Finances and the Cour des Comptes, each drew 30 per cent of their staff from the highest bourgeoisie, and the whole of the remainder from middle and lower bourgeois families.[1] The Cour has had many members whose names were patently aristocratic. The *grands corps* are an *élite* socially as well as intellectually, although the tendency of post-war recruitment methods is towards a social leaven based exclusively on merit.

The cultivation of prestige and traditionalism may in this world be negative and stultifying if it becomes an end in itself. In the

Centrales', *La Revue des Deux Mondes*, Paris, 1 January 1959. The quotation illustrates the French tradition which gives primacy to functions of 'control' rather than to those of active 'management'. The latter are largely confided to the corps of *administrateurs civils*, whose prestige and career prospects are markedly lower than those of the *grand corps*. The status of *grand corps* belongs principally to the Conseil d'Etat, the Cour des Comptes, and the Inspection des Finances, and perhaps also to the diplomatic corps. See also Chapter X below.

[1] *Parties et Classes en France*, pp. 116–17 (Assn. française de Science politique), Paris, Armand Colin, 1955. The study was carried out by the Institut national d'Etudes démographiques.

Cour des Comptes, however, it serves a definite purpose. Monsieur de Mirimonde, himself a Président de Chambre, writes that it is important to confer prestige upon the corps of auditors in order to give them authority in relation to the administrative services. Everything is directed towards this end. The Cour des Comptes is equal in standing to the Cour de Cassation, the highest court of appeal; irremovable status is guaranteed to all the magistrates; and since frequent contacts with departmental chiefs are involved, 'it is important that the magistrate who directs the audit should have, in the administrative hierarchy, a rank equal to that of the Directors'.[1]

The organization of the Cour is much more informal than is usual among official bodies. The younger magistrates are just as irremovable, and therefore independent, as their seniors. The members have considerable liberty in such matters as hours of work: ambition and *esprit de corps* appear to provide sufficient incentives and working hours nevertheless tend to be long. The Cour takes its decisions by various collegiate procedures after full debate, and this applies even to disciplinary action which might be demanded against a magistrate for alleged neglect of duty.

Audit work is divided up between five sections with the old title of *Chambres*, and is based principally upon two types of accounts. There are, firstly, the accounts of the receiving and paying officers of the *Trésor*, the *comptables* of France and its overseas territories. These constitute the customary audit material, but it is less important than formerly. More emphasis is now placed upon the second type, the so-called 'administrative accounts', which consist of a documentation of all decisions giving rise to a receipt or a payment. Their great advantage is that they are submitted separately for each ministry, local authority and other public body at home or abroad, and they therefore permit the auditors to specialize. Such specialization was scarcely possible prior to a reform carried out by decree in 1936, and the magistrates were disqualified from local audit visits until the Vichy government passed a permissive law on 4 April 1941. The modernization of the Cour, as also of French public finance generally, is a recent phenomenon. Under the Third Republic the

[1] A.-P. de Mirimonde, *La Cour des Comptes*, Paris, Recueil Sirey, 1947. A Director in a French Ministry is approximately equivalent to an Under-Secretary in Great Britain, namely the head of a major division of the whole department.

prestige of the magistrature was scarcely equalled by its technical progress. We shall see, however, how remarkable is the change which has taken place since then.

This change results mainly from the creation during the post-war years of off-shoots of the Cour to fulfil specialized but vital functions. The least important of these in practice is the Court of Budgetary Discipline, instituted in 1948[1] for the punishment of offences committed by administrators against the rules of public finance. Of far greater significance is the Central Committee of Enquiry into the Cost and Efficiency of the Public Services, which conducts the study of 'organization and methods' in France.[2] Very great interest also attaches to the Commission for auditing the Accounts of Public Enterprises, an original mechanism designed especially to meet the delicate problem of financial control for nationalized industries.[3] More will be said about these bold administrative experiments in subsequent chapters.

The Cour des Comptes is not a numerous body. At the beginning of 1961 the list of magistrates comprised 231 names, including the Premier Président, the Procureur-Général and 8 Présidents de Chambre. Of this total, 41 were on loan to a selection of important posts outside the Cour,[4] of whom 4 were apparently detached permanently. On the other hand 22 officials, mostly from the services of the Ministry of Finance, were attached to the Cour for audit duties. There was also a staff of 33 engaged upon general administration. In accordance with a tradition of the French civil service, some of the magistrates of the Cour give lectures in schools of the University of Paris, and others perform occasional advisory functions within the national administration.

Both the post-war Constitutions of France have made reference to the Cour des Comptes. That of 27 October 1946, used the following wording:

> The National Assembly regulates the accounts of the nation. It is assisted for this purpose by the Cour des Comptes. The National Assembly may charge the Cour des Comptes with any enquiries and

---

[1] Law of 25 September 1948.

[2] Decree of 9 August 1946 (See below, Chapter IX.)

[3] Law of 6 January 1948. (See below, Chapter XI.)

[4] For example, one was Minister for the Army, another was Delegate General in Algeria, a third was President of the Council of Administration of Électricité de France and a fourth was Assistant Director General of Radio-diffusion-Télévision française.

studies connected with public receipts and payments or with the administration of the Treasury.[1]

This text seemed to bring the Cour into a closer relationship with the legislature than it had ever enjoyed before, and a law of 8 August 1950 gave the Premier Président discretion to address findings of the Cour directly to the Finance Commissions of the National Assembly and the Council of the Republic.

The Cour, however, has always operated in the No Man's Land between the executive and the legislature, and has belonged to neither. The Constitution of the Fifth Republic, dated 4 October 1958, seems to accept this and states simply:

The Cour des Comptes assists Parliament and the Government in controlling the execution of the financial laws.

The Bundesrechnungshof (Western Germany)

The accounts of the German Reich of the Hohenzollerns were audited, under laws renewed every year, by the Supreme Chamber of Accounts (Oberrechnungskammer) of the Kingdom of Prussia, the greatest member state (Land) of Bismarck's Imperial federation. Each Land had its own audit body for internal accounts, but only that of Prussia was, in effect, also a national audit institution, bearing for this purpose the title of Court of Accounts of the German Reich.

After the First World War this Rechnungshof des Deutschen Reiches became for the first time the official and permanent institution for audit of Reich accounts. Its tasks, organization and procedure were laid down in the Reich Budget Law (Reichshaushaltsordnung)[2] of 31 December 1922. Its home was the Prussian Versailles, the town of Potsdam. There it occupied an old official building of neo-baroque solidity and dignity, half eighteenth-century dynastic seat and half barracks in inspiration, typical of a thousand continental edifices of state in the spacious days before Sarajevo.

Under the dispositions of the Reichshaushaltsordnung a parliamentary budget cycle was developed by the Weimar Republic. This was contemptuously distorted and perverted by the National Socialist government after the Hitlerian seizure of power in 1933.

[1] The Treasury (Trésorerie) is the banking and accounting service of the Ministry of Finance.

[2] Usually referred to under the initials RHO. It was this important statute which established full parliamentary control of finance in Germany.

The Rechnungshof des Deutschen Reiches lost some of its most fundamental functions in the process. The Rechnungshof, however, continued to exist throughout the domination of Hitler and his party until the final destruction and capture of Potsdam by the Red Army in 1945. The audit body then dissolved among the general chaos of defeat.[1]

A few of the surviving staff of the Rechnungshof were taken over by the German financial authorities in the Soviet zone. After the war the Länder of the United States zone (Bavaria, Hesse and the Free Hanseatic City of Bremen) and of the French zone (Baden-Württemberg and Rhineland-Palatinate) re-established independent Courts of Accounts, as they had existed before the centralization effected by the Nazi regime. But the nucleus of what was eventually to become the state audit body for the whole of Western Germany was formed in the British zone of occupation. In the ruins of Hamburg survived a branch office of the Potsdam Rechnungshof, and this in August 1945 received authority from the Control Commission for Germany (British Section) to continue its work, and to be responsible for audit in the entire British zone. An Order of the British Military Government, dated 1 December 1946, clarified the legal position. The Hamburg office became the Rechnungshof des Deutschen Reiches (Britische Zone), and the Military Governor assumed the rights which were attributed in the Reichshaushaltsordnung to the Reich President, the Reichsrat and the Reichstag. He was to nominate the President of the Rechnungshof and its officials and he guaranteed their independence from the German authorities which they were to audit by the provision that they were only to be removed from office upon order of the Military Government. The Hamburg Rechnungshof was to audit not only the budgetary accounts for the whole Zone but also, through local offices, those of the Länder (North Rhine-Westphalia, Lower Saxony, Schleswig-Holstein and the Free Hanseatic City of Hamburg itself).

This constructive piece of financial administration in the British Zone was noticed at the time by the Comptroller and Auditor General in the following words:

In order to improve the system of control of German public finances,

---

[1] For the history of accountability and audit under the Third Reich see Chapter XII below.

including the accounts operated by British officers, the Military Governor has approved the establishment of an independent audit branch to exercise, in relation to the German public accounts under British control, functions similar to those which I exercise in the United Kingdom. This branch will draw the Military Government's personal attention to any matters coming to notice which it is essential for the Governor to know, including any action which appears to involve improper use, or waste, of public money or stores whether controlled by British or German officials.[1]

After the fusion of the economies of the British and American Zones, the 'Rechnungshof for the Combined Economic Region' was formed at Hamburg in November 1948. This remained the principal audit authority until the creation of the Federal Court of Accounts (Bundesrechnungshof), for the whole of West Germany, by a Federal law of 27 November 1950.

The Bundesrechnungshof moved to the more central location of Frankfurt, and here a new building was erected for it, which was opened by the Federal President, Herr Heuss, on 19 February 1954. The new home of state audit in Germany is next door to the greatest monument associated with the liberal and democratic aspirations of the nation, the cylindrical church of St Paul, the *Paulskirche*, in which the revolutionaries of 1848 tried and failed to unite their fatherland as a popular and constitutional state. Whether or not the site of the Rechnungshof was chosen for its association with German democratic strivings, it is certainly historic German ground. Close by is the hall, the *Römer*, in which for generations the Holy Roman Emperors were crowned. So also is the carefully reconstructed house in the Hirschgraben where on 28 August 1749, a son, Johann Wolfgang, was born to Johann Caspar Goethe, Counsellor to his Roman Imperial Majesty.

The new Bundesrechnungshof is a set of three glass-walled, flat-roofed blocks of unequal height, in juxtaposition. The interior captures the light from every angle, and the impression of working in a pleasant greenhouse is enhanced by a great abundance of potted plants and by a surround of lawns. Lightness of construction, simplicity of fittings and the modest proportions of rooms reveal a regard for economy which was proper in the postwar years; but the building is well equipped with curtains and blinds to protect the staff against parboiling in the summer. When

[1] C. & A.G.'s Report, Civil Appropriation Accounts (Class X), 1946–7.

all the staff are present the assembly hall permits standing room only. There is an air of practicality, but there is neither space nor atmosphere for ceremonial. For the few whose experience goes so far back, there is a mural depicting Sanssouci and other famous buildings of old Potsdam in the entrance hall. But Potsdam, or what remains of it, is in the so-called German Democratic Republic, far more remote than most foreign countries. Many of the audit staff in Frankfurt were born and educated in the lands beyond the Iron Curtain, the truncated territories of the former Reich; the Bundesrechnungshof is nevertheless very much a part of the new Germany. The atmosphere of Hohenzollern Potsdam cannot be recreated, and there is little evidence of any desire to do so. In an address to his staff, the late President of the Bundesrechnungshof spoke of a hopeful and exciting future, in which they were fortunate to be able to participate. He was not, however, referring to the old German national ambitions, but to the Common Market and the new Europe which it symbolized.[1]

The work of the Federal audit body is mostly centralized in Frankfurt; but a good deal of local examination is done from time to time, as we should expect in a country without a permanent capital city. Bonn is, in fact, too small to house the whole administrative apparatus of the Bund, and this is dispersed among the principal cities. The Ministers have their headquarters in Bonn, but important subordinate departments may be elsewhere. The Federal Ministry of the Interior is, for example, responsible for the Federal Administrative Court in Berlin, the Statistical Office and the Criminal Bureau of the Bund in Wiesbaden, the Federal Archives in Koblenz, the Administration Office of the Bund in Cologne, the Federal Bureau for Acceptance of Foreign Refugees in Nuremberg, and so on. The Federal Constitutional Court and the Federal Court of Justice, the highest judicial bodies in Western Germany, are at Karlsruhe. The Patent Office is in Munich and the headquarters of the German Federal Railways—a public department—is in Frankfurt. The Second World War exploded the Berlin bureaucracy, and also the judiciary, which in Germany has many administrative functions. There is probably no other country where national administration is so scattered. But the Bundesrechnungshof does not normally maintain staffs resident with all these bodies; the auditors are based at Frankfurt, the

[1] Address given by the President, Dr Hertel, in March 1961. (The author was present.)

focal point for transport in West Germany, and visit when required.

The German audit body consisted in early 1961 of its President and 484 other persons. Out of this total, 293 were engaged upon audit duties, of whom 68 were members of the Higher Service (Höherer Dienst), which corresponds fairly closely, at least in status, to the Administrative Class in the British Civil Service, though not to the *grands corps* in France, which enjoy a unique prestige. Engaged upon general clerical and administrative work were 161 persons, including three members of the Höherer Dienst. Finally, thirty persons, half of them from the Higher Service, constituted the Consultant Section (Gutachtenabteilung) which is responsible to the President of the Bundesrechnungshof in his separate capacity as Federal Commissioner for Efficiency in the Administration.[1] This small but select group are the central experts in 'Organization and Methods' studies in the West German civil service. The Bundesrechnungshof audits not only the accounts of the Bund authorities themselves but also maintains a degree of audit control over the considerable body of industry in which the Federal Republic is a major shareholder. It carries out an audit of the Federal Railways and of the Federal Post Office, which in Germany is an important road transport operator as well as the national communications agency. But, in contrast to practice in France, there is no state audit of the Länder—which all have their own Courts of Accounts—nor of the municipal and local authorities, except in so far as they spend Federal subsidies or act as agents for the central government.

The Fundamental Law (Grundgesetz) or Constitution of the German Federal Republic, dated 23 May 1949, makes the following reference to state audit:

Article 114

(1) The Federal Minister of Finance is to render an account annually of all receipts and expenditures, as well as of assets and liabilities, to the Bundestag and the Bundesrat.[2]

---

[1] The German title is Bundesbeauftragter für Wirtschaftlichkeit in der Verwaltung. The word 'Wirtschaftlichkeit' can also be rendered as 'economy', 'good management', 'businesslike behaviour', etc.

[2] The Bundestag, or Federal Diet (497 voting members, elected by direct universal suffrage for four year periods) is the principal lawmaking body. The Bundesrat, or Federal Council (41 representatives appointed by the governments of the Länder without fixed term of office) has a limited right

(2) The account will be audited by a Court of Accounts (Rechnungshof), whose members possess judicial independence. The general account and a summary of the assets and liabilities, together with the observations of the Rechnungshof, are to be laid before the Bundestag and the Bundesrat during the course of the following financial year, for the purpose of discharging[1] the Federal Government. The audit will be regulated by Federal law.

This final provision was carried into effect by the Law concerning the Foundation and Duties of the Bundesrechnungshof, dated 27 November 1950, which began with these words:

(1) The Bundesrechnungshof is founded as the supreme audit authority for the organs and the administration of the Bund.
(2) The Bundesrechnungshof is a Highest Federal Authority, independent of the Federal Government and subject only to the law.

In the Federal Republic, all administrative authorities of the Bund and the Länder are classified according to their status. There are Higher-, Middle-, and Lower Authorities. The top classification is that of the Highest Federal Authorities. These consist only of the Federal President and the Federal Chancellor together with their private offices, seventeen Federal Ministries, and the Bundesrechnungshof, which is the only body outside the executive with this high standing. The permanent heads of the Highest Federal Authorities, including the President of the Bundesrechnungshof, hold the rank of State Secretary, which implies a status at least equal to that of Permanent Secretary in Great Britain.[2]

The United States General Accounting Office

No. 441, G. Street, in Washington, D.C., is a large uncomplicated office building of recent vintage, although prior to the glass curtain-walled block architecture which spread around the world from the United Nations headquarters in New York. It rises

---

of veto over Federal laws. Members and representatives from West Berlin do not have votes.

[1] i.e. Discharging the government from its budgetary responsibilities as laid down in financial legislation covering the year of account.

[2] The high status of the Staatssekretär is shown by the fact that his salary is greater than that of any other public servant. It exceeds that of Generals, Admirals and Presidents of the highest law courts and it very considerably exceeds that of the leading Ambassadors.

seven stories above the street and occupies an entire city block. It is the principal home of the United States General Accounting Office, the largest state audit body in the Western world.

Until the Second World War, almost the whole of the work of the G.A.O. was carried on in Washington, but the growth of military expenditures at that time led to a great dispersal, which has become a feature of permanent policy. On 30 June 1959, the General Accounting Office employed a total of 5,203 persons, of whom 3,409 were in the capital city. Forty-nine were based upon Paris, for audit duties in Europe, and twenty-four were in Tokyo. The remainder were attached to branch offices in twenty-one cities of the Union, from Boston to Los Angeles.

Five thousand seems, by European standards, a large staff for state audit work. But in April 1946, the G.A.O. employed no less than 14,904 persons. The reduction in personnel to little more than a third of the 1946 figure is indicative of the great changes which have taken place in the Office, and of the spirit of modernization which inspired them. It is not that the work of auditing the accounts of the Federal Government and its agencies has declined; it is rather that this work has been studied and reformed, in order to abolish unnecessary routine. At the same time the internal controls of the Federal departments and agencies have been systematically strengthened, as part of a Joint Financial Management Improvement Programme, a very large effort sponsored from 1947 up to the present time by the General Accounting Office, together with the Treasury Department and the Bureau of the Budget. In addition, the G.A.O. is in course of professionalization; what was formerly a miscellaneous bureaucracy as far as its staff was concerned, is rapidly falling under the domination of a cadre of qualified accountants and lawyers.

The General Accounting Office, as created by the Budget and Accounting Act of 1921, bore the stamp of two evident influences. One of these was British precedent. The status of the Comptroller General of the United States reflected that of the Comptroller and Auditor General, not only in his title, his protected tenure of office and the personal nature of his powers of decision, but also in the fact that the Congress envisaged him as its own servant, to impose the power of the purse upon the executive branch. It had long been recognized that the United States was administratively behind the times, not merely in its lack of a comprehensive national budget, but also because state audit had been entrusted to officers of the Treasury Department; that is to say to members of the executive branch. Within that branch the auditors had been subject to divided loyalties and to all kinds of career pressures, and their efforts to impose the will of the legislature in financial matters had been neither dynamic nor successful. There had been no clear pattern of accountability. As a result, the General Accounting Office came to be placed upon an exceptionally firm basis in relation to the separation of powers, at least in legal status if not in duties. It is officially part of 'the legislative branch of the Government' and is systematically protected by Congress from all influences by the executive branch. It became, 'the Congress' own agency, the great bulwark erected by the Congress against illegal and improper use of public moneys and unbridled waste and extravagance'.[1]

The form and powers of the General Accounting Office also owe much to American history. The Office, under the terms of the 1921 Act, inherited a whole collection of responsibilities which had gradually been imposed upon the Treasury Department ever since the American Revolution. These included all the duties and powers which had been conferred by law upon the Comptroller of the Treasury and the six auditors of the Treasury Department, and also the duties of the Division of Book-keeping and Warrants relating to the personal ledger accounts of disbursing and collecting officers. These old responsibilities included wide audit powers, but they also included tasks of an administrative nature, which are normally outside the scope of state audit. The title of the office perhaps gave rise to some confusion, and in fact the G.A.O. found itself saddled with a great deal of routine accounting work, not only upon the personal accounts of disbursing and collecting officers, but also, by a curious anomaly, in maintaining the general ledgers for the entire Post Office Department. It may be that the essential differences and incompatibilities between accountancy and state auditing were not very fully understood. But these home truths imposed their own logic, and since the last war the Division of Book-keeping and Warrants has been handed back to the Treasury Department, and in 1949 the Postmaster General became responsible for his own account-

[1] 'The General Accounting Office. A study of its Functions and Operations', Fifth Intermediate Report of the Committee on Expenditures in the Executive Departments, 1949. (81st Congress, 1st Session; House Report No. 1441.)

ing. It is these changes which explain much of the reduction in G.A.O. staff, although increased efficiency has also contributed.

The Comptroller General, however, still retains certain powers of practical and legal decision regarding proposed receipts and expenditures, and he is the final authority—always excepting Congress or the Courts—for settlement of claims by or against the United States. It has been argued that these powers should, by their nature, belong to the executive branch, but the Comptroller appears to have emerged unscathed from this dispute and his decisions in difficult financial settlements form a code of precedent and case law for the whole Federal administration.

A most interesting development in the General Accounting Office concerns the state enterprises of the United States, which are dignified with the title of Government Corporations. Indeed they are scarcely 'nationalized' industries in the sense of a state take-over of something which existed before. They were created, principally under the New Deal and World War II, to meet special requirements and create new facilities; their total importance, however, remains very considerable indeed. By 1945 there were over a hundred corporations, and their budgets and programmes mostly were not subject to approval by Congress; they all escaped audit by the General Accounting Office. This situation was remedied by the uniform controls introduced in the Government Corporation Control Act of 1945 which subjected them to the submission of annual budgets and to audit by the G.A.O.[1] This development had an important impact on the state audit body, as well as on the corporations, since the Act directed that the audit was to be in accordance with commercial principles and procedures. It was in response to this requirement that the G.A.O. developed techniques of 'comprehensive audit', which went beyond old routines, and engaged Certified Public Accountants on its staff for the first time. In the outcome the accountants virtually gained control of the Office, and it was found that 'comprehensive audit' could profitably be applied also to the departments and agencies of the executive branch, as well as to the corporations. The Comptroller General, Mr Joseph Campbell, appointed in 1954, is himself a professional accountant, and the G.A.O. is definitely committed to competition in the keen labour market for graduate staff who have specialized in accounting. It seems to

[1] See below, Chapter XI.

be common practice for them to obtain the actual C.P.A. qualification after entering the G.A.O. service.

The legal powers of the Comptroller General as the servant of Congress are very wide indeed. His office is increasingly used as the legislature's private information service upon all kinds of financial matters; it makes annual and other reports, it replies to enquiries from committees and individual Members of Congress, and it provides expert advisory staff as required. The Comptroller's powers in practice cover investigations of an 'Organization and Methods' type. He is the principal adviser to the whole civil service upon accountancy matters. The combination of accounting and legal decision with audit and reporting is not always an easy matter and there is, in principle, a danger that the audit, as a study of government in action, may suffer. The G.A.O., however, has since the war shown clear evidence of a dynamic spirit and a willingness to experiment. There is, at any rate, no danger of it becoming a museum-piece, which is the fate that attends state audit institutions, like other public bodies, if they cling overlong to ancient routines or lack the power to do otherwise.

The Italian Corte dei Conti

In Rome, sharing the same site as the Ministry of Finance, but with its own building, is the Italian State audit institution, the Corte dei Conti, which was established in its present form by a law of 1862, under the inspiration of Cavour.

The Corte has a considerable staff. At a recent date the establishment provided for a magistrature of 517 persons, including the President and fourteen *presidenti di sezione*. Of this total, 81 held irremovable status. There were 328 further persons employed upon audit duties but not classed within the magistrature, and finally 294 employees engaged upon general clerical and archival work; a total staff of 1139, much more numerous than that of the state audit bodies of Britain, France or Western Germany.

But the Corte dei Conti is scarcely a comparable body. To some extent its name is a misnomer; in practice it is only half a state audit institution. For the rest, its duties correspond more closely to those of an administrative court.[1]

The activities of the Corte place a heavy stress upon *a priori*, or,

[1] On this point, see Brian Chapman, *The Profession of Government*, pp. 261–3, London, George Allen & Unwin, 1959.

as it is called, preventive, control. This is applied not only to financial transactions but to all decrees issued by the Head of State and the Ministers whatever their subject (with certain prescribed exceptions), and to all decisions concerning State employees and pensions. It is a kind of censorship of all the acts of the executive, but the test applied is purely one of legality, including budgetary legality in the case of financial proposals. The Corte also has a considerable field of jurisdiction in individual cases. It 'judges the accounts' in a way broadly similar to the Cour des Comptes of France. It can make 'judgments of responsibility' against civil servants and military personnel, charging them for damages caused to the State by their actions or omissions. It hears appeals against judgments by Prefectural Councils in matters of provincial and local public finance and the responsibility of officials. It judges disputes between local tax collectors and the central authorities regarding taxes alleged by the former to be not demandable although personally liable for their amount. All these jurisdictions concern in some degree the accountability of officials to the State. But the Corte is also the tribunal for appeals against awards of State pensions, including those to ex-servicemen and their surviving relatives; this is a different kind of administrative jurisdiction, and a very important one.

The Corte, therefore, is a unique organization, many of whose responsibilities fall outside the scope of state audit. The Constitution of the Italian Republic, which took effect from the beginning of 1948, defined the functions and status of the Corte as follows:

Article 100. The Corte dei Conti exercises *a priori* control of the legitimacy of the actions of the Government, as well as *a posteriori* control of the execution of the State budget. It participates, in the cases and according to the forms decided by law, in control of the financial administration of organizations which receive contributions from State funds. It reports directly to the Chambers on the results of the control effected.

The law guarantees the independence of the Institution and its members from the Government.

Article 103. The Corte dei Conti exercises jurisdiction over everything which concerns the public accounts and over other matters specified by law.

This was an attempt to explain in simple terms a truly complex collection of responsibilities. In fact there have from early in this century been various projects for reform of the statutes of the Corte, which a recent commentator described as 'not lacking in defects and imperfections'. He concluded that reform of the duties of the Corte, as part of a general reorganization of the Italian administrative system, was a necessity.[1] The projects of reform arise not only from a demand for simplification of the regulations, 'very often antiquated and scattered among a multitude of laws', but also because the Corte is closely restricted to a control of formal legality, and has no right to examine questions of the merit of administrative and financial action.

Certainly such a restriction is a barrier to development of state audit on the lines of its world-wide evolution in the age of heavy state spending. But the existence of a demand for administrative reform within the organization concerned is not evidence of decadence; on the contrary it may suggest a basic vigour and independence of mind.

Meanwhile, the Corte fulfils a dignified role on the Italian administrative stage. Its senior magistrates are entitled to be addressed as 'Eccellenza', like a Roman prince. Its advice is sought upon all proposed legislation and measures which would modify the accounting regulations in force, the rules governing pensions, or the tasks of the Corte itself, and upon other matters where its advice is considered useful. For the purpose of *a priori* control of departments where rapidity of administrative action is particularly important, the Corte has installed certain permanently detached staffs. It has Sections or Delegations attached to the Regional Administrations of the three provinces of Italy which enjoy a degree of special autonomy under the Republic; Sicily since 1948, Sardinia since 1949, and the Alto Adige since 1951. In accordance with Article 100 of the Constitution, the Corte participates in control of bodies subsidized by the State; in this task it has no powers of *a priori* decision or of jurisdiction, but is rather a source of information and advice for both the legislature and the executive. The aim of its supervision is to ascertain not only whether public funds are used within the limitations set by law, but also whether the administration of the subsidized bodies conforms to the public interest.[2]

[1] Sepe, op. cit., pp. 27–31.

[2] Onorato Sepe. Article on the Corte dei Conti, in *Enciclopedia Forense*, vol. 2, Milan, Casa Editrice Dr Francesco Vallardi.

The Algemene Rekenkamer (Netherlands)

The General Chamber of Accounts (Algemene Rekenkamer) of the Netherlands is in the centre of the Hague, at five minutes walk from the Binnenhof, palace of the ancient stadtholders and of the States General, which is still the national Parliament. The office of the Rekenkamer is perhaps the most venerable building at present occupied by any state audit organization, which seems appropriate to a nation which was, in its age of greatness, a pioneer in the techniques of modern finance.

The Rekenkamer consists of three irremovable Members, forming a college, of whom one is the President, together with a staff of 136 persons with auditing duties and 54 administrative and auxiliary employees. As in London, the office of the state audit body is a headquarters rather than a place of audit; the auditors of the Rekenkamer work mainly inside the departments which they control. The audit co-operates closely with a permanent committee of the Second Chamber of the States General, the Committee on Government Expenditures, which has seven members. But this is not only an 'administrative' audit; the Rekenkamer retains exclusive powers of discharge for all receiving and paying officers, or 'fiscal officers', of the Kingdom.

The Dutch audit considers not only the 'regularity' of revenue and expenditure but also its 'suitability', and it has statutory power of discretion to make 'proposals and statements which in its opinion can lead to a reduction of national expenditure, to an increase in national revenue and to an improvement in the administration of the nation's money and assets'.[1] This power enables the Rekenkamer to take a wide view of its functions and to study the efficiency of administrative conduct.

The Belgian Cour des Comptes

Such a power is, however, still withheld from the Cour des Comptes of Belgium, which occupies a corner of the elegant Place Royale in Brussels.

The Belgian Cour is often classified together with that of Italy. This is because these two bodies alone base their audit activities primarily upon *a priori* control. And these two alone are closely restricted to considerations of legality and 'regularity' in state receipts and expenditures. The Belgian Cour does not, however,

[1] Article 60 of the Accounting Act (Comptabiliteitswet) of 1927.

resemble the Corte dei Conti in its guise as an administrative court.

For a small country, the Cour of Belgium is a large body; from 1908 until recent events, however, it also controlled the accounts of the Congo. The directing group is a college of twelve members of judicial status, divided between two Chambers, each with a President and five members. The separation into two chambers is on a linguistic basis; there is a Flemish Chamber and a French Chamber. The senior of the two Presidents holds the title of Premier Président and presides at meetings in general assembly. A balance of new appointments between Fleming and Walloon is maintained; this is the uneasy servitude and discipline of a bilingual state. The Belgian Cour is also unusual in that its members are nominated by the Chamber of Representatives of the national parliament, and the appointments are thus subject to party influence. Tradition, however, demands that each of the three great political parties shall be represented in the Cour, which thus constitutes a racial and political microcosm of the state.

There are 222 audit posts and 124 persons with clerical and other duties, making a total of staff not dissimilar to that of the very different Cour des Comptes of France.[1] Belgium has no nationalized industries, but the state has entrusted a whole series of tasks to various public and subsidized bodies. The control of these institutions was regulated and codified by a law of 16 March 1954; they are all subject to audit by the Cour des Comptes.

The Norwegian Riksrevisjonen

Perhaps the state audit system which most closely resembles that of Great Britain is the Norwegian. The National Audit Department (Riksrevisjonen) is directly responsible to the Parliament, the Storting. The Protocol Committee of the lower house, the Odelsting, fulfils a function similar to that of the Public Accounts Committee of the House of Commons. The Audit Department is much larger in proportion to the size of the population than is the Exchequer and Audit Department in the United Kingdom; it has a staff of about 360, of whom some 250 are engaged upon audit.

[1] The size of national audit staffs is not, of course, a very meaningful subject for comparison. It depends upon all sorts of considerations, such as the amount of routine auditing and the strength of 'internal' controls, and it is certainly no standard of efficiency. The comparative figures are, nevertheless, of some interest.

But, as in Great Britain and in the Netherlands, the auditors are dispersed among the various authorities, rather than centralized in their own permanent headquarters. About half the staff consists of local and travelling auditors—and in the extraordinary geographical conditions of Norway travel can even in modern times be an adventurous life. The scope of their control goes beyond formal regularity; the Audit Department is also 'responsible for checking the justifiability of the financial dispositions and examining these from a general economic angle, in other words a critical audit'.[1]

But no two state audit systems are alike, and there are important differences between those of Norway and Great Britain. Firstly, the Riksrevisjonen will under pending legislation become the auditor of all government enterprises[2] and is already responsible for most of them. Secondly, the structure of the Audit Department at the top follows a purely Scandinavian tradition whereby 'National Auditors' (in Norwegian, Riksrevisorene) are elected by Parliaments for a limited period. Before 1925 the five elected auditors, who were usually members of the Storting with a legal background, worked only part time, and elected their own chairman. By the Audit Act of 1918 they were charged with the direction of the new Riksrevisjonen and in 1925 the Storting decreed that one of the five auditors should be appointed chairman by decision of the legislature, and should work full time. He became the administrative head of the Audit Department, and in effect, Auditor General of Norway. But the elected auditors, chosen by the Storting for four year periods, continue to form a college, or board, which is the highest authority of the Audit Department.

In Norway, the elected auditors of Scandinavian usage have thus come to form a unit with the career auditors of the Riksrevisjonen. It was not always so. There was once a Ministry of Audit, which had staff but lacked authority, whilst the elected auditors had to work without staff. It was the Audit Act of 1918 which finally centralized all external audit in one independent department.

[1] Lars Breie, Auditor General of Norway, 'The Auditing and Control of Government Accounts in Norway' (in English).

[2] The term 'nationalized' would be inappropriate since these Norwegian enterprises have never been privately owned.

The Four Audit Departments of Denmark

In Denmark such unification did not take place, and the administrative pattern of state audit is therefore one of the most complex to be found anywhere. The career audit was reorganized by the State Accounting and Audit Act of 1926.[1] There are four Audit Departments, headed by Chief Auditors (Hovedrevisorer), who are directly subordinated to the Minister of Finance but are independent of the other state authorities and of each other. They form a college only for decisions upon questions of personnel and internal finance, although they may also discuss common audit problems.

At some time in the past, the audit authority was in most countries united with the financial branch of the executive. This situation was found to be unsatisfactory, even under absolute governments, but especially after the separation of powers. In effect it amounted to uniting controller and controlled in one corporate personality, and it left great scope for restriction of independent audit criticism through the machinery of career pressures. The last case in a major Western power was that of the United States, where state audit remained within the Treasury Department until 1921. Denmark therefore appears to constitute an almost unique survival of a state audit which is neither wholly independent nor completely external.[2]

An authority upon budget and control matters, Kurt Heinig, was a strong friend of Denmark, where he found refuge from Nazi persecution, but he nevertheless described the Danish arrangements for state audit as 'a faulty construction'.[3]

The Danish administration is, however, aware of the basic necessities of state audit action, and the four Chief Auditors in practice enjoy a considerable degree of independence. They communicate directly with the various Ministries, and they submit their own annual reports. These reach the Danish Parliament through four Constitutional Auditors elected by the legislature,

[1] This Act was based on the report of a commission which 'considered both the Roman idea of a Cour des Comptes and the English–Norwegian idea of a parliamentary audit body', but found that neither would 'fit into Danish administrative tradition'.

[2] The only other surviving example is Switzerland.

[3] A reform of the Danish audit system is now under consideration. (I am indebted to Mr Arne Johansen of the Fourth Audit Department for this information.)

who need not be members of Parliament but normally are. The elected auditors submit a report to a committee of the legislature, which in turn reports briefly to Parliament. In practice the Constitutional Auditors rely very heavily upon the reports of the four Hovedrevisorer, with whom they meet to constitute a Committee of Public Accounts, of which the Chief Accounting Officer of the Treasury is also a member.

The scope of criticism expected from the Danish audit is not a narrow one; special attention is to be paid to 'due observance of economy in the administration of Government funds and in the managements of establishments'. Most of the questions in the annual reports concern this wide field of criticism, which goes beyond considerations of 'regularity'.

The four Audit Departments employ a total of 99 'academic personnel' with university degrees, including the four Chief Auditors, who are all of equal status; there are also fourteen qualified accountants and 209 clerical staff. Audit visits in recent years have included such inhospitable destinations as Greenland, the Faroe Islands and the United Nations forces at Gaza.

The Austrian Rechnungshof

A state audit body of great interest is the Rechnungshof of the Federal Republic of Austria, not only because of the long traditions of that country's civil service, but because of the extensive tasks which are entrusted to the audit. Whereas the Länder of the German Federal Republic have their own Courts of Accounts, the Rechnungshof of Austria controls both the Federal finances on behalf of the National Assembly (Nationalrat) and the finances of the nine provinces as an organ of their parliaments, the Landtage. It also controls the accounts of the seventeen communes with more than 20,000 inhabitants and those of twenty-eight groups of communes (Gemeindeverbände). Austria has also a wide range of state enterprises, mainly basic industries, which were the object of two nationalization laws in 1946 and 1947. Shares in some of them are owned by the Federation and in others by the provinces. In either case the Rechnungshof has an absolute right of examination and audit. It also audits the numerous nationalized banks and various traditional state enterprises such as the National Railways and the monopolies of salt, tobacco, spirits and lotteries. Altogether some 240 principal and subsidiary undertakings, plus about 50 underwriters of social insurance, are subject to the attentions of the Rechnungshof.

This field of audit is one of the widest to be found in any Western country, and the Court met its responsibilities in 1960 with only 91 auditors, of whom 48 had university degrees in law or economics, and the remainder had secondary school education. It seems to have been felt, however, that an increased establishment of auditors would be justified. In addition there were 45 persons with auxiliary duties, and the Rechnungshof is entitled to call in technical experts for advice when required. The whole office is under the authority of a President, who is elected by the Nationalrat for an unlimited term. There is also a Vice-President, but the Rechnungshof is a monocratic, not a collegiate body. Whereas in most countries the head of the national audit body is a civil servant of the highest classification, the President of the Austrian institution has the full status of a Minister. In accordance with the unique dual role of this audit body, he counts as a Federal Minister for duties on behalf of the Nationalrat and as a provincial Minister when he represents the interests of a Landtag. The audit is nevertheless absolutely independent of the government.

The aims of the audit are very broad and modern. Transactions are considered not only from the point of view of 'regularity', but are also judged for their economy (Sparsamkeit), their efficiency (Wirtschaftlichkeit) and finally for their expediency (Zweckmässigkeit).

The State Comptroller's Office in Israel

Israel is an inherently Western country exported to the Middle East, which is also aware of Central and Eastern European traditions because many of its immigrants came from there. It shows an evident intention of living in the most up-to-date way that its circumstances allow, and it has enjoyed the freedom of choice of methods which is the special advantage of countries starting from scratch. It is therefore of interest to see what use the polyglot administration of Israel has made of state audit, after considering the whole range of foreign example.

It has in fact given great importance to state audit, and a whole range of foreign influence can be detected. The statutory basis is the State Comptroller's Law of 1949, as several times amended.

The State Comptroller's is a political appointment but he may not be chosen from among active politicians. He is appointed for a five years term by the President of the State upon the recommendation of the House Committee of the Knesset, the Israeli Parliament. This means in practice, we are told, that the Knesset elects the State Comptroller.[1] He is responsible only to the Knesset and is not dependent upon the Government. His rank is equated with that of a Cabinet Minister. He controls a staff which reached the figure of 416 in January 1959. He maintains contact with the Knesset through its Finance Committee and recently also through a special sub-committee for matters of State Control. A committee of Directors General of Ministries has also been set up 'in order to advance the rectification of recurring defects' revealed by the State Comptroller's Office.

This Office is responsible for 'inspection' of every Government office and every State enterprise or institution; of all local authorities; of all undertakings in which the State has a share, direct or indirect; of every holder or manager of State property; and finally, of any person or body subjected to inspection by law or agreement. In addition to tests of 'regularity', the audit is charged with examining 'whether the inspected bodies . . . have operated economically, and in a morally irreproachable manner'. The State Comptroller also has discretion to examine 'any such other matter as he may deem necessary', and he is to make recommendations for the rectification or prevention of defects. He may be charged by the Knesset, the Finance Committee or the Government, to 'prepare an opinion as to any matter within the scope of his functions'.

The conception of the State Comptroller's role combines the English idea of an auditor in the service of the legislature with a more general function of administrative inspection, which is perhaps especially desirable in the formative period of a new state. The inspectional activity probably owes something to 'State Control' as practised in Communist countries.[2] The aim is a practical one. The State Comptroller expresses the view that the most direct, and probably the chief, beneficiaries of 'State Control' are the administration and the managements of the controlled organizations, rather than the Knesset.[3]

[1] Report submitted by Israel to the Second International Congress of Supreme Audit Institutions; Brussels, September 1956.

[2] For Communist 'State Control' see below, Chapter XII.

[3] State Comptroller's Annual Report No. 7, for the Fiscal Year 1955–6.

The State Comptroller's Office, divided between Jerusalem, Haifa and Tel Aviv, is organized with an eye to modern and varied administrative techniques. Members of the Office attend courses at universities and they are encouraged to study such subjects as economics, statistics, administrative law, budget analysis and cost accounting. The State Comptroller co-operates with the Israel Association for Political Science in the sponsorship of research projects in financial administration. The Comptroller assigned a member of the staff, 'a specialist in the Public Law of the People's Democracies', to make a study of 'State Control' in the U.S.S.R., Poland and other communist states.[1]

The internal organization of the Office shows how wide the scope of control is considered to be. In addition to a normal hierarchy, which includes departments for the control of local authorities and of government corporations, there are various advisory services. These are the Legal Adviser's Service, the Efficiency Control Service, the Advisory Unit for Problems of Principle connected with Budgeting and Accounts, and the Advisory Unit for Economic Research and Economic Science. The Efficiency Control Service conducts studies of organization and methods, although all of the auditors are expected to investigate matters of economy and efficiency. The Legal Adviser also conducts inspections, and in addition he centralizes the handling of complaints reaching the Office. About 800 complaints against various inspected bodies are received from the public every year. In dealing with these complaints the State Comptroller appears to fulfil a role comparable to that of the Scandinavian Ombudsman;[2] most of the complaints in 1958 were about administrative decisions and procedures rather than purely financial questions. The Comptroller has a permanent representation in New York, for control of Israeli Missions and branches of government corporations in the United States. A unique object of state audit is the implementation of the Reparations Agreement of 1952 with the German Federal Republic, under which the latter country contributes to the economic rehabilitation of Jewish refugees. Cologne is the centre for this audit, and that of the European Missions of the Ministry for Foreign Affairs.

[1] State Comptroller's Annual Report No. 9, for the Fiscal Year 1957–8.

[2] The investigation of public complaints is also characteristic of Communist 'State Control'. See Chapter XII.

In Israel we find in operation a dynamic state control, clearly designed and intended to play a major part in shaping the administration and the economy of the country. It remains chiefly based upon the examination of accounts, but—as in the handling of complaints—the State Comptroller also has the role of a general commissioner for the public interest. His Annual Reports show that state control in Israel has been concerned with the most diverse problems. There is a survey of administrative procedure concerning burials, which 'has not yet found its proper organization in Israel'; a demand for standard conditions for public contracts and for a new Civil Service law; a survey of controversies about official apartments; a report on the place of government corporations in the national economy, with frequent reference to foreign analogy. There is a review of internal audit and 'O. & M.' in the Ministries and government corporations and another of the national 'water economy', which is the collective title for all the water supply and irrigation projects of this arid country. There is a long report on the registration of pupils in schools, a matter which had given rise to many complaints. The administrative defects of local authorities are listed 'in the light of the results of inspection'. These are both the special growing pains of a new state and the inevitable day-to-day problems which arise even in older countries.

* * * *

State audit is a worldwide phenomenon and these examples are a specialized sample; they all come from lands which allocate a very important role in government to elected assemblies, not only in theory but in actual practice. In all these places the state audit must, as a fundamental duty, examine the acts of the executive in relation to the prior decisions of the legislature. But even in these countries that is not the entire role of audit, nor, as our examples show, is there only one way of auditing on behalf of a legislature. The conclusion which emerges is one of wide diversity of method and approach, even within our Western world.

There are collegiate bodies, some of them of ancient origin, and parliamentary audits under a 'comptroller', on the English pattern. There are varying degrees of judicial audit, and countries where control is purely 'administrative'. There are audits which deal with central government finance only, and others which have responsibilities over local government as well. A majority of state audit bodies work *a posteriori*, examining transactions already effected, but there is a minority of countries in which the main emphasis is upon *a priori* control. In the great majority of cases the national audit institution has at least a limited degree of control over state enterprises and subsidized bodies, but this is not universal; the same is becoming true of administrative efficiency, or 'O. & M.' studies. In most places the audit has come to enjoy a wide discretion in the type of criticism that it may make, but in a few cases it remains confined to the investigation of questions of 'regularity'. Almost everywhere, including all the major Western countries, state audit is now a separate entity, wholly independent of the executive, at least for the conduct of its daily duties. But even this is not universal and in a very few cases state audit survives as a department of the Ministry of Finance, although with special status. Finally, there is the idea, implied by practices in Israel and some other countries, of state audit as a general guardian of the public interest; we shall note in a subsequent chapter that it may in Communist countries be conceived as the guardian of the interests of the government and of the party which dominates or is synonymous with it.

Only upon a single matter, the control of 'regularity' in the conduct of public finance, is there a measure of universal agreement as to what state audit should do. For the rest, there is a fascinating diversity and in many countries a spirit of experiment. The various national theories of state audit are almost all in a stage of development, and this is a type of administrative action which must rest upon a body of theory, however pragmatic; its task is not self-evident like that of most executive activity. Therein lies the interest of the present study.

CHAPTER IV

The Lowest Common Denominator: 'Regularity'

> 'Ten Auditors and ten Assistant Auditors are chosen by lot. Every single public officer must account to them. They have sole control over those subject to audit: they place their findings before the courts.
>
> Anyone against whom they prove embezzlement is convicted and fined by the court ten times the sum discovered stolen. Anyone whom the court on the Auditors' evidence convicts of corruption, is also fined ten times the amount of the bribe. If he is found guilty of administrative error, they assess the sum involved, and he is fined that amount, provided in this case that he pays it within nine months; otherwise the fine is doubled'—Aristotle, *The Constitution of Athens*

TO be 'regular', says a dictionary, is to be 'governed by or according to rule, law, order, habit, custom, established practice, mode prescribed, or the ordinary course of things'. In a financial context 'regularity' has a negative connotation; it implies the absence of irregularity. The word 'regularity' is here taken to mean conformity with all relevant accounting, administrative, budgetary and other financial regulations and accepted procedures, as well as with the laws of the land. Any transaction may thus be irregular without necessarily being illegal, though it may be both. All state audit, indeed all audit whatsoever, has at all times and under all regimes, been interested in the prevention, the detection and the correction of irregularity. But, except for outright fraud and illegality, there is no universal criterion to show what is irregular.

In practice, however, the audit tests of 'regularity' do not at present differ very greatly as between the various Western countries. There are basic checks similar to those of private audit. Each transaction must be 'vouched'; that is to say that sufficient documentary evidence must be readily available to show its nature, its reality and its legality. No auditor will pass receipts and expenditures which are 'unvouched', at least without very full and detailed explanations and independent corroboration. Each item of income and expense must then be properly 'posted'; that is duly entered into the correct accounts at the proper time. The accounts themselves must be correctly totalled and balanced at specified intervals of time and the balances must be carried to general accounts, the accuracy and completeness of which must of course also be tested and confirmed.

Every payment must be authorized by somebody, who personally signs a payment order. It is very rare in large organizations for such an official, whom the French call an ordonnateur and the Americans specifically designate as the certifying officer, to be also a holder of funds and a paying officer. Separation of the ordering from the paying function is a basic safeguard and in some countries it is strictly enforced by law for the public service. The auditor is interested to ensure that each transaction was ordered by an authorized person in accordance with known commitments, that the amounts appear to be correct, that if payment is for supplies they were properly furnished and if for services they were actually performed. He requires confirmation that the amount paid was duly received by the person or organization designated. Finally, the auditor is entitled to reassure himself that the sum paid corresponded either to some generally accepted scale for the supply or service, or was agreed beforehand and properly recorded then.

These are the timeless commonplaces of audit and the endless repetition of these basic tests is the only sure guarantee that any kind of financial administration is being conducted at least honestly. The failure of any voucher, in any audit, to meet a test, may be the key to a remarkable and unexpected history.

The state auditor has to consider regularity in the special context of the budgetary cycle. He has to ensure that the executive has worked within the framework of legislative authorization. For the last century in Britain and some other countries, and for a considerable period in all Western countries, this has been the most important single function of state audit, although with the development of new ideas and techniques it is now declining in relative importance. Briefly, the auditor has to ascertain that each transaction and each individual payment does not contravene the law, and in particular the budgetary law. The legislature has not only authorized the spending of a large total sum but has indicated in detail the objects upon which that sum is to be expended, and up to what total in each case. The budgetary system would be worthless if the executive ignored the authorized individual totals, even if it respected the overall total. The auditor must therefore make sure that each payment is correctly charged; so that for example money voted for the purchase of aircraft is not used for buying motor-cars. Many expenditures have to be split up between various different budgetary headings. The details of proposed expenditures are often given in estimates and budgetary laws with considerable detail and precision, and the auditor must confirm that actual expenditures correspond fully with the intention. Certain types of receipts must be surrendered to the central reserves of the state and the auditor must ensure that this is done. Some headings in the budget will inevitably be underspent, leaving a balance of authorized funds apparently available to the executive for use in other ways; the auditor has to see that this is not done without special authorization for transfer from one heading to another, which is called virement. In principle, the authorization of virement is a prerogative of the legislature which granted funds in the first place, because this constitutes a variation of the grant; in practice some delegation of this authority to the executive may be permitted within prescribed limits. In general, the auditor must see that the sums voted under budget headings are not exceeded; if for unforeseen reasons this cannot be avoided, the audit must verify the explanations given by the executive and ensure that appropriate legislative action is initiated.

In these and other ways state audit endeavours to ensure that legislative control over finance is made a reality. In the most experienced countries this has ceased to be a very difficult task; there are many tricks and devices open to an executive which seeks to evade budgetary control, but most of these were tried and detected by the auditors long ago. They are not likely to be used again. In newer countries, however, similar battles remain to be fought. But the budgetary control enforced by state audit remains in all Western countries a very important constitutional device, calling for constant vigilance. Without it, control of the purse by the legislative power would be a wholly empty phrase, and there would be very little scope for parliaments to exercise any influence over day-to-day administration. Financial discipline within the executive itself would also be compromised. If the executive must conform to the rules of the budgetary system, it must of course also be honest. As Aristotle warned, nothing is more intolerable to the public than the knowledge that its contribution to the cost of government is being dissipated for the enrichment of officials. Widespread and unchecked peculation has undermined parties, governments and whole regimes. There is nowadays little scope for this in the older Western countries, and traditions of probity in central administration have been firmly established. For this, state audit should be given a fair share of the credit. But of course the phenomenon still exists in the world; the former Comptroller and Auditor General of India reported sadly that, 'the growth of indiscipline, dishonesty and corruption both in administration and outside, is distressing', and he called for 'firmness. . .—even ruthlessness' in dealing with cases.[1]

It would, moreover, be wrong for Western citizens, and especially Western auditors, to feel over-confident and secure against corrupt practices. State auditors have direct contact principally with officials of the central executive, whose average standards of integrity are high in all the most advanced countries. But whenever these officials, and the auditors, make contacts in the line of duty with persons and bodies outside the national ministries they are apt to find that quite different standards apply. Claims of all kinds submitted by private citizens, for pensions, subsidies and benefits, or for compensation, may be fraudulent. The same applies, with greater emphasis, to matters of taxation. Especially it behoves an auditor to be vigilant in matters concerning public contracts. One cannot generalize, but in a number of Western countries morality appears to be in course of evolution; public funds, which have come to be regarded as sacred by most of the state's own servants, are still regarded as fair game by some of its contractors as well as by many other private individuals.

Questions of honesty have perhaps lost their ancient primacy among the concerns of state audit, but they retain importance everywhere, and especially along the frontier where the central administration must conduct relations with the general public, with other authorities and with the private sector of the economy. The individual dishonesty of officials, in so far as it still exists, is increasingly the preoccupation of internal audit, which has the advantage of greater proximity to the events and personalities concerned. This is particularly true in countries like Great Britain, where state audit is specifically 'administrative' and concerns itself with the collective accountability of the executive rather than the

[1] Asok Chanda, *Aspects of Audit Control*, pp. 28–9, New Delhi, 1960.

individual responsibility of paying officers. There is general agreement among state audit bodies in the advanced countries that observations involving misdemeanours represent only a fairly small proportion of their total activity. This is to some extent a tribute to their own effectiveness as a safeguard. But every state auditor should retain a healthy element of suspicion in his approach to work; at some time in his career he will find that suspicion is fully justified.

In each country, at least part of the code of 'regularity' which the state auditor must enforce is laid down by law. In Great Britain, the Comptroller and Auditor General is charged to satisfy himself 'that the money expended has been applied to the purpose or purposes for which the grants made by Parliament were intended to provide and that the expenditure conforms to the authority which governs it'.[1] He is also to ensure, when so required by the Treasury, that expenditure is supported by the authority of the Treasury;[2] in practice the enforcement of the Treasury's regulatory controls over other departments is a permanent activity of British state audit, and to this extent it is a traditional rather than a parliamentary audit. The Comptroller and Auditor General may only admit as chargeable to the accounts of a financial year sums which were actually paid within the same period.[3]

This last provision is much more important than at first appears. It may seem natural that money should be voted to meet actual bills presented within a fixed period of time. There is, however, another equally natural view, namely that money should be granted for commitments to be incurred within the same period, even if they result in payment falling due after the end of the period. In one case the vote is purely on a chronological basis; this is entitled by French theorists, *le système de la gestion.* In the second case the grant of funds is geared to anticipated liabilities, irrespective of when these will be met; the French call this *le système de l'exercice.*[4] The latter system has certain advantages for the purpose of estimating, and it is of ancient origin. But the former has the outstanding advantage in modern conditions that it permits the rapid rendering of accounts. It has long been customary in British Commonwealth countries and in Germany. Nevertheless the *exercice*

[1] The Exchequer and Audit Departments Act, 1921, Section 1 (1).

[2] E. & A. Depts. Act, 1921, Section 1(3).

[3] E. & A. Depts. Act, 1866, Section 24.

[4] The terms *gestion* and *exercice* appear scarcely translatable in this context.

still survives in a modified form in a number of countries;[1] in these places a complementary period of a few months following the end of the financial year is allowed, during which payments against debts incurred during the previous year are considered as operations of that year.

The United States is in a midway position; its budget is estimated according to the *exercice* principle, but the annual accounts are established on the basis of the *gestion;* all actual receipts and payments are included, irrespective of which budget may have originally provided for them.[2] Every annual budget is valid, in effect, for three years. After the end of the first year no new commitments may be made, but existing commitments can be honoured for a further two years. The total of actual payments in any year, therefore, comprises funds voted in three separate budgets. This permits rapid compilation of accounts, but it renders difficult a comparison of estimates with actual results.

Within the last few years France has adopted the British system of *la gestion*; the law now says:

> The receipts are charged to the budget of the year in course of which they are collected by a public *comptable*.
>
> The expenditures are charged to the budget of the year in course of which the orders for payment or money-orders are approved by the *comptables* to whom they are assigned; they must be paid against funds granted for that year whatever may be the date of the debt.[3]

Under the British system, which existed even when the state audit body was formed in 1866, all funds voted by Parliament for a financial year and remaining unexpended, cease to be available after the last day of that year, which is 31 March. No new payments may be made, although holders of payable orders made out before the end of the financial year have three months' grace in which to cash them. The system of dividing government expenditures has been widely criticized for its inflexibility; voted funds are cut off every 31 March, but liabilities continue, and the problem is especially difficult in the case of capital expenditures. Nevertheless, as long as national spending is to be based upon the cycle

[1] In 1954 these included France, Switzerland, Italy and Portugal.

[2] *La Réforme Budgétaire*, vol. II, p. 131. Paris, Les Editions de L'Epargne, 1954.

[3] Ordonnance No. 59–2 of 2 January 1959, 'portant loi organique relative aux lois de finances', Article 16.

of the annual parliamentary budget (and possible alternatives[1] to this are outside the subject of this study), there is a good deal to be said for doing it in the present way.

The basic advantage is rapidity in rendering account, which is always vital if lessons are to be drawn. The enormous time-lags of accounting and audit in the eighteenth century are well known to historians. For example, the accounts of the Treasurers of the British Navy were twenty-two years in arrears in 1780.[2] In France in 1789 the most recent year for which the accounts had been cleared was 1780; in 1766 the King had granted an amnesty to *comptables* in respect of their debts to the state which had arisen on accounts prior to 1719 and were still outstanding.[3] What is not so well known is that a situation arose in France, Belgium, Italy and elsewhere after the First World War in which accounting delays were almost equally alarming. Delays of up to ten years in clearance by the audit were common until the thirties, and the laws of discharge, which are voted by the Parliaments in most continental countries, were even more in arrears. Such delays inevitably vitiate the effectiveness of accountability and audit, and may bring the entire financial system into dangerous disrepute and ridicule. In the United Kingdom, however, extraordinary delays did not occur, except for the accounts of the actual war years; on 22 July 1924 the Public Accounts Committee had already published the last of its Reports on the accounts for the financial year 1922–3.

It is against this background that the speed of British accounting and auditing may be fully appreciated. In France it received the following unsolicited tribute:

> The British Budgetary system is characterized by a very great rapidity in rendering of the accounts . . .
>
> The centralization of book-keeping in the Paymaster-General's Office, the concentration of the financial services under the authority of the Treasury, the *a posteriori* control exercised by the Audit month by month, without waiting for the end of the year, all contribute to simplicity in establishing the accounts and rapidity in rendering them.[4]

---

[1] A general application of such alternatives would in any event have very drastic constitutional, quite apart from practical, consequences. There would probably be a very marked decline of the legislative power.

[2] Binney, op. cit., p. 145.

[3] V. de Marcé, *Le Contrôle des Finances*, vol. 1, Paris, Alcan, 1928.

[4] M. de Veyrac, Inspecteur Général des Finances, in *La Réforme Budgétaire*, vol. II, pp. 130–1.

One of the primary functions of state audit is to ensure that the executive in fact renders accounts as required by law, and renders them at the proper time. It is a role which often comes to be taken for granted, but which is indeed a difficult one in the newer countries and even in the older ones in time of emergency. In lands where individual paying officers, as well as the departments of state, render account to state audit, the national audit institution is often endowed with the power to impose fines for delay. Such sanctions cannot, of course, be used against governments, and state audit can only give publicity to lapses in the duties of accountability. What can happen is shown by the case of Brazil. For the financial year 1911, the President of the Tribunal de Contas of that country reported to the parliament that accounts had not been produced. Even in 1930 the Tribunal recorded that 'governments did not carry out their elementary duty of producing the accounts', so that for exercise of its statutory duties the audit body disposed only of 'its own accountancy'.[1] This kind of situation presents the most radical problems that state audit can face, and in such cases political and financial chaos may often go hand in hand.

* * * *

In Germany, the law requires state audit to cover the following aspects of 'regularity':

1. Whether the budget, including its supporting documents, has been adhered to.
2. Whether the individual figures in the accounts are substantiated and vouched factually and arithmetically in the prescribed manner.
3. Whether in the raising and collection of revenues and in the employment and disbursement of Reich funds, as well as in the purchase, utilization and disposal of Reich property, a procedure has been followed in accordance with the existing laws and regulations, paying attention to the relevant administrative principles and complying with the need for economy.[2]

This sets out the essence of the matter effectively, but the reference to 'economy' immediately carries the scope of audit criticism beyond the limits of 'regularity'.

United States law requires the Comptroller General to report to

[1] Report of the Brazilian delegation to the Second International Congress of Supreme Audit Institutions, Brussels, 1956.

[2] Reichshaushaltsordnung (RHO), 1922, Section 96. This is still in force.

Congress every expenditure or contract made illegally.[1] It also requires that:

> The auditing for the Government, conducted by the Comptroller General of the United States as an Agent of the Congress, be directed at determining the extent to which accounting and related financial reporting fulfil the purposes specified, financial transactions have been consummated in accordance with laws, regulations and other legal requirements, . . . and afford an effective basis for the settlement of accounts of accountable officers.[2]

'Regularity' in essence amounts to legality in the broadest sense, together with proper and correct accounting. The word covers all the basic technical questions which face state audit and all of its traditional activities. But, as we have already noted, the enforcement of 'regularity' by state audit takes place at two different administrative levels. Firstly there is, in many countries, but not in the United Kingdom or Western Germany, direct control of the individual officials charged with receiving and disbursing public funds. In the second place, the regularity of the conduct of finance by the entire executive is examined through the accounts of the ministries and departments. The former is the *raison d'être* of the judicial type of audit and is of very ancient origin. The latter, or 'administrative' type of control, is a relatively modern development, like the ministries themselves.

Audit by a court of law is an idea which appears strange in the light of recent British administrative experience. But the Anglo-Norman Exchequer conducted judicial audits from at least as early as the twelfth century. It was an expedient for the imposition of some kind of centralized finance in an age which lacked adequate central records. In eighteenth-century England it was already an anachronism, and it did not long survive. The whole concept of judicial audit disappeared with it, in a land which had ceased to think of administration as an activity in which judges could participate. The responsibility of officials was enforced through hierarchical discipline.

Such discipline was not, however, readily available at the top, on the frontiers between the executive and the legislature, and the Public Accounts Committee of the House of Commons began to occupy itself at a very early date with the problem of finding an

[1] Budget and Accounting Act, 1921, Section 312(c).

[2] Budget and Accounting Procedures Act, 1950. Section 111(d).

individual other than the minister who could be held personally accountable for the financial conduct of each ministry. In 1872 the Committee expressed the view that the appointment of an official to sign and render appropriation accounts 'should be accompanied by some formal notice or warning as to the extent of responsibility thereby conveyed and as to the additional duty imposed'. The Treasury, after stating the opinion that it was inexpedient for ministers to render accounts, in view of 'the temporary character of their tenure of office, and the burden of their Parliamentary in addition to their strictly executive duties', agreed to lay down the rule that they would, whenever practicable, 'nominate the permanent heads of departments to render the Appropriation Accounts of grants for the services under their control', with the title of 'Accounting Officer' for this purpose.[1] The practice of appointing permanent heads to render the account became in due time generalized. The responsibility of an Accounting Officer is not merely administrative but also pecuniary. In 1921 the Accounting Officer of the former wartime Ministry of Information repaid to public funds the sum of £101 *6s. 3d.* from his own pocket, at the insistence of the Public Accounts Committee and the Treasury.[2] This was an exceptional case and the personal liability of Accounting Officers is very rarely invoked. Nevertheless, individual responsibility is an essential element in the control of 'regularity'. In England this is enforced administratively through each ministerial hierarchy, rather than by the direct accountability of each paying officer to state audit. The device of the Accounting Officer ingeniously bridges the gap between the summit of each hierarchy and Parliament. The P.A.C. can if necessary subject Accounting Officers to a sort of latter-day judicial audit, in which, as the 1921 case shows, they are not inevitably acquitted. Indeed, the normal procedures of the Public Accounts Committee[3], even when the personal liability of the Accounting Officer is not invoked, are not wholly remote in spirit from the Exchequer as described in the *Dialogus* of 1179.

In many countries, however, the ancient tradition of direct accountability has been retained unbroken, as the basic safeguard of

[1] P.A.C. Second Report, 1872.

[2] P.A.C. Third Report, 1920, and Third Report, 1921. The case had been originally brought to notice by the Comptroller and Auditor General.

[3] For a detailed consideration of the P.A.C. and its activities, see Basil Chubb, op. cit.

probity and legality in the handling of public money. Each paying officer or public accountant, whose duty is to receive and disburse state funds when requested to do so by qualified persons and in the proper form, must strike an annual balance in his affairs. Such a balance, however, has no legal validity until it has been confirmed by state audit. In such a role the public accountants are more than mere subordinates in a hierarchy; each one has a degree of personal independence and is, within his own reduced sphere, an 'Accounting Officer' in his own right. The correctness of the general ministerial accounts is verified by comparison with the numerous accounts of the paying officers who made the actual transactions. The regularity of these sub-accounts is checked by the several state audits by methods which may or may not be consciously judicial, but which usually are accompanied by the power to make disallowances and to invoke the paying officer's pecuniary liability.

France is the classic case. The Cour des Comptes is, at least in form, a court of law, with a specialized administrative jurisdiction, and all members of the auditing corps are magistrates of the court. The Cour was charged by Napoleon with judgment of the accounts of receipts and payments at all levels, including the départements and communes and the military and naval commands.[1] A law passed by the Vichy government declared that all *comptables* handling public funds were subject to the jurisdiction of the Cour.[2] On the strength of this, the Cour claims the role of 'common law judge of public funds', and control by state audit is consequently more difficult to escape than in many other lands. An exception of any kind, where public funds are involved, must be established by legislation. In some other countries, including Great Britain, on the contrary, positive legislation, or at least a Treasury decision, is required to subject any organization to proper accountability to Parliament (which necessarily involves state audit), and exceptions are therefore more easily and frequently made. In France the logic that acceptance of public financial support implies accountability for that support is respected; and the accepted definition of public funds includes those of local and overseas authorities as well as of the central government.

There are, however, many thousands of *comptables* handling public funds, and despite its judicial array, the Cour does not subject

[1] Law of 16 September 1807, Article 11.
[2] Law of 4 April 1941, Article 4.

them to a formal trial in person, like a medieval Sheriff before the Anglo-Norman Exchequer. It behaves, in fact, like an audit department; it examines the accounts and vouchers submitted by the *comptables* to Paris, and deals with queries by correspondence. Indeed it does not as a rule audit the accounts of small communes at all; this responsibility is delegated to the chief financial officer of each département, who holds the picturesque title of Trésorier-Payeur Général. For each account which it has audited, the Cour finally takes a decision which has the force of law, either acquitting the *comptable* or assigning to him a specific debt to public funds. It is the same kind of judicial decision that the medieval Exchequer used to take after auditing a Sheriff's accounts.

In France, the *comptables* form a special and unique corps, which together with its headquarters in the Ministry of Finance, is known as the Trésor. 'No definition of the Trésor exists,' says a modern specialist, but 'if we wanted to give it one, we might say that it consists of the whole financial services of the State, bound together by a unity of financial resources. . . . One could compare the Trésor to a very large bank, probably one of the biggest in the world.'[1] Through this organization, a product of administrative evolution rather than of creative decision, almost all the financial operations of public bodies of all kinds are conducted; thus the State retains the handling of all public funds. It is as if the Paymaster General had a personal representative in every British town and village to whom all taxes, local as well as national, had to be paid and from whom all public payments had to be collected.

This is not merely a banking system, but a means of financial control. Every *comptable* is personally liable to reimburse the loss to public funds resulting from an irregular payment, and is in duty bound to refuse to honour a payment order which he suspects to be in any way irregular. It is a means of controlling the regularity of official finance at its source. 'It is easy to appreciate,' writes M. Devaux, 'the moral force of a *comptable* who can reply to an official ordering a payment, "Whatever may be my desire to satisfy you, I cannot carry out the operation which you propose because the Cour des Comptes would become aware of it and I should have to reimburse the amount with my own money." '[2]

[1] G. Devaux, *La Comptabilité Publique*, vol. 1, p. 146, Paris, Presses Universitaires de France, 1957.

[2] Devaux, op. cit., vol. 1, p. 82.

The essence of the French system has been stressed by the Premier Président with great clarity:

The Cour des Comptes is not only a collegiate institution, like its German equivalent, it is a judicial body: if in certain cases it judges the *comptables* themselves and can condemn a negligent *comptable* to a fine, in principle it judges the accounts and not the *comptables*.

The settlement (*arrêté*) of an account by decision of justice is a solemn procedure, which has its origin not only in the circumstances of history but also in the fact that in France the public *comptable*, agent of the Ministry of Finance, is not a simple cashier; he is also a paying officer charged, under his personal responsibility, to exercise before payment a control of regularity over the official ordering payment (the *ordonnateur*), that is to say over the administrator. In judging the account and rejecting an expenditure or ordering collection of a receipt item, the Cour enforces and lends power to the control by the *comptable* over the administrator; it thus effects an administrative control at one stage removed, a control of regularity to which is increasingly added a control of efficiency, of the good use of voted funds.[1]

It has in fact always been a problem which troubled the Cour des Comptes that its statutes specifically directed control towards the responsibility of the paying officers rather than the ministers and higher officials qualified to order payments, who were in practice absolved of personal responsibility. Napoleon's law was quite specific about this: 'The Cour may not, in any case whatever, claim any jurisdiction over administrators (*ordonnateurs*).'[2] This was clear notice that no restriction upon the freedom of action of an absolutist executive would be tolerated. It was because of this legal situation that the indirect control, via the *comptables*, was evolved and encouraged by the Cour.

However, a number of financial scandals were reported by the Cour after the Second World War and a new organism was created which aimed at the enforcement of a personal responsibility for *ordonnateurs*. This was the Court of Budgetary Discipline, founded by a law of 26 September 1948. This Court holds session at the Cour des Comptes and its president is the Premier Président of the

[1] M. Roger Léonard, Premier Président de la Cour des Comptes, in a letter to the author, dated 11 January 1960.

[2] Law of 16 September 1807, Article 18. The word *ordonnateur* has no literal translation, but refers particularly to high officials and ministers. It might best be rendered as 'policy makers'.

Cour; the members are all drawn from the Cour and the Conseil d'Etat. This new court was given jurisdiction over infractions of budgetary legality or of general financial rules which might be committed by any officials, 'civil or military', though not by ministers. The offences for which fines are prescribed include making a commitment by an official not qualified to do so; incorrect charging of an expense to hide a budgetary excess; causing an irregular appointment or promotion; and favouring a particular contractor. Actions can be initiated by the Presidents of the Assemblies, by the Prime Minister and other ministers, by the Cour des Comptes and the audit body for nationalized industries, the Commission de Vérification des Comptes des Entreprises Publiques.

But it is far more difficult to impose personal responsibilities upon administrators than upon cashiers. In the first nine years of its existence this unusual Court reached only five verdicts, involving fines against eight officials, and these were mostly for activities of a nature which might have been expected to be the concern of the criminal courts. For example, the former Director General of a state enterprise was fined a million francs in 1957 for allowing a third party to obtain excessive advantages from certain contracts. In 1954 a senior officer was fined 250,000 frs. for using voted moneys to make 'payments for his personal utility'. Again in 1957 three officials were fined for irregular sale of State property.[1] These are no doubt offences which justly call for punishment, but they are scarcely to be classified as matters of mere budgetary discipline. Perhaps the eighteen other cases which were abandoned fell more strictly into this category.

The General Accounting Office is another state audit organization with responsibilities for controlling the transactions of individual public accountants. The Budget and Accounting Act of 1921 transferred to the G.A.O. all the legal powers and duties then vested in the Comptroller and auditors of the Treasury Department. Among these is the authority to 'settle and adjust' the accounts of government disbursing officers, which means to verify their regularity by audit, with power to make permanent disallowance of payments considered to be contrary to budgetary appropriation law or in other ways illegal. The Attorney General is expected to file a claim for recovery of any such illegal expenditure,

[1] Paul Therre, 'La Cour des Comptes et la Cour de Discipline Budgétaire'. Unpublished lecture, 1957 (Library of the Cour des Comptes).

and the disbursing officer[1] is personally liable for the amount unless he can recover it from the payee.

In the first two decades of its life, the General Accounting Office's power to 'settle' accounts gave rise to much controversy. The opinion of the Comptroller General became decisive in questions of financial legality. 'He could at will substitute his interpretation of what constituted a legal expenditure for that of any administrative official, including the Attorney General of the United States. Where disagreement arose, Congress alone was able to step in and settle the issue.'[2] This was not merely a technical difficulty, especially as the first Comptroller General, John R. McCarl, who held office from 1921 until 1936, was a person of dogmatic and high-handed character, disposed to the fullest assertion of his new authority. He was also out of sympathy with the New Deal policies of President Franklin Roosevelt. Some of the Comptroller General's legal decisions were the reverse of helpful at this period. He ruled, for example, that an artificial limb was not a medical supply for the purposes of government employees' compensation, that army officers assigned to assist the Civilian Conservation Corps—a New Deal creation—were not entitled to rental allowances, and that to be legal, a travel order authorizing transfer expenses for a federal employee, had to be signed personally by the Secretary of the Interior.

Matters in fact went beyond this and constitutional issues became involved. These disputes were, however, largely symptoms of immaturity. Not only was the Comptroller's office a new one, but existing financial legislation left plenty of scope for differences of interpretation. The difficulties have been rectified, partly by clarifying and limiting legislation,[3] but especially as a result of a new spirit in the General Accounting Office, which has learned from its experiences the essential truths that a co-operative and helpful attitude is necessary in the relations between state audit and the administration, and that merely obstructive criticism defeats its own object.

The examination of 'regularity' can, as we have seen, be

[1] Or his bonding company. In France, U.S.A. and elsewhere, public officials with a pecuniary liability are nowadays covered by some sort of insurance against the possibility that the liability will be invoked.

[2] John D. Millett, op. cit., p. 181.

[3] For example, Public Law 600 of the 79th Congress, 1946, which established regulations for many kinds of routine transactions.

conducted by state audit through the accounts of the officials who actually receive and pay money on behalf of the state. This was the original form of state audit and for many centuries almost the only form. But in twentieth-century conditions it has serious disadvantages. Because very many separate accounts are involved, it is slow and unwieldy. But a worse disadvantage is that each personal account represents only a fraction, and sometimes a very miscellaneous fraction, of total state expenditures; detailed examination of each fraction gives very little help in ascertaining and understanding the financial activities of an administration as a whole.

The problem of the control of regularity has to be considered in the light of the intentions of state audit. On the one hand there is the enforcement of high standards of personal integrity in the handling of public money and property. On the other, the entire state accounts have to be understood and declared correct. To do both thoroughly and comprehensively in this age of vast public finance would be a major operation for state audit unaided, and it would require a large staff and a great deal of routine checking, even if the audit were to perform no other tasks whatever.

This dilemma has already had important consequences. The massive growth of expenditure has not been matched by a similar growth in the size of the state audit bodies, which by and large have expanded only very modestly, and very much less rapidly than the civil services generally. There has, therefore, necessarily been a major reorganization of audit work. State audit has concentrated more and more upon the ministerial and departmental accounts, which give a much better idea of important financial questions than the individual cashiers' accounts. Even in France this 'administrative' type of audit has gained ever increasing importance in relation to the judicial procedure of tradition.[1] In most countries the 'administrative' audit is overwhelmingly the most important, and there are audit departments, such as the British, whose statutes provide for nothing else.

Again, the increases in volume of national expenditures have to some degree been offset by a reduction in the necessity for all-embracing control of 'regularity'. As national administrations

[1] The Premier Président of the Cour des Comptes, M. Roger Léonard, informed the author that this was so. He added, however, that the judicial status of the Cour gave it 'a highly strategic position' from which to criticize the administration, even in a non-judicial way.

gain in experience, as their staffs grow up with the rules and improve them to provide precedents for all kinds of situations, so the risk of budgetary irregularities declines. At the same time, advances in banking and accounting techniques make book-keeping error less probable and fraud by officials more difficult. A large department is an administrative machine, and it is hard for any individual to turn a machine into an accomplice. The award of permanent status and pensions to civil servants in all the advanced countries placed them in a position where the risk involved in dishonesty was scarcely worth while. For all these reasons the control of regularity alone tended to decline into a routine. At the same time very important new state audit techniques were being developed in various countries, techniques which lie outside the traditional field of 'regularity'. The emphasis in the critical activities has changed and continues to change.

In an imperfect State, populated by fallible citizens, however, it will never be possible to abandon entirely the control of regularity. It is at once a legal and an accounting safeguard, a protection against negligent and slovenly administration as well as against actual fraud, a security for public stores as well as cash, and above all a major constitutional guarantee essential for a healthy relationship between the administrative and the political powers, between executives and lawmakers. Moreover, control of regularity is not incompatible with more 'advanced' state audit techniques. Any transaction can be considered with reference both to the fairly rigid and factual criteria of regularity and to the more subtle tests of economy, merit and efficiency. State audit is learning to combine the operations.

The fact remains, nevertheless, that the volume of public financial operations in all the greater modern countries far exceeds the capacity of state audit to make any kind of general examination at all. As a result of this, three things have happened. In the first place state audit has abandoned the attempt to check everything and has in many cases obtained legislative authority to do so. Secondly, there has been ever greater emphasis upon *internal* auditing of regularity. Thirdly, state audit has concentrated more and more upon examination of the methods and procedures adopted by administrative departments to prevent irregularities in each sphere of operations; upon the efficacy of internal audit and control. A doctrine of 'super-audit' has evolved, and there has in some countries been an increasingly precise co-operation and division of labour between state and internal audits.

In the United Kingdom the signs were indeed already visible in the Exchequer and Audit Departments Act of 1866, which gave to the Comptroller and Auditor General discretion to accept as satisfactory evidence of payment Army and Navy Account vouchers which had been 'completely checked, examined, and certified as correct in every respect, and. . . allowed and passed by the proper departmental officers'. But to do so for other accounts he required the consent of the Treasury.[1] The E. and A. Departments Act of 1921 put the matter much more simply:

> The Comptroller and Auditor General, after satisfying himself that the vouchers have been examined and certified as correct by the accounting department, may, in his discretion and having regard to the character of the departmental examination, in any particular case admit the sums so certified without further evidence of payment in support of the charges to which they relate.[2]

The C. & A.G.'s personal discretion to make a test-audit[3] was now in practice almost complete. The 1921 Act also made the audit of receipts of revenue and of store accounts a part of the audit on behalf of Parliament; the 1866 statute seems to have considered the parliamentary audit as a check of payments only. For both revenue and stores, the Comptroller and Auditor General was charged by the 1921 Act to ascertain that adequate regulations and procedures had been devised and were being applied; this attention to the quality of internal control was a new emphasis.

The German budget law of 1922 made provision for test-auditing and internal audit:

> . . . accounts are to be subjected to a preliminary audit by the responsible departments, during which . . . the vouchers are to be checked and verified arithmetically and the accounts and vouchers are to be examined from a formal and factual point of view. . . . The results of the preliminary audit are to be reported to the Rechnungshof when the

[1] E. & A. Depts. Act 1866, Sections 29 and 30.

[2] E. & A. Depts. Act 1921, Section 1(2), which however reserved to the Treasury the power to request a more detailed examination of 'the vouchers or any of them'.

[3] The French equivalent for 'test-audit' is to take 'soundings' (sondages) which is both apt and expressive.

account is submitted, together with the necessary explanations, observations and certificates.

The Rechnungshof was given full authority to restrict or dispense with audits as it saw fit, to waive the submission of vouchers, and even to limit or renounce the preliminary audits. On the other hand it could amplify or amend the preliminary auditors' observations and take its own decisions thereon. Finally, it was periodically to ensure that the administration of funds, the submission of accounts and the preliminary audit were being carried out in the prescribed manner.[1]

Here was clear evidence of a principle of 'super-audit', giving state audit precedence over internal audits, although the latter were directly regulated by the individual departments themselves. Since the establishment of the West German Republic a complete preliminary audit regulation for the federal administration[2] has been issued, in the interests of uniform procedure.

This regulation contains innovations in line with modern ideas about internal audit. Every ministry is to set up a pre-audit office, and appoint its head in agreement with the Bundesrechnungshof. The office is directly responsible to the minister, who may delegate his powers to an official for this purpose. The official should, however, be the permanent head of the department (Staatssekretär), since the appointment of a person in charge of a subordinate section might lead to a collision of interests with the pre-audit office which would limit the impartiality and independence of the audit. The department head is to protect the pre-audit's status and to ensure that errors and weaknesses reported by it are corrected. The pre-audit office is to follow the directions and guidance of the Bundesrechnungshof and to report it to any important questions which arise during the audit. The aim of pre-audit is declared to be: '. . . to prepare for the audit by the Bundesrechnungshof, and also to guarantee as complete a supervision of the execution of the budget as possible in those cases where the Bundesrechnungshof makes only a test-audit.' The scope of pre-audit covers the full legal and accounting regularity of receipts and expenditures and the administration of public property.[3] The Bundesrechnungshof can undertake local audits jointly with the

[1] RHO. 1922, Sections 92 to 94.

[2] Vorprüfungsordnung für die Bundesverwaltung, 1953.

[3] It is a sign of the times that provision is made for arithmetical checking to be dispensed with in the case of machine-prepared accounts.

pre-audit office, and can, if so requested, advise the minister in the case of any unsolved dispute between the pre-audit office and the audited department.

The points of particular interest in all this are two. The first is the emphasis upon the independence of internal audit within its parent department. The real point at issue is whether the internal auditors should be responsible to the heads of the finance or accounts branches within departments; the answer in Germany, and in the United States also, is decisively in the negative. Such subordination might place them in the position of having reason to criticize the actions and decisions of their own immediate superior, which would inevitably endanger their independence. The point is a valid one: placing internal audit in direct responsibility to the head of the ministry gives it a detachment which is a vital asset for all impartial auditing.

Secondly, the systematic dovetailing of the functions of external and internal audit, under the general supervision of the former, appears to be a rational way of utilizing limited manpower resources. It also provides a pool of audit information upon which all can draw. It clarifies and improves the status of internal audit, whilst differentiating it from that of the state audit body, with its overall responsibilities for the correctness of the state accounts and for reporting upon them to the Federal parliament.

There are indeed the best possible reasons why the main burden of examination of regularity should be borne by internal audit. This necessarily has the more intimate knowledge of the activities of its parent department. And the state audit body is freed to conduct newer types of audit, to study administrative procedures, to investigate questions of particular importance which may necessitate report action, and to consider matters of general principle. If state audit is to obtain a really clear picture over the entire field of its national responsibilities, and to do so with a small fixed staff, it must be given systematic rather than random assistance.

The same considerations are very clearly apparent in the Budget and Accounting Procedures Act of 1950, in the United States. This is part of a very large scale campaign which has been waged ever since 1947, and which is still continuing, for improvement of the entire financial administration of the Federal Government. The campaign is sponsored by the General Accounting Office, in cooperation with the Bureau of the Budget and the Treasury Department, and it was strongly encouraged by the two Commissions on Organization of the Executive Branch of the Government (whose chairman was Herbert Hoover, the former President of the United States), which reported in 1949 and 1955.

The main emphasis both of the 1950 Act and of the campaign as a whole was upon a major improvement of internal accounting and control within the departments and agencies. This in its turn permitted the abandonment of the cumbersome procedure upon which the first Comptroller General had insisted, whereby all payment vouchers and supporting details of every financial transaction had to be sent to the G.A.O. in Washington. The Hoover Commission of 1949 recommended that this be replaced by a 'spot sampling process', a test-audit.

The Act of 1950, a highly practical document, laid down that:

> The head of each executive agency shall establish and maintain systems of accounting and internal control designed to provide:
> (1) full disclosure of the financial results of the agency's activities.
> (2) adequate financial information needed for the agency's management purposes.
> (3) effective control over and accountability for all funds, property, and other assets for which the agency is responsible, including appropriate internal audit.[1]

The General Accounting Office was to co-operate with the agencies in developing their accounting systems, to review the systems from time to time, and to determine the adequacy of internal audit and control over operations. The general intention of rationalization was proclaimed to be:

> effecting orderly improvements resulting in simplified and more effective accounting, financial reporting, budgeting and auditing requirements and procedures and . . . the elimination of those which involve duplication or which do not serve a purpose commensurate with the costs involved.

The central accounting system was also to be overhauled, and the Comptroller General was authorized to waive, jointly with the Secretary of the Treasury, certain routine operations required by law. When the Comptroller was satisfied that the internal controls of the agencies were sufficient, he was empowered to discontinue his elaborate book-keeping in the G.A.O.

[1] Budget and Accounting Procedures Act, 1950, Section 113.

The influence of the accounting profession upon this comprehensive programme of modernization can probably be detected in the provision which instructs the Comptroller General to 'give due regard to generally accepted principles of auditing'. The second Hoover Commission in 1955 commented very favourably upon the G.A.O., which had begun to perform 'modern commercial-type audits at the site of agency operations' and had abandoned its duplicate records of all expenditures. 'By 1955,' says another observer, 'the Congress of the United States had acquired a powerful instrument for keeping the financial operations of government under surveillance.'[1] The General Accounting Office calls its revised methods 'comprehensive audit', in contradistinction from the old 'centralized audit', which was a routine check of the formal regularity of vouchers, entirely conducted in Washington. A well qualified foreign visitor reached this conclusion: 'The real revolution brought about by comprehensive audit is the external control by the G.A.O. of an internal control organized under its supervision and with its co-operation.'[2]

The institution of internal audit, which has existed for many years in the United Kingdom and Germany, at least in simple forms, and which has now attained greater sophistication in Germany and the United States, does not appear to exist at all[3] in the French Republic. The reason for this may perhaps lie in the highly original financial administration of France, under which, as we have described, a monopoly of public cash transactions is held by the agents of the Minister of Finance, organized in the service of the 'Trésor'. It may be that the executive departments felt it superfluous to provide for an audit of cash which they never held, and for which the *comptables* were personally responsible. The situation may also help to explain the importance which the Cour des Comptes continues to attach to its judicial procedures. It is in effect the only *a posteriori* audit organization in the French public service, and therefore no doubt feels the need for

[1] Millett, op. cit., p. 189.

[2] P. Senechal, Conseiller référendaire à la Cour des Comptes, 'Le General Accounting Office', an unpublished but valuable survey. Date about 1956 (Library of the Cour des Comptes).

[3] Unless the examination carried out by the Trésoriers-Payeurs Généraux of the départements acting as authorized auxiliaries of the Cour des Comptes can be called internal audit. But the Trésoriers-Payeurs are not full-time auditors by profession.

powers sufficient to impose and maintain a healthy respect for its decisions.

If France has nothing recognizable as an internal audit, this does not mean that it has no internal controls. On the contrary, there are a great many corps of inspection or control, which are another characteristic feature of Gallic administration. There are 'Inspections générales' of Finance and of the Administration, 'Contrôles' of the Army, Navy and Armée de l'Air, 'Inspections' of the Ponts et Chaussées, the Trésor, the P.T.T. and of various ministries. The prestige of these bodies varies considerably; that of the Inspection Générale des Finances is very high. It is one of the *grands corps de l'Etat*, like the Cour des Comptes. For the rest, the various inspectors and controllers are persons of senior rank and ill-defined duties. Their basic function is to keep their ministers informed about the activities of their subordinates; they make spot checks and inspections and report directly to their political chiefs. But they are not auditors, even though they may sometimes verify cash or stores. Their surveillance is over administrative and financial activities, but it seems that in the nineteenth century some of the corps were required to provide their ministers with confidential reports of a political nature. Thus, for example, republican Ministers of Marine could be kept informed of the activities of Admirals opposed to the Republic.

The control of regularity through inspection is a particularly French tradition, and in the case of the Inspectors of Finance, who have a very wide field of competence wherever financial action is taking place, the effect may be considerable.[1] The weakness of inspection, as compared with audit, is a certain vagueness of approach. The auditor has one incomparable advantage over all other types of fact-finder in that the accounts give him a practical basis for systematic examination and researches; if he works carefully through them from beginning to end and makes enquiries about what is not clear to him, there is little chance that anything very important can escape his notice.

The State Comptroller's law in Israel gives what is perhaps the

[1] In fact, however, more than half the members of the Inspection Générale des Finances are normally on detachment in high posts, a far higher proportion than in the case of the Cour des Comptes. The Inspection appears to be tending to forget its original functions. See P. Lalumière, *L'Inspection des Finances*, Part II, Chapter 2, Paris, Presses Universitaires de France, 1959.

clearest and most up-to-date legal definition of the concerns involved for state audit—and to a large extent of internal audit also—in the control of regularity. The State Comptroller is charged to examine whether departments have operated 'in a morally irreproachable manner', and also:

(*a*) whether every expenditure has been incurred within the limits of the legal appropriation and for the purpose for which it was assigned;
(*b*) whether the income has been received in accordance with law and is authorized by law;
(*c*) whether there are sufficient vouchers in respect of all expenditure and income;
(*d*) whether every act . . . has been done in accordance with law and by the person competent to do it;
(*e*) whether the keeping of the accounts, the drawing-up of balance-sheets, the checking of the cash-in-hand and the stock, and the voucher systems, are efficient;
(*f*) whether the method of keeping moneys and safeguarding property is satisfactory;
(*g*) whether the state of the cash-in-hand and the stock tallies with the accounts.[1]

* * * *

This general survey of the control of regularity by state audit permits a few tentative conclusions. The necessity for this kind of control is not controversial. Any type of government, liberal-democratic or totalitarian, will wish to ensure that the administration is adhering to the programme ratified by the political powers. There is no more effective way of confirming this in detail than by systematic examination of the financial accounts and records, since almost all administrative activity must necessarily be reflected there. Similarly public opinion under any regime is bound to favour the principle that public resources should be handled with scrupulous honesty, and that procedures should exist to guarantee this. The *a posteriori* control of regularity ensures not merely that an administrative machine works and works with integrity, but that it is under command.

[1] State Comptroller's Law, 1958 (consolidated version), Section 10. It may be noted that some state audit bodies, including the British, refrain as a matter of policy from making physical checks of cash and stores. In Britain this rests upon a Treasury decision of 1872 'to retain in their own hands the power of verifying balances at any given moment', in order to maintain 'the distinction between administration and audit'. (Treasury Minute 14/8/1872. *Epitome*, vol. 1, p. 30.)

This control is based upon the examination of vouchers, which are the paper record of transactions. The growth of spending and of administrative action has led to an incalculably great increase in these records. This has, however, been offset by the development of office and banking procedures which have reduced the danger that these records may be tampered with or falsified. It is unnecessary that the routine work of audit should be increased to keep step with the rise in expenditures. It is sufficient that samples be taken, to see how things are going.

The work of regularity audit can very profitably be carried out 'on the spot' by internal audit; a system which promises to be both expeditious and economical, and to provide direct audit information to heads of departments. Internal audit should not, however, be entrusted merely to anyone in an accounts branch, but should be given a proper independent status, with direct access to the head of the office. There should also be an organized relationship between internal audit and the state audit body, based upon their different responsibilities, so that one can assist the other and demand assistance if necessary, and so that duplication of work can be avoided. The tasks of internal and external audit should be treated as complementary, and organized accordingly; their stocks of information and experience should be pooled. The gain to the auditing services would be considerable; in particular the high constitutional reporting functions of state audit would benefit.

Since a state audit body cannot hope to take more than very limited 'soundings' from the general mass of administrative records, the question arises of how it should best employ its resources. Executive accountability can be considered as a matter of collective responsibility or as the sum of the responsibilities of individuals. State audit might be wise to concentrate upon the former, leaving the latter principally as a concern for internal audit. State audit needs to watch the administrative machine as a whole; internal audit can keep an eye upon the men who tend it. State audit should, and does, concern itself more and more with systems and procedures, considering whether they have been well designed for the avoidance of irregularity in all kinds of conditions.

The main new development thus appears to be the emergence of internal audit with new status and dignity as the main controller of regularity in the bulky accounts of today, and the association of state audit with it, on the basis of the doctrine of the super-audit. We saw enough of the special circumstances of France, however, to recall that administrative systems may be highly individual, and that some countries may have an approach so original that for them 'general trends' are almost meaningless.

In any case, the control of regularity is not an exciting new technique but the basic routine of state audit. It is outside the field of regularity that state audit is breaking really new ground. The increasingly widespread realization that state audit can provide positive and vital information about finance and administration, as well as a negative guarantee against irregularity, has led to some remarkable innovations.

But before we leave the question of regularity there is one aspect of it which is of sufficient interest to merit a chapter of its own. This is the attempt to achieve control before payments are made, and thus avoid irregularity altogether.

CHAPTER V

Audit as Preventive Control

'It is better to prevent than to lament'
—Old Saw

A LAYMAN'S complaint against state audit is that its observations and criticisms are too late; the errors and omissions have already been made, the misdemeanours perpetrated, the money wasted, the damage done. Action should have been taken earlier, the trouble should have been prevented and the public's resources protected. The argument is a valid one, and it demands an answer.

In a general way, all audit is preventive. The knowledge that the records created in the course of business will come under the scrutiny of shrewd and experienced auditors is a very strong deterrent to carelessness and negligence, to fraud, to defiance of law and regulation, to overspending and even to abuse of power. It is not unknown for an auditor to observe in official records an internal note from one branch to another which says, 'We would be glad to adopt the method which you propose, but cannot do so because it would expose us to audit criticism,' or words to the same effect. Thus, by the mere presence of an audit, irregularity is suppressed at its source and never comes to notice at all.

But this is begging the question. Auditors are not merely stuffed watchdogs; they must inspire respect not by their presence alone but by evidence of their alertness. If an audit is content to be passive and to cling to a negative routine, it will earn the contemptuous indifference of the administration and the auditors' own morale will decline. And just as modern state audit interests itself more and more in the financial control arrangements of others, so it must expect enquiry into its own procedures. A question which must then be expected is: 'cannot an active, and positive form of prevention be devised?'

*　　*　　*　　*

In fact, procedures for the preventive control of expenditures do exist. The idea is an old one. Such *a priori* control can be internal, within the executive or even within a department itself. The legislature may play its part. Or it can be exercised principally by state audit. Preventive control can be applied at four distinct stages before actual payment is made; during examination of the estimates submitted by departments for approval and legislative ratification, at the moment when funds are issued out of the central reserve, before a specific and binding commitment is made, and when payment has actually been ordered.

Estimates

There is a fair degree of international agreement that the control of departmental estimates is the prime responsibility of the Ministries of Finance, subject to review and revision by those legislatures which assert themselves.

Legislatures in Western countries are indeed always potential competitors of the executive in the control of departmental estimates. For many years the House of Commons aspired to achieve some such control through its Estimates Committees.[1] In the early twenties the Committee members asked for the appointment of an expert 'Examiner of Estimates' to advise them. But no such post was ever created, and the Committee's attempt to control estimates by taking the figures in turn and asking random questions was eventually conceded to be amateurish and unprofitable. Since the Second World War the Estimates Committee has adopted the technique of investigating selected blocks of current expenditure and particular problems. The practical results have proved more satisfactory, but the legislature appears for the time being to have abandoned the field of detailed estimates control and left the executive in full command.[2]

In France, the system of parliamentary Commissions de Finances created strong competition for control of preparation of the budget. Under the Third Republic especially, the Commission of the popular chamber had what has been called, 'the regrettable habit of turning the government's draft budget completely upside down in order to try to substitute its own'.[3] There has been a

[1] 1912–14 and 1921–39.

[2] See Chubb, op. cit., especially Chapters VIII and IX. There is one school of thought which deplores the decline of parliamentary control over estimates. See Paul Einzig, op. cit.

[3] Maurice Duverger, *Les Finances Publiques*, Paris, Presses Universitaires de France, 2nd edn., 1960.

strong movement of opinion away from this practice. Already the Constitution of 1946, although it recognized the traditional right of individual initiative of French republican deputies in matters of public finance, declared this right suspended during the discussion of the budget, in so far as it concerned proposals to create or augment expenditures.[1] This considerably restricted the activities of the Finance Commission of the National Assembly, but it nevertheless retained the right to modify the proposals for receipts, or in other words to influence taxation. Under the Fifth Republic the right to initiate amendments tending to increase expenditure or reduce revenues has been lost by all deputies. The law now states:

No additional Article, no amendment to a draft budget law may be presented, unless it tends to eliminate or reduce an expenditure, to create or increase an item of receipt or to improve the control of public spending.[2]

The independence of parliament in financial matters has also been circumscribed by a time-limit upon consideration of draft budgets. If no decision has been pronounced within seventy days after submission of the draft, the government can bring it into force by decree (*ordonnance*). Thus the law has moved in favour of the executive in General De Gaulle's authoritarian republic. But it should be recalled that the Members of the British House of Commons signed away their right to propose expenditures when they accepted as a Standing Order, the rule which states, 'that this House will receive no petition, for any sum of money, relating to public service, but what is recommended from the Crown'. This happened as long ago as 11 June 1713.

The Congress of the United States has traditionally retained in its purest form the power to control budget estimates. Before 1921, indeed, there was no effective scrutiny by the executive of the estimates of departments and agencies, which made direct application for funds to various Congressional committees. There was therefore no planned balance between spending and revenue; no proper budget at all. The requirements of modern administration were bound to come into conflict with this chaotic arrangement.

[1] Constitution of 27 October 1946, Article 17.

[2] Ordonnance of 3 Janvier 1959, 'portant loi organique relative aux lois de finances', Article 42.

As a result of such pressures, the Budget and Accounting Act created an executive budget system which imposed the work of drafting and presentation upon the President. For this task, the President was equipped with a Bureau of the Budget,[1] with authority to 'assemble, correlate, revise, reduce, or increase the requests for appropriations of the several departments or establishments', in accordance with rules prescribed by the President.[2] However, the President only received the power to recommend expenditures to Congress, and both the Budget Bureau and the General Accounting Office were required by the 1921 Act to assist Congress and its committees when required.[3] Nevertheless, the power of budget scrutiny is a very substantial power and in 1921 this accrued to the executive branch. Congress did not assume any obligation to accept the President's recommendations. 'Yet,' we are told, 'the fact is that the legislature only occasionally undertakes any substantial alteration in the budget estimates submitted by the President. Once expenditure plans have been put together and the whole set forth in the context of a particular set of taxation and other fiscal policies, there are powerful incentives to leave the whole structure unchanged.'[4] So, rather to our surprise, we find that even in Washington the effective control of estimates has passed largely into the hands of the executive.[5] The Congress is naturally disturbed at the loss of its former prerogatives, and a few years ago the Senate advocated the establishment of a Joint Committee on the Budget, which would have been entitled to employ as many staff as it might require. It was a response to the same urges which led to the proposal for an 'Examiner of Estimates' in England.

Considered objectively, it would seem a reasonable and logical proposition that state audit bodies, which spend their whole time in active study of the financial behaviour of departments, should be called upon in a consultant's role at the time that new estimates from the same departments are under consideration. Such a pro-

[1] At first part of the Treasury Dept., the Bureau of the Budget became part of the President's own Executive Office on 1 July 1939.

[2] Budget & Accounting Act, 1921, Section 207, as amended by Public Law 784, 81st Congress.

[3] 1921 Act, Sections 212 and 312 (*a*) to (*d*).

[4] Millett, op. cit., pp. 352–3.

[5] The legislative scrutiny of estimates nevertheless remains very thorough when judged by British standards.

cedure would strengthen and complete the machinery of the financial control cycle. Yet although both French and American laws provide in a general way for the audit bodies to assist both legislature and executive as and when required, it is only in Western Germany among the larger western countries, that a formula has been devised which provides systematically for audit advice during budget preparations.

The German budget law dating from 1922 specified that the Reich Finance Minister was to submit documents dealing with the draft budget for the coming financial year to the President of the Rechnungshof. The latter was to express opinions and make suggestions thereon, wherever the findings of audit gave reason to do so. This arrangement still has legal force, but a more recent procedure appears to be of much greater importance.

The new procedure derives from a Federal Cabinet decision of 8 January 1952, which confided to the President of the Bundesrechnungshof the title and duties of Federal Commissioner for Efficiency in the Administration.[1] The Commissioner's broad function is to advise both the Federal government and the legislature on all questions of efficiency and rationalization in the public service, with economy as the objective. To do this, he not only uses the knowledge acquired by the Rechnungshof during audit, but also conducts Organization and Methods studies, about which we shall say more in a later chapter.[2] What is interesting here is that he is to take part in drawing up the budget estimates.[3] How this arrangement works is described by the Bundesrechnungshof:

> The Federal Ministers compile an estimate for the next financial year and submit this to the Federal Finance Minister. They forward a copy of the estimate to the President of the Bundesrechnungshof in his capacity of Federal Commissioner for Efficiency in the Administration. The President has the estimates examined; the experience acquired in the course of audit is then utilized. His representatives also take part in the Federal Finance Minister's preliminary discussions of the estimates with the responsible ministers; they thus have the opportunity of contributing to an economical and businesslike estimation of budget requirements. Moreover the President of the Bundesrechnungshof, as Federal Commissioner . . . takes part in the debates upon the draft

---

[1] See Chapter III above. [2] Chapter IX below.

[3] This is laid down in para. 4. of the Commissioner's Terms of Reference (Richtlinien), approved by the Federal Cabinet in 1952.

Federal budget in the Budget Committee of the German Bundestag, or sends his representatives. In this way he is given the opportunity to report directly to the competent committee of parliament his opinion as to the necessity, the suitability and also the amount of the funds requested for expenditure. This is of great importance, particularly when the executive bodies concerned have not taken fully into account the audit observations raised by him.[1]

The law of 2 June 1960, which regulated the preparation of the budget, empowered the Budget Committee of the Bundestag to request any expert advice from the President of the Bundesrechnungshof, as Federal Commissioner. His views were henceforward always to be obtained by the committee in case of a proposal for virement of voted funds in a matter of staff requirements.[2]

The control of estimates constitutes a part of the 'planning' aspect of financial control. It leads to a positive decision—the final drafting of the budget. The other three stages at which preventive intervention can take place prior to actual payment are, however, occasions for the examination of decisions already made. Control of the issue of funds, of commitments and of payment orders is intervention between decision and execution, whereas conventional audit is subsequent to both. It is called *a priori* control, but is so only in relation to the executive act. Such *a priori* control by state audit could not be fully discussed in the study of a single country's audit arrangements, because in no one country does the audit intervene at all three stages, namely before issue, commitment and payment. Indeed some national audit bodies reject all *a priori* control as a matter of principle. But in an international study examples can be shown of such control operating at all three stages, although not all in the same country.

Issues

The first of these stages is the moment when voted funds are to be issued to the executive for use. Control by an audit body at this juncture is peculiarly a tradition of the English-speaking countries. When, until recent centuries, funds were necessarily held in

[1] From an internal memorandum, 'Übersicht über die Aufgaben und die Stellung des Bundesrechnungshofes', August 1958.

[2] Gesetz über die Feststellung des Bundeshaushaltsplanes für das Rechnungsjahr 1960; 2 June 1960, Sections 20 and 32.

the form of precious metals, the ceremony of opening the state's money-chests for issue was a solemn one, surrounded by precaution and protocol. The advent of modern banking has long since changed the scene; the issue of money is a simple book-keeping operation, it is credit rather than cash which changes hands—and the bank is responsible for strict adherence to its instructions. Nevertheless issues from the national treasuries have been subjected to a form of control by state audit in both America and Britain.

The United States, which as we tend to forget is quite old as a political organism, appears to have historical priority here. Although the power to countersign Treasury warrants was only vested in the Comptroller General in 1921, it was first given to the Comptroller of the Treasury in 1789. The control was based upon the constitutional provision that 'no money shall be drawn from the Treasury, but in consequence of appropriations made by law'. The warrants were issued by the Secretary of the Treasury and, when the Comptroller had certified their legality, they authorized the Treasurer of the U.S. to withdraw money from the Treasury and transfer it to disbursing officers.

In England, control of issues from the Exchequer existed through the centuries according to an elaborate procedure, but it was not embodied in a system sanctioned by Parliament until 1834, when the office of Comptroller General of His Majesty's Exchequer was created. His main function was to verify the legality of issues—by that time made from the Bank of England—to public officers, and to do so for the first time on behalf of Parliament rather than of 'the Crown'. The duty was incorporated in the office of Comptroller and Auditor General, created in 1866. In principle, the Comptroller is the guardian of the Exchequer account at the Bank of England, into which all revenue is paid, and he should have a constant record from the Bank of the receipts and issues. The Treasury regularly raises a formal requisition for funds, but this cannot give rise to an issue until credit has been granted by the Comptroller, when he has decided that such issue is authorized by statute. The procedure has scarcely changed since 1834.

The original motives of these British and American controls of issue are more obvious than their utility in modern conditions. There was very naturally a sentiment among legislators in an age when legislative supremacy over finance was a battle slogan rather than a reality, that public money should be paid out only for purposes accepted by the legislatures. There was then also a real danger that it would be paid out for other purposes.

The essential difficulty in the present age of complex government is that one can hardly know anything about the final destination of a sum of money at the time of its requisition and issue. When a department receives a lump sum to the credit of its votes, it will expend the funds upon a wide range of different purposes. If none of these expenditures are irregular it will be because of the controls which are known to follow payment and not because of anything which might have happened before issue was made from Exchequer or U.S. Treasury. If there is irregularity it cannot be prevented at the issue stage, when the irregular intention cannot be declared or even known at all. 'The Comptroller', wrote a student in the United States, 'has no way of knowing from the warrant whether the money will be spent legally or not. As a result, this countersigning of warrants has, in effect, become a . . . duty which is of no real consequence in controlling the expenditure of appropriated funds.'[1] In 1902, Lord Welby, a former permanent secretary of the Treasury, told the National Expenditure Committee substantially the same thing. He had, he said, always been struck by the fact that the House of Commons had remained for so long under the misconception 'that it could control expenditure by putting checks on the issue of money from the Exchequer instead of ascertaining how the money had been spent'.[2]

The survival of this somewhat illusory kind of control is not, however, a matter of major public importance. The view has sometimes been expressed that it still represents a reserve power of potential utility in the event that a government should resort to arbitrary or unconstitutional expenditure. The staff engaged upon Exchequer control in Great Britain is in any case only a small fraction of that employed upon state audit duties. In the United States, the Budget and Accounting Procedures Act of 1950 permitted the Comptroller General and the Secretary of the Treasury discretion jointly to waive the existing legal requirement that 'warrants be issued and countersigned in connection with the receipt, retention and disbursement of public moneys'. It does not,

[1] James A. Hare, in a paper entitled, 'The Comptroller General: Watchdog or Wolfhound?' (Cornell University, 1958).

[2] Quoted from H.C. 387 of 1902 by Chubb, op. cit., p. 14. See also the comments of Einzig, op. cit., p. 176.

however, appear that the practice of countersigning appropriation warrants has been discontinued.[1]

Commitments and Payments

With the control of commitments we come to a real problem of practical administration. The commitment stage is a decisive one; it is at this point that errors and irregularities, as well as sound policies, become binding and irrevocable. Thereafter, the moment when actual payment is impending provides the final opportunity for prevention of errors. Various devices have been invented for preventive control of commitments and payments. The executive generally holds the field, without serious challenge from the legislatures. In a few countries, however, state audit is a competitor. And there are several solutions to the problem of how far departments should be autonomous within the executive itself.

In the English-speaking countries the concept of control of commitments is not very clearly developed. It is mainly in countries of what might be called the Latin administrative tradition that control routines have been devised which are applied by independent officials to all draft contracts, proposed engagements of staff and other future liabilities. This is not quite the same thing as the requirement of prior Treasury approval in the United Kingdom for such things as increases of establishment, of salary, of the cost of a service, and of new works and services not specifically voted by Parliament. Any British department will be well advised to seek such prior approval before it embarks upon any new activity which will involve liabilities. But the approval will usually be for the new policy or activity as a whole, and there is no machinery for control of specific commitments made under cover of the general approval. Indeed we are told that British administrators have considerably more freedom to make commitments than their American counterparts; they can, for example, make binding contracts which will involve payments in future financial years, for which no funds have yet been voted by Parliament. They are also less strictly dependent upon statutory sanction.[2]

[1] This practice was still mentioned by the General Accounting Office as its 'initial control of appropriated funds' in U.S. Government Organization Manual, 1957–8, pp. 35–6.

[2] Beer, op. cit., pp. 45–56. The power to commit funds not yet voted is certainly exceptional. In Germany, for example, a contract (other than for a matter of recurring routine) requires approval in the budget if it commits

The control of actual commitments in Great Britain is therefore a matter for the individual departments, acting with unusually wide discretion within the framework of voted funds and Treasury approval. This involves an especially great departmental responsibility in the placing of contracts, and for this some advice on general principles is available from the inter-departmental Contracts Co-ordinating Committee. There is also a body of precedent in the Epitome of the Reports of the Committees of Public Accounts. For the rest, departments must use their own discretion, even in contracting for very large sums and with industries not remarkable for competition in pricing. Professor Beer appreciated the freedom of manœuvre of the British executive to incur liabilities, but he added that it was 'also the opportunity to act thoughtlessly, incoherently and with extravagance'.

In France, on the other hand, the Minister of Finance has, since 1922, had his own representative, the *contrôleur des dépenses engagées*,[1] in every ministry. No contract or other document creating a commitment is valid without the 'visa' of this senior official, and if he refuses his visa it may be granted solely by the Minister of Finance. His control is essentially one of regularity only. But this is only the formal aspect of the matter; in practice the *contrôleurs* have a wide range of duties. They maintain records of their visas to assist control at the payment stage, and they report regularly to the Minister of Finance and give opinions upon all the financial projects of the ministry to which they are attached. In their fact-finding and advisory functions they are not confined to considerations of regularity.

In France also there is a *Commission consultative centrale des marchés* for the study of contracts. In contrast to the Co-ordinating Committee in the United Kingdom, which is concerned only with general policy, its function includes giving advice upon all draft contracts involving really large expenditures.

In Western Germany preventive control is confided to a specially appointed 'Official responsible for the Budget' (Sachbearbeiter des Haushalts) in every department. He is, however, a member of the internal staff rather than an agent of the Finance

---

future budgets, though the Finance Minister may approve exceptions. (RHO. Section 45(b).)

[1] The title *contrôleur financier* has been recently used.

Ministry. The situation is therefore not radically different from that in the English-speaking countries.

Only in Italy is the state audit department responsible for a control of commitments. This is part of a general duty of 'preventive control of the legitimacy of the actions of the government', under article 100 of the Constitution of 27 December 1947.[1] A commitment is not legally valid without the visa of the Corte dei Conti, which exercises this control through officers responsible for each major department and in some cases working within it. The most important preventive control is that of contracts, but the test in all cases is purely one of regularity. If the visa is refused on a point of law, the Council of Ministers can order the Corte to grant a 'visa with reserve'; such cases are reported to parliament. But if the Corte alleges a budgetary violation its refusal of visa is in such a case absolute; a provision which suggests what really mattered to the nineteenth-century law-makers who devised the system.

This unique Italian control machinery derives from the founding statute of the Corte in 1862, passed very soon after the unification of Italy, whilst Turin was still the capital. It was a product, therefore, of exceptional times, when pan-Italian conformity to the legal and administrative standards of Piedmont was a vital objective for the legislators. The parliamentary system itself was a recent creation, for which a strong control of finance and of executive acts represented both self-assertion and self-defence. The Italian preventive control is not a forward-looking administrative experiment but a product of the historical influences of the Risorgimento.

It has, nevertheless, often been examined with interest. The principles which it involves were studied and discussed by a magistrate of the French Cour des Comptes as long ago as 1890.[2] He considered not only the control of commitments and other acts of the executive, but also the visa control of payment orders, which the Corte exercises *a priori* and with the same criteria of legal and budgetary regularity. This student's conclusions still have validity, not only for Italy but for *a priori* control of commitments and payments by state audit in any imaginable context.

[1] See above, Chapter III.

[2] Victor de Marcé: *La Cour des Comptes Italienne*, Paris, circa 1890. (Library of the Cour des Comptes.)

De Marcé agreed with the principle that prevention was desirable; but should it, he asked, be entrusted to a Cour des Comptes? Such control in fact existed everywhere, but was administered by other authorities. In Italy it was felt that Parliament could not trust the loyalty of the ministries, subject as they were to solicitations for increased expenditures and arbitrary acts. Ministerial responsibility was therefore subjected to constant surveillance by 'an independent body—and one without responsibility'. 'In general,' wrote de Marcé, 'it does not seem to us in perfect harmony with a rigorous conception of the parliamentary system.' The ministers were responsible not only to Parliament but also to the Corte, which could impede their actions and in some cases annul them. The Corte also appeared to compromise its own liberty to criticize and render judgments during normal audit after payment; there had in fact been an abortive attempt in 1877 to remove the preventive control from the Corte on the ground 'that it was important to free the action of the supreme tribunal of accounts from all appearance of prior decision'.

There were also practical problems. The *a priori* control procedure took time; an average of three working days was claimed, but this was for routine approval. In cases where difficulties arose the Corte could either yield so as not to hold up the administrative action—in which case its control was ineffective—or debate for an indefinite time, ending with a veto (on a budgetary point) or visa with reserve (on any other issue). Thus if control was to be effective delays were inevitable.[1] The Corte also had to maintain fairly complex accounting records; it was essential to have note of all grants of visa, for comparison during *a posteriori* audit. Thus the state audit body became involved in the accounting system, with resulting duplication of work. Moreover, the control of commitments and payment orders in Italy was far from being comprehensive; there were various procedures by which it was frequently avoided altogether. Indeed it had been said in 1877 that preventive control of payments embraced hardly a fifth of budgetary expenditure; the prior examination of local payments presented apparently insoluble problems. Again, no *a priori* control could guarantee a correct charge to the budget; transfers and

[1] De Marcé noted that in Belgium, where the Cour des Comptes maintained a comparable visa-control of payment orders (though not of commitments), the civil courts had in some cases awarded damages against the state for delays in payment arising from the control procedure.

virements could be effected by the executive before submission of the final accounts. Finally, the visas in practice jeopardized the accountability of the ministries and the paying-officers, by acknowledging the regularity of their acts in advance. It was, concluded de Marcé, a hybrid system, inconsistent with logic, and of very moderate efficacy.

This was a weighty and well based judgment, whose validity has not diminished with time. In 1946 it was estimated that the preventive control of a ministerial act was completed in an average of nine days, but that if the Corte had an objection it took a further 41 days merely to obtain the comments of the originating department. 'Thus,' it has been said, 'if preventive control was exercised in full the public services would rapidly be paralysed.' So, in Italy and also in Belgium expedients have been devised to lighten the control, and in the latter country it is only directly applied to about twenty per cent of total state expenditures. In both countries, 'the preventive control of the Cour des Comptes has only been able to maintain itself on condition that it is only very partially applied'.[1]

It was considerations like these which led the French Cour des Comptes to reject the idea of a visa-control. A former Premier Président once stated, 'when preventive control was instituted in France, the Cour was asked whether it wished to be responsible. It refused for two reasons: it considered that such a thing would greatly retard the conduct of business and it was also afraid that this control would enfeeble its audit criticism because the Cour would already have committed itself.' The preventive control was therefore deliberately left to the *contrôleurs des dépenses engagées*.[2]

No such proposal was ever made in Britain, but the Treasury in 1872 expressed a similar point of principle when it wrote:

> It is most important that the difference between administration and audit should be clearly defined. The auditor . . . when the time for his interference arrives, that is to say, as soon as the accounts are delivered to him, should have uncontrolled power to make any enquiry that he may consider necessary, but he should be in no sense accessory to the facts of which he will be the judge.[3]

---

[1] *La Réforme Budgétaire*, vol. II, p. 195. Paris, 1954.

[2] Ecole Nationale d'Administration. Lecture on the Cour des Comptes by M. Pierre Brin, then Premier Président, 12 October 1950.

[3] Treasury Minute, 14 August 1872. *Epitome*, vol. 1, p. 30.

This has rightly been a constant guiding principle for the Exchequer and Audit Department.

In the United States the position is less clear. The Comptroller General conducts nothing comparable to the visa-control of Italy or Belgium, but in certain circumstances he does nevertheless intervene before payment. He inherited from the Comptroller of the Treasury the duty, arising from the Dockery Act of 1894, of rendering advance opinions on the legality of proposed expenditures at the request of individual officials responsible for making the payments. This is far from being merely a formal duty; since disbursing officers are personally liable, they make extensive use, for their own protection, of the Comptroller General's opinions, which are binding upon the G.A.O. and the administration—though not upon Congress and the Courts. An expert legal staff prepares the Comptroller's decisions in the Office of the General Counsel of the G.A.O.; the 'Opinions of the Comptroller General of the United States' are published regularly as a code for the guidance of the administration. In the year ended on 30 June 1959, no less than 6,422 new legal decisions were issued.[1] Many decisions are naturally upon minor questions, but there have been some *causes célèbres*. There was the case of the liner 'United States', which cost the Federal Government $78 millions and was sold by the Maritime Commission to United States Lines for $28 millions. On 27 May 1952, at the request of the Secretary of Commerce, the Comptroller General reviewed the case and gave his opinion that the contract of sale was not 'binding and unavoidable', the price being abnormally low. After transmission of the file to the Attorney General the price was increased by $4 millions. On another occasion the Comptroller decided, on a question from the Department of Justice, that an official could receive compensation from the German government for damage caused by the Nazis without violating the provision in the Constitution which prohibits civil servants from accepting an emolument from a foreign state.[2] An example of a decision which may have a very wide application was one rendered during the fiscal year 1959[3] to the Postmaster General, declaring that postal savings deposits were

[1] Comptroller General of the U.S. Annual Report, 1959.

[2] Cases quoted by Senechal, op. cit. The prohibition of foreign emoluments is in Article 1, Section 9, of the Constitution.

[3] I.e. the year ending 30 June 1959.

subject to levy for 'delinquent taxes' in accordance with the Inland Revenue Code.[1]

This decision service is a device whereby a country without administrative courts is enabled to interpret its own administrative law. If the frequent use made of it is a fair test, it appears to work well, and it saves the various departments from maintaining large legal staff to enquire into the legality of expenditures. It is an advisory service rather than a system of *a priori* control on the Italian or Belgian model; it does not therefore hold up the general conduct of business, because only cases which involve difficulties are referred to its notice, and these would be slow of settlement in any case.

There seems for these reasons to be a good deal to be said in favour of this unique arrangement. It has, nevertheless been criticized, often together with the procedure for direct settlement of claims by and against the government, which is another duty inherited by the G.A.O. from the Comptroller of the Treasury. In the settlement of claims the Comptroller General not merely advises but actually takes over the whole task himself.

If it is felt that the legal opinion and claim settlement services are in themselves desirable, the question still remains; should they be entrusted to an audit body? The anomaly is clear; they were the legacy of the Comptroller of the Treasury, who was an official of the executive. A critic has put the matter in this way:

> An auditor must have no prior connection with the transactions which he is supposed to audit. The Comptroller General is intimately involved in a number of transactions which he is supposed to audit, either through his countersignature on warrants, his advance opinion on proposed payments, or his direct settlement of disputed claims. The Comptroller General could be either an auditor or a controller, but he cannot be both.[2]

Nevertheless, the General Accounting Office *does* have things both ways, and this may be one of those cases where the argument that a system actually works can be stronger than the theoretical objections to it.

On balance, however, the tide of opinion is visibly running against the intervention of state audit for control of commitments and payments. The problem has been discussed by the Belgian

[1] C. G. of the U.S. Annual Report, 1959, p. 227.

[2] Hare, op. cit., p. 14.

Cour des Comptes,[1] whose preventive control of payments dates from as early as the creation of independent Belgium in 1830.

The Belgian Cour admitted that its system of prior approval did slow down payment; although the procedure was said to take less than eight days. For fear of infringing ministerial responsibility the Cour could take only the strictest regularity into consideration in deciding whether to refuse a visa. There had, moreover, been judicial embarrassments. It had been ruled by the civil courts that a refusal by the Cour des Comptes to pass a payment on the grounds of illegality was a decision of a purely administrative nature, which neither deprived the creditor of his right to request a court to order the fulfilment of the contract, nor the court of its power to do so.

But it is a poor organization which cannot find justifications for its own prerogatives. The Cour claimed that its visa control was a bar against favours to contractors; that it had often stopped payments which could not easily have been recovered, such as pensions and compensation; that it was a protection against double payment, and that its action had resulted in 'considerable' savings. It strengthened the hand of the executive against importuning; the Cour had written in one Annual Report:

> While, in some cases, the system of prior approval is a hindrance for the Honourable Ministers, the same system is, in other circumstances, used by them as a justification for refraining to make decisions for which they are being solicited.

—But this was in 1863!

The Cour stated that the authorities sometimes sent to them documents of doubtful regularity 'which, for want of a proper check or of a will to make a decision, are left to the verdict of the Cour des Comptes'. This was put forward by the Cour as a justification of the system. Another interpretation is, however, possible.

The Cour maintained that the preventive procedure was of such significance that 'even the persons who, a few years ago, concluded that it should be shelved' now favoured its replacement by an identical system 'entrusted to regular civil servants'. This would, however, lack the guaranteed independence possessed by the Cour. A way out of the judicial impasse was also suggested.

[1] Paper submitted to the Second International Congress of Supreme Audit Institutions, Brussels, 1956.

Since rights were acquired by third parties as a result of government commitments, even if irregular, it was simple logic that the commitments themselves should be controlled. It is true, as the Belgian Cour maintained, that 'the control of payment-orders loses part of its significance when there is no organized control over the commitment of expenditure'. Only the Italian system, in fact, has the full logical advantages of visa control and its full practical disadvantages.

* * * *

One must guard against dogmatism in administrative matters, and against seeing things outside their national context. It seems, nevertheless, that some unusually clear conclusions may be drawn about *a priori* control of expenditures; there is unanimity of opinion from a variety of sources.

Preventive control of all important transactions is a sound idea and it meets an obvious need. To be really effective such control must be applied at the commitment stage, since all later examination is dealing with accomplished facts. And like all worthwhile control it should enjoy substantial independence from the immediate hierarchy; a controller who is responsible to the same superiors as the controlled is part of the management rather than a check upon it. The control of commitments becomes ever more desirable with the growth of spending. A single contract may create a vast obligation with untold consequences; to take a second opinion from outside the chain of common decision before placing such a contract would seem to be a wise precaution. Yet it sometimes happens that very large commitments are made as a routine consequence of approved policy and with very little last-minute reflection. There is still real scope here for the complete prevention of avoidable waste and extravagance.

Such control is not however, a task for state audit. This was admirably argued by de Marcé and others, and the strength of their case has increased with the complexity of administration, which can even less tolerate delays than formerly. The arguments have never been effectively answered. State audit hampers administration and damages itself by intervening before payment. It comes into conflict not only with the executive but with the judiciary also. In order that its position should not be wholly untenable, the audit department has to permit evasion and dilution of its preventive control, which can only bring the whole procedure into disrepute. Meanwhile even the *a posteriori* audit is compromised.

There is another very strong argument which was not stressed by de Marcé and other critics. Preventive control by state audit can only be a check of regularity. But regularity has in practice ceased to be the most important consideration for state audit, which must now judge the financial consequences of policy and draw from the operation lessons of value for administration and government as a whole. This can only be done by systematic study after payment. The modern state auditor is basically interested in the consequences of commitments, rather than in the regularity of individual transactions, which is increasingly the concern of internal audit. One commitment may involve ten thousand transactions; often the full extent can scarcely be foreseen. Still less can it be understood by the piecemeal verification of regularity of the separate transactions. The auditor must nowadays be able to report 'the things which really matter'. He must see administration steadily and see its consequences whole. He must be able to open a dossier which begins with the record of an executive decision and a commitment, and ends with a judgment on the full result, which may not be concluded and clarified until years later. This is a historian's operation, and historians can only work after the events.

In the interest not only of the administration but also of the quality of audit itself, the *a priori* control of commitments and payments should therefore be left to the executive. The French innovation of the *contrôleurs des dépenses engagées* is one way to reinforce prevention within the executive. If a department wishes a firm second opinion upon its commitments and cannot, under the rules, obtain it from state audit, there is scarcely anyone else to ask but the Ministry of Finance. There is much to be said for this liaison being as close as possible, so that nothing may escape the attention of the Finance Ministry until it is too late.

Both logic and experience impose a division of labour between *a priori* and *a posteriori* control. The limited procedures of the General Accounting Office remind us again, however, that even the most inescapable administrative conclusions may co-exist with minor exceptions to the rules which their logic imposes.

Control of issues is a separate matter. No weighty arguments suggest that this is a task which is inappropriate and damaging to state audit control. The only question is whether in modern circumstances this is a task which is required at all; the verdict is at present 'not proven'. It is in any case not a procedure which involves great administrative cost, nor does it have major adverse consequences. Perhaps it has scarcely any consequences at all.

The only *a priori* intervention by state audit which may be considered both unobjectionable in theory and beneficial in practice is that of advice upon the budget estimates, as practised in Federal Germany. This is not participation in a domain sacred to the executive and the legislature if the audit body merely reports from its own experience, and does not share in the final decisions. Audit is a study of administration which is undertaken with the intention of being useful. It is a crucial problem for all national audit to find ways by which the findings can be translated into remedial action. Except for certain matters of regularity in some countries, state audit is without, and rightly without, executive powers. It can only report, and in some cases recommend. It is vital therefore that the auditors should be enabled and encouraged to report and recommend in ways which will be most effective. The method of advising in preparation of the budget seems to be such an effective way; it is merely an extension of the auditor's reporting function. The state cannot afford to waste the financial knowledge of servants whose only task is to acquire such knowledge.

CHAPTER VI

The Advance Beyond 'Regularity'

> 'As when a master of a family, in taking an account, casteth up the sums of all the bills of expense into one sum, and not regarding how each bill is summed up, by those that give them in account; nor what it is he pays for; he advantages himself no more than if he allowed the account in gross, trusting to every [*sic*] of the accountants' skill and honesty: so also in reasoning of all other things, he that takes up conclusions on the trust of authors, and doth not fetch them from the first items in every reckoning . . . loses his labour; and does not know any thing, but only believeth'
>
> —Thomas Hobbes, *Leviathan*

> 'Administrators' mistakes cost more than those of accountants'—Article in *Statistiques et Études Financières*, no. 136

THE control of regularity constitutes the whole of the formal and traditional function of an auditor. It is a function essential for the maintenance of order and discipline in administration and the conduct of finance.

But it has a very serious inadequacy, especially within the complicated pattern of activities of the modern state. As has been said, regularity is a negative criterion; it is the absence of technical irregularity. A form of control which considers only strict regularity is therefore negative also. It is not concerned with the efficiency, nor even in a broad sense with the economy of administrative action. It has no interest in improvement, in simplification, in rationalization or reform; in a word, the application of common-sense to public business. It is solely responsible for enforcing the rules, or bringing to light infringements of them, and can take no objective thought for the public interest.

If a Department had a large sum voted for 'purchase of (unspecified) supplies' and cared to spend it entirely upon green and yellow budgerigars, this would not be an infringement against regularity, provided that the proper authorizations were obtained and the birds were actually received. Their utility to the nation would be 'an administrative question' outside the competence of a state audit body charged with the sole control of regularity. The Minister concerned might have to face parliamentary criticism of his aviary, but the chances are that its very existence would not become known, since the auditors would not report a matter which was within the formal rules. In this way the confusion of control of regularity with a proper state audit often has covered, and in a few countries still does cover, a multitude of administrative sins. It has also obscured the meaning of audit to the state, by an oversimplification of its role.

The truth is that control of regularity is not merely insufficient but terribly inadequate in this epoch of heavy spending. Offences of irregularity are more often than not of minor financial importance in themselves, although their correction is necessary in order that confidence in the accounts may be maintained. Much of this control can and should, however, be the duty of internal audit in the accounting departments. Aberrations of administrative conduct, however, whether due to negligence or simple error, are sometimes distressingly costly in this era of millionaire policies and enormous contracts. The most wasteful, extravagant, foolish and ill-planned activities are frequently 'regular' in a technical sense. Indeed the standards of traditional regularity may be quite irrelevant to a rational critique of modern administration.

In almost all the major Western countries, national audit has, in the twentieth century, been liberated from the cramping limitations of regularity and thus allowed to play at least some positive role in solving the awesome administrative problems of the modern state. This has rather been an instinctive readjustment to the growth of 'big government' than a conscious decision in favour of such a liberation. Neither the issues nor the nature of the liberation have been clearly presented. The statutes of some state audit bodies remains as they always were; their liberation is wholly extra-statutory and a matter of practice rather than theory. It remains, nevertheless, one of the most important consequences for state audit of 'big government' in the twentieth century. It releases the energies of national audit to make a growing contribution to the development of public administration and government as a whole—a contribution which no other organ of the state could possibly make. State audit always had to obtain a wide picture of administrative activity even in order to control regularity; it is no longer obliged to suppress its unique knowledge but can make good use of it in a critical role which is fundamentally constructive. The potentialities of this role are still only being tentatively explored in the various countries. They are, however, already seen to be very considerable, although state audit may itself have to change in order to realize them to the full. A new and significant element is evolving in national administration. The liberated state audit is still rather a clumsy fledgling, but there is no doubt that it will learn how to fly.

In the nineteenth century, regularity was everywhere the rule. In France the Cour des Comptes was restricted by its Napoleonic statute to control of the *comptables*, whose discretion could be exercised only in the enforcement of regularity.[1]

In England it is doubtful whether the idea of an audit going beyond consideration of regularity was ever even considered in the early days of parliamentary control of accounts. The need for a reconstruction of the whole system of public accounting and financial control was great and the identity of audit with control of regularity appeared axiomatic, as in private accounting. There was nothing in the Exchequer and Audit Departments Act of 1866 which gave the faintest hint of any broader duty for the Comptroller and Auditor General than the control of regularity. He was, nevertheless, charged to 'certify and report upon' the accounts, and the scope of such reporting was not circumscribed. He was from very early days admitted in practice to have considerable discretion in the conduct of his duties.

The experience of strict audit was an irksome novelty to most of the departments of state. In particular the great military and naval departments, accustomed to far more deference and autonomy than any agency of state enjoys in the twentieth century, and by far the biggest spenders, took unkindly to the new discipline. Before the full rigours were applied to the War Office accounts in 1876, even their Lordships of the Treasury were really alarmed. 'It is evident,' they informed the Comptroller and Auditor General, 'that the task before you is of some delicacy, and

[1] The Cour was disabled from 'refusing to paying-officers its approval of sums disbursed by them, against payment-orders provided with the prescribed formalities, and accompanied by receipts from the payees and the supporting documents designated to be annexed thereto.' (Act of 1807, Article 18). Control was thus specifically confined to form rather than content.

that it will be most desirable to secure, as far as possible, the co-operation of the great department, which is about to be subjected to a check more stringent than has hitherto been imposed upon it.' The current administration of the department should not be impeded. The C. & A.G. was in no way to 'interfere with the discretion which the law gives to the Secretary of State' nor to 'weaken or impair his authority'. The Treasury finally stressed 'the necessity for cautious and considerate action in the first instance'.[1]

These warnings were not groundless. The Army and Navy conducted brisk skirmishes with the Comptroller and Auditor General over many years. It was largely in these military and naval combats that the powers of the Comptroller were consolidated and extended, in alliance with the Public Accounts Committee, and also, as it proved, with the timorous Treasury. In 1877 the Accountant General of the Army expressed the opinion that the C. & A.G. had 'nothing to do with the Royal Warrants' under which pay and allowances were regulated. The P.A.C. disagreed, and considered that it was open to him 'to state his opinion to Parliament on any points which he may think necessary, in his Report upon the Army Appropriation Account'.[2] In a case concerning seamen in 1881 the Treasury insisted that:

The Comptroller and Auditor General is alone competent to say what information is necessary for the discharge of his statutory functions, and must exercise his discretion as to communicating to Parliament any information in his possession that is relevant to the accounts upon which he is reporting.[3]

In 1887, the War Office took the offensive. The C. & A.G. had enquired why a contract for ribbon had been placed at 20*s*. with one supplier after the cancellation of another firm's contract at 14*s*. The military department declined to reply on the ground that the E. & A. Departments Act did not empower him 'to enter upon matters of administration'. The P.A.C. thereupon made the important declaration that:

If, in the course of his audit, the Comptroller and Auditor General becomes aware of facts which appear to him to indicate an improper expenditure or waste of public money, it his his duty to call the attention of Parliament to them.

---

[1] *Epitome*, vol. 1, p. 62. [2] Ibid., p. 72. [3] Ibid., p. 108.

The Treasury clarified the situation further:

My Lords think it important that the Comptroller and Auditor General should have great freedom in drawing his reports to Parliament. He may draw attention to any circumstance which comes to his knowledge in the course of audit, and point out its financial bearing. As, however, he is the officer of Parliament, he will naturally have no disposition to question anything that Parliament has already sanctioned, and if he reports on a matter of administration from the point of view of its effect on the public purse, it will be for the purpose of bringing before Parliament something which would otherwise pass unnoticed. It is impossible to deny that it will always be his right, and will often be his duty, to take this step.

Departments, added the Treasury, were bound to furnish information to establish the regularity of their payments. But,

If questioned why the money was spent, with due authority, in one way rather than another, the Department may refuse to answer the question. But it, of course, must be prepared to justify such refusal to Parliament, if necessary.[1]

The War Department had emerged bruised from the encounter and provoked a precedent which greatly strengthened the Comptroller and Auditor General's personal position and widened his discretion. However in 1891 that Department returned to the assault. The C. & A.G. made a studiously polite request for 'any observations which the Secretary of State might desire to offer' concerning discrepancies in numbers of Yeomanry troops estimated to have cost an additional £5,000 per annum. The only reply was that the subject was 'one of administration, on which Mr. Secretary Stanhope must decline in any way to recognize the right of the Comptroller and Auditor General to invite his observations'. This ungallant declaration called forth a brisk counter-attack from the P.A.C., who expressed their trust:

that, in performing the important and necessary work entrusted to him by Parliament, the Comptroller and Auditor General will in future be met with invariable courtesy, and furnished by the War Office, as well as by every other Department, with all the information which he may need....

He was not to be deterred from further pursuing the matter and if necessary reporting upon it again. At another place in their

[1] *Epitome*, vol. 1, p. 207.

same report, and still dealing with an Army account, the Committee made the following sally:

The assistance afforded by a thorough system of audit deserves a welcome which it does not always receive from those who are responsible for administration.[1]

The War Department had suffered another humiliating reverse, and in 1895 it was the Admiralty which took up the struggle; both strategy and tactics were, however, different. The C. & A.G. was now known to be a formidable opponent, and he had been making enquiries about differences between the cost of shipbuilding in the Dockyards and by contract, and also as between different Dockyards. This was a new line of research which went far beyond issues of regularity and touched upon the merits of administrative policy. The Admiralty contended, quite rightly, that the questions were not strictly within the primary objects of the audit as laid down in statute, but it appeared that in any case they could not provide explanations of cost differences, being themselves without information. The P.A.C., despite the nature of the C. & A.G.'s enquiries, took the opportunity of declaring that his action had been 'completely justified . . . and in obvious discharge of his public duty'. The Treasury concurred and added that:

The differences between the cost of similar ships, according as they are built by the Government, or by the trade, or in one Government yard rather than in another, are matters of much public interest, and the Comptroller and Auditor General was clearly within his right... when, in the exercise of his discretion, he called attention to them.[2]

Here was the full approval of the representatives of both legislature and executive for an observation which was clearly not based upon regularity and which touched very closely upon departmental policy.

There was no further frontal collision until 1911, when the War Office was once again in action. The C. & A.G. had observed important price discrepancies between the various Army commands for the purchase of horses, and when he enquired whether the advisability of obtaining competitive tenders in all the commands had been considered, he received the riposte that this did 'not appear to be a matter of audit of accounts'.

The Public Accounts Committee's defence began by a denunciation of one of the Army commands for incurring considerable

[1] Ibid., pp. 290–2.

[2] Ibid., pp. 376–7.

extra expenditure. The P.A.C. then proceeded to deal with the War Office, and obtained an admission from its Accounting Officer that although an explanation had been withheld under the discretion accorded to Departments by the Treasury in the 1887 case,[1] there had been no reasons of public policy why one should not have been given. The Committee 'regretted' that this had not been done, and noted that the Army Council had since written to the Comptroller and Auditor General promising 'when questions of an administrative character are raised, to furnish explanations in all ordinary cases'. The C. & A.G. had 'consented' to this.[2] It was the final capitulation of the department which in 1876 had held even the Treasury in awe. It was also a great vindication of the right of state audit to ask questions which concerned departmental policies, irrespective of their technical regularity.[3]

This right was thus established before the First World War; the attempts of Departments to place limits upon the C. & A.G.'s discretionary powers had failed. This was chiefly due to the resolute protection of his prerogative by the Public Accounts Committee, which was thus indirectly protecting and even enlarging its own powers. A veteran Committee member said in 1902 that the functions of the P.A.C. extended 'beyond the formality of the expenditure, to its wisdom, faithfulness and economy'. At the same time the C. & A.G. himself said that 'with the encouragement of Parliament' he had begun to make a feature of questions of this nature.[4]

Here was an almost unlimited field for research, and at least the test cases had established the right of state audit to conduct it.

But too much should not be made of the actual achievement at this early date, although it is true that the South African War offered great scope for the P.A.C. The audit remained geared to its

[1] p. 106 above.

[2] *Epitome*, vol. 1, pp. 543–4.

[3] It is of the greatest interest to note that in 1958 the U.S. Departments of the Air Force and the Navy began to create difficulties for the General Accounting Office in obtaining access to certain information and records deemed to be 'sensitive' or 'privileged' and therefore limited to internal use. Elaborately 'censored' administrative documents were submitted to the Comptroller General in response to his requests to the Secretaries of the Air Force and the Navy. The Comptroller referred the matter to Congressional committees on the grounds that his statutory functions were being obstructed. The outcome is not yet known; it is clearly a test of very great significance (Annual Report of C.G. of the U.S. 1959, pp. 77–82).

[4] Quoted by Chubb, op. cit., p. 78.

statutory function of regularity control, and even the new Exchequer and Audit Departments Act of 1921 gave no indication whatever that the emphasis had changed. In all the hundreds of cases cited in the volume of the Epitome of P.A.C. reports from 1857 to 1937, the examples which do not in some way arise from considerations of regularity could be counted on the fingers of both hands.[1] Perhaps this was because, as the C. & A.G. admitted in 1902, the audit body was deficient in high specialization and 'the machinery was not built for the job'.[2] Perhaps it was because habits change more slowly than leading ideas; the long-continued resistance of the armed service departments showed in itself that the idea of regularity as the limit of audit was not readily superseded.

The real change of emphasis came much later, during and even shortly before the Second World War. The second volume of the *Epitome*, covering the period from 1938 to 1950, is almost the opposite of the first one; cases of pure regularity have by now become a rarity. The basic question being asked has ceased to be 'Was this payment duly authorized and properly accounted for?', and is now 'How did the Department satisfy itself that the price paid was fair and reasonable?' In the age of 'big government', and in its relationships with an often monopolistic big business, this is one of the most pregnant of all questions in administration. The published reports of the C. & A.G. since the last war show how complete has been this silent and unlegislated revolution in the audit of British government accounts; the cases of mere regularity have almost disappeared.[3]

When the Cour des Comptes reported on its control functions in 1949 to the French Commission on Budgetary Reform, it was

[1] Including some of the test cases with War Office and Admiralty, mentioned above. It is true that the *Epitome* is only a digest of particular cases raised by the C. & A.G. In his actual reports the emphasis was perhaps rather less strictly upon regularity. See Chubb, p. 79.

[2] Chubb, op. cit., p. 79.

[3] For the new subjects of Report, see the two following chapters. Cases of technical irregularity of course continue to be dealt with by state audit, though they seldom are considered worth mentioning in Reports. (The formal annual reports of state audit bodies to the legislature or other constitutional authority are quite commonly accorded the capital R, in token of their dignity as major official documents, in the same way as, for example, an Act or a Writ).

able to point to 'an evolution which, in recent years, has been more profound than during the whole course of the nineteenth century'.[1] This referred not only to the creation under post-war legislation of devices and procedures for extending control to nationalized industries, the social security organizations, and to the organization and methods of the public service. It applied also to what the Cour described as its duties of superior financial control—to distinguish them from the traditional judicial audit.

The judicial control was prevented from providing a satisfactory means of criticizing administrative conduct by its strict confinement to matters of regularity in the founding statute of 1807. The Cour was, however, also charged with preparing a report annually for the personal attention of Napoleon, and—as in the case of the Exchequer and Audit Departments Act of 1866—the content of the report was not specified in the law. This report may be taken as the origin of the 'superior financial control' function of the Cour, in its most vital manifestation, the task of 'informing and enlightening' both the government and the legislature. But fulfilment of this duty also was hampered by the limitations imposed upon the auditors. Not until the reforms in the last few years of the Third Republic were the ministerial accounts—as distinct from those of the *comptables*—submitted to the Cour in a coherent form and without serious delay. Not until 1941 were the auditors permitted by law to travel and undertake local enquiries. Until these changes made wider horizons visible, the control and the reports of the Cour of necessity remained principally judicial and therefore dominated by the ideas of regularity and personal liability. But that is no longer the case, and since 1938 the Report of the Cour has been printed in the *Journal Officiel* and thus made available to public opinion.[2] Each Public Report is a remarkable document, which exhibits no inhibitions whatsoever about the discussion of 'matters of administration' in the broadest surveys and the frankest terms. Since the war the Cour has sought to report general administrative weaknesses, irrespective of their formal regularity. In the hard years of post-war shortages and reconstruction it set itself the task of denounc-

[1] M. A. Saramite and M. J. Hamelin, 'Les contrôles exercés par la Cour des Comptes', in *La Réforme Budgétaire*, vol. 1, p. 221.

[2] The Cour's reports during the German occupation were suppressed by the Vichy Government.

ing 'useless public works and luxurious purchases' which the country could ill afford.[1]

It was a magistrate of the Cour who penned the stimulating passage which follows:

In its most rudimentary form, state audit limits itself to checking the total of the account, to comparing the balance with the cash in hand, to ticking the vouchers which guarantee the reality of transactions. It does not permit itself to judge these transactions on their merits, much less to evaluate through them the performance of administrators; it will discover among the records, without making any comment, the receipt of taxes which are ruinous to production and whose costs of collection are disproportionate to their net product, the making of useless payments rendered regular by the mere fact that they are charged to voted funds and supported by vouchers. In its most developed form, on the other hand, state audit. . . pursues its investigations on all levels and by every means, in order to inform the Prince about the quality of administration. Under such a system it does not suffice that transactions are legal or regular, they must also be in conformity with the demands of a healthy conduct of business. Indeed, an operation which is irregular in form but inspired by the desire to safeguard the interests of the State will be considered with more indulgence than a wasteful action rendered legal by a deficiency or a lack of precision in the law.

The control of the Cour des Comptes, originally rudimentary in the extreme, has constantly improved, without, however, having attained the most highly developed form.[2]

The same might be said of state audit in nearly all the advanced countries. The only places where the limitations and restraints of strict regularity are still imposed upon the auditors are those same countries, notably Italy and Belgium, which conduct an *a priori* control by state audit of commitments or payments. This is no accident; visa-control is incompatible with any standards other than those of regularity. It may be admissible to stop a payment on the basis of legal fact; on the grounds of a value judgment by the auditor it would be intolerable. Advanced criteria and sophisticated tests of administrative actions can only be applied after the facts, when their full history and consequences can be discovered and assessed.

The United States and Western Germany differ from Great

[1] Submission by the Cour des Comptes to the First International Congress of Supreme Audit Institutions, Havana, 1953.

[2] E. Chalandon, 'Que peut la Cour des Comptes?' *Revue de Paris*, November 1950.

Britain and France in that their basic budgetary statutes provide expressly for a wide range of discretion in the conduct of state audit.

The Budget and Accounting Act of 1921 charged the Comptroller General to 'investigate . . . all matters relating to the receipt, disbursement, and application of public funds'.[1] The story is that the word 'application', which opens the way to a control of efficiency, was added at the request of a Senator who was anxious to grant the Comptroller vigorous powers, beyond the control of regularity. In the same section of the Act, the Comptroller General was directed to make reports to Congress, and to the President upon request, in which he was to make, 'recommendations looking to greater economy or efficiency in public expenditures'. The field was therefore wide open to discretionary audit upon the broadest principles.

Yet the General Accounting Office in its teething years was unimaginative in the approach to its duties; it gradually amassed a huge staff engaged upon a routine 'tick-and-turn-over' audit of vouchers in Washington, an audit which in the main accepted regularity as the limit of its vision. The first Hoover Commission was stern with the G.A.O.; it complained of the allocation of financial authority which made that Office responsible for introducing accounting systems and settling claims. These, according to the Commission, should have been duties of the executive branch of the government. And not only was the G.A.O. reproached for doing other people's work, but also for doing it badly:

> Instead of accomplishing an important task, the agency has passed its time in checking millions of receipts and credits which had already been administratively checked and paid and in splitting hairs about matters which were perfectly in order down to the tiniest detail. The Congress should be very severe about the rarity of substantial audit reports which have reached it from the G.A.O. since its creation.

The Commission thought that the G.A.O.'s proper but unfulfilled role was to be 'the powerful ally of the Congress in the hunt for waste and abusive employment of public funds'. This was only the climax of criticism which had been directed at the American audit body for a good many years and from many sources.

Congress, however, feared that by adopting proposals to reduce

[1] 1921 Act, Section 312(a).

the Comptroller General's powers it might enfeeble its own, and reform took place on a more conservative basis. The G.A.O. founded its new position upon the joint programme for accounting improvement which had been initiated together with the Bureau of the Budget and the Treasury Department in 1947. An integral part of this programme was the modernization of the G.A.O.'s own audit by gradual reduction of the old 'centralized audit' of regularity in Washington and its replacement by a programme of 'comprehensive audit', to be carried out primarily at the point of local operations.

What is 'comprehensive audit'? It originated as we have seen, in an attempt to fulfil the requirement of the Government Corporation Control Act of 1945 under which all wholly owned corporations were to be audited on commercial auditing lines by the G.A.O.[1] For this purpose qualified accountants were recruited, and 'comprehensive audit' may perhaps be regarded as a professional reaction to the problems encountered at that time, against a background of G.A.O. procedures which were admitted to be archaic. It was a very natural step to extend 'comprehensive audit' from the government corporations to the departments and agencies of the Federal Government, and this extension was part of the meaning of the Budget and Accounting Procedures Act of 1950.

The purpose of 'comprehensive audit' was described by a Director of the G.A.O. in 1954 as follows:

To determine to what extent the agency under audit has discharged its financial responsibilities, which imply equally the expenditure of public funds and the utilization of materials and personnel, within the limit of its programmes and activities and their execution in an effective, efficient and economical fashion.[2]

It would be difficult for an objective to seem more remote from mere audit of payment regularity; it went, in fact, much further in scope than was customary in private professional audit.[3] Ways of conducting comprehensive audit included:

1. Preparatory study of the laws.
2. Critical examination of the agency's methods.

---

[1] See above, Chapter III, and below, Chapter XI.

[2] Mr Long, Director of the Division of Audits, quoted by Senechal, op. cit.

[3] Despite the fact that in the United States private auditors are said to be tending to widen their audits and to make them 'real instruments of administrative control'.

3. Examination of practical procedures and organizational formulas.
4. Examination for each activity of receipts and payments, tending within the budget limits towards an appreciation of cost and efficiency.
5. Check of individual operations, certification of balance, physical stocktaking.[1]

Finally a report on the audit would be sent to Congress or, as required, to agency heads and to co-ordinating departments such as the Bureau of the Budget.

The central concern of this type of audit seems to be the examination of administrative efficiency. In any case it was a success. And the General Accounting Office itself and its personnel were thoroughly renewed; a state audit which had fallen into disrepute through a prosaic control of regularity was vindicated.

It was during the Comptrollership of Mr Lindsay C. Warren, between 1940 and 1954, that the most decisive changes took place in the General Accounting Office. This was, wrote the Assistant Comptroller General after Mr Warren's retirement,

> a period during which there had to be a complete change in the thinking and approach of the G.A.O. if it was to meet the challenge of the times. Mr Warren's extensive and thorough revisions in the internal operations of the Office and his insistence on improved service to the Congress and to the executive branch, at the lowest possible cost to the taxpayers, have made the General Accounting Office an efficient, hard-hitting agency.[2]

Mr Warren had been a Member of Congress and he understood the requirements of the legislature and its committees, and the capacity of the G.A.O. to meet them. He gave high priority to the work of reporting to and assisting Congress. The latter, in its turn, welcomed this policy because it was aware of its own need for the services of an effective audit body. The number of individual audit and investigation reports submitted to Congress increased from 180 in 1940 to 967 in 1954, and the quality of the reports is said to have improved as well. The G.A.O. also undertook researches and provided staff to assist various congressional committees, in accordance with Section 312(b) of the 1921 Act. It made many recommendations concerning or proposing legisla-

[1] Mr Long, quoted by Senechal, op. cit.

[2] Annual Report of the C.G. of the U.S., 1954, p. vi.

tion. Finally the G.A.O. provided an enquiry service for individual members of Congress, which was used 'several thousand' times in 1954 alone.[1] Mr. Warren's declared aim was so to gear the operations of the General Accounting Office as to be of real assistance to the legislature.

Thus the work of state audit in America underwent a refreshing modernization. Meanwhile the quality of staff recruitment was raised and the numbers cut by more than half in a few years.[2] 'I felt', wrote Mr Warren, 'that I could not criticize wasteful and extravagant practices observed in audits and investigations of other Government agencies if my own house was not in order.'[3] In his farewell message upon retirement, he said, 'together we have revolutionized the Office, raised its stature and made its influence felt for good throughout the Federal Government'.[4] It was a proud claim and there is considerable testimony to the effect that it was justified.

When the German budgetary code, the Reichshaushaltsordnung, was passed into law in 1922, it was against a background of post-war chaos, political, economic and financial. This is no doubt one reason why the code did not confine the German Rechnungshof to a control of regularity. It directed the auditors to examine not only whether the procedures for raising revenue and for utilization of Reich funds and assets were 'regular', but also whether they satisfied the need for economy. The Rechnungshof was to investigate in particular,

> Whether institutions have been maintained, posts retained, or other Reich expenditures incurred, which could have been eliminated or reduced without jeopardising the aims of administration.[5]

The Rechnungshof under the Weimar Republic thus had a full mandate for the pursuit of administrative efficiency and economy, and this mandate has passed to the Bundesrechnungshof.[6] Already in 1925 it was said that this control represented 'an important

[1] Ibid., 1955, p. 14.

[2] The reduction included the transfer of whole sections of the G.A.O. to the Treasury Dept. and the Post Office Dept., see Chapter III above.

[3] Annual Report of C.G. of the U.S., 1953, p. 2.

[4] Ibid., 1954, p. vi.

[5] RHO. Section 96(4). Section 26(1) also directs that 'budgetary funds are to be administered in an efficient and economical manner'.

[6] There was, naturally, little effective constitutional control of this or any other kind under the Third Reich. See Chapter XII below.

broadening and increase in profundity of the audit function'.[1] It constituted probably the major part of the entire state audit activity, and in addition, the President of the Rechnungshof was appointed Reich Economy Commissioner (Reichssparkommissar) in 1922, with special powers and a personal staff.

There is a difference of emphasis in the application of this type of control at the present time, as compared with the 1920s. Then, stress was placed upon the achievement of direct economy by (as the law clearly suggested) the abolition of official posts and whole establishments. It was inspired by the contemporary mentality typified by 'the Geddes axe' in Great Britain, which sought a return to pre-1914 standards and cost of administrative activity and tended to place the blame for economic crises upon failure to achieve this. At the present day both public opinion and the public services in the highly developed countries have gained in wisdom and caution. The way out of economic difficulties for a nation is no longer conceived to be through mere cuts in public spending, at the price of unloading surplus personnel upon a stagnant labour market. In any case powerful labour movements make such policies impossible. But administrative efficiency remains a keenly sought objective. It is believed that even if direct and immediate economies may be hard to show, the long-term gain will be very great. Not only will an administration be restrained from swelling in size as a direct result of its own inefficiency, but it will do its job much better. The present emphasis, in Germany and elsewhere, is therefore upon rationalization, rather than upon 'axeing'. There has also been a development of control techniques, based on the one hand upon a refined audit of accounts, and on the other upon 'organization and methods' studies. The defence against the dangers inherent in Professor Parkinson's Law is a patient and painstaking control of efficiency, together with unflagging criticism of infringements of the rules, not merely of regularity, but of a sound conduct of business.

The President of the Rechnungshof of the Free Hanseatic City of Hamburg, which is a Land of the Federal Republic, has recently had this to say:

> Audit following the formal rules . . . today holds its legitimate place in the structure of state, but it no longer represents the sole field of

[1] *Handwörterbuch der Staatswissenschaften*, vol. 6., 4th edn., Jena, 1925 (article on Verwaltungskontrolle).

activity of the audit bodies. In the breast of the national auditors beats more than the keyboard of an adding machine. Evolution has led to consideration of the execution of the budget, not only from the point of view of legal and arithmetical correctness, but also of the economic rationality, the efficiency, shown in carrying out administrative duties. . . . Several of the Länder have passed laws assigning to their audit departments the task of general surveillance over the entire budgetary and commercial activity of the administration. All the audit departments have in practice assumed this duty and the Parliaments have insisted that they should.[1]

The situation at national level in most of the greater Western countries corresponds, as we have seen, to that in the German Länder. In the United States and the West German Federal Republic state audit has been assigned by law a very wide general surveillance over all administration which has any financial consequence—and there is very little administration which has none. In some other countries a fairly wide general control has evolved independently of the law. In Great Britain this development has had the full support of the Public Accounts Committee.

It is clear that in some places actual practice is far in advance of organic law, and this is of interest. The remarkable evolution beyond standards of regularity, which took place separately and independently in different countries and without anything which might be called a general theory for guidance, suggests a kind of inevitability arising from the pressure of modern administrative problems.

The executive, however—like the British War Office before the First World War—could scarcely be other than jealous of its ancient prerogatives and immunities. It is perfectly true that Ministries and Departments have ultimately much to gain from the stimulus of an audit conducted upon broad principles, but the idea of accountability for business efficiency was bound to be accepted only rather gradually. It offended against the deeply ingrained feeling that administrators actually on the job know best, and that feeling has only been weakened and not eradicated by many thousands of solid audit observations which have demonstrated that it is not invariably true. Occasionally officials of the

[1] Dr H. Weichmann, 'Die Tätigkeit der Rechnungshöfe im modernen Staat', an address to the XI Congress of the International Institute for the Administrative Sciences, Wiesbaden, 2 September 1959.

executive welcome a constructive audit, like the Assistant Commissioner of the Bureau of the Public Debt, who told a Congressional committee that certain suggestions made by the General Accounting Office represented 'a fresh look at some of the old problems that we have been confronted with'.[1] This attitude is, in fact, less rare than might be expected, for many a senior official has been impressed by the salutary effect of an intelligent audit on his subordinates.

For the rest, however, there remains a certain nervousness. This has sometimes been reflected in a reluctance to define the nature and scope of the actual control being practised. This has been the subject of comment in the Netherlands:

> The audit as a control of efficiency has for a long time been treated in a rather vague fashion both in the Accounting Act and in practice. One still frequently encounters the opinion that control of this kind is not a part of the responsibilities of an independent auditing body.
>
> The Netherlands Algemene Rekenkamer regards the control of efficiency as an integral part of its task.
>
> ... It seems possible that more money is lost in the government services through lack of efficiency than through fraud, duplicate payments, etc., so that there is good reason to accord an important place to efficiency control.[2]

In certain cases state audit, or the legislature alerted and informed by it, can induce a branch of the executive to do something which is manifestly in the public interest but which for its own reasons the department did not want to do. That is precisely one of the great virtues of a rigorous audit. And yet auditors are trained to believe that a pre-requisite for any achievement is the maintenance of good relations with the establishment under examination, and to act accordingly.

This is certainly correct and necessary during the actual conduct of audit work. But a state audit body should not be deterred from raising substantial issues on the grounds that they are controversial. Whilst observing the courtesies, it should, like the Public Accounts Committee in defence of the Comptroller and Auditor General, be ready for a fight if needed in a good cause. The total absence of friction and controversy is by no means necessarily a token of effective performance by a state audit body.

[1] Annual Report of C.G. of the U.S. 1953, p. 8.

[2] From 'Budget Execution and Government Accounting in the Netherlands', The Hague, Dept. of Economic Affairs, 1952.

The temptation to adopt a passive role may be very strong. Yet a state audit has everything to gain by being diplomatic but firm; to temporize is to hurt morale as well as prestige. 'Is painless control possible?' asked one student of the subject. 'There are people who seek a control method which hurts nobody. That is no control. . . . To be quite painless, that's impossible!'[1]

Since a little sporadic friction with the executive may be hard to avoid, and may indeed be a sign that the audit is doing its duty, the alliance between audit and legislature in Western democratic countries assumes special significance. How strong this alliance can be was shown by the decisive defeat of the British War Office in its attempts long ago to intimidate the Comptroller and Auditor General. In Washington it is shown many times every year in effective collaboration between Congressional committees and the General Accounting Office. The alliance is, in fact, a device peculiar to liberal democracies; a function of the separation of powers. It is especially useful when audit evolves beyond the control of regularity and takes up questions which are really vital and controversial. Properly understood and exploited, the alliance offers the possibility of a real contribution by the legislature to the control of day-to-day administration; an art which in some countries has been lost.

The advance beyond control of regularity offers to state audit the possibility of probing into the dark corners and crannies of a ramified administrative system, and of posing whatever questions may seem to be merited by its discoveries. *Dat ordinem lucendo* is the legend upon a medal struck by the French Cour des Comptes. This investigative function, exercised on behalf of a popularly elected assembly, is fundamentally democratic. Upon this, a magistrate of the French Cour has had something striking to say:

> Control is a function the very essence of which is to be independent of executive authority, of decision . . . it is a function of discovering, of criticizing, and its very existence is associated with the imperfection of other people.
>
> That is why it is frequently suspect. . . . For authoritarian and conformist epochs and minds . . . the distrust of 'control' goes together

[1] Kurt Heinig, 'Die Rechnungsprüfungsbehörde und ihr Verhältnis zu Exekutive und Legislative im internazionalen Vergleich', in *Der öffentliche Haushalt*, Heft 2/3, 1954.

with hostility towards 'the critical spirit', a major heresy in the eyes of all the orthodox, proclaimed 'negative' and 'destructive'. Considered from this aspect . . . the function of control inclines towards the citizen rather than towards authority. This is not its least merit.[1]

Indeed there is a perpetual battle to avoid accountability and to keep the dark corners and crannies secret and inviolate. This is an extension of the ancient struggle to end the secrecy of state accounting and administration, against the tradition that the state's affairs are a private and esoteric mystery for specialists. Whatever pretext may be given in any individual cases, every grant of exemption from control is a small reverse for democracy, a triumph for authoritarianism and conformism over the critical spirit and a protection of vested interest and privilege.

There is an awareness in modern thought that accountability has not yet been extended nearly far enough, that it is too unevenly distributed and applied, and that there are too many dark nooks and crannies effectively protected from public investigation. This situation is beginning to be regarded not only as undemocratic but also as economically inefficient. 'The requirement of democracy,' says a contemporary economist, 'is that power should be balanced and that it should be accountable to the community. . . . There is certainly a need for exploring ways of making all big organizations, be they business enterprises, trade unions, or Government departments, more fully accountable.'[2]

This takes the matter beyond the scope of the present study, the principal concern of which is the Western democratic state, which still does not regard itself as coterminous with the entire economy. There is no legal sanction at present in any liberal and constitutional country for proper accountability on the part of organizations whose funding does not derive from the common public purse.

For institutions which do draw their resources from national or local taxation, however, public and political opinion has long been inured to the idea of accountability and overwhelmingly demands it. Why, indeed, should a taxpayer think otherwise? The present work sets its sights upon the limited objective of 'no subsidy without accountability', as a rule to be applied impartially to all kinds of bodies, whatever their function and legal status, and

[1] Therre, op. cit.

[2] Michael Shanks, *The Stagnant Society*, London, Penguin Books, 1961.

irrespective of whether they receive income directly from centrally voted moneys, from state-guaranteed loans or in the form of subsidies, grants to local authorities, and so on. They should all be obliged to show that they make good and efficient use of the public contribution, and moreover that they really need it. This is the least that should be asked, yet in a large number of instances even this is not asked. Money is doled out from the public treasuries and at the end the most that the central constitutional powers have to show for a good deal of it is a meaningless collection of receipts for lump sums granted to a variety of beneficiaries. It is one of the essential tasks for the modernization of government that the state should find out what really happens to all of its money. It is for the legislatures, which provide the money in the first place, to realize that in many cases the fate of public funds cannot be coherently investigated and may often not be known at all, and to provide a statutory framework within which this situation may be remedied.

It is not the task of state audit to apply the ultimate control, but it must be the source of information upon which control is based. The state audit bodies should ensure that they are themselves equipped for a more complex role. If they are not, this fact will be used—as it often has been in the past—as a pretext for the avoidance of accountability. State audit is, however, capable, with statutory authority, of adapting itself to varied circumstances and needs; a great deal of adaptation has already been achieved in some countries.[1] State audit must be prepared not only to vary its tactics but to study its targets; to consider what it is trying to achieve now that enforcement of regularity is not the sole and self-evident intention. It must be prepared to examine ways of utilizing specialized skills; this is a way towards added effectiveness and prestige.

Control of regularity is a useful form of employment but not an imaginative one. Strict concentration upon this aim tended in the nineteenth century to reduce state audit to the condition of a quiet backwater. It seems even likely that this condition was in

[1] 'Methods of control need constant revision to match changes and developments in the subject-matter of public expenditure.'—Sir Edmund Compton, Comptroller and Auditor General: 'Control of Public Expenditure', address to the annual conference of the Institute of Municipal Treasurers and Accountants, London, 15 June 1960.

some instances deliberately intended by the founding legislators. The 1807 statute of the Cour des Comptes is a case in point:

> . . . It was forbidden ever to criticize the activity of the administration; still less that of the government. The subordinate and auxiliary character of the task confided to the Cour was indirectly recognized by Napoleon. At the time of the creation of the Cour he said that it was destined to 'increase the splendour of the throne and shelter the dignitaries of the Empire.' Hence the division of the Cour into two hostile categories; that of the présidents and counseillers-maîtres, endowed with dignified sinecures; that of the référendaires, charged with the thankless work of auditing accounts. That distinction, now disappearing, existed for a long time.[1]

Barbé-Marbois, the first Premier Président of the Cour des Comptes, had incurred the displeasure of Napoleon as a Minister and had been persuaded to resign. When the Emperor nominated him for the new post he is recorded as saying, 'There at least he won't do any harm!'

* * * *

Thus the strict control of regularity effectively limited state audit to a relatively minor role by prohibiting the consideration of matters of real importance. This was not without its psychological effect upon the audit; a certain feeling of futility and impotence due to having the material for major criticisms and being obliged to suppress them. State audit is now allowed and even encouraged to make these criticisms, but sometimes a shadow of the old mental attitudes still lingers, and may be detected in the attitude of the executive to the audit. It is not the least requirement of the changed circumstances that the auditors themselves should come thoroughly to believe in their new mission.

What is the essence of this mission? The duties of the national audit bodies apart from the control of regularity, are not self-explanatory and they are in course of evolution. They touch the whole of administration at many points, but these are not the same points in every country; they vary in accordance with the development of ideas and practical techniques in each locality, and in relation to each constitutional, legal and economic environment. In comparison, the ministries and other executive departments present a degree of sameness from place to place; their duties are much more self-evident.

[1] Chalandon, op. cit.

But there is one common factor besides the control of regularity, and this may well be the key to an assessment of the state auditor's essential mission. This is the reporting function. It is the duty of state audit to seek out the complex facts of modern administration and inform legislatures, the heads of the executive and even public opinion about them, without fear, favour or partiality. A President of the Bundesrechnungshof has described his staff as 'a reconnaissance patrol in the dense undergrowth of financial administration'.[1] Comptroller General Warren said that he was keenly aware of 'the absolute necessity for the Congress to be fully informed on the financial operations of the Government and the import of proposed legislation.'[2]

The reporting function is not nowadays even tied to criticism. It may bring to light unfortunate aspects and consequences of administrative policy and legislation which have escaped notice and could not have been foreseen, and which therefore do not reflect adversely upon anybody. Using his unique statutory powers of access to records of all kinds, the state auditor is most of all interested in finding out what the late Comptroller and Auditor General, Sir Frank Tribe, once called the 'things which really matter'. After the Second World War it was observed that the emphasis of the Comptroller and Auditor General's report had altered.

> Subjects mentioned tended to be less concerned with detailed points of automatic or formal accounting and more with general questions involving important issues or with matters which would otherwise escape Parliament's attention. In addition, more and more paragraphs of his report were included for information, explaining complicated and hidden expenditure.[3]

The modern state auditor is no longer a policeman, merely enforcing the rules of regularity, although he must still take reasonable note that they are observed. He is not even confined to the role of a critic, although his critical sense should be very strongly developed. He is above all an impartial and studious general fact-finder about government.

[1] Dr Guido Hertel, at Frankfurt University, 1961.

[2] Annual Report, C.G. of the U.S., 1952, p. iv.

[3] Chubb, op. cit., pp. 141–2.

CHAPTER VII

The Published Reports, Part I: Fraud, Waste and Extravagance

'Unprofitable expenditures are those whose consequences are irrelevant to the public interest, which serve no useful purpose, bringing no security for the State, no greatness nor prestige to the king; and since vanity is limitless, the examples of such expenditure are innumerable'
—Giovanni Botero:
Della Ragion di Stato, Venice, 1589

WE now need to look at what the state auditor actually finds in the various national accounts and records. This will give us a clearer idea, not only of his function but of the need for it. The efficiency of administration is too often assessed by a simple value judgment, without supporting evidence. The reports of state audit fortunately present a great deal of evidence. We shall not use this to attempt any general assessment, but merely to consider the unsuccessful side of administration and the forms in which failure is apt to manifest itself.

When a state auditor discovers something which attracts his observations he does not immediately inform Parliament or the government. He first of all carefully studies the case and follows it through all its ramifications; then he writes his own internal brief for the audit department itself. Minor criticisms and queries may be cleared up in discussion with the accountable authority; bigger ones will involve an exchange of letters; definitely important ones will be taken up in writing with some show of formality and at high level. In London a senior representative of the Comptroller and Auditor General will send a 'Reference Sheet' to the appropriate Accounting Officer. In Paris the Premier Président will adress a 'Référé' to the responsible Minister.

Matters are thus first of all brought to the notice of the executive authority concerned, which is given every opportunity to explain the circumstances and justify itself. The procedure incidentally provides an insurance for the state audit body that its facts are absolutely correct and its observation well founded, before the matter is taken any further.[1]

To take the matter further means, as a rule, to include it in the published report which is issued periodically under statute by every state audit department in constitutionally governed countries, apparently without exception. Under absolute rule there may well be an official report also, but it will be in strict confidence for central authority, as was that of the Cour des Comptes for Napoleon. What is secret cannot be discussed; our interest here is in the reports which are printed and published in Western countries. They provide potential source material for all kinds of administrative study; the most that can be done with them here is to take samples to show what kinds of observation are raised.

The constitutional reports reflect the evolution of state audit itself. They seem to have been at first considered as an appendix to the declared accounts of government, indicating deviations from the prior instructions of the budget-making power; a kind of extended reservation to the auditor's certificate. In France, Germany and elsewhere, it remains constitutional practice for the budget-making power to grant 'discharge' to the executive for its conduct of finance in each budgetary year. This discharge is recorded in the form of a law or formal resolution.[2] The audit report may then form one of the documents upon which the act of discharge is based.[3]

Although, as we have seen, the nineteenth-century statutes of French and British state audit did not indicate what the content of the reports should be, their primeval characteristic was that of a commentary upon regularity, a list of exceptions to the rules. The German budgetary law of 1922 specifically charged the state audit department to report whether the accounts had been properly vouched and maintained and also:

Whether deviations from the budget and its supporting documents have occurred, and in what cases the laws relating to Reich receipts

---

[1] This might be called 'European' procedure. The General Accounting Office appears to submit its complete individual audit reports directly to Congress after each major auditing operation.

[2] Loi de règlement, Entlastung der Bundesregierung, etc.

[3] In France the document which serves this purpose is the *déclaration générale de conformité*, not the audit report.

and expenditures or the purchase and administration of Reich property have been infringed.[1]

The trouble with audit reports of this type is that they tend to be unreadable and therefore to remain unread except in the strictest line of duty. The observations made are very important in the formative era of any country's budgetary system, when each case may establish a general principle. But after a pattern of state accounting becomes well set, the reporting of infringements of regularity—often concerning small sums of money—tends to become an unprofitable routine, which merely establishes that the auditors are still alive. Unless they involve new principles, or large amounts, it is better that cases of formal infringements should be dealt with outside the published reports.

In the major countries of the West this lesson has already been learned. There is far too much of general importance in the present-day national accounts for it to be necessary to pad annual audit reports with trivialities. The whole of state administration is spread out before the eyes of the auditor, and he has become interested in the detailed interpretation of this broad picture. When he reports at the end of examining a year's accounts he will still refer to individual cases which he has found; but these cases are usually cited as illustrations of a broader theme. The old type of report still survives, but not in the larger and busier countries. There it is evolving into a document conveying lessons about government; a document sometimes so rich in instructive experience that it may exceed the capacity of the constitutional machinery to absorb and act upon its contents. Only American law seems really to have contemplated this type of reporting from the outset; the Comptroller General was always intended to play a constructive, rather than a merely regulative role in the machinery of state. The Budget and Accounting Act of 1921 directed him to:

make to the President when requested by him, and to Congress at the beginning of each regular session, a report in writing of the work of the General Accounting Office, containing recommendations concerning the legislation he may deem necessary to facilitate the prompt and accurate rendition and settlement of accounts and concerning such other matters relating to the receipt, disbursement and application of public funds as he may think advisable. In such regular report, or in

[1] Reichshaushaltsordnung (RHO), 1922, Section 107.

special reports at any time when Congress is in session, he shall make recommendations looking to greater economy and efficiency in public expenditures.[1]

The same sort of thing has been spontaneously achieved elsewhere, in advance of the auditors' statutes. The impulsion has come from the serious and sometimes even startling nature of discoveries made by the auditors whilst reviewing matters which in a formal sense were perfectly 'regular'. This reported information, unavailable from any other source, has been welcomed by legislatures and by the organs of public opinion. In England, France and Germany the reports of state audit have received much attention in the press since the Second World War.[2] In France one report of the Cour des Comptes was a 'best-seller' in its time, and the press cuttings which derive from the reports of the Cour form very large bundles indeed.

* * * *

The presentation of audit reports differs from country to country. In Great Britain the Comptroller and Auditor General's reports appear as a kind of foreword to the various published accounts of which he is the statutory examiner; these include not only the civil and military appropriation accounts but trading accounts, White Paper accounts[3] and the accounts of a number of semi-public bodies such as the Greenwich Hospital charity.

This form of presentation, with the reports in the same volumes as the accounts to which they refer, is no doubt highly practical and convenient from the point of view of the Public Accounts Committee, which has to consider them and recommend action if it thinks fit. It perhaps also makes for prompt submission, since accounts and reports can be printed piecemeal as they become available. On the other hand the reports are not readily accessible as material for record and research; a complete set of reports for a single year is dispersed among many official publications and a full collection is difficult to assemble.[4]

[1] 1921 Act, Section 312(a).

[2] In Britain the press sometimes uses the separate reports of the Public Accounts Committee, whose commentaries are of course very largely based upon the disclosures of the Comptroller and Auditor General in his reports.

[3] For example the White Paper accounts of the hospitals under the National Health Service.

[4] The possible advantages of printing a single volume containing all the C. and A.G.'s reports (or preferably these and the associated reports of the

The reports are essentially factual and of precise accuracy and detail. They almost always incorporate a précis of the explanations furnished by Accounting Officers in reply to the Reference Sheets of the Exchequer and Audit Department. Since as a rule the Comptroller and Auditor General eschews all comment, leaving the facts to speak for themselves, the observations are austere and cannot be criticized for overstatement. This restraint is perhaps a source of strength.

The C. & A.G. rarely makes any kind of recommendation in his reports, leaving this to the Public Accounts Committee. But, as cases in the *Epitome* show, he has frequently expressed his own views and advice in evidence before the Committee.[1] The C. & A.G. has, in fact, always been the trusted personal adviser of the Committee, but hitherto principally upon matters of pure accounting. It might now be a timely reform if he were given statutory instructions to make recommendations in his published reports when he sees fit.[2] Such advice would guide and help the P.A.C. without committing it in any way, and it would greatly encourage the auditors to approach their task in a constructive spirit. It would help to close the gap in the financial control cycle, by enabling such conclusions as may be drawn from the accountability phase to be freely expressed and used for the guidance of future budgetary planning.

In France the report of the Cour des Comptes, was ordered by a law of 1832 to be printed and distributed to the Chambers of the legislature. By this act, the Cour, born as an instrument of absolutist control, became under the monarchy of Louis Philippe a source of information for the legislative power. In 1938 the reporting procedure was further liberalized; the report henceforward was to be 'placed upon the table of the Chambers and published in the *Journal officiel* . . . at the same time that it is presented to the President of the Republic'. Thus, the report has been

---

P.A.C. combined) but without the accounts, might repay consideration. The accounts themselves are of very slight interest indeed, either for reading or for reference.

[1] See for example *Epitome*, vol. I, pp. 41, 104, 120, 129, 133, 153, 208, 210, 228, 260, 278–9, 282–3, 391–2, 472–3, 599–600, 671, 716. Vol. II, pp. 11, 91, 112, 121.

[2] The C. & A. G. would, strictly speaking, be entitled to make recommendations under his existing discretionary powers, but he has no statutory instructions to do so and there is no precedent.

addressed to the Head of State since 1807, to Parliament since 1832 and to public opinion as a whole (this was the deliberate intention of publication in the *Journal officiel*) since 1938. The Cour calls its report the 'Public Report' and regards the appeal to public opinion as legitimate democratic strategy in a country which still proclaims that national sovereignty belongs to the people.[1]

> The Cour's independence from Government and Parliament has permitted it, after having informed the Assemblies, to put matters directly before public opinion through its Public Report. Thus it possesses a very effective means of campaigning for the solution of problems which it cannot modify within the limits of its judicial control.[2]

The Public Report is published in a single volume, covering various spheres of auditing activity. For example the report for 1955–6 was in four parts; the State Administrations, the Local Authorities, the Public Hospitals, and Social Security. The headings, however, vary; sometimes attention may be focused upon subsidized bodies, the administration and finance of overseas territories, etc. The reports are not tied to the annual accounts of the various services; they form a general rather than a closely related commentary. Indeed they have not appeared annually since the last war, and a biennial rhythm seems to have established itself. This is not necessarily a disadvantage; the very rarity of the reports seems to increase their impact and to make their publication an event.

The Cour is very frank in its criticism of administrative behaviour and of legislation which it believes to be inadequate, unsound or unworkable. The explanations furnished by ministries and other public bodies are printed in full at the back of the report volume. The Cour's observations are exceptionally lucid and readable and sometimes reflect very detailed research, but occasionally its conclusions seem to lack adequate factual support. The text contains recommendations, exhortations, admonitions and suggestions for administrative reforms of all kinds. The reader may however feel vaguely disquieted by what seems like a

[1] This republican doctrine is retained in Article 3 of the Constitution of 4 October 1958.

[2] Report of the French delegation to the First International Congress of Supreme Audit Institutions, Havana, 1953.

certain imprecision of objective. It is for debate whether state audit is more effective with a flail or with a scalpel.

In Germany the report is an annual volume published as a Bundestag paper by the Federal Finance Minister, who submits it to the President of the popular assembly in connection with the 'discharge' of the government's responsibility for a completed financial year. The report is usually in four sections. Firstly the Bundesrechnungshof submits its observations (Bemerkungen) upon the Federal budgetary accounts for the year awaiting discharge action.[1] The Observations are mostly matters of detailed regularity. There is a considerable time-lag behind the events; for example, the report submitted in December 1959 contained Observations upon the accounts for the financial year 1956.

Secondly, however, the President of the Bundesrechnungshof submits in the same general volume a personal Memorandum (Denkschrift) setting out the most important findings of audit.[2] This is prepared with much more freedom than the Observations; the cases cited are not necessarily matters of regularity and they may be much more recent in date. The Memorandum submitted in December 1959 contains audit findings arising during the financial years 1957 and 1958 as well as 1956. The views of the departments responsible are incorporated in the texts of both the Observations and the Memorandum, and, as a further refinement, the German reports contain the comments of the Bundesrechnungshof on the departmental statements. There are signs of official caution; names and locations are not often quoted. In general, the reports lack the clarity of the French ones, which explain the broad context of everything reported. The recommendations of the Bundesrechnungshof are however stated firmly and they often require the reimbursement of sums alleged to have been paid in error. A feature of the German reports is a list of amounts recovered or otherwise saved; a total of thirty-five million Deutschmarks is recorded for the financial year 1956.

The third section of these documents is the Report of the Bundesrechnungshof on the Audit of 'Enterprises with their own Legal Personality.'[3] The German Republic has no fully national-

[1] In accordance with RHO., Section 107(1).

[2] RHO., Section 107(6).

[3] RHO., Section 107(3)2 (re nationalized industries, see Chapter XI below).

ized industries but it holds shares in industrial and financial concerns and is in some cases the sole shareholder. This report follows up the administration of these federal resources.

Finally there is a Report by the President of the Bundesrechnungshof upon his activity as Federal Commissioner for Efficiency in the Administration. This is a highly interesting record of studies in the field of administrative organization and methods.[1]

The Annual Reports of the Comptroller General of the United States differ from those in Europe in that they do not contain new observations but are digests of cases already brought to the notice of Congress in reports upon individual authorities. There is little doubt that the number of audit observations made by the General Accounting Office far exceeds that in any other Western country[2] —just as the United States budget is by far the biggest. A single report containing details of all the more important observations would be extremely cumbersome. However that may be, it is the policy of the General Accounting Office, as the servant of Congress, to keep the legislature and its committees continuously supplied with information, and not merely at one season of the year. This it achieves by submitting numerous audit reports every year to the appropriate committees as soon as each one becomes available.[3]

[1] See Chapter IX below.

[2] This impression may be gained from any Annual Report of the Comptroller General.

[3] In the 'fiscal' year which ended on 30 June 1959, reports were furnished by the G.A.O., as appropriate and as requested, to: The Offices of the Senate and the House of Representatives; The Senate and House Committees on: Appropriations, Armed Services, Agriculture, Banking and Currency, Government Operations, Interior and Insular Affairs, Interstate and Foreign Commerce, the Judiciary, Post Office and Civil Service, and Public Works, the District of Columbia; The House Committee on Foreign Affairs and the Senate Committee on Foreign Relations; The Senate Committee on Aeronautical and Space Sciences and the House Committee on Science and Astronautics; The Senate Committee on Labour and Public Welfare and the House Committee on Education and Labour; The House Committees on Merchant Marine and Fisheries, Veterans' Affairs, and Ways and Means; The Joint Committee on Atomic Energy; Joint Economic Committee, and Joint Committee on Reduction of Non-essential Federal Expenditures; The Select Committees on Small Business; The Senate Select Committee on Improper Activities in the Labour or Management Field. The reports were not merely distributed for information but were addressed to the appropriate committees for specific action.

State audit thus provides the committees with an impartial fact-finding team. Nothing really comparable to this remarkable co-operation has been evolved in a European country, despite the scope which it offers for a renewal of parliamentary interest in administration. Perhaps something of this sort was envisaged by the French Constitution of 1946, which provided in Article 18 that the National Assembly might 'entrust to the Cour des Comptes any investigations or studies concerning public revenues and expenditures or the administration of the treasury'.[1] (This provision does not reappear in the Constitution of the Fifth Republic, which diminishes the prerogatives of the legislature.)

The Comptroller General's annual reports are a summary of General Accounting Office activity rather than working documents. They contain an impressive account of very extensive operations in audit, legal advice, and assistance to Congress and the Bureau of the Budget. The presentation, however, has disadvantages. The reports are primarily a justification of the G.A.O. and its functions, and a very ample justification they have been in recent years. But because of their purpose they occasionally approach the tone of an advertiser's announcement or a public relations circular. The cases cited in them are often of great interest but not much detail is given and there is sometimes no mention of the views of the departments criticized.

Like the Bundesrechnungshof, the General Accounting Office is proud of its cash recoveries, which greatly exceed the cost of the Office itself. In the fiscal year 1956, $68 millions was collected from audit and the settlement of claims, whilst the G.A.O. cost $31.5 millions to maintain. In 1959 the corresponding figures were $60.5 millions and $36.8 millions.

Another characteristic of General Accounting Office reporting is that much of it arises outside the general conduct of audit, as a result of studies and investigations requested in accordance with the statutes of the Office. There is a great deal of reporting upon proposals for new legislation. The Comptroller General records the reporting activity in the fiscal year 1959 in the following figures:[2]

---

[1] A law of 1950 also permitted the Premier Président of the Cour to report audit findings directly by letter to the *Commissions des Finances* of the two parliamentary chambers.

[2] Annual Report, C.G. of the U.S., 1959, p. 253.

To the Congress:		
Accounting, auditing and investigation reports	138	
Other	4	142
To officers of the Congress:		
Audit reports on Senate and House activities	11	
Other	6	17
To committees:		
Reports on bills	638	
Audit and special reports	76	714
To individual Members:		2,930
Informal contacts with Members and committees:		4,290
To the Director, Bureau of the Budget:		
Reports on bills		95
	Total	8,188

* * * *

What sort of observations do state audit bodies consider of sufficient importance to include in their published reports? In recent years the material is so plentiful and varied that it brings to mind a saying of the German budgetary specialist Kurt Heinig that 'state budgets are the cash books of world history'. One can only adopt the procedure of the modern state auditor; make a test examination and take soundings.

Where should soundings be taken? Some sort of classification of reported audit findings, however approximate, may be a guide.

What interests us in the present chapter is the loss of public resources through dishonesty or squandering. The prevention of corruption and waste is essential to the stability of governments, as Aristotle warned. This is an endless campaign against undying enemies. In the age of Gladstone it may have been imagined that waste in administration was no longer a danger if 'regularity' was ensured; at any rate no powers were given to state auditors to look for wasteful expenditures as such. In the twentieth century, it has become clear that 'regularity' is not a protection against waste.

Fraud

Fraud is familiar in all ages. It is the prototype of all audit observations. Within the public service itself, cases of dishonesty have in most countries become a comparative rarity since the development of permanent careers and pensions for officials. They are, however, still common enough where the persons concerned have a more 'tolerant' tradition and little in the way of career prospects to lose, or where accountability has been inadequate for a long time. It is on the ill-lighted fringes of the public sector, remote from the central administrations with their high degree of accountability, that the oddest things happen. In fact a great deal more fraud is detected than finds its way into the public reports of state audit; the internal auditors, whose check comes first and is more detailed, make most of the discoveries. The state auditors may also consider that cases of dishonesty do not usually merit reporting because they involve no issues of principle.

Nevertheless, a selection of fraud finds its way into the reports, and some kind of classification of it is possible.

Cases of plain theft, embezzlement or corruption, whether by servants of the state or members of the public, may be taken as the first class, the 'direct' frauds. A typical case is that of the official whose larcenies become a long undetected routine. As an example, a certain Cosset, assistant cashier of the Paris Opera, was found guilty of embezzling more than a million francs during the war years. The Cour des Comptes found it difficult to understand how the crime continued undiscovered for so long, and commented with acidity:

> No doubt one should not reproach the administrators of the *théâtres lyriques nationaux* for placing artistic questions in the forefront of their preoccupations. They should not, however, neglect the financial aspect of their authority, even when a chronic and perhaps inevitable deficit has accustomed them to count on the subsidies of the State.[1]

In Britain, a conspiracy between an official in charge of egg transport on behalf of the Ministry of Food and an accomplice, between 1948 and 1954, involving the use of false invoices, resulted in losses to public funds exceeding £37,000. Both the culprits were sentenced to seven years' imprisonment.[2]

The history of the mental hospital of Lafond, near La Rochelle,

[1] C. des C., Rapport, 1948–9, p. 163.

[2] C. & A.G.'s R., Civil Appn. A/cs. (Cl. VI–X), 1954–5. (This is the first of various summarized examples taken from Reports of the Comptroller and Auditor General. There is no intention of assessing the importance of individual cases, and the relevant comments of the Public Accounts Committee, if any, have not been considered. The purpose is merely to show what sort of things may be reported.)

after it was requisitioned by the Germans in 1941, was a curious record of corrupt practices. Although the 1,200 patients were dispersed and some of the stores looted, most of the staff was retained; out of a total of 170, there were still 112 in 1947. They performed only occasional duties. The director and his wife used six persons, whose wages from public funds in 1948 were over 1.3 million francs, for their own domestic purposes. The director and staff received allowances for qualifications which they did not possess and for services which they did not perform. The produce of the hospital farm disappeared mysteriously; among the beneficiaries as a result were the Prefect of the département and his staff, as well as senior hospital personnel and members of the supervisory board. Following a local investigation by the Cour des Comptes, the director was transferred and downgraded. Immediately after his replacement in 1948 the declared farm yields increased suddenly. Production of milk, fruit and poultry appeared to have doubled; vegetables became six times as abundant.[1]

The Cour des Comptes also reported the extraordinary exploits of a food purchasing mission which was sent to Germany on behalf of the Lyons region after the end of the war. The members did not vouch properly for the money advanced to them, nor for their expenses. The quantities of food which were taken on charge after the mission showed serious losses compared with what had been bought. A certain Dr. Gorjux, having acquired 75,100 kg. of butter, proceeded to Switzerland and exchanged it for 2,001 piglets, at a net loss estimated at about seven million francs! The Cour not only criticized the principle of a mission on behalf of a single locality, but asked that legal action be taken against the members and 'reimbursement sought for the sums irregularly withdrawn from the treasury for their personal profit'.[2]

A second group of frauds, and one of the commonest types of all, are offences connected with contracts. These occur both during the financially delicate operation of tendering and afterwards when one of the competitors has received and is executing a firm order.

After the last war an armament directorate of the French Ministry of National Defence placed contracts for timber with a group of associated firms. Investigation later revealed evidence

[1] C. des C., Rapport, 1948–9, pp. 192–3.
[2] Ibid., p. 157.

of fraudulent complicity between the contractors and the official in charge of the Ministry's Timber department:

lack of competition; excessive benevolence in the conditions and the contract settlements; over-valuation of agreed prices and violation of controlled price limits; invoices quoting fictitious or already paid amounts; obtaining by means of false certificates public funds exceeding the liabilities of the State by 93 million francs.[1]

At that time the French timber trade appears to have been particularly unreliable. The Cour des Comptes found that a number of timber contracts placed by the Ministry of Public Works had resulted in substantial losses from fraud, bankruptcy, short deliveries and inadequate quality.

All the contractors had close relations with each other, and throughout extremely complex transactions, in contracts entangled, cancelled, transformed, or modified, one perceives a veritable network of complicity with the sole objective of obtaining funds by the game of obtaining advances without counterpart in services rendered.

The Cour reported action taken against the contractors and officials concerned, and criticized the law itself for being too liberal on the subject of contractual advances.[2]

Contracts for 'wiping cloths' for the United States Navy were the subject of fraudulent deliveries. The Comptroller General tells how it was done:

. . . by the process of switching bales during and after inspection, wiping cloths in great quantity definitely not meeting specifications were shipped to the Navy and paid for. This was done with knowledge and under instructions of the responsible officers of the respective companies. In one instance Government personnel received gifts, loans of money, payment of hotel rooms and other gratuities.[3]

The effrontery of this contractor was surpassed by that of a French firm which, in June 1946, was awarded a contract by the Ministry of Reconstruction and Town-planning for 20,000 sleeping-bags and 15,000 bolster cases for workers' camps. The full price, over 11 million francs, was paid after proper invoices had been submitted and certified—all by the same official. Later investigation revealed that only 1,151 bolster cases had in fact been delivered, and no sleeping-bags at all! The Cour des Comptes

[1] C. des C. Rapport, 1948–9, p. 161.

[2] Ibid., pp. 165–7.

[3] Annual R., C.G. of the U.S., 1954, p. 46.

reminded the administration that the issue of false certificates was a penal offence and requested appropriate action.[1]

Fraudulent deliveries arise even in international contracting. An interesting case was investigated by a General Accounting Office team in the Far East at the request of the Government Operations Committee of the House of Representatives. At a time when world prices for strategic materials were high, contracts had been placed with mining companies in Thailand for the supply of 268,000 units of tungsten ore at $65 per unit—a total of over $17 millions. The world price was then about $70 a unit but it later fell to around $45.

> During the period that the world market price was above the contract price the suppliers did not meet delivery schedules. As soon as the world price dropped below the contract price, deliveries began to exceed contract requirements. The investigation revealed that much of the ore furnished to the United States by the contractors was purchased on the open market and excessive profits were realized.

The contracts were suspended after about $5½ millions had been paid, but it was estimated that this figure already included more than $1 million paid in excess of the world market price.[2]

Thus contractual deliveries can be unscrupulously manipulated in quantity, in quality and in price.

A third common type of fraud is that which draws undue advantage from schemes designed for the benefit of the public or sections of it, whether in the form of social security and welfare or subsidy and compensation. West Germany has had an unusually large number of such schemes since the war, as a consequence of its unprecedented reconstruction and rehabilitation problems. It also has had to combat frauds.

There were fraudulent officials. The Bundesrechnungshof recorded the case of a senior civil servant of a Land who was in charge of the funds for housing loans and was also in private life a member of a limited company dealing in housing. The manager of the company was the official's father; later the official himself and his wife were also appointed to the management. The company benefited from housing loans to the extent of hundreds of

[1] C. des C., Rapport, 1948–9, p. 171.

[2] Annual R., C.G. of the U.S., 1955, pp. 80–1.

thousands of Deutschmarks 'under unusually favourable conditions'. Proceedings against the official had been instituted.[1]

There were also fraudulent claimants. In the hard times of unemployment and short-time work in the earlier post-war years, 'black work', undeclared by workers claiming unemployment assistance, was a serious problem to which the Bundesrechnungshof devoted attention.[2] More recently, the grant of resettlement compensation and loans to exiles from Eastern Germany has offered scope to ambitious claimants. The broad intentions behind such financial aid have been to ensure the refugees a livelihood, to relate assistance to actual losses suffered, to maintain former social levels and to restore previous occupations. The administrative difficulties involved when the evidence in support of the claims was mostly behind the Iron Curtain, may be imagined. The case of a furrier seems to have been aggravated by administrative clumsiness. He was granted a loan of 90,000 DM. to assist his new business in Western Germany, but this turned out to be overloaded with debt and had fraudulent books. Whilst liquidation proceedings were pending he received a second loan of 35,000 DM., and the Bundesrechnungshof reported that he had since gone abroad.[3]

The Cour des Comptes recorded fraud among beneficiaries from French family allowances, which are perhaps the highest in the world. The 'sole income allowance' is, as the name suggests, available to husbands only if their wives do not go out to work, and it was indeed originally designed to encourage mothers to stay in the home. So common was the fraudulent concealment of wives' employment that the resulting overpayment a decade ago was estimated by the Cour to be of the order of ten milliards of francs yearly.[4]

Since under the French social security system industrial accident benefits were higher than those for illness, there was a strong incentive for misrepresentation of the causes of claims on the part

[1] Denkschrift for financial year 1955, p. 37.

[2] Denkschrift for financial years 1949 and 1950, p. 125.

[3] Denkschrift dated 12 August 1958, pp. 85–6.

[4] Owing to devaluations of the franc, it is extremely difficult to express French expenditures in terms of pounds sterling, except for those made since the currency stabilization of the Fifth Republic. As a very rough guide, a milliard (a thousand million) francs was approximately a million pounds during the last years of the Fourth Republic. In the immediate post-war years it was, however, a great deal more.

of the sick and their doctors. When an experiment in strict medical control was made among the Marseilles dockers a substantial reduction in accident costs resulted, until trade-union protests led to a relaxation, after which payments again rose immediately.[1]

In Britain the Comptroller and Auditor General has reported fraudulent or at least very loose interpretations of the rules by claimants for farm subsidies of various kinds. The Ploughing Grants (Scotland) Scheme, 1958, provided for grants of £7 an acre for ploughing up land under grass sowed before 1 June 1955. The state auditors observed certain cases where fields stated to have been under grass had also been the subject of another kind of subsidy, 'deficiency payments' for oats, barley and mixed corn. The Department of Agriculture for Scotland then checked all ploughing grants against deficiency payments and discovered overpayments totalling £8,200, and also a case of fraud inside the Department involving nearly £1,000.[2] The C. & A.G. had previously reported on the subject of 'deficiency payments', based upon acreages of barley, oats and mixed corn sown and harvested. Out of 177,000 farmers' claims received in Great Britain, a proportion had been checked by local officials, mainly by field inspection. About 17 per cent of the claims checked were amended, with a net reduction of 20,733 acres, which would otherwise have attracted substantial payments.[3]

Finally, there may be collusion between corrupt officials and dishonest claimants. In West Germany, claims for compensation in connection with the allied forces stationed there have in recent years been dealt with by Defence Cost Offices (Verteidigungslastenämter). At one of these the representatives of the Bundesrechnungshof discovered numerous cases of collusion with claimants, as a result of which compensation payments had been assessed which were wholly or partly unjustified. The officials concerned received long terms of imprisonment. About 700,000 DM. of improper compensation payments was recovered following action by the Bundesrechnungshof.[4]

The fourth class of fraud is that which arises from official travel. The travelling claim, which officials in all countries submit

[1] C. des C., Rapport, 'La Sécurité Sociale', 1950–1, pp. 51–5.
[2] C. & A.G.'s R., Civil Appn. A/cs. (Cl. VI–X), 1958–9.
[3] Ibid., 1954–5.
[4] Denkschrift dated 24 October 1959, p. 100.

after return from a duty journey, is the nearest thing that civil servants have to an expense account, and presumably most organizations have to accept the existence of a small element of overclaiming which they cannot disprove.

But travel frauds are not always small, and occasionally one or two cases find their way into the national audit reports.

A Bordeaux doctor was employed upon itinerant vaccination and inoculation duties, and the Cour des Comptes studied and reported upon his journeys:

For vaccinations, he goes long distances daily; for example 302 kilometres on 10 April 1956 and 248 kilometres on the 25th. But under the heading of inoculations he also obtains reimbursement for even longer distances, covered on the same day. Altogether on the 10th April, 648 kilometres are alleged to have been travelled, and 676 on the 25th, in the course of which a dozen vaccination sessions are said to have been completed.

The good doctor apparently made two separate visits to each village on the same day and returned to Bordeaux after every session.[1]

When claims for travel go beyond the bounds of probability or evident utility, the cause may be abuse of the privileges of authority. Such a case was that of the director of a public corporation charged with regional development in Germany, the Emsland Company. In 1954 he made a journey which was 'supposed to be for the purpose of examining development measures in Italy'. He pursued this plausible intention, however, for almost seven weeks in the early summer, and he did so in a chauffeur-driven official car. Moreover, he went to Switzerland and the French Riviera as well as the whole of Italy and Sicily.[2]

One of the very commonest kinds of petty fraud is indeed the misuse of official cars or of private cars charged on public account at a fixed rate per mile. As the result of the discovery of such cases by an internal auditor, a strange drama came to the notice of the Bundesrechnungshof. In 1955 the head of the audit section of a trading organization subsidized by the Federal Ministry of Food, Agriculture and Forests was given notice. The dismissal was at first justified on the grounds of matters of internal administration, but the case came before a Labour Court and the official

[1] C. des C., Rapport, 1957–8, p. 55.

[2] Denkschrift dated 24 October 1957, p. 79.

maintained that the chief reason for his dismissal was that he had raised audit criticisms concerning the use of service vehicles by members of his Board. The legal action resulted in a compromise based on a payment of compensation for dismissal. In 1956, however, the Bundesrechnungshof took up the matter after receiving a petition from the official. The state audit body was concerned that 'an unhindered conduct of audit must be protected against the pressure of unreasonable influence'. The auditor's observations were examined in detail and found to be justified. They concerned motor journeys which gave rise to doubt whether their purpose was official or even whether they took place at all; there were journeys on Sundays and holidays, and in some cases official cars were alleged to have been used at the same moment as the Board members' own private cars. A Board member told the Bundesrechnungshof that the real complaint was about the type of audit; the official should know how to distinguish between 'important' and 'unimportant' matters. The state audit body commented that it looked upon this attitude as one likely to influence staff charged with auditing duties. It therefore proposed for the future that the appointment and removal of heads of audit sections should be reserved for the approval of the Minister, after consultation with the Bundesrechnungshof. The unfortunate official in the case was not forgotten; the Bundesrechnunshof recommended to the Minister that he be given a career placement, since it took the view quite openly that injustice had been done. But apparently the action of the Board members was not wholly unsuccessful, since the principle of restoring the auditor to his old post does not seem to have been mooted.[1] The case shows the vulnerability of internal auditors in the face of their own managements.

The fifth and last major category of frauds in public finance is that connected with the revenue system, both for direct and for indirect taxation. The audit of government income is one of the oldest activities of state audit. It was the principal task of medieval bodies like the Exchequer and the Chambre des Comptes of Paris, but nineteenth century auditors turned from it to the examination of expenditure. Probably in the twentieth century too little is done by the state audit bodies by way of revenue studies. Their reports are potentially an excellent factual guide to the reform or adaptation

[1] Denkschrift dated 19 August 1958, pp. 55–6.

of tax regulations. In the words of a specialist from the Cour des Comptes: 'Public opinion needs to be informed about the irregularities or anomalies which may have arisen in the collection of revenues.'[1]

Some useful reporting about the difficulties and problems of revenue collection and tax law does in fact take place. The Cour des Comptes gives a degree of importance to it, and in the process records the nature of frauds discovered.

In 1952 the Cour reported that social security for French peasants was mainly supported by an indirect tax on agricultural produce; cereals, meat, sugar-beet, wines, tobacco, timber and certain alcohols. The collection of this tax was found by the auditors to be subject to 'massive and generalized fraud'. Among the expedients used were failure to record corn and timber deliveries and a systematic understatement of turnover in the meat trade. The public thus paid the tax, but much of it did not reach the treasury.

> Incorporation of the tax in the selling prices transforms various sorts of tradespeople into tax-collectors, who sometimes retain a part of the amounts deposited with them.[2]

A very complicated type of commercial trickery was discovered by the General Accounting Office, in which manipulation of the customs regulations was combined with the wrongful collection of subsidies. It thus encompassed two major categories of fraud. During audit at the United States Bureau of Customs in 1952, the Comptroller General's staff observed that wheat in large quantities was being imported from Canada at a reduced duty applicable to grain unfit for human consumption; it was then being milled into flour and exported. Export subsidy payments were being claimed from the Commodity Credit Corporation. The Comptroller General reported the matter to Congress and to the Senate Committee on Agriculture and Forestry. Cases involving no less than twenty-four companies were referred to the Department of Justice. About $1 million was recovered from the improper subsidy payments. The Customs also revised their regulations. The Comptroller finally noted 'a decline in importations of this

[1] Pierre Viot, 'Les Attributions de l'organisme supérieur de contrôle en ce qui concerne les recettes'. (Paper prepared for the Third International Congress of Supreme Audit Institutions, 1959.)

[2] C. des C., Rapport, 'La Sécurité Sociale', 1950–1, pp. 21–2.

type of wheat from 30,602,327 bushels in 1952 to 4,399,556 bushels in 1953 following our disclosures'.[1]

* * * *

There are other types of administrative mishap which are costly without being fraudulent. Waste may be taken as the consequence of neglect, inefficiency or maladministration. Extravagance is the result of a deliberate decision to do things in an expensive way, or of the absence of a decision to reduce exorbitant costs. Unsound projects are those which show a very evident lack of forethought and common sense. All these categories are outside the limits of 'regularity'. According to nineteenth-century ideas they should not be the concern of state audit at all, because they involve 'matters of administration'. But at the present day they constitute the main types of published criticism, and the examples of them in state audit reports vastly outnumber the cases of formal irregularity, including fraud.

Waste

The general heading of waste may be sub-divided into three groups; firstly neglect and carelessness; secondly, technical inefficiency, and finally general maladministration.

The Comptroller General of the U.S. has reported a number of cases in which what should have been done had not in fact been done. For example, in the Virgin Islands, G.A.O. auditors discovered in 1954 that the charges of the municipal hospitals had not been revised since 1938 and were so ridiculously low that they only covered about five per cent of operating costs.[2]

The Puerto Rico Reconstruction Administration, which had been set up after a hurricane, was reported several years later to be quite superfluous. On the basis of G.A.O. recommendations, Congress enacted its abolition with an estimated total saving of $7 to 8 millions.[3]

Another odd fact which came to the American state auditors' notice was that the official table of distances used for road travel payments by Federal departments was in fact based upon railway routes, which were mostly longer. The difference was estimated to cost more than $1 million a year.[4]

[1] C. G. of the U.S. Annual Reports 1953, p. 20, and 1954, p. 25.

[2] Ibid., 1954, p. 26. [3] Ibid. [4] Ibid., p. 38.

Over-estimation of requirements involves a deliberate decision and is therefore to be classed as extravagance rather than waste. But when members of the Exchequer and Audit Department visited a military depot they found a case of over-estimation which was not deliberate but the result of a careless mistake. The Army was found to be in possession of a stock of 1,400,000 feet of brass tubing, in 33 sizes, with an estimated value of £276,000 and with no known requirement for issue. The total length to be obtained for all sizes had been taken as the requirement for each size. The War Office decided to dispose of all but 38,500 ft. of the tubing even before the future requirement, 'if any', was re-assessed.[1]

Operational trials of an air navigational system developed by a private firm, were, under a special arrangement, to be provided by 150 flying hours, estimated to cost £40,000, with Ministry of Supply aircraft from an Experimental Establishment. The actual cost up to 31 March 1959, however, was assessed at £300,000, involving 615 flying hours. The Ministry informed the Comptroller and Auditor General that through an oversight the Experimental Establishment had not been told of the financial limit prescribed and had not been given instructions to record costs.[2]

The West German auditors came to the conclusion that the system of employing free-lance architects and engineers on building projects for the forces of the allied powers was unsatisfactory; they were repeatedly found to have failed to carry out their duties properly. The Bundesrechnungshof examined two projects closely and reported 'considerable constructional defects and gross errors in the accounts.' The drains were found to be completely blocked by mud at many points. Incorrect calculation of quantities had resulted in substantial invoice discrepancies for earthworks, reinforced concrete and drainage installations. The Bundesrechnungshof calculated a minimum overcharge of 500,000 DM. for the two projects, but as a result of its action at least 150,000 DM. of this would fall upon the contractors. The remaining loss would have been avoided by proper works supervision, and only well-proven architects should be commissioned in future. The auditors proposed to raise certain claims against the consultants responsible.[3]

[1] C. & A.G.'s R., Army Appn. A/cs., 1957–8.
[2] C. & A.G.'s R., Civil Appn. A/cs. (Cl. VI–X), 1958–9.
[3] Denkschrift for financial year 1954, p. 85.

Failures of technical control have been reported from two British Commonwealth territories. During the 1940's a dam was built in Jamaica at a cost of about £475,000, mainly in the form of an interest-free loan from British funds. Unfortunately it was found in 1948 that the reservoir would not hold water. The supervising engineer had set aside some of the advice of consulting engineers and 'owing to a major error of judgment' the floor and banks had not been sealed. The work of making the reservoir watertight necessitated a further loan of £100,000.[1]

Over £60,000 was issued by the United Kingdom to the Government of Nyasaland from Colonial Development and Welfare funds, for the construction of a new secondary-technical school which was completed in 1956. There was extensive wasteful expenditure due to lack of proper technical supervision, resulting in poor workmanship throughout. The use of mud mortar instead of cement had resulted in damage from white ants. The electric wiring had been condemned. Repairs had been carried out at an estimated cost of £12,000 but in the opinion of the Director of Public Works only complete demolition and rebuilding would suffice.[2]

Technical inefficiency is not confined to engineering. It can, for example, appear in specialized financial administration. The Federal Crop Insurance Corporation, a body associated with the U.S. Department of Agriculture, was reported by the Comptroller General to have continued to insure crops in some areas with records of almost continuous high losses. In eighteen counties of Colorado, New Mexico, Oklahoma and Texas the losses from 1948 to 1953 totalled nearly $10 millions. 'Operations of this nature,' commented the Comptroller, 'are in the nature of a subsidy and are not consistent with the expressed intent of the Congress that the Corporation's insurance operations be developed on a self-sustaining basis.'[3]

In another case, the Comptroller General reported the results of a bad technical specification, the consequences of which were aggravated by administrative carelessness. Trouble arose with the packing, at a cost of $7,600,000, of 178,000 jettisonable aircraft fuel tanks for the U.S. Air Force. The packing work was done in accordance with instructions but,

early in the programme, reports were received from domestic and

[1] C. & A.G.'s R., Civil Appn. A/cs. (Cl. I–V), 1953–4.

[2] Ibid., 1957–8.

[3] Annual R., C.G. of the U.S., 1955, p. 50.

overseas depots that the tanks, after being stored for short periods of time, were found to contain water, sand, soot, and other foreign matter; tank parts and fittings were corroding and some of the tanks were punctured.

Whilst this situation was being studied, further contracts for 117,000 tanks were placed. Despite the adverse reports which had been received, the same inadequate packing specifications were used for the new tanks, with a packing cost of $5,400,000.

At the time of our investigation, (wrote the Comptroller General) the tank refurbishing and recrating programme had already cost the Government an additional $1⅓ million; also, a large but undetermined quantity of tanks remained to be refurbished and recrated at domestic and overseas depots, which would cost an even greater sum in labour and money.[1]

When expenditures are high, an oversight may be very costly. The Comptroller General reported that timely cancellation of a contract for aero-engines, following a change in requirements, might have saved $3½ millions. Of this amount, about $1 million was actually saved as a result of audit action.[2]

Waste can, finally, arise as a result of errors so wide-spread that they can only be summed-up as general maladministration. A case in point was a French organization created during the confused post-war period, with the intention of facilitating foreign trade. This was the Société des importations et des exportations ('Impex'), which was very severely criticized by the Cour des Comptes and has since been abolished. The entire administration and staffing of this makeshift organization appeared to the Cour to be 'disjointed'. As for its activity, Impex was a vast 'middleman' agency; it did not buy, but merely took all French imports on charge at frontiers and ports, distributed them to addresses furnished by the ministries and collected payment. The task was difficult; at the beginning of each operation Impex did not know who were either the suppliers or the purchasers. The accounting fell heavily in arrears, and, lacking an adequate staff of its own, Impex, by 'a singular expedient', created a limited company, Servimpex, to prepare invoices for a fee. This permitted the employment of a further 554 persons without increasing the voted

[1] Annual R., C.G. of the U.S., 1954, pp. 49–50.

[2] Ibid., 1956, pp. 53–4.

establishment. Impex was not in contractual relations with the addressees of consignments, who sometimes demanded discounts or even refused to take delivery. It was also the victim of foreign exchange losses arising from successive devaluations of the franc, to the great profit of importers. Owing to this price mechanism various ministries took advantage of an arrangement which enabled them to transfer part of their costs to the Impex account; 20 milliards of francs of unvoted expenditures were incurred in this way before the loophole was stopped in 1948. The Impex account was used as a hidden subsidy for various transactions; imports from Switzerland, exports to U.N.R.R.A.; electric power imports from Germany, which alone involved a deficit of over one milliard. When the account finally came up for liquidation, ten milliard francs remained to be recovered from private clients, and invoices covering seven milliards had not been issued. Legal disputes related to more than two milliards. The Cour's basic criticism was of the very nature of the Impex account itself, 'open to arbitrariness, disorder and waste'.[1]

Extravagance

Cases of extravagance in state audit reports are even more numerous than examples of waste. Extravagance may arise from an overestimation of requirements, from a taste for luxury and operations on a large scale, or from a breakdown of normal rules and controls. Or it may simply involve expenditures which need not have been incurred at all.

Several examples of the last type of extravagance, of unnecessary spending, have been reported by the General Accounting Office. In June 1951, the U.S. Air Force had $\$1\frac{1}{2}$ millions to spare at the end of the financial year and, rather than surrender it to the Treasury, purchased 142 miles of chain-link fencing. The state auditors found eighteen months later that over 70 per cent of the fencing remained unused.[2]

A notable case of misplaced largesse was the gift by a U.S. Army Depot of 523 unused warehouse tractors to various educational establishments. The tractors, which had cost $479,000, were described as surplus property, but the G.A.O. discovered contracts for hundreds of similar tractors which had

[1] C. des C., Rapport, 1948–9, pp. 174–84.

[2] Annual R., C.G. of the U.S., 1953, p. 43.

been placed at a date subsequent to the gift. The Secretary of Defense told the Comptroller General that the tractors given away were of a type which had been superseded, but he promised that in future stocks of superseded items would be used as far as possible.[1]

In an intensely practical audit observation, the Comptroller General reported to Congress that in 1957 and 1958 dried milk and processed cheese had been packed in tin cans by the Commodity Credit Corporation for donation abroad. This cost about $7 millions more than packing in plastic bags inside cartons.

Only minor damage (said the report) has resulted in the past when these products were packed in plastic bags. For this reason we believe that almost all the additional $7 million cost incurred by packaging in tin cans was unnecessary.[2]

Again, the General Accounting Office considered that the issue of sea duty pay to naval personnel operating on the Great Lakes was unnecessary. The point was accepted and the regulations were revised to preclude this in the future.[3]

A case of unnecessary motor vehicle maintenance was reported in Germany. The Bundesrechnungshof was concerned to note that the Federal Post Office (Bundespost) had from 1953 onwards placed contracts for the maintenance of some 2,000 Volkswagen vehicles on a scale which appeared to be greatly exaggerated. They were to be greased weekly and sprayed down every two weeks; according to the makers' manual the former was required only every 2,500 kilometres and the latter only occasionally in winter. On the basis of average usage, greasing was needed every 44 days but the 26 spray-downs a year were not justified at all. Following audit observations, a new maintenance regime was established in 1956, involving an annual economy of between 260,000 and 400,000 DM.[4]

The Cour des Comptes reported a very interesting case of extravagance. The old 100-franc pieces issued under the Fourth Republic were of cupro-nickel, in which the nickel content was only 25 per cent. The Cour noted that no difficulty had been experienced with this alloy, which was much less costly and easier to work than pure nickel. It had, nevertheless, been decided to

[1] Annual R., C.G. of the U.S., 1953, p. 51.
[2] Ibid., 1959, p. 57.
[3] Ibid., 1954, p. 39.
[4] Denkschrift dated 19 August 1958, p. 100.

strike the one-new-franc piece of the Fifth Republic in pure nickel, and moreover, 'for reasons completely unrelated to the technique of money manufacture', in nickel from the French island of New Caledonia, the price of which was above the world market level. The Cour estimated that this policy would involve an additional 1,078 millions of old francs, doubling the cost of the whole operation.[1]

Luxury in public expenditures often concerns buildings and accommodation: the Comptroller and Auditor General drew attention to the fact that the Residency compound for the Political Resident in the Persian Gulf, at Bahrein, which was built between 1948 and 1954, cost about half a million pounds.[2]

The U.S. State Department was taken to task by the Comptroller General for carrying out a 'de luxe' housing project at Bonn in 1951, for the staff of the American High Commissioner in Germany. The ambassadorial residence cost $240,000 and five houses for senior officers $151,000 each. There were 458 apartments, a church, two schools, a shopping centre, a theatre and a recreation centre with swimming pool. The total cost, $16,750,000, was incurred without specific Congressional approval, and it was 'nearly three times the amount authorized by Congress for the world-wide operations under the Foreign Service Buildings Act for the same year'.[3]

A curious case which arose during the last war, and was reported by the Cour des Comptes after the Liberation, was the acquisition by the French Navy of a large estate near Toulon which was under sequestration because its owner was a Jew. The ostensible reason for the acquisition was to provide an officers' rest home and a holiday camp for children. 'But a few weeks later a decision of the "Minister of the Navy", dated 22 March 1942, transformed the estate into a summer residence for the Admiral of the Fleet, who was, incidentally, none other than the Minister himself.' This was Admiral Darlan, who was to die at the hand of an assassin in Algiers within the year.[4]

Many cases of extravagance in accommodation were reported by the Cour after the War, sometimes with wrathful commentaries.

[1] C. des C., Rapport, 1957–8, p. 32.
[2] C. & A.G.'s R., Civil Appn. A/cs. (Cl. VI–X), 1953–4.
[3] Annual R., C.G. of the U.S., 1953, pp. 43–4.
[4] C. des C., Rapport, 1940–5, p. 8.

The Chateau de Saint-Victor at Marseilles, which had been purchased for purposes of social service, was taken over by the general commanding the region as his headquarters. The Cour described this as 'highly reprehensible' and 'evidence of a singular lack of scruple'.[1] During an audit of Radiodiffusion française, the Cour found that many members of the staff were unnecessarily receiving free lodging, including the former Director General, more than a year after his retirement.[2] The General Staff was criticized for holding the magnificent Hotel Continental, behind the Rue de Rivoli, on requisition. It was only partly occupied, and the use of the hotel restaurant involved a heavy subsidy from public funds. This observation was part of a campaign by the Cour des Comptes against the uncontrolled use of requisitioning after the Liberation, which in August 1945 involved over 15,000 housing units in the Paris region.

> There is no need (it wrote) to stress the immense handicap which this seizure by the administration of numerous premises, formerly in private use, has imposed upon the economic life of the country, nor to say with what impatience it is tolerated at a period when the housing crisis is particularly grave.[3]

An example of construction on the most lavish scale was the U.S. Air Force Academy at Colorado Springs. The Air Force, said the Comptroller General, had not made a full disclosure to Congress of the complete requirements and cost of the project. The legislature had indicated its intention that the total cost should not exceed $126 millions, which had later been increased to $139·8 millions. In fact the Academy was expected to cost not less than $256 millions. Of this $3·48 millions had been improperly charged to other appropriations. About $2·2 millions had been incurred for certain facilities in advance of congressional approval, which, when later requested, was refused. Over $6 millions which had been justified to Congress for family housing had been used for other purposes. The G.A.O. submitted a list of facilities which had been considerably increased in scope and cost after approval by Congress. The Air Force Academy seems to be almost a classic example of the breakdown in the age of big government of the traditional controls over public expenditure.[4]

[1] C. des C., Rapport, 1948–9, p. 154.
[2] Ibid., p. 158.
[3] Ibid., 1940–5, pp. 19–20.
[4] Annual R., C.G. of the U.S., 1959, pp. 121–4.

Accommodation is the commonest but not the only object of luxurious expenditure. When the Comptroller and Auditor General twice reported upon the cost of the College of Aeronautics it was the upkeep rather than the housing which seemed to him sumptuous, or at least out of all proportion to income from students' fees. The College's net expenditure in the year ended 31 March 1952 was £286,269, so that on the basis of 130 students the cost of maintenance per student averaged £2,200. The fees charged to United Kingdom students were, however, only £200 per annum. The staff of the college numbered 374. In addition 75 men were normally employed on upkeep of buildings and services.[1] In the year ended 31 March 1955, the net maintenance expenditure had risen to £381,669, the average maintenance cost per student to £2,495 and the staff to 463 plus 70 men engaged on upkeep. The fees of £200 per annum had remained unchanged since 1946.[2]

The specification of stores can be excessively luxurious. The Bundesrechnungshof commented upon the decision to provide members of the West German armed forces with expensive kapok mattresses instead of palliasses filled with palm fibre, which had been tested and found highly satisfactory. This was expected to increase the cost of German rearmament by ten million Deutschmarks, without taking subsequent replacements into consideration.[3]

Sport and recreational facilities were the subject of a striking American observation about luxurious spending. The General Accounting Office reported in 1953 that Armed Forces recreational activities in Hawaii cost about $2·5 millions a year in appropriated funds, in addition to other money accruing from post exchanges, etc. There were 23 athletic fields, 5 golf courses, 8 gymnasiums, 24 theatres, 7 beach recreation areas, 16 service clubs, 18 swimming pools and 80 tennis courts.[4]

Overestimation of requirements is a perennial source of very great extravagance in public spending. It is one of the most costly of all types of administrative aberration, because a single overestimate may result in the useless expenditure of millions. This

[1] C. & A.G.'s R., Civil Appn. A/cs. (Classes I–VIII), 1951–2.
[2] Ibid. (Classes I–V), 1954–5.
[3] Denkschrift dated 24 October 1959, p. 94.
[4] Annual R., C.G. of the U.S., 1953, p. 44.

happens everywhere, but the General Accounting Office has encountered some of the most remarkable cases.

The G.A.O. discovered, for example, that the U.S. Air Force was purchasing substantially more J-47 aero-engines than it in fact needed. As a result it was possible to cancel an order for additional engines and stop another in the negotiation stage, with a total estimated saving of between $60 and $70 millions. Conversion of older engines was expected to save a further $8 millions.[1]

The requirement for troopships had also been overestimated. During the first seven months of the fiscal year 1956, 17 troopships of the Military Sea Transportation Service had been retained idle, at a cost estimated at over $5 millions. The G.A.O. did not therefore hesitate to make proposals which concerned high strategy.

> Based on the high cost and known passenger requirements we recommended to the Commander, M.S.T.S., that at least 10 troopships be inactivated. We were advised that although this would result in savings to the Government, it would seriously affect the ability of M.S.T.S. to meet mobilization and emergency requirements established by the Joint Chiefs of Staff. However, in order to minimize cost . . . the Commander has requested the Chief of Naval Operations to consider the establishment of a ready reserve of troopships. Vessels in this category would be essentially dead ships but would be maintained at such standards as to be ready on short notice.[2]

The financial consequences of these overestimates were, however, dwarfed by those of another case. The Comptroller General criticized the U.S. Navy for consistent overestimation of material for ship overhaul and conversion work:

> As a result, enormous quantities of surplus material have been accumulated which experience shows will ultimately be disposed of at a fraction of their cost. During the last 3 fiscal years, a sizable amount of Navy inventories have been classified as excess to its needs. This included nearly $850 million worth of electronic and shipboard equipment and ship repair parts which are used almost exclusively for overhaul and conversion of ships.[3]

In Britain the auditors visited an Army clothing depot and discovered that the stocks of women's clothing were in many cases sufficient for over twenty years' peacetime consumption,

[1] Annual R., C.G. of the U.S., 1955, p. 20, and 1956, pp. 52–3.

[2] Ibid., 1956, p. 49.

[3] Ibid., 1959, p. 114.

although some articles had an estimated store life of less than seven years. The War Office informed the Comptroller and Auditor General in response to his enquiries, that it had been decided to dispose of almost all stocks of underclothing, valued at £287,000 in 1955, and that other reserves would be substantially reduced.[1]

It is just as easy to overestimate requirements for staff. The Cour des Comptes, for example, has referred to the veterinary service of the French Army. In 1913 the Army had 175,000 horses and mules and 522 veterinary officers. The Cour found that it now had less than 12,000—plus 4,500 dogs—but the veterinary service still numbered 180 officers and 123 *aspirants*.[2]

Accommodation may also be subject to overestimation. This seems to have been the case at Fort Logan in Colorado, a huge army camp with 200 buildings and 973 acres of land. When the G.A.O. took an interest in 1955, the camp had been unused since 1951 and the vacant buildings were deteriorating despite an expense of $135,000 annually for maintenance. Nevertheless, an offer to purchase the camp for $11 millions had been rejected because it still met a presumed requirement and had not been declared surplus.[3]

There are, finally, a limited number of cases due to a temporary failure of financial control. The regulations seem in such cases to have at least momentarily lost all proportion and to provide for payments which are clearly excessive.

In the early days of the National Health Service, the scale of payments for British dentists was notoriously out of balance. It had been designed to provide a fair income, but it was soon found that dentists were earning much more. By the end of 1948, 22 per cent of all dentists were receiving from the Health Service alone gross incomes exceeding £6,000 a year. The Comptroller and Auditor General made a special mention in his report of a Scottish dentist who achieved the record. For the period of less than six months between the establishment of the Health Service and the end of 1948 he was paid £18,077, including £4,686 for the month of December alone.[4] The trouble was not due only to the

[1] C. & A.G.'s R., Army Appn. A/c., 1955–6.

[2] C. des C., Rapport, 1957–8, p. 24.

[3] Annual R., C.G. of the U.S., 1955, p. 83.

[4] C. & A.G.'s R., Civil Appn. A/cs. (Cl. I–IX), 1948–9.

over-generous payment scale. The Public Accounts Committee of 1950 noted that remuneration of dentists was substantially higher than that of doctors, and also that there was 'some evidence of scamped work and even of fraud.' Six dentists' names had been removed from dental lists.[1]

The Bundesrechnungshof expressed disquiet about the decisions taken on some refugees' claims for loss of lands and property beyond the Iron Curtain. In a number of cases, some of them involving very large claims, the compensation awarded in West Germany was based on a valuation much higher than that put forward by the claimant himself. One expellee claimed on a rateable value of 97,100 Reichsmarks and was assessed at 150,000. The former owner of a very large manorial estate, of which two-thirds was in cultivation, claimed a figure of 625,000 RM. for the whole property, but the value of his arable land alone was assessed at 805,000 RM. The Bundesrechnungshof commented that such cases should be very rare, because in its experience claimants did not knowingly understate the rateable value of their property.[2]

Financial control can break down during a foreign aid scheme. The General Accounting Office found something like this when it examined the aid furnished to the Chinese government in Formosa (Taiwan) through the International Co-operation Administration. The audit report drew attention to the use of an exchange rate which overvalued the Taiwan dollar and to the fact that the Chinese were depositing less local currency in the counterpart account, provided for in the bilateral agreement, than had been collected from private importers. The Comptroller General concluded that this resulted in 'hidden budgetary support to the Chinese Government'. After the issue of his report the exchange rate was revised.[3]

Some expenditures recorded in state audit reports deserve mention merely as examples of the bizarre. Payments for odd and anachronistic reasons are not very uncommon in the records of ancient states. They may be a picturesque residue of history.

One such survival reported by the Comptroller and Auditor General was the annual payment to the Sultan of Muscat of £6,480. This subsidy was established in 1856 in compensation for

[1] C. & A.G.'s R., Civil Appn. A/cs. (Cl. I–VIII), 1949–50.

[2] Denkschrift dated 24 October 1959, pp. 111–12.

[3] Annual R., C.G. of the U.S., 1959, p. 166.

renunciation of the Sultan's claims to Zanzibar. From 1873 until 1948 the grant was 'for various reasons' paid by the Government of India, on condition that the Sultan should 'manifest his friendship towards the British Government'. In 1948, after Indian independence, payment was taken over by the United Kingdom. 'I understand,' wrote the C. & A.G., 'that the subsidy is regarded as payable in perpetuity, subject only to the Sultan's observance of his engagements.'[1]

Contemplating the financial anarchy of the Vichy Government, the Cour des Comptes discovered many bizarre activities. It must suffice here to mention one of them. The auditors noticed the purchase by the département of the Côte d'Or of part of a famous vineyard at Beaune. Although unusual, the acquisition was not irregular in itself. What was astonishing was the motive for the purchase. The Prefect of the Côte d'Or intended to rename the property 'the Marshal's Vineyard' and present it to the Head of State, Philippe Pétain. The gift was made with due formality at Dijon in June 1942. The Cour commented that it could not help drawing attention to such an example of 'political servility' and misuse of money raised by taxation.[2]

The significance of publicity

Most of the examples of waste and extravagance, and of course all the cases of fraud, are in some way reprehensible. If left to themselves, with no external audit, the authorities concerned would certainly not have drawn public attention to them. What is the significance of the publicity which these cases receive through state audit?

The simplest answer, as far as the purely critical material in state audit reports is concerned, is that publication is *useful*. It is so in a general sense, as expressed by a member of the Cour des Comptes:

> It is certainly useful that light, full light, is shed upon the conditions in which the taxes, which impose heavy sacrifices upon every citizen, are employed. . . . Light is the prerequisite of good order.[3]

More specifically, public reporting of the faults of administrative bodies is *effective*. This is for two reasons; firstly because it may

[1] C. & A.G.'s R., Civil Appn. A/cs. (Cl. I–IX), 1948–9.

[2] C. des C., Rapport, 1940–5, p. 22.

[3] Pierre Escoube, 'La Cour des Comptes', *Revue des Deux Mondes*, 1 October 1958.

create a movement of opinion in favour of remedial measures, and secondly because the exposure of errors will in any case serve 'pour encourager les autres'. Publicity given to the foibles of administration is a mild but adequate form of reproach. The reports rarely mention personalities and the only responsibilities invoked are the collective ones of the authorities concerned. Such a form of censure is infinitely preferable to a search for individual scapegoats.

There is good evidence of the effectiveness of public audit criticism. The Cour des Comptes has used it in a very direct and outspoken way, addressing the report to public opinion as 'the final recourse in a democracy'.[1] Gilbert Devaux, as a high official of the executive, naturally had slightly mixed feelings about this, but he had no doubts concerning the reality of its influence:

> The reformers (of control procedures) have hit upon the idea of an appeal to public opinion, with the secret intention of forcing the hands of the Assemblies and the heads of hierarchies. They have tried to give the errors committed by administrators a certain amount of publicity. It is beyond doubt that this method can often exert a more effective influence than an administrative punishment or a fine. Nothing is more disagreeable to an official—and this applies with even greater emphasis to a politician—than the public exhibition of his weaknesses. . . . This consideration explains the development which the Public Report of the Cour des Comptes has undergone since the end of the war.[2]

Professor Duverger says almost the same thing, although he has no axe to grind for the administration, and he evidently approves:

> There is such a thing as a diffuse and unorganised kind of punishment, which results from the reprobation of society. . . . That is why, despite its imperfections, the report of the Cour des Comptes is of great importance; the fear of being mentioned in this report inspires a certain wisdom among administrators.[3]

The effect of publicity is salutary even if it arises 'accidentally' and not intentionally, as in France. The audit reports in most Western countries do not make a direct and deliberate appeal to public opinion as the Cour des Comptes does. But they are in any case constitutional and public documents, often cited in the press.

[1] Paper submitted by the Cour des Comptes to the Brussels Audit Congress, 1956.

[2] Devaux, op. cit., vol. 1, pp. 74–5.

[3] Duverger, *Institutions Financières*, p. 417.

The experience of the late Sir Frank Tribe was curiously similar to that of the French:

It surprises me sometimes what publicity I get in the newspapers. I can assure you that I have never raised a little finger to secure any publicity for any reports, and yet you will constantly see the subject matter of my reports mentioned in the evening Press and often in the morning Press as well. I can only imagine that the newspaper editors think that criticisms of waste and extravagance will make interesting reading for their patrons. Of course, it is a very healthy procedure because the last thing in the world which the departments want is to be held up to ridicule in the public Press. I believe they sometimes think it is worse than being criticized by the Public Accounts Committee.[1]

The chief auditor of a Western country is in his constitutional function a kind of popular tribune, and without him there would be no knowledge of or sanction against cases of waste and extravagance.

There has been some complaint by the executive, 'that it is only their mistakes . . . that are noticed: when all is well the best that they can hope for is to be ignored'.[2] The Cour des Comptes has tried to forestall this kind of grievance by repeatedly pointing out in the preambles to its public reports that these are, by their very nature, critical documents. It has added that the weaknesses disclosed are happily the exception and that it would be a mistake to interpret them as a general estimation of departmental conduct.

The Cour discovered that its criticisms were sometimes reported in the press in 'an inexact and tendentious manner'. An anonymous writer even suggested that the Cour might be encouraging revolution! He explained this surprising fear as follows:

In the sometimes distorting mirrors of the press and before a public which is often more impassioned than well-informed, its observations risk being misappropriated to serve as attacks against personalities, against authorities, against the administration as a whole, or even against the regime.

The commentator, however, reassured himself by adding that:

The objectivity and measured tone of the Public Report permit all such fears to be dismissed. Its moderation seems to have increased since it

---

[1] Address to the London and District Society of Chartered Accountants, 5 January 1954 (*The Accountant*, 23 January 1954).

[2] Sir E. Compton, Comptroller and Auditor General; op. cit., p. 17.

began to excite general interest. Proper names appear more rarely . . . no criticism which might have political repercussions is ever inserted.

This critic suggested that the Cour, thanks to its 'incomparable facilities for obtaining information', might provide 'a general view of the State's finances, not excluding the favourable aspects'.[1]

The Cour des Comptes has not adopted this policy and it continues to point out in the reports that it has not been given 'the mission of dispensing eulogies'. It nevertheless began a recent public report with a general encomium:

These observations cannot without misuse be invoked to cast discredit on the Administration as a whole, which, at all levels of the hierarchy, carries out its task in a generally satisfactory and sometimes exemplary way.[2]

This is in fact a useful corrective. If there are any national administrations which live permanently under the stars of blunder, confusion and corruption, they are not those of the major Western countries. The existence of free and public audit criticism is itself an aspect and a token of sound national administration. No regime will permit its weaknesses to be publicized if they are the rule rather than the exception.[3]

On the other hand, Western public authorities have various occasions for justifying and explaining their policies, through Ministerial reports and statements, through public announcements, replies to parliamentary questions, answers to state audit queries and so on. It is only through the published reports of national audit bodies and of legislative committees that informed criticism is introduced at all. Were it not thus, legislatures and the public would have to take the executive at its own valuation, or live upon a diet of gossip and rumour.

It is essential under all regimes that machinery should exist to make public authorities aware of their own imperfections. Without this, by a kind of natural law, they tend to develop a myth of infallibility. Even Communist states are well aware of this danger

[1] Article on the Cour des Comptes, signed 'XXX', in *Revue des Deux Mondes*, 15 August 1957.

[2] C. des C., Rapport, 1957–8, p. 1.

[3] The public will in such cases hear criticism in the form of rumours. (All sorts of stories of corruption and inefficiency circulated in Turkey under the Menderes Government even though the state audit body was 'muzzled'.)

and arrange controlled bursts of publicity to counteract it. In constitutional countries such publicity is achieved through freer processes; the press carries criticism on its own initiative, rather than on that of the government.

There is, nevertheless, a danger that we may create genteel societies in which all criticism is stifled. This is the age of competing interest groups, political, commercial, professional, trade-union and the rest. Such groups are much more highly organized than in the past; they have paid officials, card indexes, common funds and the right to punish dissentients by exclusion. They are also concerned to present an amiable face to the world. This is the responsibility of 'public relations'. Each private interest is concerned to appear as a champion of the public interest. There is of course contradiction in this, but the issue is glossed over. Vital facts remain unmentioned if they might be unfavourable to the desired image. All open announcements therefore tend increasingly to take the form of sales-talk, propaganda, press conferences, company reports, public relations handouts, the dicta of official spokesmen. Information is not given, it is 'released', or even 'leaked'. Uncomfortable truths remain in the files. Commercial sales techniques are applied to life as a whole.

Even legal and administrative procedures may serve to protect the public images and create a criticism-free society. In Britain, it has been suggested that the rules against contempt of court prevent criticism of judicial proceedings, that the libel laws result in omission from the press of reports which should have appeared, and that the Official Secrets Act is 'now used quite cynically to protect the reputations of Ministers and, above all, of civil servants'.[1]

In a society in which *informed* criticism is increasingly rare, the few prime sources of impartial reporting and comment based upon inside information are therefore of especial value. The list is a short one, and high upon it must figure the published reports of state audit. These are checked and double-checked for accuracy and are issued by officials who enjoy statutory protection against the pressures to which the citizen is exposed through authority, hierarchy and association. State audit is not a participant in the decisions of power, and it examines their consequences without involvement.

[1] Mr Cecil King, quoted in the *Guardian*, 5 June 1962.

CHAPTER VIII

The Published Reports, Part II: Unsound Projects and Complicated Policies

> 'Whoever wishes to study the living State, whoever seeks familiarity with the administrative manner of our age, whoever would understand the principal relationships of public life, cannot ignore audit control and its task. . . . This allows a glimpse into the very heart of the State, revealing its points of strength, but also its frailty'
> —Dr Guido Hertel, President of the Bundesrechnungshof, at Frankfurt University, 1961

IN the last chapter we have cited various examples of projects and policies which went wrong as a result of some kind of inefficiency or dishonesty in execution. These schemes were mostly quite sound in conception and plan and would not have evoked criticism if properly executed.

There remains, however, an important category of projects which were from the very beginning unsound in idea or in plan or in both. There was carelessness or lack of forethought in the original decisions, or even in the framing of the long-term administrative policies of which the projects formed part. The significance of audit criticism here is deeper than in the case of the sound projects which miscarried. When projects prove to be unsound, and especially when this happens repeatedly, there is something wrong with the basic direction of affairs. There is a failure of planning in the field concerned, and by showing this state audit is playing its part in the financial control cycle.

Acquisition of buildings and land

The acquisition of buildings and land has often proved to be ill-advised as well as wasteful. Among the worst offenders in this respect were the new hospital authorities of the National Health Service in Britain, and their nearest equivalents in France, during the later nineteen-forties.

The National Health Service was established in 1948 and almost immediately many hospital administrations hastened to acquire property and buildings for various purposes, in some cases without any clear ideas about utilization. Hotels and large private estates were the commonest types of acquisition. In numerous instances the responsible authorities found that their resources were inadequate to cover adaptation of their new (and often unsuitable) properties and to maintain them in regular use. In other cases the difficulty was simply to decide what to do with them. The existence of a substantial group of unused hospital properties gradually came to the notice of the Comptroller and Auditor General as a result of audits conducted at Regional Hospital Boards. For several years his reports mentioned selected cases of large premises which were costing money for maintenance but were nevertheless empty and deteriorating.

For example, the auditors discovered that in one South Coast town, although one hotel was already retained unused by a local hospital, a second hotel was purchased in 1950 for £46,500 by another hospital authority, and this also remained empty. By 1953, after thousands of pounds had been spent upon abortive adaptation schemes, the first hotel was sold and it was agreed to dispose of the second, without either of them having ever been used for hospital purposes.[1] In another case, a country house in the Midlands, with a large estate of over 200 acres, was bought for £25,500 as a recovery home for 70 patients in 1950, on the understanding that there would be an early sale of surplus land. No such disposal in fact took place; nor was any use made of the property for hospital purposes. In 1954 it was transferred to another public department as surplus to hospital requirements. The Treasury expressed the opinion that the property had been 'improperly purchased, without proper regard to the real need for accommodation and the alternative ways of providing it'.[2]

Other properties were converted for specific purposes at considerable expense but remained empty nevertheless. Still others were only partly used. After the intervention of the Comptroller and Auditor General and the Public Accounts Committee, various properties were sold, often at a loss, and the Ministry of Health and the Treasury announced new procedures to control acquisitions in future.[3]

Events in France were strangely similar. Social Security and

[1] C. & A.G.'s R., Civil Appn. A/cs. (Cl. I–VIII), 1952–3.
[2] Ibid., (Cl. I–V), 1953–4.
[3] Ibid., (Cl. I–VIII), 1951–2, 1952–3 and (Cl. I–V), 1953–4.

public assistance bodies purchased huge estates, especially in 1946 and 1947. The Cour des Comptes stigmatized this as 'the chateau policy', and complained that it had been carried out without studying local requirements or measuring the cost of adaptations. For example, in 1946 the Marseilles public assistance authorities took a chateau on lease with the intention of turning it into a maternity home. But they never occupied it, 'the possibilities for hospital use proving to be delusive'. By the time that the property could be sublet, in 1954, over twenty million francs had been spent on repairs alone, without any corresponding advantage.[1] Another example was the Chateau de Beaulieu-Morancé, near Lyons. It was purchased in 1946 for use as a health colony for children, but this scheme was found to require a conversion costing 190 millions and was therefore abandoned. After prolonged consideration of other possibilities, it was finally decided in 1950 to adapt it for use as a 'preventorium' at a cost of 82 millions. The Cour found this case typical of this species of administrative error, in which:

> Instead of purchasing or constructing a suitable building to fulfil the most urgent requirements as defined beforehand, long years are spent searching for a use for acquisitions made wilfully and without any coherent programme.[2]

Not only hospital authorities have been guilty of mistakes in acquiring property, however. The Bundesrechnungshof recounts the case of a group of buildings and a large parcel of land in Bavaria, which were purchased in almost indecent haste on the very last day of the financial year 1954–5. The intention was to create accommodation needed for the Federal Frontier Guard. After the purchase had been effected it was learned for the first time that the site was in fact divided into two pieces by land belonging to another proprietor; it was therefore necessary to buy this land also. Enlargement of the buildings was at first estimated to cost 800,000 DM., but no construction work was begun until 1958, by which time the estimate had risen to 1·32 millions. When work began it was found that the existing buildings had been heavily attacked by that arch-enemy of vacant property, dry-rot. In December 1959, no use had yet been made of the accommodation. The report suggests that no real need for the property

[1] C. des C., Rapport, 1955–6, p. 50.

[2] C. des C., Rapport, La Sécurité Sociale, 1950–1, p. 86.

existed in 1955, that the price paid was more than the estimated value, that the authorities concerned were not fully aware of the condition or the legal situation of the premises, and that the cost of adaptation was underestimated. The total damage to the interests of the state could still not be calculated because no final decision had been taken about the use of the property and it was therefore uncertain what further costs would be incurred.[1]

An error of judgment for which extenuating circumstances might be pleaded, was made in 1945 by the French reconstruction services. They conceived the idea that temporary buildings in the British Isles, which had served for the accommodation of troops and workers throughout the war, might be dismantled and re-erected in France to provide emergency housing. Fifty camps were therefore acquired in Britain and the hutments were dismantled by French labour. But the defective condition of the materials was noted even before they were shipped, and the official charged with their acceptance recorded that they were 'severely worn and often unsuitable for any purpose'. Prolonged storage in France pending choice of sites resulted in further deterioration, and in the end only 1,206 huts out of 2,147 sent from England were ever erected.[2]

Construction and public works

The French Ministry of Reconstruction also subsidized the construction of a building which in England would be called a 'folly', the eccentric *tour Perret* at Amiens. This drew its inspiration from the characteristic belfreys of Flanders on the one hand and from American skyscrapers on the other. The tower was designed to contain two flats on each floor, and prospective 'volunteer' tenants were found among persons left homeless by the war. 'The creation of a building which must be the tallest residence in Europe poses various special problems,' remarked the Cour des Comptes. The flats, in fact, cost much more than conventional constructions. What was really serious was that as general reconstruction progressed and other types of accommodation became available the waiting list of 'volunteers' for the tower faded away. Its use for housing had therefore to be renounced; any alternative, however, posed difficult problems. When the building had been

[1] Bemerkungen for financial year 1956, pp. 11–15.
[2] C. des C., Rapport, 1951–2, p. 19.

made weather-tight, the Ministry therefore withdrew its support from this 'ruinous enterprise' after contributing 225 millions.[1]

Another experimental project subsidized by the same Ministry was unsound only in the sense that its technical planning and cost estimating were faulty. This was the celebrated neighbourhood unit at Marseilles, the work of Le Corbusier called the *Cité radieuse*. The declared purpose of this piece of architecture was not only to provide a better, healthier and more pleasant life, but also to demonstrate that 'by extreme rationalization of construction . . . the building time as well as the unit costs could be considerably reduced'. Whatever the artistic and social value of this pioneer work, the Cour des Comptes discovered that as a planned economic project it called for 'serious reservations'. The approved cost in 1947 was 350 million francs, and completion in one year was predicted, 'thanks to a rigorous analysis of the work'. In fact construction took almost five years, and the cost at the end of 1952 had risen to 2,045 millions. This the Cour evaluated at an increase of about a hundred per cent over the approved cost, even after allowing for five subsequent devaluations of the franc. As for causes, it was concluded that:

> The excess costs result essentially from the inadequacy of advance design work, which considerably prolonged operations and made necessary various unforeseen modifications and adaptations.[2]

Such a conclusion is almost a commonplace among state audit observations in the post-war period. Inadequate planning and cost estimating seems to have become an occupational disease of architects and surveyors in every Western country. Scarcely any major product seems to have kept even nearly within its budget. Time and again, public authorities commissioned major works without adequate information about their scope and cost, and were therefore partly themselves to blame. It has sometimes been suggested that some of the trouble may be attributable to the architectural profession and its scales of fees proportional to total construction costs, which give little incentive to economy. One wonders whether the great architects of the past were good administrators.

The smooth and economical conduct of a building operation is impossible without thorough planning and preparation. The same

[1] C. des C., Rapport, 1951–2, pp. 27–8.

[2] Ibid., pp. 28–9. (The report does not mention Le Corbusier by name.)

applies to public works. An example of the confusion which may otherwise result is the case of the bypass road for the city of Münster, as reported by the Bundesrechnungshof. Total construction costs for this project were quoted in successive budgets as follows:

Financial year	*million DM.*
1952	3·8
1953	4·9
1954	5·5
1956	9·5
1957	15
1958	17·5

The Deutschmark is a stable currency, and the Federal auditors made strong comments about these snowballing costs. Construction projects should, they wrote, be entered in the budget only when plans and cost estimates made the financial consequences of the work quite clear.

In this case planning was inadequate; the necessary traffic surveys were not made, the cost calculations were fragmentary. . . . The inclination of road construction authorities to put through building schemes in the budget by understating their first requests for funds and counting on a subsequent vote for the further amounts necessary, should in the opinion of the Bundesrechnungshof be resisted.[1]

Industrial ventures

The same sort of failures in planning are sometimes apparent in industrial projects. The conversion of British locomotives from coal to oil firing between 1946 and 1948 seems, in retrospect, to have been due to unsound policy. The scheme was undertaken at the instance of the Ministry of Fuel and Power, with the object of saving coal. It was planned to convert as many as 1,200 locomotives and provide the necessary oil storage depots. In fact only 93 engines were converted and the British Transport Commission stated in 1948 that these alone would cost an additional £279,000 a year to operate; for the full programme the extra operating cost would exceed £3½ millions annually. There was, moreover, a shortage of oil as well as coal, and as a result, the conversion was stopped and it was decided in May 1948 to reconvert the oil-firing locomotives. The Ministry of Transport estimated that,

[1] Denkschrift dated 19 August 1958, pp. 75–6.

including the cost of storage depots, they had incurred a total expenditure of nearly £3 millions.[1]

The Cour des Comptes has several times complained that the state was incurring losses by the grant of subsidies to failing industrial enterprises. A loss to public funds of between 600 and 700 million francs was anticipated following loans to a heavy tractor company which went bankrupt.[2] An interest-free advance of 130 millions failed to save the Salmson motor company.[3] The Société des schistes bitumineux d'Autun was a domestic producer of petroleum, but on a very modest scale. The firm produced only a thousandth part of the national consumption and at three times the cost of other petrols. It required about 500 millions of public money annually to keep this puny enterprise in business; it had been said that it would be cheaper to transform the workers into paid loungers. In 1955 the Cour informed the parliamentary Finance Committees that studies had shown that no economically viable activity appeared to be possible. Yet the pressure of local interests was such that operations were not stopped until June 1957.[4]

Overseas development schemes

Schemes for development in tropical countries have repeatedly proved to be unsound. The most famous of these was the Tanganyika ground-nut plantation scheme of the British Ministry of Food. This was an economic *débâcle* so spectacular that it came to public notice in other ways besides the state audit reports. It was, nevertheless, reported upon more than once by the Comptroller and Auditor General, whose representatives visited East Africa in 1948. They then recorded that the insufficiency of port facilities, water supplies and road and rail communications was greatly impeding work in the clearance areas hundreds of miles inland. Only second-hand tractors and land-clearing equipment were available and repair and maintenance facilities were inadequate. In the circumstances heavy losses of operating time and increased costs were being incurred.[5] The situation scarcely improved thereafter, and ultimately advances made from the United

[1] C. & A.G.'s R., Civil Appn. A/cs. (Cl. X), 1947–8.
[2] C. des C., Rapport, 1953–4, p. 47.
[3] Ibid., 1955–6, p. 17.
[4] Ibid., p. 18.
[5] C. & A.G.'s R., Civil Appn. A/cs. (Cl. X), 1947–8.

Kingdom Exchequer to the tune of £35,871,125 were written off, subject to some relatively minor repayments.[1]

Great Britain was not, however, the only country which followed the mirage of quick yields from the African continent in the post-war period of European poverty. The French government invested over seven milliards in the Gabon and Cameroun Companies, founded for the exploitation of jungle timber resources. It is unlikely to recover any of the money. As the Cour des Comptes observed drily:

The Compagnie française du Gabon and the Compagnie française du Cameroun are united by close bonds of connection; same founders, same administrative headquarters in Paris; one may add same errors committed, both having found themselves unable to cover their financial liabilities.

Like the Tanganyika ground-nut farmers, the French lumbermen found that all their difficulties and all their expenses had been underestimated. The mother country had to throw more and more good money after bad. Even when a modest sawmill output was achieved it was very difficult to find a market for it. The Gabon enterprise just managed to survive, but the Cameroun company went into liquidation in 1953.[2]

The General Accounting Office, in examining United States foreign aid programmes administered by the International Cooperation Administration, discovered other breakdowns of financial control besides that in Taiwan, mentioned in the last chapter. It also encountered failures of planning. The auditors who visited Laos concluded that:

the disproportionate size of the aid programme tended to strain the internal facilities of the country, provide more goods than the country could readily absorb, and lead to malpractices by importers and suppliers.

The supply of aid had been continued at a high level,

for overriding international political and military considerations. . . . despite the inability to overcome major administrative shortcomings and the disclosure of numerous abuses of aid funds after they had been turned over to the Laos Government.[3]

---

[1] Ibid., (Cl. I–V), 1953–4.
[2] C. des C., Rapport, 1953–4, p. 49.
[3] Annual R., C.G. of the U.S., 1959, p. 167.

This seamy side of American foreign policy also appeared in the Pakistan aid programme, in which the Comptroller found serious deficiencies in administration. It was recognized that 'a number of decisions and actions not consistent with sound financial management' might be attributable to foreign policy considerations. The auditors, however, blamed the basic difficulties upon what they called 'unsound programming concepts'. As a result, there had been premature commitment of funds, ineffective use of some equipment, an accumulation of unclaimed commodities in warehouses, and apparently also an aggravation of inflationary conditions in Pakistan, all in addition to malpractices by local businessmen and officials. The local support services were overstaffed and had a motor fleet in excess of requirements. The Comptroller General expressed his opinion of the whole matter with great frankness. It was that, 'The annual level of aid was beyond the technical and financial capacity of Pakistan and the administrative ability of the United States.'[1]

Research and development

A disturbing number of unsound projects have come to notice in the field of scientific research and development. There have been cases where work proved to be fruitless and cases where research costs were very seriously underestimated. Clearly, a percentage of failures must be expected in experimental work; what may be accepted as reasonable is a matter of opinion. But evidence of repeated waste may be a sign of misdirected effort. The Exchequer and Audit Department has been particularly active in following up such evidence, and the observations of the Comptroller and Auditor General are the best of this type.

Special attention has been drawn to heavy and in some cases unproductive expenditures upon various types of aircraft, several of them of a 'prestige' nature; £11,580,000 on the 'Brabazon' aeroplane;[2] over £8 millions on the 'Princess' flying boats, of which only one ever flew;[3] over £10 millions for Comets I and II with associated equipment, including certain redundant airframes;[4] some £40 millions for the 'Swift' fighter, which was not accepted for full operational service;[5] nearly £5 million on development of

[1] Annual R., C.G. of the U.S., 1959, pp. 168–9.

[2] C. & A.G.'s R., Civil Appn. A/cs. (Cl. X), 1947–8.

[3] Ibid., (Cl. VI–X), 1953–4.

[4] Ibid., 1954–5; P.A.C. 6th R., Session 1955–6, paras 54–7.

[5] C. & A.G.'s R., Civil Appn. A/cs. (Cl. VI–X), 1955–6.

the 'Orion' engine, support for which was finally discontinued; and £8.8 millions for developing the 'Avon R.A.29' engine, compared with an original commitment of £2.36 millions.[1]

Recent reports have referred increasingly to military research and development projects. Some of these were merely discontinued without result. For example, the Ministry of Supply placed a contract for the development of an airborne radio set at an estimated cost of £114,000, but after some £240,000 had actually been spent it was decided to purchase a modified commercial radio set instead.[2]

The same sort of fate met certain researches whose intended purpose was other than military. Development and production of a type of instrument landing system, ordered in 1946, cost £488,000. But by the time that delivery took place in 1950–1, the equipment failed to meet either the International Civil Aviation Organization's specification or the latest standards of the Ministry of Civil Aviation. The Ministry of Fuel and Power spent £275,000 upon the development of a gas turbine intended to burn peat, and £114,000 on a contract to develop equipment for use with a coal-burning gas turbine. In 1957 both development schemes were terminated.[3]

The costliest and most celebrated of the abandoned development projects was the 'Blue Streak' missile, which in 1955 was tentatively estimated to cost £50 millions over a period of ten years, up to the test firing stage. By early 1960 the estimate for development and test firing had risen to between £280 and £310 millions. It was foreseen that the cost of production and the construction of launching sites might bring the total cost up to some £500 or £600 millions. It was then decided to discontinue development of the missile as a weapon; total expenditure on the scheme at the end of March 1960 amounted to about £67 millions.[4]

One cause of the abandonment of the 'Blue Streak' weapon, or alternatively of its adoption in the first place, appears to have been a serious underestimate of development costs. The same thing has happened in a number of military schemes which were not abandoned.

Development of the 'Sea Vixen' aircraft was authorized in 1953, at an approved figure of £1,325,500. By 1957 the cost had risen to well over £4 millions, and the production cost per

[1] Ibid., 1957–8.
[2] Ibid., 1953–4.
[3] Ibid., 1956–7.
[4] Ibid., 1959–60.

aircraft under a separate contract placed in 1955, had increased by some 85 per cent. Further substantial cost increases occurred in 1958.[1]

The development of a radar scanning unit gave rise to a cost increase which was particularly great in relation to the original estimate. The development contract increased from the approved figure of £60,000 in 1951 to £350,000 in 1953, £742,000 in 1954, £1·25 million in 1955, £1·63 million in 1956 and finally £1·9 million in May 1958. There were then 17 development models and 16 prototypes compared with a total provision for three in the original contract. In 1953 a production contract was placed with the same contractor but the major part was cancelled in 1956. The estimated unit cost of the remaining equipment on order had by then risen to eight times the original figure.[2]

In his report on the 1958–9 accounts the Comptroller and Auditor General referred to three types of guided missiles for which development costs had originally been approved at a tentative figure of £8 millions. At the time of the report the total development cost of the missiles was estimated at £110 millions.[3]

The construction of a large research establishment in Cumberland was approved in 1956 at a cost of about £10 millions, plus a possible 10 to 15 per cent. By July 1959 the latest estimate had risen to £20·4 millions.[4]

In reporting all these and still more cases of snowballing or unproductive research costs, the Comptroller and Auditor General was not simply compiling a dismal and fruitless catalogue. He was conducting a campaign for the better control of expenditure on research and development. How he did this is an interesting study in the working of state audit.

While considering the £40 millions spent on the 'Swift' aircraft, the C. & A.G. asked the Ministry of Supply a number of searching questions. Why had early deliveries been accepted unconditionally although they were below specification? Had sufficient information been given by the contractor of continued lack of success in overcoming the defects of the aircraft? Had there been adequate control of the increasing cost of the airframes? Finally, and most important, the C. & A.G. asked whether any changes in the procedure for controlling contracts for aircraft had

[1] C. & A.G.'s R., Civil Appn. A/cs. (Cl. VI–X), 1957–8.
[2] Ibid. [3] Ibid., 1958–9.
[4] Ibid.

been introduced. The Ministry replied that some changes had been introduced; contractors had been asked to make their technical reports on flight tests 'more informative'. There were now contractual provisions for early test flying by the Ministry, and concerning the acceptance of substandard aircraft. Development Project Officers would be appointed and there would be improved control of the early stages of production.[1]

Continued use has been made of the technique of asking difficult questions and then reporting the result. In general, the questions have been better than the answers. For example, the C. & A.G. asked, in view of the 'substantial discrepancy' between the original estimate of £2·36 millions and the ultimate liability of £8·8 millions for the 'Avon R.A. 29' engine, what check had been applied to the first estimate. The Ministry replied that it had been examined and thought reasonable, but added rather lamely that 'the fact that the estimate was only a partial one was not revealed by the Company'.[2]

The Comptroller and Auditor General brought these matters before the Public Accounts Committee, which in Session 1958–9 drew attention to bad estimating and financial control defects in certain contracts for development of aircraft and engines. In Session 1959–60 it found similar failures in contracts for developing guided weapons, and commented that development contracts on the present scale were something new in British financial history. 'Open as they must be to abuse', they clearly called for new methods of supervision and co-ordination at the highest level. The Ministry of Aviation responded by announcing interesting new measures of internal control. In appropriate cases preliminary contracts for design studies would be placed, in order 'to define with greater accuracy the object of the development contract and assess more accurately the time scale and probable cost'. In addition, some real financial planning and control powers were being transferred from the administrative to the technical side of the Ministry.[3]

The problem of armament research and development has been followed up, though perhaps less intensively, by other state audit bodies. In 1958, the General Accounting Office began a review of the Air Force ballistic missiles programme, which it described as 'the largest single procurement programme ever undertaken by

[1] Ibid., 1955–6.
[2] Ibid., 1957–8.
[3] Ibid., 1959–60.

the Nation'. The auditors studied 'the management approach to development of the Thor weapon system by the Air Force and the technical contractor'. They also surveyed flight test operations in Florida. In 1959 the Atlas and Titan missile programmes were reviewed, and comparisons were made between the development of Thor by the Air Force and the Jupiter missile by the Army. A report was made to Congress in that year.[1]

The Cour des Comptes reported the waste of more than 300 million francs on a wind-tunnel at Toulouse, shortly after the war. The construction contract was cancelled in 1948 after the facilities for wind-tunnel experiments elsewhere in France had been taken into consideration. All that resulted from the expense was 'a site containing vast foundations, open drainage works and the rusting skeletons of steel framed buildings'.[2]

In its report on the financial years 1957 and 1958, the Cour stated that for some years it had been concerned about the conditions in which armament programmes were prepared and carried out. It had, in particular, observed:

> the costly consequences of an inadequate co-ordination of development and design studies, and the grave difficulties caused by incessant modifications to orders in course of execution.

Armament policy in the post-war period had 'suffered from the absence of any real long-term programme, based upon the financial resources available'. The consequence had been 'fragmentary projects, with little co-ordination and in some cases little relevance to the total of public funds on hand'.

For example, the separate development of anti-tank rockets by two different research bodies should have been avoided. At one time it could have been argued that such a dispersal of effort might result in a healthy spirit of rivalry; 'but at the present time the very high cost of research justifies a concentration of resources'.

Ten years of development of Hotchkiss half-tracked vehicles had proved inconclusive. The first directive asked for a light model, later ones requested a heavier and yet heavier design, and finally there was a return to the principle of a lightweight vehicle,

[1] Annual R., C.G. of the U.S., 1959, pp. 120–1. (Publication of the detailed audit findings on the missile programme seems to have been prevented by security considerations.)

[2] C. des C., Rapport, 1948–9, p. 165.

although with many variations. Such chopping and changing not only revealed indecision about the general intention but inevitably had wasteful consequences.

Development of 'Parca', an anti-aircraft rocket, was continued long after its conception had become obsolescent. It was finally abandoned after having cost 15 milliards. Similarly, about 2,500 million francs were spent upon a type of radar which was never put into production. Design studies for a self-propelled gun cost 700 millions, 'despite the fact that it was realized from the outset that the weapon would be far too costly to permit large-scale production'.

Troubles had also arisen as a result of premature manufacture of new weapons. An armoured reconnaissance car was put into mass production on the basis of inadequate drawings and even before a prototype had been completed. Several thousand corrections had to be made and a large number of parts scrapped. After three years, production was interrupted pending improvement of the design. Contracts covering thousands of another type of light reconnaissance vehicle were placed on the basis of an imperfect prototype. The extra costs for modifications as a result totalled well over 1,000 millions. The Cour remarked that these cases showed the interdependence of development and production programmes, which therefore needed to be harmonized within a more clearly defined general framework. It also warned against the dangers of making loose commitments to contractors without any clear idea about eventual costs or the availability of funds. In particular, the disadvantages of 'stop-go' financing ('coups d'accordéon') were stressed. Economy drives by the government had repeatedly stopped production lines. This not only disorganized industry but was very costly. Moreover, the reduction or cancellation of a large order could not produce the intended economies until at least a year later.[1]

* * * *

One essential lesson may be inferred from all these audit observations, as well as from many of those recorded in the last chapter. This is the lesson of sound planning. If public bodies embark upon new policies and important projects on the basis of ad hoc judgments, unrelated to a larger national or even international context, without the benefit of the latest specialized knowledge or

[1] Ibid., 1957–8, pp. 24–7.

the experience of other authorities, and without co-ordination of resources or requirements, they run serious risks of incurring losses and unproductive expenditure in the age of big government. Every major project needs careful and often prolonged preparation; this applies equally to building works, to technical development schemes, to the acquisition of property, to production contracts, and to many other things. Moreover, each large project—and this is a relatively new consequence of the inflated scale of government operations—must be related to other similar projects, even if sponsored by separate authorities. It may need to be seen in terms of the national economy as a whole. A parochial attitude to public spending is not only inefficient in a broad sense but positively wasteful. Lack of co-ordination and forethought is almost always financially harmful, sometimes even disastrous.

Such principles are fairly obvious but difficult to apply and easy to overlook when they create difficulties. Detailed planning of expenditures is a clear administrative responsibility but sometimes the pressures of urgency take precedence. In other cases the necessary techniques of planning are not clearly and widely known, either because they are experimental and new or because the wider context has not been studied. In the present age, failures of planning represent the most important single cause of waste in state expenditure. It is this fact which constitutes the crisis of planning in financial control, and it is related to the even wider crisis of economic planning.

The task of state audit, therefore, is to identify, explain and show the consequences of failures in planning. It is only in this way that talk of the need for planning can be backed up by evidence. Only from such case-studies can the practical requirements of planning be examined. These requirements are not the same in every field of administration. New economic, military and scientific developments rapidly create new planning needs. Unless the results of failures are widely known it is scarcely likely that new planning techniques will be evolved with the necessary speed.

Another creative activity of audit is the study of complicated administrative policies, so that their financial implications, foreseen and unforeseen, may be explained in the published reports. Such 'narrative reporting' is to be found at great length in most modern state audit reports, and the following examples indicate the sort of topics which often furnish material.

Public contracts

A subject in which all state auditors must acquire expertise is that of public contracting. How to ensure that supplies and services are purchased at fair and reasonable prices is a perpetual problem which challenges the ingenuity of modern administrators. In the nineteenth century, when state budgets were modest in scale, the problem was relatively simple; save for military and naval supplies, which in any case were largely provided by government arsenals and dockyards, it was a matter of entering the competitive open market and obtaining the best price available. The growth of public requirements in the twentieth century has enormously increased the difficulty, as well as the amounts of public money involved.

Over a wide range of products the state is now a monopoly purchaser. A whole selection of industries has grown up to supply governments and must sell to them or die. Governments cannot therefore obtain the guarantee of fair prices which is assumed to be available when competitive tenders are received. Monopoly buyer and monopoly suppliers must do the best they can to negotiate tolerable arrangements for prices and controls, even when astronomical sums of money are involved. In the fiscal year 1960 the United States military departments alone dealt with a volume of purchasing amounting to some twenty billion dollars, about 30 per cent of the entire Federal budget, and of this total as much as 80 to 90 per cent was expected to be under negotiated, not competitive, contracts.[1] In 1951–2, the British Ministry of Supply alone placed contracts to an estimated value of £466 millions without competition, and within this total were contracts for £406 millions which provided for the settlement of prices after work was begun.[2]

Meanwhile, industry as a whole is not so competitive as formerly. Companies are much larger and some of them practically represent a whole industry. In other cases, firms have turned the competitive tendering procedure into a farce by submitting identical prices or prearranging their respective bids. In 1951–2, tenders in the United Kingdom for bulk supplies of motor and aviation fuel to the value of over £20 millions were submitted at the same prices by all the 'competing' firms.[3] The same was, with

[1] Annual R., C.G. of the U.S., 1959, p. 85.
[2] C. & A.G.'s R., Civil Appn. A/cs. (Cl. IX), 1952–3.
[3] Ibid., (Cl. I–VIII), 1951–2.

minor exceptions, true in the case of tenders for central purchases of drugs for National Health Service hospitals.[1] In 1951 it was found that the majority of suppliers of asphalt to the Ministry of Works had an arrangement for deciding who should submit the lowest tenders.[2]

Society has difficulty in protecting itself against such practices. It may limit collusion between companies by anti-trust laws,[3] or it may conduct the slow and delicate investigation of monopolies,[4] jealous of their trading and financial secrets. But these measures alone will not guarantee fair prices. There is plenty of chance evidence that contractors are quite prepared, if they have the opportunity, to overcharge for government work.[5]

The best solution to the price problem in conditions where competition is defective or non-existent is to send government cost accountants, and also in some cases technical cost estimators, to examine the contractor's books, records and manufacturing processes and either ascertain his actual expenditures upon completed work, or estimate them in the case of work in hand. Such cost figures can usually be established with some degree of accuracy, and they then form a solid basis upon which to negotiate prices. In wartime, such a procedure was normal for a great number of contracts, especially for defence work, and the Comptroller and Auditor General took a very close interest in ensuring that everything possible was done to establish the fairness of prices and profits.[6] In 1940 the Public Accounts Committee recorded its emphatic opinion that no industry should be exempt from an obli-

[1] C.& A.G .'s R., Civil Appn. A/cs. (Cl.I–VIII), 1950–51, and Civil Appn. A/cs. (Cl. I–V), 1956–7.

[2] Ibid., (Cl. VI–X), 1954–5. (The Ministry made a new arrangement with the asphalt firms as from 1 January 1953.)

[3] In Britain a Restrictive Practices Court was established under the Restrictive Trade Practices Act, 1956. The court is responsible for deciding whether a restrictive agreement is in the public interest as defined in the Act. If the court is not satisfied it has powers to declare the agreement void.

[4] The Monopolies Commission was set up by the Monopolies and Restrictive Practices (Inquiry and Control) Act, 1948.

[5] See, e.g., *Epitome*, vol. II, pp. 81–2, re warship construction, and C. & A.G.'s R., Civil Appn. A/cs. (Cl. I–V), 1953–4, re the National Health Service Drug Tariff.

[6] See numerous cases in *Epitome*, vol. II; e.g. pp. 24–5 (purchasing of 'Anderson' air-raid shelters), pp. 48–9 (prices of light alloys purchased by aircraft firms), pp. 49–50 (contracts for army stores), and pp. 123–4 (price-fixing in the electrical and woodworking industries).

gation to submit its costs to investigation by Government accountants for the purpose of determining the prices to be paid under non-competitive contracts with Government Departments.[1]

In addition to accounting checks upon prices, the weight of wartime public opinion was heavily opposed to 'profiteering', and this must have influenced industry itself. In peacetime, however, the matter is much more difficult. Unless governments are prepared to make use of powers providing for compulsory cost investigation in the absence of competition—and in Great Britain they usually are not—contractors are entitled to refuse to allow access to their books. In practice they do this unless they have accepted a clause in their contract providing for 'costings'. Such clauses are rare in peacetime except in a proportion of defence contracts.

But an important case reported by the Comptroller and Auditor General shows that even negotiation based upon access to a manufacturer's records and technical processes is not an infallible safeguard against excessive prices. The contracts concerned were for guided weapon electronic equipment, and the press referred to the matter as 'the Ferranti case'—although it is not the C. & A.G.'s policy to refer to contractors by name. The C. & A.G.'s officers observed a large discrepancy, which had been overlooked by the Ministry of Aviation, between the labour costs as estimated by the Ministry's technical cost estimators (which were the basis for price negotiations) and as ascertained by the Ministry's accountants for the purpose of calculating overhead rates. The Public Accounts Committee investigated the case and published a special report which was fully debated in Parliament. This report disclosed that the contractor had made an estimated profit of 63 per cent on cost, amounting to some £4·5 millions, which the P.A.C. considered to be excessive.[2]

[1] *Epitome*, vol. II, p. 25.

[2] C. & A.G.'s R., Civil Appn. A/cs. (Cl. I–IV), 1962–3, paras. 49–53, and P.A.C., Second Report, Session 1963–4 (Guided Weapons Contracts placed by the Ministry of Aviation with Ferranti Ltd.). A subsequent enquiry in greater detail was made by a specially appointed committee headed by Sir John Lang, which obtained access to the company's books. The first report of this committee placed the profit as high as £5·77 millions, or 82 per cent on cost. The committee complained of 'a lack of direction and a lack of drive' in the branches of the Ministry which had dealt with the contracts, and of an absence of effective collaboration between them. The technical costs and accountancy directorates had 'lived in separate ivory towers'. The con-

The American government has wide general powers of access to contractors' records and factories. It appears from the reports of the Comptroller General that such access is usual if not invariable in non-competitive transactions. Moreover, investigations at contractors' factories are frequently carried out by the audit staff of the General Accounting Office itself. The G.A.O. has the right to examine any pertinent books and records of contractors holding contracts negotiated without advertising, under authority contained in the Federal Property and Administrative Services Act of 1949, the Armed Forces Procurement Act of 1947 and other laws. The same right applies to the records of sub-contractors engaged upon work related to the main contracts.[1] During the fiscal year 1959, local examinations were made of the records of 118 companies holding contracts with the Department of Defense, 53 under contract to the Atomic Energy Commission and 48 working for other departments. 'Factory audits' were also conducted in the cases of fourteen sub-contractors and even of one described as a sub-sub-contractor.[2] The practice of direct investigation at the factory enables the G.A.O. to obtain a view of contractual problems which is not available to European audit departments.

The Comptroller General has reported the discovery of excessive prices negotiated for both prime contracts and sub-contracts. In most cases these were attributed to deficiencies in pricing control by departments, and by both departments and their prime contractors in the case of sub-contracts. In particular, cost data available to price negotiators had not been adequately considered. In some cases, prime contractors had submitted excessive cost estimates, including inflated sub-contract prices substantially in excess of figures already negotiated with sub-contractors; the reviews conducted by departments had, however, been insufficient to disclose these discrepancies. The departments had made some improvements in their costing and negotiating procedures in response to the recommendations of the G.A.O., and in certain cases had adjusted prices, but the Comptroller

tracts directorate had 'failed to measure up to the high standard required . . .' ('First Report of the Inquiry into the Pricing of Ministry of Aviation Contracts', Command 2428, July 1964). The Minister of Aviation announced in the House of Commons on 28 July 1964, that the contractor had agreed to repay £4·25 millions to the state.

[1] Annual R., C.G. of the U.S., 1959, p. 3.

[2] Ibid., pp. 293–8.

believed that a further strengthening of pricing controls was necessary.[1]

Ordinary contract audit, confined to examination of departmental documents, produces observations concerning lack of or defects in competitive tendering, deviations from the terms of the contract, excessive advance payments and a variety of other things. But through its factory costing operations the G.A.O. is able to show more. It found, for example, that a contractor had accounted for certain expenses both as direct costs and as overheads; that work contracted with one firm for $164,000 had been subcontracted to another for $58,000, and that a contractor had himself initiated design changes which greatly increased costs.[2] It was discovered from surveys at aero-engine plants that substantial savings could be obtained if petroleum products required in the manufacturing process were furnished from government sources.[3] Examination of European contractors' records disclosed taxes charged contrary to an agreement between the U.S. and the country concerned.[4]

Contract prices for spare parts for B-52 aircraft were found to be about $5 millions higher than those agreed by the contractor with sub-contractors and not disclosed. The same applied to C-130A airframe components, with a discrepancy of over $4 millions. Target prices for two radar contracts had been overestimated by half a million dollars. B-52 stabilizer assemblies were ordered by a prime contractor at a firm price totalling $6·32 millions from a sub-contractor who actually incurred costs of only $4·62 millions. A contractor for B-52 fire control systems refunded $1,133,500 after the G.A.O. had established that this represented the cost of excessive quantities of components. Another contractor refunded $75,000 when G.A.O. auditors showed that his costs had been overestimated in price negotiations by nearly $1 million. The actual costs incurred by a contractor for naval aircraft were about $6 millions less than the amount contemplated in price negotiations, and the Comptroller General recommended the Secretary of the Navy to press for more than the refund of $1·2 million agreed by the company.[5] The G.A.O. showed that several of these discrepancies could have been recognized at the price

[1] Ibid., pp. 85–9.
[2] From C.G.'s Reports, 1953–6.
[3] Annual R., C.G. of the U.S., 1956, p. 26.
[4] Ibid., p. 46.
[5] Ibid., 1959, pp. 89–96.

negotiation stage if there had been an adequate review of cost data already available.

When prices are based directly upon factory costs incurred, governments have an obvious and immediate interest in the efficiency of manufacture. Contractors unfortunately do not. The G.A.O. endeavours to ensure that proper regard is paid to this situation:

> Our audits (says the Comptroller General) include a review of the contractors' organization, procedures and business methods for the purpose of evaluating the protection which has been afforded to the Government's interests.[1]

Observations of an 'Organization and Methods' type have been raised after such audits. For example, a contractor to the Atomic Energy Commission was stated to be maintaining offices unnecessarily in two cities, to perform tasks which were done adequately in a third.[2] Some firms revised their purchasing arrangements. One contractor was buying certain materials through a middleman who took a commission of 23 per cent, rather than directly from the manufacturer; a change of method in this case saved $300,000 in the first six months.[3] Another contractor incurred excess costs by 'splitting his coal purchases among an unwarranted number of suppliers'.[4] Business efficiency has sometimes been called into question. A contractor was persuaded to maintain only one set of stock record cards instead of two, and eliminated 35 office posts as a result.[5] Another saved an estimated $250,000 on one contract by re-using containers furnished by a sub-contractor instead of destroying them and providing new ones.[6] The principle of an efficiency audit of government contractors is far in advance of anything in Western Europe, where such a principle has not yet everywhere been accepted even for the government service itself. It is also apparent that in the U.S.A. the principle of free competition is not incompatible with the acceptance by the government's contractors of a considerable degree of discipline.

The modern purchasing methods of public departments are a study in themselves. When contracting reaches an unprecedented scale and degree of technical specialization, the traditional methods

[1] Annual R., C.G. of the U.S., 1956, p. 23.
[2] Ibid., 1955, p. 77.
[3] Ibid., 1953, p. 30.
[4] Ibid., 1954, p. 37.
[5] Ibid.
[6] Ibid., 1953, p. 26.

of price determination sometimes become completely unrealistic and may operate against the interests of the state. Even when competitive tendering is available, the offer which should be accepted is not necessarily the cheapest but that which, taking all the circumstances into consideration, is the most economical. More public funds are spent through contracts for supplies and services than in any other way, and they will always form a fruitful source of observations for any state audit which has really full access to tendering and price negotiating documents and information. Prices are, however, often a very delicate subject, and as we have seen, a completely unrestricted access to information about their build-up is easier to grant in theory than to obtain in practice.

Subsidies

Another very important field for audit studies is that of state subsidies of all kinds, industrial, commercial, educational, agricultural; subsidies and grants to local authorities and to a whole range of other institutions at home and abroad. Here is another way of spending public money which calls for vigilance against accident, error and abuse, as well as against the dangers of plain fraud which we noted in the preceding chapter. It is a type of expenditure which scarcely existed in the nineteenth century. It is also another field in which adequate information about the actual employment of state funds may be hard to come by, or even, in the present statutory situation, sometimes impossible.

Already before the last war the accounts of the British Sugar Corporation were audited by private auditors and the Public Accounts Committee complained of a lack of information in connection with the beet sugar subsidy.[1]

Expenditure by local authorities which is chargeable to Votes of Parliament is audited by the District Auditors appointed by the Minister of Housing and Local Government.[2] In 1948–9 the Public Accounts Committee considered eleven grants-in-aid, mostly to bodies with scarcely any other income. Parliamentary and even ministerial control appeared in most cases to be slight. The Committee's recommendation was that 'certain changes should be made with a view to giving Parliament fuller information about the way in which these large sums are being used'.

[1] *Epitome*, vol. II, pp. 13–15 and 27.

[2] L. H. Helmore, *The District Auditor*, London, Macdonald & Evans, 1961.

This was the principle of 'no subsidy without accountability'. The P.A.C. also suggested that, 'the degree of Government control must depend on the proportion of Government grant to total income'.[1]

But the resistance of some grant-aided bodies to even limited accountability was very determined. Notable among these was the University Grants Committee, which has received rapidly increasing amounts from the Exchequer since the war. In 1932–3 the grant in aid to universities was only £1·68 millions. In 1947–8 it was still less than £10 millions.[2] By 1959–60 it had risen to £57·9 millions, including £19·7 millions for capital expenditure, and was still rapidly increasing. Yet despite repeated requests by the Public Accounts Committee, these grants are still exempt from any audit on behalf of Parliament. The Comptroller and Auditor General stated in his report:

> I have no access to the books of the universities or to the records of the University Grants Committee. This therefore constitutes an exception to the principle laid down by the Committee of Public Accounts of Session 1950–51 and generally accepted by the Treasury that the books and accounts of all bodies which receive the greater part of their income from public funds should be open to my inspection so that I may if necessary report on them to Parliament.

The curious position at present is that the C. & A.G. can obtain some information about capital grants indirectly from the University Grants Committee through the Treasury. Information about the employment of maintenance grants, which totalled £38·2 millions in 1959–60, does not appear to be available at all.[3] The justification given for this dogged opposition to accountability, in a situation when the British universities are moving towards almost total dependence upon the taxpayer, is the fear of interference with academic policy. Such interference would, however, be outside the purpose and terms of reference of state audit, and the impression is unfortunately bound to be created that the universities' administrative houses are not in order and that they have something to hide.

There was, however, no need to struggle for access to information about subsidies which are directly administered by ministerial agencies, and the audit reports reflect some detailed studies of them.

[1] *Epitome*, vol. II, pp. 165–6. [2] Ibid., p. 195.

[3] C. & A.G.'s R., Civil Appn. A/cs. (Cl. I–V), 1959–60.

Agricultural subsidies are a typical case. The Comptroller and Auditor General examined the basis of the principal subsidy payments and brought several anomalies to notice. The assessment of subsidies often depends upon the periodical establishment of standard units of price and quantity. Even small variations in these standards have large financial repercussions; for example, a variation of 0·1*d.* per gallon on British milk retailers' margins costs over half a million pounds a year.[1] The estimation of standards is a hazardous commercial calculation subject to human error of judgment.

Farm subsidies fall broadly into four main types. Firstly there are bonus payments for specific services, such as ploughing, cultivating particular crops, or increasing numbers of livestock. The second type consists of price-supplement payments, when market prices for agricultural produce are considered to be below an economic level, or when governments decide to keep them low for policy reasons. Thirdly, subsidies may be in the form of purchases by the state of unsaleable farm surpluses, or of crops and animals ruined by blight and disease. Finally, artificial shortages may be created in order to support the market price, by marginal purchases of produce which might otherwise have created something like a glut. The choice of a particular kind of subsidy may depend upon national agricultural policy; for instance the first type is suitable when a changeover of crops or livestock production is favoured. Some subsidies are administered through 'middleman' organizations with a monopoly of purchasing and resale.

Ploughing and cultivation grants can, as we saw in the last chapter, offer scope for fraudulent claims by farmers. The other types of subsidy are subject to misadventure, due to the inherent difficulties of prediction in agricultural matters. In most spheres of administration the cause of trouble is usually the lack of a firm plan fixed in advance; in farming, where so much depends upon imponderables like the weather, the pre-established programme may on the other hand prove to be an embarrassment.

The Comptroller and Auditor General in his report on the 1955–6 accounts explained the milk subsidy in England and Wales under which the Milk Marketing Board made nominal profits above a 'lower price' per gallon fixed by the Minister of Agriculture. These profits rose suddenly from £1·25 million in

[1] Ibid., (Cl. VI–X), 1956–7.

1954–5 to £4 millions in the following year. But the C. & A.G. considered that these results had arisen not so much from the Board's efforts as from 'extraneous circumstances, including an under-assessment of the lower price'.[1]

In the following year a study was made of the potato subsidy. In April 1956 there was a market collapse. Under the arrangements then in force the Potato Marketing Board were obliged to purchase all potatoes offered to them up to the end of May. These amounted in 1956 to some 43,000 tons, most of which could not be sold and were left on the farms. The Ministry agreed with the Comptroller and Auditor General that this was 'unsatisfactory'. Revised regulations were being made which should prevent a recurrence.[2] In 1957–8 the egg subsidy exceeded the estimate and rose to a total of £46·6 millions. This was because the subsidy, calculated in advance, had been based on an estimated market price of 2*s.* 10*d.* a dozen, whereas in fact the price rose to an average of 3*s.* 1·3*d.* a dozen. As a result, an excess subsidy of 3·3*d* per dozen was paid, which amounted to about £8·8 millions on 7,650 million eggs. Of this, the state recovered £1·7 millions but the Egg Marketing Board retained over £7 millions.[3]

The Comptroller and Auditor General noted that the fertilizer subsidy rose from £12 millions in the year ended 30 June 1955 to an estimated total of £28·5 millions in the year ended 30 June 1960. He therefore asked the Ministry how, in the absence of price control, they satisfied themselves that prices of subsidized fertilizers were fair and reasonable, and received the reply that they had insufficient information about production and distribution costs to be able to judge. A report on the fertilizer industry by the Monopolies Commission was awaited.[4]

The General Accounting Office has reviewed various agricultural subsidies administered by the Commodity Stabilization Service and the Commodity Credit Corporation. It found that in 1958–9 cotton export prices had been maintained at levels in excess of competitive world prices; the Secretary of Agriculture was recommended to adjust the export prices periodically. For the purpose of price support, a type of cotton no longer representative of current production was specified by law as the standard grade, and this had the effect of supporting the price of all qualities at an artificially high level. This legal provision was

[1] C. & A.G.'s R., Civil Appn. A/cs. (Cl.VI–X), 1955–6.

[2] Ibid., 1956–7. [3] Ibid., 1957–8. [4] Ibid., 1958–9.

repealed, as the G.A.O. had proposed, and it was announced that as from 1961 subsidies would be based on the average quality of the crop. The Commodity Credit Corporation lost $167 millions in three years as a result of a cotton sales procedure which permitted regrading at the purchaser's request after sale; the Department of Agriculture informed the G.A.O. that after 1 August 1959 cotton would be sold without an option to the purchaser to have it reclassified.[1]

The hidden subsidy is a varied and elusive phenomenon which the state auditor must seek out and expose. The Comptroller General found that borrowers of loans from the Rural Electrification Administration were receiving one, because for some years their interest rate had been below the average U.S. Treasury rate, so that in effect the difference was met by the government.[2]

The Cour des Comptes examined agricultural subsidies in its report for 1955–6. Price support operations for meat had been entrusted to a semi-independent organization, which was exempt from audit. The Cour, nevertheless, showed that this body had repeatedly granted assistance against official advice to firms whose businesses were unsound. More than one of these had gone into liquidation. It was discovered that the manager of one of the firms had been arranging the purchase of his own cattle at inflated prices fixed by himself. The Cour demanded 'measures which would make possible at least some protection of the rights of the treasury', since the amounts voted by Parliament were 'obviously not intended to refloat companies in difficulties or with a management deserving severe criticism'.

In 1953–4, 1,800 tons of Danish butter were imported into France under a trade agreement. It was, however, kept out of the market because the price of butter was falling, and it was eventually re-exported about a year later. The firms concerned were granted compensation which, together with the cost of storage, cost the state nearly 500 million francs for the whole abortive operation.

In general, the Cour warned against the financial risks of an automatic price support system, which might commit the State to costs of an unforeseeable magnitude.[3]

The Bundesrechnungshof observed that the German egg subsidy was calculated upon an average laying capacity per hen of 145

[1] Annual R., C.G. of the U.S., 1959, pp. 55–60.

[2] Ibid., p. 63.

[3] C. des C., Rapport, 1955–6, pp. 18–27.

eggs annually. By making enquiries in various areas, however, the auditors reached the conclusion that this should be between 164 and 175 eggs per year. A further problem arose from the fact that only marked 'standard' eggs were eligible for subsidy. The Bundesrechnungshof had information to the effect that subsidies had also been paid for unmarked eggs.[1]

We may conclude from these varied cases that agricultural subsidies are exceptionally difficult to calculate or negotiate, and easily susceptible to abuse and fraud. Some of this applies also to housing subsidies.

Study of such subsidies by the Exchequer and Audit Department in Scotland produced some surprising figures. About 45,000 houses had been built by the Scottish Special Housing Association since the war; the state paid an average subsidy of nearly £33 a year for each house and it also had to meet a further deficit on income account, averaging £21·6 per house. The Comptroller and Auditor General therefore asked the Scottish Home Department whether rents were considered to be adequate; he was told that the level of rents was considered to be a matter of general policy, not to be determined by what would be needed to eliminate the Association's deficit.

Exchequer equalization grants to local authorities in less prosperous areas were found to be affected by housing accounts in a curious way. The total grant in any year was determined in relation to various local expenditures, including the meeting of deficits on housing revenue after crediting the normal housing subsidies. 'It follows', wrote the C. & A.G., 'that if rents are unduly low, the housing deficits and relevant expenditure are correspondingly greater and therefore a larger Exchequer equalization grant is payable.' Subsidies, in their various guises, are temperamental administrative devices, and in this case they provided an incentive to the maintenance of uneconomic rents. Rents charged by local authorities in Scotland in 1959 averaged only 8*s*. 8*d*. per week for permanent houses. Some twenty authorities had not reviewed their rents for five years or more, and one last did so in 1937. The average annual rent in one locality was as low as 2*s*. 10*d*. a week, or £7 7*s*. 4*d*. per year, compared with an average gross annual cost in 1958–9 of £73 6*s*. 7*d*. per house.[2]

[1] Denkschrift dated 10 December 1959, p. 84.

[2] C. & A.G.'s R., Civil Appn. A/cs. (Cl. I–V), 1959–60. (The problem of rents for Scottish council houses, to which the C. & A.G. had drawn at-

One form of housing subsidy in France is by the grant of state loans to the organizations for Homes at Moderate Rents (Habitations à Loyer Modéré, H.L.M.). The Cour des Comptes found that some of the housing provided in this way, and also by direct subsidy, was being allocated to social classes other than those for which it was intended. In one large estate, four per cent of the tenants were in a high surtax group; 50 out of 178 tenants of a block of Paris flats were well-to-do. 'It seems', says the Cour, 'that this clientele has often been received with favour and even attracted by the administrators of the H.L.M. groups, with the intention of facilitating the collection of rents and favouring good upkeep of the premises.' Provision of a category of housing for this wealthier social group was suggested by the Cour, 'in order to restore these organizations to their vocation, which is to provide homes for the classes of small means.'[1] To subsidize the affluent is wasteful, and it becomes intolerable when those who really need the subsidy remain unrelieved.

After the war the Cour des Comptes conducted a campaign against unvoted subsidies, in the form of what was called 'parafiscal taxation'. This consisted of a range of privileges which had been granted by the executive to various trade associations, permitting them to collect fees, duties and other additional charges as part of the selling prices of their members' products. These were intended to provide not only various subsidies but also to cover the cost of services such as apprentice training. But, as the Cour pointed out, the charges had an obligatory character, like proper taxation, and yet were outside the control of Parliament. They imposed upon the country a charge at once substantial and hidden. Parliament had not been informed of the amount levied in this way, but the Cour believed after enquiries that it was well over 50 milliards of francs a year, and that it increased the price of corn, wine, milk, meat, fruit, vegetables, beet-sugar, tobacco, timber, wool, leather, the cinema, and a wide range of industrial products. The report added that Parliament had shown a will to reduce the volume of these subsidies and to establish a general statutory regulation of them; but the administration, which made use of parafiscality as a way around its own budgetary controls,

---

tention, was remedied by the Local Government (Financial Provisions) (Scotland) Act, 1963.)

[1] C. des C., Rapport, 1955–6, p. 14.

showed no signs of haste in submitting a draft law.[1] Parafiscality was finally subjected to control by Parliament a few years later.[2] The number of levies diminished and those which remained were brought under surveillance.

Welfare and health services

Another costly and delicate aspect of modern administration is that of welfare and social security schemes, including nationalized health services.

In Britain the Comptroller and Auditor General has reported at length, year after year, about levels of prices and remuneration in the National Health Service, and about general aspects of financial administration in the hospital service. The subjects covered have included purchasing arrangements; remuneration of medical consultants, general practitioners, dentists, chemists and opticians; the cost of drugs and dressings to hospitals and on prescription; ambulance services; store accounts and inventories; capital investment, and many more things. The reports have recorded steady and sometimes startling increases in costs, the progress of slow and difficult negotiations with professional and trade associations aiming at discovering actual rates of profit and at agreeing upon fair prices and fees. They have favoured rational purchasing procedures and shown how wasteful it is for hospital authorities to buy in small quantities, without obtaining competitive tenders, rather than to co-ordinate requirements within a locality. The reports drew attention to heavy losses of stores, especially blankets and other textiles, in the early days of the health service; effective remedies against this were improved inventory records and the prominent marking of textiles with woven identifications.

The economies which would result from the prescribing of equivalent pharmaceutical preparations rather than proprietary products have more than once been stressed in audit reports. For example, it was shown that in 1951 about £400,000 was spent on a proprietary product for slimming. 'The same substance', wrote the C. & A.G., 'could have been prescribed under its standard name for £158,000.' [3]

Various official questions which had been sent by the auditors to the Ministry of Health were recorded in the annual reports.

[1] C. des C., Rapport, 1948–9, pp. 197–202. [2] Law of 25 July 1953.

[3] C. & A.G.'s R., Civil Appn. A/cs. (Cl. I–VIII), 1951–2.

There were queries about action ('I asked the Ministry whether they had given doctors any additional information on comparative costs of proprietaries and the equivalent standard preparations').[1] There were requests for up-to-date information, sometimes with an implied criticism between the lines ('I have enquired of the Ministry as to the evidence upon which they based their assumption, used in calculations, that receipts from private practice have remained at a total of £2 millions for years subsequent to 1950–51').[2]

The financial negotiations for the National Health Service have been and remain a dour struggle between the Ministry on the one hand and a number of tough, well-organized and secretive commercial and professional interest groups on the other. When the history of the National Health Service is written the part played by state audit, by its constant vigilance and its regular publication of objective information, will be found to have been an influential one. Indeed the Comptroller and Auditor General's reports, together with those of the Public Accounts Committee, will be essential source material for the historian.

French social security is based upon a contributory scheme, compulsory for all employed persons, providing comprehensive benefits to the contributor and his immediate family, including pensions and family allowances. It is not, however, universal and equal in its application. It covers less than full costs (for example, it leaves about 20 per cent of medical expenses on private account), and it varies considerably between different elements of the population. There is a general regime for wage earners, an agricultural regime, and a number of special regimes for miners, railwaymen, gas and electricity workers, civil servants and other groups. Most self-employed persons and employers are compulsorily associated with the general regime. And since the principle of participation is employment, persons without regular means of support receive assistance under other schemes. The intention in the early days after the Liberation was to establish a social security scheme open to all, but, in the restrained words of the Cour des Comptes, later legislation 'tended to replace the notion of national by that of professional solidarity'.

Diversity means complexity, and in 1950–1 the Cour dedicated

[1] Ibid.

[2] Ibid., (Cl. I–V), 1954–5.

itself to an intensive study of this whole varied administrative structure, in an attempt 'to obtain a clearer view of that still vague entity which constitutes our social finance'. The Cour looked 'behind appearances', in order to 'trace out the actual distribution of social burdens'.[1]

The report showed the practical consequences of fragmentation in social security. Collection of the various contributions gave rise to all kinds of abuse. Employers' associations openly drew the attention of their members to the possibilities of reducing contributions by paying part of wages in the form of 'bonuses'. There was no liaison between the tax authorities and those charged with collection of contributions; moreover the system of separate collecting by social security and by family allowance bodies added to administrative costs and to paper work for employers. By its complexity it also favoured fraud. Very great difficulty had been encountered in obtaining information upon which to base contributions from professional people; the Cour found that in various regions up to 16 per cent of doctors and dentists and 21 per cent of lawyers and architects were not on the books of social security at all. The answer in this case, said the Cour, was to have contributions collected by the tax authorities, who already had the information which the social security bodies could not obtain. Audit researches in a dozen départements led to the conclusions that nine per cent of workers in receipt of family allowances had not paid contributions, and that only about 82 per cent of the known total value of wages was assessed for social security.

On the expenditure side, the Cour had more to say. It was important to reduce day-bed costs at public hospitals, yet a considerable number of these had low proportions of occupancy. For the whole of the provinces the average bed utilization was only 59 per cent and in six départements it was below 45 per cent. This left 'the impression of a complete unsuitability of the existing hospital organization to the needs which it must satisfy'; the Cour had therefore asked for a full census of public and private hospital resources in France, and this was being undertaken.

It had also been noted that prescription costs were rising steeply. Doctors often over-prescribed and took insufficient note of the cost of medicines. The Cour's comment was outspoken:

the irresponsibility of the prescribing practitioner is encouraged by the

---

[1] C. des C., Rapport, 'La Sécurité Sociale, 1950–1, p. 102.

notorious inadequacy of medical controls and by the existence of a powerful professional organization.

As in Britain, proprietaries were frequently prescribed instead of equivalent laboratory preparations, and the Cour suggested that the price of the latter might be used as a maximum for reimbursement by social security. Wholesalers' and chemists' margins were very high, and amounted to as much as 50 per cent of the cost of proprietaries. Fees charged by medical practitioners to their patients were not in practice tied to social security rates of reimbursement; in the Paris region and elsewhere fees had so risen that the contribution of patients, instead of being 20 per cent, as intended by legislation, was about 50 per cent on the average. Certain friendly societies (mutuelles) had signed agreements with doctors, providing for fees far in excess of the social security rates:

> thus, (said the Cour) actual competition sometimes operates between the friendly societies and the social security organizations, which cannot fail to strengthen the position of the medical profession when it claims increased rates.

In the dental field the magistrates of the Cour had done some cost-accounting. In various towns the social security bodies had established dental clinics, which were opposed by private dentists, using the argument that these clinics did not maintain proper cost accounts, so that their real costs per treatment were unknown.[1] The Cour examined fourteen clinics and found that this was true. However, after making numerous amendments to the cost accounts, the auditors were able to establish that the actual costs per treatment were in fact very considerably below the local social security fees for private dentists. It was concluded that if the cost accounts of clinics were improved, their resulting figures would be a useful guide to the bodies charged with establishing rates of private fees.

Of particular interest were the findings of the Cour on the relationships between social security benefits and the various

[1] It is a common administrative experience that public authorities when calculating the unit costs of their operations, often overlook such expenses as rent and rates, heating and lighting, which they do not pay themselves. In the absence of such charges, however, their unit cost figures are useless for purposes of comparison with those of private bodies, which may be the main motive for maintaining cost accounts. The difficulty is sometimes minimized by the insertion of notional figures to cover the missing expense items.

income groups. The fact that patients had themselves to advance the cost of treatment and to bear part of it on their own account operated strongly in favour of the more well-to-do. Researches in four regions showed that the expenditures of social security for individuals in the highest income groups were four times greater than for the poorest, under the headings of medical, surgical and dental treatment, and two and a half times as high in the case of prescriptions. For hospital costs, however, the reverse was true; wealthier persons mostly used private nursing-homes. Spa treatment under social security applied almost exclusively to the more affluent groups; this in particular seemed to the Cour to demand reform. Specialists, with their higher fees, were consulted much more regularly by persons of higher income. Thus, at any rate a decade ago, the French system had not made a revolutionary change in the traditional social pattern of medical treatment; this was fundamentally a conservative scheme.

The special miners' regime had proved less conservative. Doctors were salaried in proportion to the number of their patients and did not charge fees; prescriptions were free or nearly so. But the Cour showed that the quality of treatment suffered; doctors had about 7,500 patients each in the northern coalfields, 'an absolutely excessive figure, since an average medical clientele is of the order of 1,000 persons'. Prescribing seemed to be a source of perquisites; diet foods, tonic wines, beauty preparations, even products intended for animals. The tradition of miners' self-help made the imposition of controls all the more difficult.

The stark reality behind the social policies of the German Federal Republic is one of the most tremendous population changes of which history has any accurate record. The figures are astonishing:[1]

Population of the same area on 17/5/1939	40,247,500
War losses	− 4,600,000
Expellees and refugees, up to 3/12/1959	+ 12,864,000
Natural population increase, etc.	+ 4,537,000
Population on 31/12/1959 (excluding West Berlin)	53,048,500

There have, as a result, been all sorts of 'post-war social charges'

[1] Quoted by Professor Helmut Arntz in *Réalités Allemandes*, a Federal Government publication, 1961.

(soziale Kriegsfolgelasten); emergency measures for coping with the huge army of refugees. We can get some inkling of the size of these operations at their peak, when the Bundesrechnungshof tells us that:

> general relief measures consisting of transport, camp accommodation and support of expellees, evacuees, newcomers from the Soviet zone of occupation and Berlin, foreigners, stateless persons and repatriated soldiers, up to the point of permanent housing in the reception area, were conducted during the financial year 1950 in more than 2,000 separate camps in the Federal territory.[1]

In 1949, after the establishment of the Federal Republic, an Immediate Assistance Law (Soforthilfegesetz) was passed, providing for the relief of refugees, victims of political persecution and other impoverished persons. This aimed not only at the provision of subsistence but also, as far as funds permitted, at help towards economic independence. It was eventually replaced by the shrewdly named 'Equalization of Burdens Law' (Lastenausgleichsgesetz). The Bundesrechnungshof studied the special taxes established under this law and emphasized the difficulty of collection owing to their complexity, which in turn was due to the fact that the law was a compromise between opposing political, economic and social ideas.[2] Year by year there has been comment on equalization expenditures. Pensions for War Victims (Kriegsopferversorgung) were also the subject of a considerable study. At the end of 1954, 4,296,000 persons (1,517,000 disabled, 1,185,000 widows, 1,253,000 orphans and 341,000 parents) were war pensioners. Three years later the total had declined by half a million, but the cost was still about a tenth of the entire budget. The emphasis of the audit report was upon the methods by which this great mass of pensions was controlled.[3] Thus the liquidation of old wars may create as many financial problems as preparation for new ones.

State audit as research

One of the weaknesses of modern government is that, despite its huge scale, it tends to be carried on with very little systematic research. The state auditor, in his new capacity as a researcher, is

[1] Denkschrift for financial years 1949 and 1950, p. 198.
[2] Denkschrift for financial year 1955, pp. 48–55.
[3] Denkschrift dated 19 August 1958, pp. 62–74.

helping to remedy this situation, and his statutory powers of access to records give him an excellent working basis upon which to do so. He builds up his picture of administration, not from the statements of interested parties but from the original records.

Publication of state audit reports has becomes a recognized part of the democratic process in constitutionally governed countries. When the reports contained little but isolated matters of 'regularity' they were of minor interest except to persons directly concerned with budgetary control. In the present age, they help Parliaments and the public to take an informed interest in administration. They also serve the government machine itself. By revealing cases of fraud and showing where there is scope for further fraud, the reports encourage greater precautions where they are needed. By exposing the failures of planning and the consequent waste of public resources they conduct a campaign in favour of a more thorough and better informed preparation of public policy. They are a help to administration as well as a critique of it. This, in the age of big government, is their positive and growing contribution to the financial control cycle.

All of which may entitle us to deal with two well-known arguments used by the inveterate opponents of all external control of administration. It is said, firstly, that the need to answer queries obliges public authorities to keep voluminous records. This requires little comment; they need not, in fact, maintain more records than they would in any case require for their own purposes of reference. No large administrative body nowadays could itself dispense with voluminous records.

The second argument is a more considerable one. It is that fear of criticism discourages bold action by administrators and induces them to be cautious and negative in their approach to business. *A priori*, this is a strong case. But in the light of state audit findings it looks very different. As we have seen, the outstanding single cause of administrative waste is the failure to plan policies and transactions with due efficiency and thoroughness. Thus, if the word caution means the careful planning of action it is all to the good; the planned policy is usually the sound one. If boldness means more unplanned activity, it will end up as increased waste. The 'bold', ill-considered, actions will end up in the state audit reports and deserve to do so. The audit reports are an indication whether administrators really have taken proper thought on the basis of full information, and whether they have sought skilled advice. The public's millions cannot be soundly administered on the basis of brash and arbitrary decisions; as the reports show, it is precisely these whose results are often 'negative'.

CHAPTER IX

The Control of Administrative Efficiency

'The development of the modern form of organization of corporate groups of all kinds is nothing less than identical with the growth and continually widening extent of bureaucratic administration. . . . Its development is . . . the most crucial phenomenon of the modern Western state'—Max Weber: *The Theory of Social and Economic Organization*

THE cost of maintaining offices and paying officials is the principal overhead of government. Officials are not in any obvious sense a productive force, and the net cost of services performed by a government is, approximately, the total of revenue devoted to those services less the cost of the authorities administering them. Such administrative expenses are inevitable and necessary. But it is equally inevitable that when political and public opinion calls for cuts in state expenditure attention should be directed largely upon the overheads, in the hope that the same services might be rendered to the public despite a reduction in gross cost. The idea is deceptive, if only because the administrative overheads do not amount to more than a small percentage of total spending. And yet when statistics show, as they do in all major countries, that the state employs hundreds of thousands, or even millions, of office staff, the public is entitled to take an interest in what they do.

The approach to the problem is, however, very difficult. Public opinion in most countries believes that civil servants are far from dynamic, and it is true that rigid official structures often give them little incentive to be so. In England it has been said that 'the public service is particularly lacking in many of the natural forces which conduce to efficiency'.[1] In France, M. Edouard Bonnefous, after experience as 'Minister of State charged with administrative reform', defined the problem with greater precision. Whilst paying tribute to the French civil service at all levels, he reached the conclusion that, 'the services of the State cost dearly, in money, in

[1] Chubb, op. cit., p. 252.

useless work, in misused material, in time wasted, without however giving full satisfaction to those served by them'.

M. Bonnefous has described some of the symptoms which led him to take this view. 'Being stimulated neither by competition nor by a financial system based upon a sense of economy,' he says, 'the services have the tendency to preserve their old methods, even when they no longer correspond to changed circumstances.' The administration is, in his view, 'orientated more towards formal correctness and legality than towards efficiency. Manifold obstacles slow down and impede its action, whether it is a question of the regulation which confines it, of the tradition which stifles it, or of the necessity to come to terms with national or international opinion.' There are 'rich ministries and poor ministries. There are generously endowed services and others reduced to a wretched pittance.' Similarly, 'the qualities of an official do not ensure him a career unless he is in a favourable channel which will lead him to positions corresponding to his potentialities'. There is, 'a general climate which does not sufficiently favour the spirit of initiative and the productivity of the services'. 'Conservatism (the attitude of persons who profit from a given state of affairs) has', says Bonnefous, 'impregnated a large part of the Administration.' Meanwhile, 'the citizen demands a more effective and more economical administration, the official hopes for an improved status and more modern equipment'.[1]

In the United States a note of alarm can also be heard. For example, the second Hoover Commission on Organization of the Executive Branch of the Government, 1953–5, worked from the premise that the 'sprawling and amorphous mass of overlapping and extravagant agencies of our Government is difficult to supervise and almost impossible to control. Its sheer size and the variety of its impact make it easy to evade responsibility.'[2] The problem is important enough to be a major political issue, and it has been said that,

> In substantial part the reputation of a President or Governor today depends upon the satisfactory performance of (the) public service. An executive's political career can be broken by a failure or by a major

[1] Edouard Bonnefous, *La Réforme Administrative*, pp. 4, 23, 45–9, Paris, Presses Universitaires de France, 1958.

[2] Neil Macneil and Harold W. Metz, *The Hoover Report 1953–55. What it means to You as Citizen and Taxpayer*, p. 7, New York, The Macmillan Coy., 1956.

breakdown in the performance of governmental administrative activities. Furthermore, tax and budget pressures are such that waste in the operation of the public service becomes more and more intolerable. It is no longer a relatively simple matter . . . to have numerous employees on the public payroll who perform little if any public service or who perform public service at a relatively low level of competence. The public service has become too important for this. An executive today has as a major political concern the need to advance the professional competence of all public service.[1]

The former President of the Bundesrechnungshof was certainly right when he told his radio listeners that, 'The call for administrative simplification is to be heard everywhere in the world where the development of the modern Mass State has brought the consequence that new tasks have accrued to or have been taken over by the administration. The desire for administrative simplification is not therefore a specifically German preoccupation.' [2]

The need for properly conducted studies of administrative organization and efficiency would thus seem at first sight to be obvious and beyond question. But a contrary view has been developed, perhaps as a defensive reaction on the part of administrators against the excessive zeal and insufficient knowledge which have certainly been shown by some investigators. This is a kind of latter-day theory of laisser-faire applied to the administrative field. No rules of procedure and organization are universally valid, it is argued. An arrangement which is bad according to some *a priori* standard may in practice work satisfactorily. Habit appears to the exponents of this theory to be almost as elemental a force as gravity itself. One must therefore muddle through without any fundamental change or reform and hope that perhaps confusion will somehow sort itself out. One may even take a pride in the situation, discovering an empirical wisdom in petrified and inexplicable procedures. To attempt to amend confusion in a systematic way will in any case merely create fresh confusion.

It has also been shown, with more justification, that the accumulation of custom behind the older administrations often gives them the power, as well as the will, to resist change. This is perhaps scarcely surprising; the strength of what is customary,

[1] Millett, op. cit., p. 331.

[2] Dr Guido Hertel, talk on the Bavarian Radio, 16 February 1959, entitled, 'Can the administration be simplified?'

especially if its origins are uncertain, is familiar to the medieval historian. 'It might well seem', says Professor Millett, 'that organization is by the inherent nature of its human relations inflexible once it has acquired some history and continuity of operations,' and he fears that this may appear to be 'a counsel of despair'.[1]

The defensive arguments are not wholly without foundation, and the conservative nature of administrative institutions, especially the older ones, is undoubtedly a factor to be considered. Administrators, moreover, are distrustful of commercial business efficiency methods and particularly of what have been called the management sciences; they doubt whether these things are relevant to their own activities, except at the level of routine work. They feel almost instinctively that 'scientific' solutions to their problems of organization must be both pretentious and shallow, and they have little incentive to share the spirit which inspires the 'scientific' approach. Even the type of figures produced for industry by cost accountants are only of marginal help in public administration; there are whole sectors of operations for which the production of unit cost figures for work done is a permanent impossibility, since no standard unit of work exists.

There is, on the other hand, no reason to suppose that administrative institutions and their activities are incapable of improvement; nor, *a fortiori*, to believe that, by some mysterious mechanism, the highest efficiency will be obtained by allowing each separate organization to control itself in isolation from every outside influence. The reaction of public bodies to the growth of big government has been, in general, a greater willingness to expand than to adapt. Yet it *is* inefficient, and it may even be impossible, to do a specific job with the wrong kind of administrative organization. Offices have been much behind factories in realizing the impact of organizational problems on their work; the idea is not an obvious one and it is much better understood when applied to particular cases.

The study of administrative efficiency and organization is sometimes delicate and difficult, but it offers the best hope of ensuring not only that the size of the huge modern armies of officials corresponds approximately to the work requirements, but that the work itself is rational and necessary. This viewpoint has been

[1] John D. Millett, *Management in the Public Service. The Quest for Effective Performance*, p. 199, New York, McGraw-Hill, 1954.

accepted, sometimes under political pressure, in all the advanced countries. But it is only part of the general problem; it must also be decided what shall be the aims and methods of the efficiency studies, who shall conduct them, and who shall deal with their results. A brief history of this form of control shows the variety of solutions and expedients which have been adopted to meet this challenge to administrative ingenuity; it is a history which increasingly concerns the state audit bodies in most countries.

Control of efficiency is a twentieth-century specialization, like so many other advanced techniques. It was scarcely of great interest before administrative bodies became really large employers of staff. In 1861, a century ago, for example, the central civil service in the United Kingdom comprised only some 32,000 persons; this was less than a quarter more than in the year of Waterloo, and it had actually declined by about 7,000 since 1851.[1] In France the public services may have begun to develop to their modern scale rather earlier, and the census of 1866 listed no less than 288,000 persons, including 32,000 women, as employed in the 'public administrative services'; many, perhaps the majority, of these were, however, members of the teaching profession rather than office workers. They also included many other persons engaged upon what in Britain would have been 'local authority services'.[2] There has been a steady increase ever since in all countries; the figures are difficult to compare because they classify persons and professions differently. But they everywhere provide ample confirmation for the view—which is not likely to be questioned—that the present century is the age of big public services. The British central services employed 710,600 officials ('non-industrial' civil servants) in the war year of 1943 and 635,600 in 1955. If the 'industrial' employees of the state are added to the latter figure, the total is 1,058,200.[3] On 30 June 1954 the United States Federal Government employed about 2,350,000 persons.[4] If state and local government employees are added, the total is very much greater;

[1] Figures quoted by W. J. M. Mackenzie and J. W. Grove, *Central Administration in Britain*, p. 7, London, Longmans, Green & Co., 1957. (The figures are only approximations, owing to ambiguities in the sources.)

[2] Alfred Sauvy, *La Bureaucratie*, p. 23, Paris, Presses Universitaires de France, 1956.

[3] Mackenzie and Grove, op. cit., pp. 23 and 25.

[4] Macneil and Metz, op. cit., p. 31.

in 1950 it was over seven millions.[1] M. Bonnefous has a list of all persons drawing their income from the budgets of the State, the nationalized industries and the local authorities of France in 1956:

Established state officials	755,800	
Other full-time state officials	287,800	
Part-time state officials	59,400	1,103,000
Military regulars		490,000
Staff of nationalized industries and establishments, social security organizations, etc.		1,275,000
Local authority personnel		380,000
		3,248,000

An even larger number of persons (3,296,000) were drawing pensions earned by military or civil service to the state. M. Bonnefous estimated that for every five workers in the 'private sector' of the economy there were two dependent on the state and its varied agencies for employment or subsequent pension.[2] This is probably a fairly average pattern among Western countries. When families are taken into consideration, it seems likely that in each of the major countries the public purse and public enterprise between them directly maintain populations greater than those of even the very largest cities.[3]

The history of efficiency studies

It was the First World War and the post-war economic crisis which gave the first impulse to the examination of administrative efficiency. The motive, however, was not efficient performance for its own sake, but rather the reduction of public spending. Everywhere the war was followed by an outcry for the cutting of official establishments, from a public opinion disillusioned to find that the peace did not bring with it a return to pre-war tax levels. The purpose was therefore an essentially negative one and the

[1] Quoted by Millett, *Government and Public Administration*, p. 9.

[2] Bonnefous, op. cit., pp. 19–20. The figures should be regarded as a guide only. The very fact that precise figures of this kind are hard to come by, is an indication of the variety and huge numbers of persons involved.

[3] *Indirectly*, of course, through health, welfare and social security organizations and state institutions of all kinds, through pensions to persons who have never been in state employment, etc. (to say nothing of the staffs of firms working for the government), public resources maintain very many more people.

measures taken to achieve it were inevitably influenced by this fact; in the main their aim was quite frankly to make cuts, and only incidentally to improve the administrative machine in the process. It was not a phase calculated to inspire confidence in the minds of state employees.

In its fourth report of 1920 the Public Accounts Committee announced the 'imperative necessity for securing economy in every department of public life, if national bankruptcy is to be avoided'. In 1921 two by-elections in wealthy constituencies were won by 'Anti-waste' candidates against the government, which responded to public demand by creating the Committee on National Expenditure, more celebrated as the Geddes Committee. This did achieve a substantial reduction of the civil service, but rather by a rapid review of the estimates, followed by ruthless 'axeing', than by a systematic study of organization and procedures.[1]

Already during the later war years, however, the Select Committee on National Expenditure,[2] which met from 1917 to 1920, had made reviews of government departments as a whole, which often included questions of organization, staff and financial control. It was the Committee's experiences in this almost unknown field of research which led to the Reports of the Haldane Committee on the Machinery of Government in 1918, and of the Bradbury Committee on Organization and Staffing of Government Offices in 1919. Their recommendations led to the creation in 1919 of an Establishments Department in the Treasury and the appointment of Establishments Officers in government departments.[3] The Bradbury Report also resulted in the engagement of a few specialists, known as Treasury Investigating Officers; it is in this development that the Organization and Methods branches of the British civil service may perhaps be found in embryo. In subsequent years these officers gave more attention to surveys of organization, but at first they were specifically regarded as experts in the supply and use of office machinery. Before 1939

[1] Chubb, op. cit., pp. 111–14.

[2] And the Public Accounts Committee also. See Chubb, op. cit., pp. 81–2.

[3] A Treasury circular of 1920 laid down that the Principal Establishments Officer of each Department was to be appointed with the consent of the Prime Minister on the advice of the Secretary of the Treasury. This mode of appointment ensured him a degree of independence within his own Department.

there were never more than four Investigating Officers, and the real impulse for the creation of 'O. & M.' branches came only with the Second World War.

Meanwhile the United States Government was feeling its way in the same general direction. The Budget and Accounting Act of 1921, that vital landmark in the development of modern administration in America, created the office of Comptroller General and charged its holder with several powers concerning organization in the government service. He was to 'prescribe the forms, systems and procedure for administrative, appropriation and fund accounting in the several departments and establishments'.[1] He was, in reports to Congress, to 'make recommendations looking to greater economy or efficiency in public expenditures'. He was to report to Congress upon 'the adequacy and effectiveness' of internal audit and inspection arrangements. Departments were to furnish such information to the Comptroller as he might require regarding 'the powers, duties, activities, organization, financial transactions, and methods of business of their respective offices'.[2] It was clearly intended from the start that the General Accounting Office was to interest itself in questions of operating efficiency, as the agent of a Congress which was itself interested in these matters. But the Act also provided for a strengthening of control over administrative departments by the President, acting through the new budget machinery, and it established the Bureau of the Budget to assist him. The Bureau, when so directed by the President, was to:

> make a detailed study of the departments and establishments for the purpose of enabling the President to determine what changes (with a view of securing greater economy and efficiency in the conduct of the public service) should be made in (1) the existing organization, activities, and methods of business of such departments and establishments, (2) the appropriations therefor, (3) the assignment of particular activities to particular services, or (4) the regrouping of services.[3]

This sounded like a programme for drastic administrative reform, based upon the researches of the Bureau, but the Act went on to specify that the President might submit his recom-

[1] 1921 Act, Section 309. (In U.S.A. there is greater emphasis than in Europe upon accounting methods as a means of achieving general administrative efficiency.)

[2] 1921 Act, Sections 312(a), 312(d) and 313.

[3] 1921 Act, Section 209.

mendations on these matters to Congress; he did not, in other words, have powers to make changes himself. In fact, little was done in the early years.[1] General Dawes, the first Director of the Bureau, created a number of committees to promote 'housekeeping' economies in printing, transport, purchasing and office arrangements, but the structure of administrative authorities was a subject which had to await the presidency of Franklin D. Roosevelt in 1933. In that year centralized agencies were created for the purchase of supplies for the federal administration, and for the improved management of public buildings. This was perhaps the first of a very long series of administrative reforms in the United States, extending into the nineteen-fifties; it established the nuclei of the General Services Administration, formed in 1949, which provides something like a comprehensive centralized service for government offices.[2]

The Bureau of the Budget does not appear to have had any permanent apparatus for organizational questions until, in 1939, it enlarged its staff and created a Division of Administrative Management, on lines favoured by the 1937 report of the President's Committee on Administrative Management. The emphasis for at least the first decade was upon the improvement of 'management' activities in such matters as purchasing, personnel and accounting procedures. The first Hoover Commission in 1949 complained that the Bureau had not integrated the work of 'management appraisal' with the review of departmental estimates; the job of ensuring management efficiency in government agencies still remained to be done.[3] More emphasis should be placed on the management research function, said the Commission, particularly as the Government was 'entering upon a period of vigorous reorganization'.[4]

In France the idea of general administrative reform was also a

[1] Both the staff and the annual cost of the Bureau remained remarkably constant at about 100 persons and $200,000, between 1922 and 1938. Mr Bell, Acting Director, complained that the Bureau had not been properly equipped to carry out Section 209 of the 1921 Act (quoted by Heinig, *Das Budget*, vol. 1, p. 207).

[2] The G.S.A. combines many of the functions which in the United Kingdom are fulfilled by the Ministry of Public Building and Works, the Stationery Office, the Public Record Office and some other departments.

[3] Millett, *Government and Public Administration*, pp. 362–3.

[4] The Hoover Commission Report (1949), pp. 46–7.

by-product of the First War. As from 1922, the 'year of the axe' in many countries, a series of commissions dealt with the problem; almost all of them included senior magistrates of the Cour des Comptes. The Commission Louis Marin (1922–3) thus defined its objective:

France should have an Administration which is a motor, instead of a perpetual brake, which instead of 'grinding without corn' and collecting useless files, has an increased and a controllable efficiency.

This Commission produced a report recommending considerable reforms of both structure and detail. It was so controversial that nothing was put into effect at that moment. Parliament in 1924 instituted for the first time the procedure of extraordinary powers. The Poincaré government was authorized for four months to make decrees effecting 'all such administrative reforms and simplifications as will permit the achievement of economies'. Poincaré did not in fact use these powers in 1924, but in 1926 they were renewed in circumstances of financial crisis, and he then made more than 80 decrees comprising a major reform of administrative structure. Many changes were made in the local organization of departmental services; 106 sub-prefectures, 227 courts of first instance and 318 gaols were among the institutions abolished. There was some decentralization of powers to local authorities. A further 41 decrees achieved 'minor but useful' changes in the Ministries. From this time onwards most administrative change in France has been brought about by governments using decrees under extraordinary powers.[1]

In the thirties 'administrative reform' became a euphemism for a deflationary policy within which the cutting of expenditure on administration, and especially on personnel, became an end in itself. Indeed something similar was happening in Britain at the same time. This was a period of what M. Bonnefous calls 'false reform', and the very idea of reform became compromised among civil servants by the abuse of it. There was a reaction against all administrative reform. When the Popular Front government, which had widespread support among rank-and-file civil servants, nationalized the railways, the war industries and the Banque de France, this 'was not the occasion for a redistribution of functions, staff and resources between the various authorities; it even led in

[1] Bonnefous, op. cit., pp. 59, 66.

some cases to the creation of services which superimposed themselves upon the existing structures'.[1] An atmosphere unfavourable to constructive reform had been created, and even when efficiency came to be sought for its own sake, after the war, there remained a suspicion of the motive behind efforts to improve administration.

The events under the Weimar Republic, prior to the seizure of power by Hitler, are of special interest. As in U.S.A., the post-war years were a time of basic budgetary reform, and the Reichshaushaltsordnung of 1922, like the American Act of the previous year, charged the state audit body to seek economy within the field of administrative organization. The Rechnungshof des Deutschen Reiches was to seek cases where institutions and individual posts were not essential or where any other economies seemed possible without compromising the policies pursued.[2] But this was considered insufficient, and Germany became the only country at this time to create a professional organization which aimed specifically at the achievement of economy through administrative rationalization. This innovation was associated with the national audit body.[3]

A Cabinet decision in November 1922, provided that the President of the Rechnungshof should act on the government's behalf as Reich Economy Commissioner (Reichssparkommissar). He was to make recommendations to the Cabinet, on the basis of investigations in each Ministry—for which he was provided with a staff —as to how administrative work could be reduced and staff decreased. He was given the right to participate as an adviser at meetings of the Cabinet. This new post, and its incumbent Dr Saemisch, were a success, and the work continued until the advent of the Nazi regime.[4] It was in essence aimed, in the spirit of the times, at economy rather than efficiency. It was another product of the 'year of the axe', and largely as a result of the Sparkommissar's work a great decrease in personnel employed by the

[1] Bonnefous, op. cit., p. 75.

[2] RHO. Section 96 (actual wording quoted on p. 115, above).

[3] An Economy Commissioner was first appointed in 1920, but was attached to the Finance Ministry. 'This organizational solution proved a failure' (Dr Guido Hertel, in an address to the Academy of Administrative Sciences, Speyer, 15 February 1960).

[4] It was terminated by a law of December 1933.

Reich was ordered in October 1923.[1] Nevertheless the unusual character of this post, together with the personality of its holder, raised it above the achievements of the 'axeing committees' of the time. Dr Saemisch developed and published a set of general principles of administrative organization which have retained influence in the German civil service until the present day. His functions were broadened into 'a general mandate to maintain a watching brief over the efficiency of the Reich administration, to make recommendations about it and to participate in an advisory capacity during the preparation of legislation. His activity extended also over the Länder and the local communes. His participation in the formation of the budgets of Reich and Länder gained steadily increasing importance.'[2] His reports were probably the first published accounts of investigations of an 'O & M.' type in any country. 'O. & M.' was established under the Weimar Republic as an independent external control, closely associated with state audit and operating at the highest level.[3] A tradition had been founded which was to re-emerge after the ordeals of dictatorship and war.

Recent Developments

The close interest of state audit in questions of administrative efficiency is, however, chiefly a development since the Second War. The War itself and the years immediately following it also produced the development of Organization and Methods as an internal service of the executive. A new approach to efficiency studies has everywhere gradually resulted from improved economic circumstances. The urge to make 'cuts' for reasons of financial politics has not disappeared, but it has been far less acute than in the crisis years of the early twenties and early thirties. A calmer and more creative type of study has increasingly become practicable. It has been seen that efficiency involves much more than the immediate salary bill of departments. It concerns their service

[1] F. F. Blachy and Miriam E. Oatman, *The Government and Administration of Germany*, p. 248, Baltimore, Johns Hopkins Press, 1928.

[2] From 'Stellung und Aufgaben des Bundesrechnungshofes und seines Präsidenten', an unpublished memorandum, August 1959.

[3] The Sparkommissar idea was fashionable in the twenties. In England, Henry Higgs, in 1922 and later, proposed a detective type of Inspector General of Finance, acting as the servant of Parliament, with a free hand and the use of whatever statistical and economic help he needed (Chubb, op. cit., p. 106).

to the general public and their contribution to national productivity. Efficiency satisfies the aspirations not only of citizens but also of many officials. And in the long view if not the short one, it offers real economies.

By the middle of 1940 the British Treasury had over twenty Investigating Officers; in 1941 their section was given the title of 'Organization and Methods Division' and the staff continued to increase. Their facilities were available to other government departments, which in the later war years began to establish 'O. & M.' branches of their own. By 1945 most of the large ministries were equipped with their own sections. In 1953, seventeen departments employed a total of over 250 'O. & M.' personnel, and the Treasury retained a further 55, many of whom served smaller authorities with no facilities of their own. In every case the 'O. & M.' branches were subordinated to the departmental Establishments Officers, so that they were in no sense in a position of independence, even within their own departments.

In France a decree dated 6 January 1945 permitted the formation of administrative organization bureaux in government offices. In 1956 there was an average O. & M. staff of about seven persons in each of seventeen departments reviewed in an enquiry by the Institut Technique des Administrations Publiques. It was said that the O. & M. branches always reported at high level in the department concerned, in contrast to British practice.[1]

The function of the O. & M. officer is to examine and analyse all existing activities in a department. He may apply a number of basic tests to each official post. Firstly, is the particular job really necessary? Is it worth what it costs in manpower? Is the official fully employed? Could his work be simplified or more effectively performed elsewhere? Is there any duplication of work? Does the official's rank correspond to the notional 'quality' of the work? There may be an attempt to estimate quantities of work and the numbers of staff required to handle them. Functional matters are a concern of O. & M. study; in particular the design and use of forms, filing systems and records, the routing of correspondence and office mechanization. Within such typical limits the O. & M. officer may have considerable scope, though his field has not the

[1] Paul Klein, 'O. & M. in the Public Service in France', *O. & M. Bulletin*, December 1956.

same extent everywhere.[1] Questions of hierarchical organization, departmental structure, regional branches, allocation of responsibility for work both inter-departmentally and within the office, and similar matters, tend to be more 'sensitive', and at the highest level there are problems which have political aspects. The O. & M. service works best at the level of routine operations and is intended to do so.[2] There are in any case certain questions whose implications are too wide to permit of a useful approach through any kind of administrative study except the purely explorative; for example, the creation, amalgamation or abolition of major departments of state. When such things take place the motive is usually political.

But between the 'political' and the 'routine' level there is a rich stratum of administrative problems, offering great scope for study. The question is how these matters are best approached; the O. & M. branches may in some cases lack the independence necessary.[3] The promotion of effective research into administrative efficiency is a major problem of organization and methods in itself.

To allow state audit to take cognisance of the administrative performance of the departments which they audit is to bring office management within the compass of public accountability. There is in principle no reason why it should not be so. Government departments are granted very considerable sums of public money for the conduct of business and the upkeep of their establishment. State auditors have always examined this expenditure from the formal standpoints. They have, for example, reassured themselves that each official on the pay list has received no more than his entitlement under the regulations. But this is the 'regularity' aspect of the expenditure; it teaches nothing about whether the department is so managed as to be efficient in the handling of operations and to give value for public money. The

[1] In the U.K. for example, the relationships between work on the one hand and numbers and ranks of staff on the other may be handled separately by 'Staff Inspectors'.

[2] Though a 'Machinery of Government' branch was set up in the U.K. Treasury in 1946 and later incorporated in the O. & M. Division (Mackenzie and Grove, op. cit., p. 361).

[3] M. Bonnefous notes that O. & M. offices have had appreciable success in France and elsewhere and that much useful progress is due to them; 'but they tend to direct reform towards measures of purely material character and local concern, neglecting the broad aspects of the matter' (op. cit., p. 163).

auditors may in any case gain some impressions about this during the conduct of their duties, but if they are not permitted to go beyond matters of regularity their impressions will not be followed up and will remain superficial.

The U.S.A.

The General Accounting Office does not appear to have worried unduly about the niceties of this matter. At least since the adoption of the procedure of 'comprehensive audit',[1] an examination of office management practices has been a normal part of a full audit. It was the 'comprehensive' policy which first led the G.A.O. to carry out audits at the site of agency operations, and certainly an efficiency study cannot be carried out anywhere else. The broad aim is to assess how the agency has fulfilled its financial responsibilities, and for this purpose the audit covers not only expenditures but the use made of staff and property and the efficiency of the conduct of work.

It has been G.A.O. policy to seek inefficiency through the accounting mechanism, by means of such comparative cost figures as can be obtained. Assessment of efficiency on the basis of costing results is intended to provide 'irrefutable objective criteria' and thereby to avoid the need to make value judgments. 'In other words the administrative unit must be based on the accounting audit.'[2] It is an idea which is very attractive in theory. In many large establishments and depots it may well have a wide application, especially with the G.A.O.'s staff of certified public accountants to manipulate such cost data as may be available. It must nevertheless be stressed that very many administrative organizations all over the world conduct operations of such a nature that cost accounting cannot possibly solve the difficulty of assessing their efficiency. The cost accountant's technique is a useful one in a limited number of cases; for administrative study it will never have universal relevance. The state auditors, including those of the United States, are frequently obliged to make value judgments based upon experience and common-sense.

The General Accounting Office has audited its own efficiency. Comptroller General Warren reported in 1953:

> Of prime importance has been the exhaustive analysis of the organization and operations of the General Accounting Office, directed by me

[1] See Chapter VI, above, and Chapter XI, below.

[2] P. Senechal, op. cit.

and performed by highly competent personnel reporting directly to me. I asked those in charge of the review to leave no stone unturned to develop the potentialities for economy and improved procedures and to bring to attention any existing cases of duplication or overlapping operations, either within the General Accounting Office or between the Office and other Government agencies.[1]

The Comptroller expressed the view that comprehensive audit, which related budgetary accounting to 'overall management improvement', could 'contribute immeasurably toward improving efficiency and economy in Government'.[2] Such audits would include:

A review of the laws, to ascertain congressional intent as to the purpose and scope of the activities of the agency, the manner in which to conduct them, and the extent of the agency's authority.

A review of the agency's own policies 'to determine whether they conform to the intent of Congress and are designed to carry out the authorized activities in an efficient and reasonable manner.'

A review of procedures, practices, forms of organization and other elements of departmental control, to determine whether they ensure accuracy, regularity, and operational efficiency.

A review and analysis, by activities, of revenues, expenditures, and the utilization of assets, 'evaluating the effectiveness with which public funds are applied.'

An examination of individual transactions and checking of balances. (This is the 'regularity' audit, necessary as always, but reduced to a subordinate role.)

Presentation of recommendations for corrective action by Congress, by the agency head, 'or other interested agencies of the Government'.[3]

Some of the most notable results, from a financial standpoint, were, wrote the Comptroller General, obtained from audit findings which improved efficiency and reduced expenditures, rather than those which led to recoveries of money already spent.[4]

For example, the auditors studied the issue, withdrawal from circulation and destruction of paper money by the Treasury Department Fiscal Service. They recommended that the checking and destruction processes could be combined with work performed

[1] Annual Report, C.G. of the U.S., 1953, p. 2. It is clear from the results of the reorganization of the G.A.O. (See Chapter VI, above, and Chapter X, below) that Mr Warren meant what he said. His principle was to find 'new ways to do a better job with high calibre but fewer personnel'.

[2] Ibid., p. 7.

[3] Ibid., pp. 17–18.

[4] Ibid., p. 19.

by Federal Reserve Banks, with a considerable saving from the elimination of dual handling. The Treasury Department accepted the recommendation, which involved an estimated economy of $500,000 annually.[1] The G.A.O., together with the General Services Administration, made a survey of electrical business machines throughout the federal service, at the request of the Committee on Appropriations of the House of Representatives. They reported 'many areas of uneconomical use of equipment, and made numerous recommendations for better utilization of the machines, elimination of unnecessary work, and rental reductions'.[2] During 1953–4, the entire organization of the Atomic Energy Commission was subjected to comprehensive audit. As a result the contracting practices were criticized. Some staff reductions were effected in the Commission's Washington office, and even in the offices of a large contractor. Information from the G.A.O. to a 'task force' of the House Committee on Appropriations was useful in supporting the force's recommendation for a reduction of $106,000,000 in the Atomic Energy Commission's budget estimates for 1955.[3]

With the aid of technical consultants, a special study of government wind tunnels and their operation, was undertaken by the G.A.O. for the Senate Committee on Appropriations.[4] Numerous and detailed recommendations for improvement in the financial management of the postal service were accepted by the Post Office Department in 1953–4.[5] Similarly, assistance in developing administrative and financial procedures for the execution of foreign aid programmes was provided for the Foreign Operations Administration, then newly created.[6] The huge military purchasing operations of the defence departments have constantly been reviewed from an administrative as well as a financial point of view.

The G.A.O. does not hesitate to enter the field of industrial administration. A review of Department of Defence shipyard operations resulted in various recommendations 'for general strengthening of procedures to enable the yards to adhere more closely to their advance scheduling of jobs and reduce costly last-

[1] Annual Report, C.G. of the U.S., 1953, pp. 8, 20.

[2] Ibid., 1954, pp. 8–9. [3] Ibid., pp. 20–21. [4] Ibid., p. 28.

[5] Ibid., p. 29. Recommendations addressed to the Post Office Dept. are cited in all Annual Reports of the C.G.

[6] Ibid., p. 30.

minute revisions in work plans'. The mechanization of much record-keeping was proposed. Most of the recommendations were accepted.[1] At an arsenal the costs of the motor transport service were unduly high. It was found that taxis as well as buses were being operated and that skilled mechanics were performing minor routine work. Substantial economies were later effected.[2] An audit of the Army Chemical Centre in Maryland resulted in a report to Congressional Committees and the Department of the Army containing no less than 70 observations, some of them directly financial and others of an 'O. & M.' nature. The Assistant Secretary of the Army for Financial Management later stated that 55 of the items reported had been corrected, that further defects in organization had been disclosed, and that a complete reorganization of the Centre was planned.[3] Among the findings of an audit of the Alaska Road Commission was 'the existence of two Federal road-building organizations in Alaska, each having different concepts of road construction'.[4]

A report which the G.A.O. transmitted to Congress upon the School Lunch Programme, administered by the Agricultural Marketing Service, amounted to a full review of legislation and policy as they were proving themselves in actual operation in the various States. The discovery of excessive charging by the contractor for distribution in Illinois was only an incident of the survey as a whole.[5] A mechanized payroll system for that legendary body, the Federal Bureau of Investigation, was developed and approved by the Comptroller General.[6]

The G.A.O. has often assisted Congressional Committees engaged upon the study of government agencies and services. It assisted the Senate Committee on Government Operations in the reorganization and modernization of the Passport Office of the Department of State.[7] It made investigations for the Senate Committee on Post Office and Civil Service in the course of a review of the administration of the Civil Service System.[8] During studies which resulted in legislation 'liberalizing' retirement benefits for civil servants, testimony and recommendations from the G.A.O. were heard by the Senate and House Committees concerned.[9]

[1] Ibid., 1955, pp. 23–4.
[2] Ibid., p. 26.
[3] Ibid., pp. 31–2.
[4] Ibid., p. 43.
[5] Ibid., pp. 50–2.
[6] Ibid., p. 70.
[7] Ibid., 1956, pp. 12, 113–14.
[8] Ibid., p. 14.
[9] Ibid, pp. 14, 128.

Audit of an Ordnance Depot and a Chemical Depot in Utah led to a complete reorganization and integration of the two depots by the Department of the Army, resulting in a reduction of over $1 million in annual operating costs and the cancellation of over $6 millions of approved construction contracts.[1] A similar review of two Air Depots in France was expected to lead to their amalgamation and the cancellation of requisitions for stores to the value of some $5 millions.[2] In a survey of 'cowboy industries' licensed by the Bureau of Land Management, the auditors found that many Federal ranges were being grazed well in excess of their estimated carrying capacity and that the grazing fees charged were inadequate to cover administrative costs.[3] The Bureau of Reclamation, Department of the Interior, and the Army Corps of Engineers, which handle and sometimes compete for the bulk of American water engineering projects, especially dams and canals, were thoroughly reviewed. Changes in their legislative powers were proposed, and the Chief of Engineers, who was 'very receptive' to the recommendations, achieved substantial economies by adopting practical suggestions.[4] Procedures for payment and reconciliation of cheques drawn in the government service upon the Treasurer of the United States at an average rate of about a million a day, were reorganized on the basis of using high-speed electronic equipment, following a joint study by the Treasury Department, the Bureau of the Budget and the General Accounting Office. This was expected to be faster, highly accurate and far more economical. The G.A.O. assisted in training the staff.[5] The Comptroller General complained that the Bureau of Customs did not possess a modern internal audit. The functions of audit were performed by miscellaneous management staffs, which resulted in lack of independence, duplication of work and unnecessary costs.[6] During review of the Coast Guard Yard it was found that relatively low use had been made by the Coast Guard of vessels, aircraft, shore facilities and vehicles. Some immediate replacements were deferred and a board was set up to examine utilization policy.[7]

No part of the Federal government is privileged and inviolate. Among 'centralized audits', i.e. audits chiefly on the basis of

[1] Annual Report, C.G. of the U.S., 1956, pp. 43–4.
[2] Ibid., p. 54.
[3] Ibid., pp. 64–6.
[4] Ibid., pp. 66–71.
[5] Ibid., pp. 91–2.
[6] Ibid., pp. 96–7.
[7] Ibid., pp. 98–9.

accounts and vouchers forwarded to the G.A.O., are those of the White House and the President's remuneration, the Supreme Court, the U.S. Court of Appeals and the lesser Federal tribunals, the Senate (including 'salaries, mileage and expense allowances of Senators'), the House of Representatives, and the General Accounting Office itself. During the financial year 1956, audits of salaries and allowances of Members of the House of Representatives and of the Senate and House Restaurants were made 'on site' and presumably with greater thoroughness. The Government of the District of Columbia was examined comprehensively.[1]

All reports submitted to Congress by the Comptroller General are referred to the Senate and House Committees on Government Operations, which have the duty 'to study the operation of Government activities at all levels with a view to determining its economy and efficiency'.[2] Many Congressional Committees make use of the G.A.O. to obtain information about broad aspects of policy. For example, a special analysis was undertaken, at the request of the Senate Committee on Interior and Insular Affairs, of the Missouri River Basin power marketing programme, together with 'an evaluation of the benefits to the Nation from project operations for power generation as opposed to navigation'.[3] For the Senate Committee on Interstate and Foreign Commerce, the G.A.O. made a full analysis of expenditures on international air transport by American and foreign carriers.[4] For the Joint Committee on Atomic Energy, the federal auditors reviewed the terms of a proposed agreement with the United Kingdom for the exchange of atomic material.[5] Meanwhile in the financial year 1959 important comprehensive audits, resulting in many observations upon management policies, were made of the Foreign Agricultural Service, the Bureau of Public Roads, the Federal Maritime Board and the Maritime Administration, the Federal Aviation Agency (which found the G.A.O.'s recommendations 'sound and constructive'), the Bureau of Indian Affairs, the Bureau of Mines, the General Services Administration, and many more official bodies.[6]

The above examples from the Comptroller General's reports, indicate more effectively than can be suggested by theorizing, the existence of a major field for administrative study at intermediate

[1] Ibid., pp. 122–3.
[2] Ibid., 1959, p. 21.
[3] Ibid., p. 26.
[4] Ibid., p. 27.
[5] Ibid., p. 33.
[6] Ibid., passim.

level. Some of the observations reported by the G.A.O. are within the range of matters usually associated with O. & M. studies, but the majority of them are on a higher and wider level of application. The range is extremely varied and therefore elusive of definition, but it concerns what official bodies do as much as how they do it. The reasonable American assumption is that where administrative policies, as well as the procedures for carrying them out, appear to be inexpedient, outmoded, unco-ordinated with other policies, unproductive, ineffectual or unnecessary, they will also be wasteful. The proposition seems so obvious to Americans, perhaps on the analogy of private business, that it is rarely justified in words. Just as there are no exempted authorities, there is no ban upon the study of any subjects; if the unsuitability of legislation is considered to be at the root of wasteful administration the Comptroller General recommends to Congress that the law be changed. The full scope of the work of the General Accounting Office when it decides to undertake a thorough survey of an agency, a subject or a policy, has been expressed as follows: 'The object of the survey is to search out the basic facts, bring to bear an informed judgment, and produce a useful, definitive appraisal as the groundwork for legislation or administrative reorganizations,' which may be 'of the most fundamental character'.[1]

Yet despite this the G.A.O. does not usually work on the very highest level, except as an agent at the request of Congress. It does not question the existence of at least the major departments and agencies. For years in the forties and fifties the stage was occupied by the Hoover Commissions, which surveyed the entire Government service from the elevation of politics. The G.A.O. provided the Commissions and their 'task forces' with considerable assistance,[2] and its normal audit reports may have suggested avenues of research. But there was no hint of any overlapping of study activities. The Commissions, with all the prestige of their Chairman and the support of the government,[3] were specifically charged to investigate the whole administrative field and were ex-

[1] Annual Report, C.G. of the U.S., 1954, p. 45.

[2] Ibid., p. 15.

[3] The Hoover Commissions of 1947–9 and 1953–5 were each composed of twelve members: the President, the Vice President and the Speaker of the House of Representatives nominated four each. The Commissions were almost equally Republican and Democrat in membership, and in practice, non-partisan.

pected to propose sweeping reforms. The first Commission made 273 recommendations for reorganizations in the government service; the second made 314. Most of these were implemented either by administrative action or by legislation.[1] The impact of the first Commission upon the General Accounting Office itself, and its activities, was very great. If the G.A.O. is often positive and dynamic rather than timid and traditional in the approach to its duties, that is largely because Herbert Hoover and his Commission favoured a vigorous state audit.

The work of the G.A.O. in the field of administrative efficiency is inevitably less spectacular than the Hoover Commission's surveys. The Federal services are enormous and are said to operate at 'more than 10,000 specific sites'.[2] As the auditors go their rounds they must take one unit of authority at a time, examine it more closely than the Commission could do, and recommend such changes as would appear to promote efficiency and therefore economy. The effect of such work must be gradual and cumulative, and it remains orientated towards the financial and accounting aspects of administrative work. The Comptroller General has statutory powers to make directions for the executive departments regarding the principles, forms, standards and system of accounting[3], and for nothing else. For all other general administrative matters he can only recommend such changes as may seem to him expedient. Indeed, since the Budget and Accounting Procedures Act of 1950 he can only issue accounting directives after consultation with the Secretary of the Treasury and the Director of the Bureau of the Budget.[4] This triple responsibility was not new but dated from the decision of these three high officers of state, in December 1947, to establish a joint accounting programme.

This triumvirate of senior public servants and their departments has had a fruitful result in the Joint Financial Management Improvement Programme,[5] which has been in continuous operation

[1] Macneil and Metz, op. cit., Chapter 1.

[2] Annual Report, C.G. of the U.S., 1954, p. 44.

[3] Budget and Accounting Act, 1921, Section 309, as modified by Budget and Accounting Procedures Act, 1950, Section 112(a).

[4] Statutory consultation between named departments as a prerequisite for administrative action of certain types is a device very commonly used in many countries. It perhaps gives an element of 'consent' to administrative regulation which is lacking in an 'arbitrary' directive.

[5] Originally known as the Joint Programme to Improve Accounting in the Federal Government.

since 1948. At first, emphasis was placed on improving basic accounting techniques in federal departments. Later efforts were directed towards improvements in financial management functions, in association with modernized accounting, especially on a cost basis. Accounting was to cease being a mechanical routine and be developed to the point where 'meaningful data on the cost of operations' could be 'used effectively as a tool of management at the various levels of Government'.[1] The general intention was expressed in the Budget and Accounting Procedures Act of 1950:

> It is the policy of the Congress . . . that the accounting of the Government provide full disclosure of the results of financial operations, adequate financial information needed in the management of operations and the formulation and execution of the Budget, and effective control over income, expenditures, funds, property, and other assets.

The Act laid down that there was to be:

> integrated accounting for the Government, full disclosure of the results of the financial operations of each executive agency and of the Government as a whole, and financial information and control necessary to enable the Congress and the President to discharge their respective responsibilities.[2]

An amendment to the act directed that 'as soon as practicable' the accounts of executive agencies were to be 'maintained on an accrual basis to show the resources, liabilities and cost of operations . . . with a view to facilitating the preparation of cost-based budgets'.[3] There were to be 'adequate monetary property accounting records' and 'appropriate internal audit'. The benefits of professional accounting developments were to be made available to the administration and the political powers. The head of each executive agency was responsible for making the necessary changes in his own department, but was subject to principles and

[1] Joint Financial Management Improvement Programme, Annual Report, 1960, p. 5.

[2] 1950 Act, Sections 111(a) and 112(a).

[3] Public Law 863, 84th Congress. (Under the 'accrual basis' of accounting, expenditures are recorded in the financial period during which they are incurred, whether or not payment is made during the same period. Income is recorded when earned, whether received in the same period or not. In commercial accounting this system may be a more accurate guide to the state of a business than accounting on a cash basis. Its advantages for ordinary government accounts are less obvious, but this is a question outside the scope of the present study.)

standards prescribed by the Comptroller General, and to review by him from time to time.[1] It was a major programme of administrative reform, but it was to be effected 'as an evolutionary process rather than by making drastic changes'. In 1948 the Comptroller General created in the G.A.O. a staff of specialists in systems work, to formulate basic accounting requirements, review systems, forms and procedures, and provide technical assistance to agencies.[2] At the end of financial year 1960, out of 125 executive agencies with separate accounting, 38 systems had been approved in their entirety and 17 in part, by the Comptroller General. A further eleven agencies of the legislative and judicial branches had received the Comptroller's approval. For the 1961 budget, 56 per cent of all appropriation items, covering expenditures of $33·5 billions, were presented by agencies in the form of cost-based estimates, produced by modernized accounting methods.[3] Thus considerable progress has been made in this operation which aims to increase general efficiency through accounting. Mechanization with automatic data-processing equipment has gone on simultaneously. At the end of June 1960, about 310 computers were in use in business and management control systems in federal agencies, compared with 200 the year before.[4]

The difficulties inherent in the utilization of cost accounting for bodies engaged upon administration rather than physical production have inevitably been encountered in the Improvement Programme. It has now been realized that the applicability of the new accounting methods 'will vary with the kind of operations conducted by the agency. . . . There are no exemptions . . . but there is recognition of a need for varying degrees of application in individual agencies.'[5] The system cannot therefore be comprehensive, but within its limits there is reason to hope for an improved standard of budgeting and control, and an important increase in the accountability of individual administrative units. All these things must contribute to general administrative efficiency.[6]

[1] 1950 Act, Section 112(c) and 113(b).

[2] 'The General Accounting Office'. Fifth Intermediate Report of Committee on Expenditures in the Executive Departments. 81st Congress House Report No. 1441, 1949.

[3] Joint Financial Management Improvement Programme, Annual Report, 1960, pp. 6–7.

[4] Ibid., pp. 12–13.

[5] Ibid., pp. 18–19.

[6] 'The whole programme should result in a very substantial reduction of red tape and related paper work . . .' (81st Congress House Report No. 1441, p. 11).

On the other hand there is possibly a danger of mistaking streamlined accounting procedures for an efficient administration of public funds. There is no necessary connection between the two, and in the last resort the objective of state audit must be the latter rather than the former.

In the United States the national audit body has responded to pressure from Congress as well as the Hoover Commission to take a broad view of its responsibilities. The General Accounting Office had been endowed at its foundation with extensive powers. In the spendthrift years following the last war it was told to go out and use them. The comprehensive audit was the result; the auditors were to find all the facts and make recommendations 'for the better protection of the interests of Congress and of the Government as a whole', including 'changes in organizations and methods when necessary'.[1] The incorporation of a study of administrative efficiency, understood in a sense far wider than mere matters of office routine, does not seem to have caused any heart-burning.

* * * *

The European attitude has been different; or rather, the European attitudes, for there are more than one.

In Great Britain there has been some concern to resist the development of an efficiency audit, as an external and independent control.[2] The subject remains for the present as the exclusive responsibility of the Organization and Methods Branches of the larger departments and of the Treasury. Their activities do not offer scope for practical discussion based upon actual cases, since no reports are published about them and the existing internal and dependent status of the O. & M. branches would seem to preclude independent reporting. The findings of organization studies in Britain repose in the confidential files.[3]

[1] 81st Congress House Report No. 1441, pp. 17–18.

[2] See the late Sir Frank Tribe's lecture to the Royal Institute of Public Administration entitled 'Efficiency in the Public Services' (reprinted in *O. & M. Bulletin*, August 1949) in which it was suggested in effect that an efficiency audit was an impracticable idea.

[3] The Comptroller and Auditor General, Sir Edmund Compton, has recently said, 'I realize that I may be asking for the impossible, but it is a pity that the spending Departments, or the Treasury on their behalf, cannot find some way of regularly reporting the year's operations in the field of O. and M. and staff control with positive indications, where these can be

There is, however, much to be said about post-war developments in France and Germany. Both of these countries have built up organizations for the study of administrative structure and efficiency which are closely associated with their state audit bodies without being completely part of them. They have preferred the view that this study is best regarded as slightly different in principle from the rest of state audit, requiring the use of new techniques to obtain the necessary information, and modified machinery to gain acceptance of the findings. But the new bodies are aware that the protected status of the state audit guarantees their own independence and that its practical co-operation and stored knowledge of the various departments are valuable guides for their own researches.

Developments in France and Germany have had that much in common. For the rest, their new efficiency study institutions are almost completely different.

France

France was endowed, by a decree of the government of Georges Bidault, dated 9 August 1946, with an official body called the Central Committee of Enquiry into the Cost and Efficiency of the Public Services (Comité Central d'Enquête sur le coût et le rendement des services publics). It was the successor of a long line of administrative reform committees, but it was nevertheless an innovation.

> This Committee, (says Edouard Bonnefous) by its composition, which is more of civil servants than politicians, by the object of its mission which is research and not decision, and by its permanent character, differs from the bodies which preceded it. It soon asserted itself and its authority has never stopped increasing. Now, after ten years in existence, it is an essential element in any reform undertaking.[1]

The constitution of the Central Committee, as established by the decree, was certainly unusual. It was composed of most of the various high officials responsible for the practical and financial efficiency of the public service, together with members from Parliament and from civil service trade unions. The actual

---

measured, of the year's gains in economy and efficiency' (Lecture to the Institute of Municipal Treasurers and Accountants entitled, 'Control of Public Expenditure', 15 June 1960).

[1] Bonnefous, op. cit., p. 90.

composition, as modified by a decree of 14 October 1960, is now as follows:

The Premier Président of the Cour des Comptes, Chairman (with casting vote).

Two members each, from the Commissions des Finances of the National Assembly and the Senate.

A member of the Conseil d'Etat.

A member of the Cour des Comptes.

The Secretary General of the Government (Secretary to the Prime Minister and the Cabinet).

The Commissioner General of the Plan for Equipment and Productivity.

The Director of the Budget (a senior officer of the Ministry of Finance, with substantial personal powers).

The Director General of the Administration and the Civil Service (an independent official with rather vague powers of co-ordination and research).

A member of the Inspection générale des Finances.

A member of the Inspection générale de l'Administration.

A member of the Inspection générale de la France d'Outre-Mer.

A member of one of the corps of control of the Army, the Air Force or the Navy.

A member of the Inspection générale de l'Economie Nationale.

A member of the corps préfectoral.

A delegate of each of the most representative civil servants' trade unions, chosen from a list of three names proposed by each union.

The members are nominated by formal order (*arrêté*) of the Prime Minister. The Chairman can divide the Committee into working groups, in which specialist non-members can participate. The terms of reference, in the wording of the 1960 decree, are:

to seek and recommend measures appropriate to reduce the cost and improve the efficiency of ministries, public establishments, local authorities and bodies of all kinds which are charged to maintain a public service. Its competence also covers companies or organizations in which the State owns a financial interest greater than 20 per cent of the registered capital, or which have benefited from subsidies, advances or guarantees from the Treasury.

The Committee is to make periodical enquiries into the duties, the structure and the operating conditions of the ministerial departments.[1]

The Committee's working and investigation methods are of

[1] Decree No. 60–1099 of 14 October 1960, Article 2.

special interest. Everything is examined on the basis of on-the-spot enquiry, followed by report to the Committee. The investigators (*rapporteurs*) are placed temporarily at the Committee's disposal from among the personnel of, 'the Conseil d'Etat, the Cour des Comptes, the corps of control and the central administrations of the various ministries, the members of the University and the magistrates of the judicial order', and also from the senior staff of public enterprises and retired civil servants. They also are appointed by *arrêté* of the Prime Minister and they act in his name, by virtue of letters of mission signed by him and countersigned by the ministers directly concerned; they hold the widest powers for both documentary and local investigations. The *rapporteurs* sometimes work alone, but more often in teams.[1] Two or three months is an average duration for an investigation.

This system has the obvious disadvantage that the *rapporteurs* can only devote a limited time to study projects on behalf of the Committee; it has, on the other hand, two notable advantages. Firstly, the Committee is able to choose *rapporteurs* with qualifications and experience, administrative, legal, financial or technical, appropriate to each task in hand. Secondly, it has the considerable psychological advantage, for an institution charged to seek economies, of obviating the need to create new posts for its own service.

In practice, however, the Central Committee, like any other body, requires a small secretariat. This is furnished in the Cour des Comptes, which supplies a kind of permanent staff, headed by the Premier Président of the Cour, as Chairman. Two other magistrates of the Cour are respectively Secretary General[2] of the Committee and *chargé de mission* with it. These particular men have had long continuity of office and constitute a close link between the two organizations. Comparison of the reports of the Cour and those of the Committee shows that the latter often follows up the findings of the former and not rarely quotes its comments verbatim. The Chair of the Committee has always been taken by the Premier Président, and a decree of 1954 made this tenure automatic;

[1] In February 1961, 16 investigations were being conducted by a total of 44 *rapporteurs*. Six of the investigations were each the responsibility of a single *rapporteur*, the remainder the task of teams. The largest team was of seven *rapporteurs*.

[2] There is also a post of Assistant Secretary General, held by an Inspecteur des Finances.

this, says M. Bonnefous, was done 'in order to assert the independence and authority of the Committee'.[1]

The reports from the *rapporteurs* are considered by the Committee, whose conclusions, 'supported in appropriate cases by drafts of proposed legislation', are addressed to the Prime Minister, to the Minister charged with Administrative Reform, to the Minister of Finance and Economic Affairs, and to the ministers directly concerned. From the beginning, the Committee has been linked administratively to the Prime Minister's Office.[2] This may originally have been intended to indicate that its mission was interministerial; it had been considered that comparative investigations on this level 'could not always be left to the corps of control alone, acting within the framework and for the benefit of a single ministry'. The researches also 'required total independence of the directorates and services whose reform was to be considered'.[3]

The link with the Prime Minister has, however, had another consequence. It has perhaps helped to interest the political powers in questions of administrative reform. It has at any rate provided a tool ready for the hand of any Prime Minister who by experience or temperament might be interested in the organization of the public services. Government is not only a political, military, diplomatic and economic process but an administrative one also. The majority of heads of governments in all countries tend, however, to think that administrative services run themselves.[4] The 'administrative' Prime Minister is a rare species; in Britain it is doubtful if there has been one since Gladstone, or before him since the younger Pitt. In Michel Debré, however, France had such a Prime

[1] Bonnefous, op. cit., p. 91. An interesting proposal was made by Sidney Webb as long ago as 1918 for the creation in Britain of an organization in some ways comparable to the Comité central. This was to be a permanent administrative organ, a 'Board of Efficiency and Economy', with a Minister as chairman, and members including accountants, business men and representatives of heads of departments. It was to have its own expert staff, and was to review the estimates from the point of view of efficiency. (Quoted by Chubb, op. cit., p. 106).

[2] Formerly called the Présidence du Conseil.

[3] *Cent-Cinquantenaire de la Cour des Comptes*, 1807–1957, p. 121. Paris, Imprimerie Nationale, 1957.

[4] The rule which is strictly enforced in Britain and a few other countries, whereby civil servants are debarred from all political activity, has had the automatic result that parliaments and parties are deficient in experience and understanding of practical civil service administration. Politicians therefore are often credulous in such matters.

Minister from 1958 until 1962. In 1957 Edouard Bonnefous had written, 'The Prime Minister alone exercises authority over the Ministers. It is therefore up to him to promote administrative reform. It is no longer a question of studies and reports but of authority.'[1]

Michel Debré made a parliamentary reputation under the Fourth Republic for inflammatory right-wing utterances about Algeria; after May 1958, he became known as the faithful and even subservient retainer of the great President of the Fifth Republic. There is another side to his character. In 1945, Debré, who was both a public servant (an officer of the Conseil d'Etat, and therefore a member of one of those *grands corps* which dominate the French civil service) and a politician from the Resistance, directed a 'mission for the reform of the public service'. It was this mission's work which resulted in comprehensive reform of the recruitment and status of the higher civil service. M. Debré is regarded as the creator of the École Nationale d'Administration, the *alma mater* of the post-war generation of high officials. It is hardly surprising that as Prime Minister he took a personal interest in the state of the public services.

His influence can probably be detected in the decree of 14 October 1960 concerning the Central Committee of Enquiry, which adds several provisions strengthening the efficacy of that body. The Prime Minister, the Minister charged with Administrative Reform, and the ministers directly concerned, may henceforward confide to the Committee the study of any measures of rationalization or projects of reform. There is a new discipline to facilitate the Committee's enquiries and give effect to its observations. For each study undertaken, the minister concerned will nominate to the Chairman of the Committee one or more senior officials to be responsible for following up the Committee's work and the practical application of its conclusions. After receiving notification of these conclusions the ministers concerned are to convey their comments to the Prime Minister, the Minister charged with Administrative Reform, the Minister of Finance and Economic Affairs and the Chairman of the Committee, within three months. 'In case of a divergence of views, the Prime Minister will arbitrate as necessary, and will . . . prescribe time-limits and conditions for carrying into effect the measures to be taken by each department concerned.' There is an authoritarian tone in this which accords

[1] Bonnefous, op. cit., p. 123.

with the hopes of M. Bonnefous, as well as with the spirit of General de Gaulle's regime.

The Central Committee has published five large general reports,[1] from which an impression can be gained of the scope and results of its work. The first Report, in 1947, contained a note on the conditions which gave rise to the Committee: it responded to a permanent need, which was particularly great at that time, because of the widened tasks of the State and the shortage of revenue, and also because of the effects of the German occupation. During that ordeal heads of departments had 'renounced possible economies, sought pretexts to bring back officials who were prisoners, avoided dismissing employees who would have been in danger of being sent to Germany, even created services to justify the employment of staff in order to withdraw them from forced labour'.

The work of the Committee was, said the first Report, to be systematic and of long duration. There was a naïve enthusiasm for the 'new' idea of cost accounting: there would be 'as methodical a determination as possible of the prime cost of each service and of each subdivision of a service'. This would be 'a means of replacing competition between profit-making organizations' and 'perhaps even lead to actual emulation between divisions and establishments in the same category'. A sounder notion was that cost should be understood in the broadest sense: 'It will not suffice to ask oneself merely what some official formality costs in salaries and materials, one must also consider what it costs to members of the public, how much of their time it demands, what further red tape it involves for them.' The rather ingenuous faith in cost accounting has since declined with experience, and the Committee has tended to leave its *rapporteurs* to follow more pragmatical methods; but the wise view that unnecessary inconvenience to the general public is a costly form of administrative inefficiency has continued to hold the members' favour.

Enquiries were to be thorough; 'not the kind which is satisfied with an examination of papers and a chat with the boss'. Work should be observed in progress at every level: 'To understand the Customs, one should have accompanied a Customs captain, a cor-

[1] The published Reports have not hitherto been addressed to anybody, but were rather by way of a general record for public information. The decree of 14 October 1960, however, states, 'This report is addressed in particular to Parliament, to the Prime Minister and to the Members of the government.'

poral, an overseer, during their tours of frontier duty. One should have seen what a night watch is like. . . .' Consideration of the most modest type of work was not to be disdained. The often artificial barriers between different authorities were not to stop the investigators, who were always to study departments other than their own, 'in order that no reflex of habit may hinder their judgment'. This did not mean that they would lack competence; there were general administrative and technical considerations which were valid for any public service, but which were nevertheless often lost sight of. 'Progress achieved by one set of authorities', said the Report, 'has very often consisted of the adoption of methods employed by others.'

The role of the *rapporteurs* was to discern, firstly, any 'localized' defects, which they were immediately to bring to attention. They were to note whether a normal, well-organized control of the service existed, and whether the numbers of personnel and the needs of the work appeared to coincide. If organization and working methods were defective, remedies should be sought; small improvements were not to be neglected nor major reforms feared. Services which were insufficiently useful in relation to their cost should be reported; 'for example, road maintenance is most useful, but the cost of upkeep of a road with very small traffic may exceed its value to the public'. Duplication of work due to defects at high level was a matter for report. So were costly and troublesome formalities; 'for example, does the use of papers bearing a stamp duty, by the formalities it imposes on both officials and users, cost the public very dear in relation to the revenue obtained?'

Three categories of research method were recommended to the *rapporteurs*. Firstly, all available background information was to be obtained independently. There were the studies of earlier commissions, the reports of the ministerial corps of control,[1] the views of the *contrôleurs des dépenses engagées*[2] and those of the Budget Directorate of the Ministry of Finance, besides the reports of the Cour des Comptes. More surprisingly, the Central Committee declared that the trade unions had already proved 'a precious source of information about the needs of a service and the ways of improving it'.

The second research category was the on-the-spot investigation

[1] See above, Chapter IV, p. 79.
[2] See above, Chapter V, p. 92.

itself. In certain cases the investigators might reach the conclusion that a service was almost useless; the Committee had already adopted reports recommending the suppression of several bodies of this type.[1] Or the service might be useful but the effectives too numerous. The study of the historical background of departments, and particularly that of their staff establishments, was recommended. This would help to distinguish the useful from the purely hampering elements of tradition.

Study of the evolution of an administrative body, of its role and its organization can furnish valuable information. Only this historical analysis may explain certain peculiarities for which no logical foundation can be found. There are freaks of survival in the administrative field, as well as the biological, services which subsist because they were useful at a given moment, methods which continue to be employed solely because they corresponded to the structure of the public services under the First Empire or the ancien régime.

The Committee anticipated that most services would appear at first examination to be genuinely useful and without excessive staff. They should nevertheless be carefully analysed by structure, division of work, geographical responsibilities, routing of business (with a note on delays in transmission) and by the most precise and varied unit costs obtainable. If this analysis revealed localized inadequacies these should be followed up on the spot. In a department with dispersed services several should be studied locally. This was particularly stressed: 'Nothing can replace the information which can be given by the officials of local branches, who are familiar with the practical needs of their service and anxious to see the conditions of its operation improved.' The points of direct contact with the public and with local authorities should be personally investigated.

The third and final category of research method was comparison of the service examined with other services of the same ministry or of other ministries. This might show defects of inter-service liaison or duplication of work. Where operations under different authorities were basically similar the most effective and least costly system might be identified. Different study teams should maintain contact for this purpose.

The Committee which gave these imaginative directions to its

[1] This corresponded to the 'post-liberation' phase and is very rare in recent years.

rapporteurs was certainly not lacking in self-confidence. Indeed, it included enough officials of the highest rank to justify a certain buoyancy. It has, nevertheless, had to experiment to find the most suitable techniques and the levels at which it can achieve the best results. In 1946 and 1947 it undertook nothing less than a comprehensive review of military manpower, at a time when France was maintaining large armies in Indo-China and Germany, as well as at home and in North Africa. It recommended, among other things, the reduction of the occupation force across the Rhine from 90,000 to 45,000, and a service of two years for half the conscripts called-up. The Committee was perhaps out of its depth here, and its complaint that 'these conclusions have either not been put into effect at all, or only to an inadequate extent',[1] is scarcely astonishing. Similarly, its early zeal to establish a statistical basis for efficiency audit led to an evident lapse of discernment. It suggested as at least limited criteria for measuring the quality of a service: 'for a teaching establishment, the percentage of successes in examinations, or in the case of primary education the percentage of illiterates; for a law court the percentage of sentences altered on appeal; for a penal administration the percentage of escapes'[2] (*sic*)!

In its third report, a huge volume of 609 pages, published in 1950, the Committee reviewed the progress achieved. This was, it claimed, not to be minimized. An effort was being made to codify and simplify regulations. Measures of partial reorganization had been implemented. Often the investigator's visit and 'the mere obligation to specify problems' had permitted departments to see the need for reform. In some other countries the Committee's work had been followed with attention. Belgium had created a comparable body in 1949, charged to seek reforms in the services of the State 'which would reduce their cost by improving efficiency'.

But inertia had, inevitably, been encountered. The proposals put into effect had been those 'within the framework of the existing structure and traditional habits'. On the other hand, 'the recommendations which had as their objective a profound transformation of structure, the suppression of out-of-date methods, or a real effort of rationalization' had frequently remained without response. Too often, costly practices were continued 'in the name of traditions which are sometimes no more than routines', and

[1] Comité Central d'Enquête, 2nd Report, 1948, p. 45.

[2] Ibid., p. 14.

more efficient procedures were 'rejected as dangerous innovations'. Improvement of the productivity of the public services demanded 'intellectual investments as well as material ones'.

The Committee then delivered a memorable reproof:

> The French administration served for a long time as example and model for the nations of Europe. The time has come when its very history gives it a duty to realize that the respect for received ideas no longer constitutes the highest wisdom and the spirit of reform the supreme folly.

What had to be aimed at was 'the veritable transformation of a state of mind'.

While exhortations rarely create much impression upon public servants—who have perhaps heard them before—it should nevertheless be noted that the French civil service has shown a more dynamic and creative spirit since the war than it did previously.[1] There has been a new feeling that public servants ought to have ideas and should plan the country's future in a positive way, rather than contenting themselves with an impassive managerial role. The causes of this change are a matter for debate; the 'spirit of the Resistance' (from which emerged a generation of officials), rapid economic development, the 1945 reform of recruitment, even the loss of empire followed by what the French have called 'the rediscovery of the homeland'—all these have probably contributed. Perhaps the Comité Central d'Enquête has, by its innovating spirit, added something to the creation of a progressive atmosphere. It is, at any rate, itself a typical product of that atmosphere.

The fourth report of the Committee coincided with that body's tenth anniversary. During the ten years it had tried to carry out a planned investigation programme and it had also responded to requests for help from the government, the Commission des Finances of the National Assembly, and Parliament itself.

There was a tone of something like disillusionment; the Committee was finding its own level a little lower than it had expected.

> The lessons of history, as well as those which the Committee has been able to draw from its own experiences, prove, that except during

[1] I am obliged to M. Pierre Viot of the Cour des Comptes for pointing this out. It is admittedly an opinion, but it is a widely held one, for which some evidence can be cited. For example, civil servants have not only participated in French economic planning but have provided a great deal of the enthusiasm and impelling force behind it.

exceptional periods the modification of administrative structures is particularly difficult. . . . In these conditions, studies aiming at a revision of the number and structure of the ministries and of the organic laws which govern the public service, have little chance of retaining anything but a doctrinaire value for long: that is why the Committee, without forbidding itself such enquiries, has considered it opportune to present suggestions which are less ambitious but more easily put into effect. Administrative life is in any case sufficiently rich and diverse; subjects for consideration within it are abundant enough for studies limited in this way to remain assured of an incontestable utility. There is no doubt that the efficiency of the public services can be improved in many fields, and their operating costs can be reduced, even without applying fundamental transformations to them, which could only be derived from broad political decisions that the Committee is not qualified to take.

This passage shows a gain in realism and a growing understanding of the way in which such a Committee can function usefully even during periods when it receives no political encouragement. The power to go further can only be constructively exercised in the presence of a reforming government.

The Committee claimed that, '*The permanent search for a minimum of information about the activities of the public services*[1] is of absolutely prime interest.' It had in passing, aptly defined its own basic function, and (if 'activities' are qualified by the adjective 'financial') that of modern state audit in general.

The Committee noted with satisfaction that its proposals for reform of the budget estimates had been put into effect. In 1957, for the first time, an appendix to the draft Finance Act presented information about the cost and efficiency of some public services.

Reform of the presentation of both budget estimates and annual accounts is in fact an approach to administrative efficiency which has found international favour. The aim is, very broadly, to achieve 'a breakdown of figures which permits measurement of the cost of public intervention or investment in favour of one activity or another'.[2] It is an intention much more simple to express than to achieve. It involves not only problems of accounting technique but the established financial procedures of all public bodies. Only long term efforts can hope to overcome the innumerable difficulties. The American efforts in this direction have been noted. In

[1] Author's italics.

[2] Annex to the French Budget for 1959: Coût et Rendement des Services, Publics, p. 9.

France the principles involved were studied between 1947 and 1952 by a Budgetary Reform Commission under the chairmanship of Robert Jacomet, Controller General of the Army.[1] In the United Kingdom a new layout for Estimates has been accepted by the government and applied to the Civil Departments' Estimates as from 1962–3; one intention is to effect a link-up between the estimates and accounts of the state and those for the whole national economy.[2]

The fifth report of the Comité Central, published in 1960, reflected the impulsion of the new government, the head of which since 1958 had (from an administrative point of view at least) been M. Debré. The Committee's recent conclusions had already had appreciable results; the situation described in the previous report had been considerably improved 'by the effort of reform pursued on the government level'. Both the political conditions and the fact that the government held full powers had permitted the achievement of measures which in some cases were inspired by earlier recommendations of the Committee. Nevertheless, the Committee still renounced investigations into fundamental problems of administrative structure in cases when, 'it seemed that the reforms, although desirable, had little chance of being tackled by the public powers'. In a whole range of proposals, on the other hand, the Committee, 'convinced of the current importance of these problems', had 'applied itself to define the framework and the means for a policy of economic expansion and country-wide planning (*aménagement du territoire*)'.

Including subjects raised in the fifth report, the Committee had since its creation adopted conclusions on over two hundred separate investigations. These were in the earlier stages often organized as enquiries into single departments or services, for instance

[1] See *La Réforme Budgétaire*, 2 vols., Paris, Les Editions de l'Epargne, 1954.

[2] See 'Control of Public Expenditure' (the Plowden Report), p. 11. Command 1432, July 1961. On the general problems which must be faced in the task of modernizing government budgetary accounting, see also Jesse Burkhead, *Government Budgeting*, New York, Wiley & Sons, 1956. A study, hitherto unpublished, entitled 'Budget Expenditure; The Methods of Coordination and Control', was made a few years ago at Nuffield College, Oxford, by Mr A. H. M. Mitchell of the Treasury. A case for reform is briefly made by Kenneth S. Most, 'Management Accounting and Government Accountability', *The Accountant*, 22 February 1964, whose editorial stresses the point and stigmatizes government accounts as 'little more than a series of meticulously kept petty-cash books'. (The special problems of government accounting are not, however, adequately considered.)

the Directorate of Instruction in the Ministry of Agriculture, the Foreign Exchange Office of the Ministry of Finance, and the diplomatic and consular services.

There has, however, been an increasing tendency to undertake studies on a subject, rather than an organizational basis. It is this kind of research which is most characteristic of the Comité Central, in contrast to the efficiency auditing bodies in America and Germany, whose enquiries are almost exclusively classified departmentally. The classification by subject permits a highly informative approach; it amounts to a study of a whole administrative problem, and the resulting report will, if it is a good one, be of value to all concerned, from local officials to the responsible politicians, for purposes of information and record even if no immediate action is approved.[1]

Examples of 'subject' studies are numerous. Within the general field of responsibility of the Ministry of Finance, for instance, the Committee examined the questions of surplus stores, the manufacture and sale of tobacco and matches by S.E.I.T.A. (the

[1] The Select Committee on Estimates of the House of Commons, and its wartime replacement, the Select Committee on National Expenditure, have since about 1937, conducted studies of single aspects of administration which invite comparison with those of the Comité Central. There is an obvious and fundamental difference. The British Committees have (except for some war-time experiments) always worked by the traditional method of taking direct oral evidence from the various heads—and often only the heads—of the departments, branches and establishments concerned. The Comité, on the other hand, sends its reporting teams behind the scenes within the departments, to obtain information wherever they see fit and form their own impressions. Ever since the early twenties, the Estimates Committees have repeatedly considered the possibility of obtaining some kind of staff to conduct enquiries on their behalf but this has been refused them. The verdict of Professor Chubb, the leading student of financial control by parliamentary committees, was as follows: 'Whereas the Accounts Committee functions at the culminating stage of a long professional examination, the Estimates and Expenditure Committees perform for themselves the only external investigation of efficiency that is made. Indeed, an expert and scientific review of the process of administration . . . is, as yet, hardly attempted even internally by the Treasury. But such an "efficiency audit" would be an essential preliminary to any parliamentary inquiries which are to be more than the present amateur general reviews' (*The Control of Public Expenditure*, 1952, p. 227). It should not be inferred that reports of the Comité Central always create a greater impression of depth and sagacity than those of the Estimates Committee; this is not the case. The Comité, however, is able to cover a wider field, and when its *rapporteurs* produce reports of high quality the amount of inside information at its disposal is greater.

state monopoly), and the operation of five nationalized banks, including the Bank of France. In the Ministry of Foreign Affairs it studied French cultural relations and operations abroad. Within the field of Defence, it produced conclusions on the winding-up of old enemy contracts, the social services of the military ministries, aircraft production policy and the nationalized aircraft companies, and the policy of the Ministry of Marine with regard to real property. Under the general headings of Reconstruction and Housing, the Committee reported upon war damage, the problem of official accommodation in the Paris region, the simplification of formalities in connection with the construction of housing estates, and 'architects and building technicians in their relations with the State and local authorities'. The National Education Ministry's field produced interesting subjects; historical monuments and sites, the national theatres, scientific and technical research, and 'the simplification of administrative formalities which university regulations impose upon students'. Similarly, under Industry and Commerce, 'the simplification of official formalities imposed upon commercial and industrial firms' was the basis of a report and conclusions. At the Ministry of the Interior, subjects of interest were the electoral list and 'the organization and work of schools for the Police and the Sûreté Nationale'. In the realm of the Minister of Justice, both 'the organization and working of the Courts' and the penal administration were considered, together with 'the administrative formalities for registration of births, marriages and deaths, and the simplifications which could be applied to them'.

Among noteworthy studies in other fields were, 'the problem of Indo-Chinese labour in France' and 'the cost of alcoholism to the public finances'. A number of reports have been of concern to several ministries and departments; under the general heading of 'the State and its Suppliers', purchasing policy for textiles, fuels, vehicles and office supplies was considered in detail. Office mechanization, civil servants' housing and 'the delimitation and regrouping of administrative regions in metropolitan France' were further problems common to various departments. So indeed was 'the reclassification of civil servants repatriated from North Africa and the French Community' (there were more than 32,000 of them from Morocco and Tunisia alone). No less than 34 reports on different types of 'parafiscal taxation'[1] appeared in

[1] See above, Chapter VIII, pp. 187–8.

the Committee's fourth report. A statement of conclusions entitled 'the organization of work in public authorities and enterprises' dealt with the results achieved by their various internal O. & M. branches.

The Comité thus provides the convenience of a permanent source of information upon administrative problems of all kinds. Often they are important, but would scarcely have been vital enough to merit the appointment of special ad hoc bodies to consider them. Even the relevant basic facts and statistics essential for a broad view of any administrative problem may be dispersed or unavailable, and one of the most useful functions of the *rapporteurs* is to gather them together. This is one notable way of providing regular guidance for government.

As for the type and quality of the Comité Central's conclusions, no generalizations are possible. Often the recommendations are modest in scope and proposals for radical changes tend to be exceptional. Among the various conclusions which are set out in its fourth report, are cases where the Committee had asked for regrouping of various scientific research bodies in the overseas territories, for the suppression of 35 local gaols, for reorganization of the sales service of the tobacco monopoly, for modification of policies adopted for a statutory housing loan system[1] and for 'transformation of the budgetary and accounting rules in force in state industrial and commercial establishments, in order to permit them to function in conditions closer to those of private enterprises'.

A study incorporated in the same report may be taken as an example of actual procedure. This was an enquiry by a member of the Conseil d'Etat, as *rapporteur* for the Committee, into a troublesome problem, the organization of the authorities charged with construction of schools and universities. A number of offices were concerned, but their responsibilities conflicted at various points and the matter had been the subject of repeated but inconclusive studies within the Ministry of National Education. The *rapporteur* produced a comprehensive and fully documented report of 180 typed pages and recommended the creation in the Ministry of a Directorate of Educational Construction with unified powers. He felt that this was a relatively modest reform, but an indispensable minimum, because 'retention of the existing organization and methods would not seem to permit the rapid

[1] The *fonds national d'amélioration de l'habitat.*

and economical execution of a major programme of school building'. The Committee supported this proposal and it was accepted by the government. A directorate broadly conforming to the suggestions, but with a different name, was created by decree in 1956.

The proposal to create a new organization, even if it takes over staff and responsibilities from existing ones, may meet relatively little opposition. The Committee, however, investigated a declining institution, the public pawn-offices called Caisses de Crédit Municipal, but better known under the traditional name of *monts-de-piété*. Their creation, said the Committee, resulted from historical circumstances, but their retention was not always justified by contemporary economic needs. Their loan operations and their staffing arrangements were examined. The picture was one of gradual decay. The Committee's proposals for a reduced and more realistic general organization were mostly given effect by decree.[1]

Sometimes the reports, even if they have no striking recommendations or if their proposals are not accepted, contain a flash of administrative insight. Thus, when criticizing the operation of subsidized vocational training centres, the Committee comments: 'Under these conditions, the State pays out subsidies without being in a position to judge the merit of the expenditures, and it authorizes these without itself controlling how they are spent.'[2] In another case, the Committee gave expression to the following significant opinion: 'In this field, as in many others, it is less advisable to seek immediate and apparent economies than to endow the services with such real resources as they require to cope with the tasks which are entrusted to them.'[3] Administrative minds have broadened since the days when Committees on organization were appointed solely to make 'cuts'. It is not now rare for them to sympathize with the plight of minor bodies and defend them against uninformed criticism. The object is to make institutions work, whilst ensuring that their activity is rational; organizational change is the remedy only when, even if given adequate means, they cannot work efficiently.

It might have been supposed that the Comité Central's usefulness would decline with the end of post-war confusion and the return to 'normality'. On the contrary, the reports give an im-

[1] Comité Central d'Enquête; Fourth Report, pp. 228–35.

[2] Ibid., p. 282.

[3] Ibid., p. 287.

pression of increasing effectiveness as the Committee learned its delicate task. The quality of observations in the fifth report surpasses that of its predecessors. The observations on regional economic planning were particularly valuable and had a considerable influence on the Commissariat Général au Plan as well as in legislation. The Comité pointed out, for example, that although fully detailed economic information had become available for the country as a whole, there was no such data on a regional basis suitable for the planning of a proper territorial distribution of economic activity. The under-developed areas were precisely those about which there was least information. The fact also had to be faced that the *département* was no longer a unit always suited to administrative realities. Grouping into regions was desirable for various purposes, but the regions should as far as possible be the same for all services.

The Committee sounded a note of alarm about the 'disarrangement' of the Paris region by increasing over-population and lack of regional authority, which had 'permitted the particularist tendencies of the various technical and administrative services, both national and local, to manifest themselves openly'. In 1955 a Commissioner of Construction and Town Planning for the Paris Region was appointed. One of the earliest acts of the government of General de Gaulle, in July 1958, was to give this high official adequate powers, as proposed by the Comité Central. The creation of a single administrative authority for the whole Paris region is under consideration. The Committee's views were followed when the legal, administrative and financial status of local authority hospitals was reformed by the new government in December 1958. The Committee recommended a drastic, and apparently well-justified[1] reform of the National Immigration Office; the report does not quote the outcome. But when, on much weaker grounds, it proposed the suppression of the National Office of Navigation, a canal and river authority, this was not accepted.[2]

This unusual but now well established investigating body thus enjoys an influence much greater under the present regime than ever before. It may lose it again under a new government, but it

[1] The Office had been established in 1945 to recruit foreign labour and provide it with temporary housing. Both these functions had lost most of their importance, and the Office had engaged in what the Committee calls 'substitute activities'—a familiar administrative category.

[2] Comité Central d'Enquête; Fifth Report, 1960, passim.

will even then presumably continue to do what it can to introduce new ideas into the administrative services and maintain at least their debate even if their realization is more difficult. It will thereby help to counteract that 'lack of fresh air' against which public servants have with reason been warned.[1]

Germany

In choosing their post-war approach to the problem of administrative efficiency, the Germans were able to base themselves upon a successful precedent in the Sparkommissar of the Weimar Republic. Already during the formation of the new Federal civil service the President of the Bundesrechnungshof had been called upon to act in a consultant's capacity. The Act which founded the Bundesrechnungshof, dated 27 November 1950, provided that the President was, 'at the request of the Bundestag, the Bundesrat, the Federal Government or the Federal Minister of Finance, to give his expert opinion upon questions of importance for the control of public funds'. He could perform the same service for public corporations,[2] and for the Länder. Under the terms of the old Reichshaushaltsordnung of 1922, which remained in force, the Bundesrechnungshof was in any case charged to make recommendations for a more economical and rational organization of the administration,[3] as a function of the general audit.

In 1952, the Federal Cabinet decided that something like the old post of Sparkommissar should be revived. What was necessary, said the Cabinet Decision document, was an office whose holder could, on his own initiative, make general proposals for economy and efficiency which were not connected with the rendering of the accounts and were even in advance of the actual expenditures. The President of the Bundesrechnungshof, Dr Meyer, was charged with the duties of 'Federal Commissioner for Efficiency in the Administration'. In 1957 the two posts were made automatically concurrent for the future.

The Commissioner was furnished with a set of Guiding Principles (Richtlinien) for his activities. He was to advise the Federal Government 'on all questions of simplification and economy in the administration, with the object of diminishing its cost and raising its efficiency'. His responsibility extended over

[1] E.g. by Mackenzie and Grove, op. cit., p. 200.

[2] The German term is *Juristische Personen des öffentlichen Rechts.*

[3] Under Section 96(4) of RHO. See above, Chapter VI, p. 115.

the whole Federal Administration, including the post office and the railways[1] and all public bodies and establishments which handled funds subject to audit by the Bundesrechnungshof. He was to make efficiency audits, and his attention was especially directed to the division of responsibilities between the various Federal authorities and between the Federal government, the Länder and the communes. He was to make recommendations at the request of Parliament,[2] the Government, or any of the Federal Ministers. He could, however, also make investigations and recommendations on his own initiative—an important element of strength in his position. In drafting his recommendations, which were to be addressed directly to the bodies or persons which had asked for them, he was to be 'independent of any kind of directions whatsoever'. The heads of every department which engaged the Commissioner's attention were ordered to assist him or his representatives with information, the production of files, or in any other way, and were on request to appoint an official as co-worker in the investigation. The Federal Ministries were to make the Commissioner a party to 'organizational or financial measures of major monetary significance'. The Commissioner was to be concerned in the preparation of the budgetary estimates, no doubt partly because this would give him the opportunity to criticize the expenditures of departments which neglected his recommendations.

The Federal Commissioner could also, on request, act for the Länder in a similar way, and could obtain such information about local authorities as he required, subject to their assent. He could, on the motion if any Federal Minister, be present as an adviser at sittings of the Federal Cabinet when matters within his terms of reference were being considered; he was entitled to submit proposals on such matters to the Cabinet. He was also authorized to attend or send representatives to sittings of the Bundestag, the Bundesrat and their committees. Finally, he was to co-operate with the Finance Minister by notifying him of all the requests to undertake investigations which he received from other sources and by sending him copies of all recommendations and proposals made.

[1] In Germany the Federal Railways are organized as a direct government service, not a nationalized corporation. See Chapter XI, below.

[2] Since 1958 the Budget Committee of the Bundestag, which reviews departmental estimates, has also been entitled to ask for the Commissioner's recommendations.

Much of this was handed down from the time of the Sparkommissar. That officer had, however, been allowed to recruit a personal staff from outside the civil service. The Federal Commissioner was not permitted to do this but was directed to make use of the existing President's Section (Präsidialabteilung) of the Bundesrechnungshof. This is now the small but strategically placed headquarters staff of organization and methods studies in Western Germany. In early 1960, this Section consisted of only thirty persons, but with an exceptionally high proportion of senior ranks. This is not accidental; these men are employed as efficiency auditors, to participate in actual missions, and it is intended that their studies should concern the highest as well as the subordinate ranks in each authority examined. Indeed, the President of the Bundesrechnungshof, in his capacity as Federal Commissioner, frequently participates personally in the missions for part of the time. In principle, the rank of each examiner is equated roughly with that of the officers interrogated, for apparent psychological reasons. O. & M. in Germany thus starts at the top. In fact, as far as the Federal Commissioner and his staff are concerned, it often stops in the middle ranks; minor posts are usually regarded as a question for the chief organization officer (Organisationsreferent) of each Ministry. This is not an invariable rule, however.

German O. & M. is thus an external and independent control, and it can give weight to its conclusions both through the Federal Commissioner's published reports and through his function of advising during the preparation of estimates.

The Federal Commissioner's investigations are more in the nature of 'traditional' organization and methods studies than those of the French Comité Central d'Enquête. They are in fact overwhelmingly 'departmental' rather than 'subject' studies. They take into consideration the whole range of internal activities and problems. The following questions are mentioned as normal matters for examination: departmental responsibilities, distribution of duties, conduct of business, regulations, office services, cash handling and accounting methods, personnel management, accommodation, purchasing and supply arrangements, and office mechanization. For the last of these the Bundesrechnungshof employs specialists as examiners. Other experts may be employed during studies of technical departments, such as research establishments. They may criticize equipment and machinery on grounds of unsuitability. Economists also participate in certain missions. These consultants are often borrowed from specialist departments or from among retired officials.

The procedure followed on missions is different from that of the French *rapporteurs*, and from that of the General Accounting Office, which combines all aspects of audit in the same operation. A team operating on behalf of the German Federal Commissioner might in a typical case consist of about ten men. They would make a preparatory study, principally from documents such as the organization plan of the department concerned. The actual investigation would follow in two separate stages. The first stage might last for two or three weeks. During this time every departmental officer from the highest down to routine level should be questioned about his duties, and the responsibilities of every division and section noted.[1] When the basic fact-finding is complete the examiners take a break in which to sort their material and discuss it, sometimes in the presence of the Federal Commissioner, who is in any case kept constantly informed of progress. The second stage of the mission, lasting about two more weeks, permits a follow-up of particular lines of research suggested by the findings of the first stage. The mission ends in a final conference with the heads of the department examined; in this the Federal Commissioner normally takes part. He then prepares his recommendations, which are addressed to the sponsor of the enquiry if there was one, or to the responsible Minister if there was not. The Minister is in any case solely answerable for the conduct of his department and for acceptance or rejection of recommendations within his field of authority. Copies are, however, sent to the Budget Committee of the Bundestag, which can use its influence when the estimates are submitted for approval, and to the Federal Chancellor, who has general powers of organization in the administration. The recommendations therefore carry weight and receive careful attention.

They are usually in two parts. The first is a general one covering the tasks of the department examined. The second contains detailed recommendations about organization and methods. These cover the normal questions of quantity and 'quality' of work,

[1] In Germany all ministries are divided into a limited number of Abteilungen and subdivided into numerous Referäte. There is no such precise nomenclature in Britain, but a translation of Abteilung as division and Referat as section suggests their relative importance.

numbers of staff and of divisions and sections, office machinery, and so on. In general, no post is assumed before a mission to be necessary, except that of the permanent head of a ministry (Staatssekretär). All subordinate posts and branches, beginning with the highest, are considered as to necessity, volume of work and position in the official structure. The quality of individual personnel is not assessed, but if the examiners consider that the staff is excessive because of inadequate performance the result may be a recommendation to reduce the establishment. The Commissioner normally includes what he considers to be a rational and justifiable organization plan in his conclusions.

The association of this efficiency audit with the Bundesrechnungshof is deliberate. In the first place, there is close co-operation between the President's Section, with its special responsibilities, and the general auditing Sections of the office. This involves not only the auditors' advice, based upon their experience of the departments scheduled for efficiency study, but also their actual participation in the 'O. & M.' missions. The President is permitted by law[1] to transfer senior officers from the 'audit side' to his own Section for temporary duty, and this permits considerable strengthening of the teams. In the second place, the state audit body already possesses the indispensable assets of statutory independence and right of access to information. The third main consideration is the personal authority of the President of the Bundesrechnungshof, in his multiple role. He is able to follow up different aspects of the same general problem in his separate published reports. He can exert some influence through the Federal budget machinery. He or his representative take part in both the Finance Minister's preliminary discussion of estimates and their later debate in the Budget Committee.

The President and Federal Commissioner's position is further strengthened by a third important function. He is also Chairman of the Federal Civil Service Committee (Bundespersonalausschuss), established in 1950. This Committee represents an effort towards 'democratization' of traditional German staff management in the public service, which formerly consisted of leaving to each Minister wide general responsibility and independence for personnel matters in his own field, subject to an oversight of regulations by the Ministry of the Interior and of remuneration by that of Finance. The Committee was created to advise upon 'excep-

[1] RHO. Section 125(3).

tional cases in staff management', and to take decisions in certain circumstances, powers formerly enjoyed by the Interior and Finance Ministries. The Federal Civil Servants' Act of 1953 assigned new powers to the Committee. It was to decide the qualifications to be demanded of candidates for the civil service from other professions. It was also given an important general task, namely that of 'forming an opinion about complaints from civil servants and rejected candidates in cases of fundamental significance, and making proposals for remedying shortcomings in the application of civil service law'. Every government official was accordingly granted the right to submit petitions and complaints to the Federal Civil Service Committee, which thus responded to the need for a sort of court of equity for public servants. It has developed a code of precedents in cases concerning individuals and it exerts a formative influence upon the personnel management of the administration generally, by its participation in the drafting of civil service regulations on recruitment, training and other subjects. 'It is not an accident that the President of the Bundesrechnungshof is the Chairman of the Federal Civil Service Committee. The reason lies in his judicial independence, which qualifies him to be a wholly impartial Chairman.'[1] His work as Federal Commissioner must also give him insight into many of the problems of staff management.

This is a remarkable combination of powers, responsibilities, connections and possibilities of asserting influence, all combined in one independent person with three interconnected roles as chief state auditor, examiner of administrative efficiency and senior regulator of staff management for the whole Federal civil service. The opportunities for an experienced, judicious and tactful man to improve the tone of the public service must be considerable. This is especially true when set against the background of post-war Germany, which has had to reconstruct its civil service in circumstances of exceptional difficulty. In addition to the physical destruction and political dismemberment of the country, these difficulties included the doubts and suspicions of denazification, the reversion to federalism after a highly centralized Hitlerism, the influences of old authoritarianism and new politics, the stresses of Allied occupation and business ambition, the rivalries of religion, and the tension between a stern career tradition on the

[1] The Private Secretary to the President of the Bundesrechnungshof in a letter to the author, dated 21 February 1961.

one hand and the need to find employment for armies of refugees on the other. The isolation of Berlin, home of the pre-war officialdom of the Reich, has added a major complication. It is not astonishing that there have been jealousies, talk of corruption and party pressure and other unedifying symptoms.[1]

The audit of efficiency appears to be working satisfactorily. The published reports of the Federal Commissioner, far from giving the impression of an immature experiment, strike a note of greater cogency than his more traditional audit reports. They are shorter but more vital in content. The efficiency audit apparently enjoys a higher prestige and priority in endeavour; it is here that the greatest advances are being made.

The former Federal Commissioner Dr Hertel expressed views on the nature of his duties,[2] and some of his points are of special interest. The term which he preferred was 'administrative simplification', which must, he considered, be differentiated from 'administrative reform'. By the latter he understood, 'only such changes as affect the fundamental realities and laws of the administration, which have political importance, and which regulate anew the relationship of the citizen to the public service and thereby ultimately to the state'. Such changes were landmarks in the development of any civil service; they were as rare as they were significant, and they were definitely measures in the political field. Administrative simplification lay more in the spheres of organization and efficiency, within which improvement, economy and a reduction of complexity might be achieved by limited measures.[3] Not only the general public but even officials themselves tended to be in favour of this; the Federal Commissioner cited the example of a trade union, the Federation of German Tax Officers, which had made proposals for simplifying tax legislation and collection.

Legislation was in fact, according to the Commissioner, an important field for simplification measures. The principle that

[1] On the post-war German civil service, see, for example, Robert G. Neumann, *European and Comparative Government*, pp. 417–21, New York, McGraw Hill, 1955.

[2] The late Dr Guido Hertel, in a radio talk: 'Kann man die Verwaltung vereinfachen?' and in several monographs.

[3] The distinction between 'reform' and 'simplification' is a useful clarification. The French, for example, use the term 'administrative reform' in a way which encompasses measures of simplification, which are nevertheless quite different in character from fundamental legislative changes.

laws should be simple, clear and lucid was unfortunately not always respected. The more this could be achieved, the better in general would the public service function, since administrators work among the laws and by means of them. But one type of recent legislation alone had led to the issue of about a thousand regulations in a few years, and officials were obliged to find their way through 'a labyrinth of implementing rules, supplementary orders and amendments'. An 'attic-clearance' of laws had been successfully begun, and amongst the still valid laws passed since 1867 'a very high percentage had been found to be absolutely superfluous'. The Commissioner considered it especially important that there should be 'a careful administrative examination of laws before they are passed, from the points of view of their practicability, the cost of their execution, and especially whether they will require the creation of new administrative bodies'.[1]

The late Commissioner Hertel suggested that it would mean an important simplification if the principle of annual budgets could be relaxed in favour of budgets embracing two financial years. It was his general view that 'a simplification within the administration usually leads also to an alleviation in the sphere of the private citizen'.

But the structure of the administration itself was his principal concern. There should, he said, be a greater 'simplification at the top'. Such rationalization had been achieved wherever the chance appeared. Rearmament had, for example, been undertaken through a single Federal Defence Administration; more progressive and economical in manpower than a return to three independent branches of the forces, for land, sea and air, each with its own private administrative service. Civil Defence had also been placed under undivided authority.

The reports of the Federal Commissioner show the efficiency audit in operation. Most of the missions are undertaken at the request of the ministers directly responsible, the Minister of Finance, or the Budget Committee of the Bundestag. Often the requests

[1] 'I have several times stressed that draft laws not merely require scrutiny from the point of view of their legal form, but that their administrative content must also be reviewed' (Dr Hertel, in a talk at Speyer, 15 February 1960). The Report of the former Commissioner, Dr Meyer, dated 29 June 1956, indicates that something of the sort already operates: 'The drafts of laws and Cabinet orders of the Federal Government (about 1,200 annually) are forwarded to me. As far as may be necessary, I make proposals for the simplest and most appropriate execution of the measures contemplated.'

arise when departments ask for increased staff, and in such cases the Budget Committee, when considering departmental estimates, pays very close attention to the Commissioner's recommendations.

In the case of the Federal Institute for Labour Exchanges and Unemployment Insurance (Bundesanstalt für Arbeitsvermittlung und Arbeitslosenversicherung), negotiations with the government about the cost of administering unemployment assistance upon an agency basis reached deadlock, and this gave rise to an investigation by the Federal Commissioner. His representatives visited the Institute's head office and many labour exchanges, and he made use of the findings of regular audit by the Bundesrechnungshof. The result was a number of recommendations of basic importance for the Institute. There should be co-operation and pooling of staff between the 'exchange' and the 'assistance' sections; personnel transfers should follow seasonal requirements, to the former in the summer and the latter in winter, with a consequent substantial reduction in the use of temporary staff. The headquarters should be considerably decentralized; the internal control branches could be reduced. More assistance might be paid fortnightly instead of weekly. The Commissioner's 'target plan' recommended that the staff requirements of the Institute be reduced within a limited period by several thousand permanent and temporary officials. For the administrative costs of the Institute, he proposed 4·5 per cent of expenditures on assistance; the Institute had asked for as much as 7 per cent, amounting to a settlement of 316 million Deutschmarks for four years' work. On the basis of the recommendations this figure was reduced to 166 millions. Despite the fairly radical nature of these findings, both parties to the negotiation undertook to accept them.[1]

When the Federal Ministry for Food, Agriculture and Forests requested substantial staff increases, the Commissioner found that a good deal of work was being done which could be carried out by subordinate or private bodies, or reduced in volume. One whole division, two sub-divisions and 28 sections of the Ministry could be dispensed with. The total staff should be slightly reduced forthwith and further posts marked in the budget as 'pending suppression'. Some temporary staff of high rank could be replaced by permanent officials of lower grade. The budget for 1957 took these proposals into consideration.[2]

[1] Report dated 29 June 1956, pp. 69–71.

[2] Report dated 4 July 1957, pp. 108–9.

A study of the administration of the Federal Post Office amounted to several years' work for a team with expert advisers. Among their numerous recommendations was the abolition of six Communications Equipment Offices. Spare parts for communications equipment were held in twenty separate depots: 'that', said the Commissioner, 'is uneconomical and inexpedient. I have proposed that the parts be placed in a single store and issued by post.' In March 1955 there were 1505 independent Post Offices; this number was considered so large as to complicate administration and stand in the way of the best arrangements for transport of mails. The Commissioner recommended that the small offices should become Branch Post Offices, grouped under larger ones, reducing the total of independent offices to less than a third. The powers of Head Postmasters (Amtsvorsteher) could then be broadened and the regional Post Directorates relieved of a burden. Four small Directorates could in fact be dispensed with altogether. After reorganization in one city instead of dispersal in two, the Central Office for Communications Technology could be reduced in staff. The administrative areas for Post and Communications should in future be the same. An organization plan for the Ministry itself provided for a reduction of 14 out of 67 sections. Most of the changes were incorporated in the 1957 budget and more were expected in 1958.[1]

In considering the organization of the Ministry of the Interior, the Federal Commissioner, 'carefully bore in mind' its historical development and traditions, its exceptional influence and its comprehensive functions. He found nevertheless that a number of its tasks could be transferred to subordinate bodies. The Ministry had, on its own initiative, abolished one of its divisions during the audit. The Commissioner proposed the abolition of 20 of its sections and advocated a total staff of 794 compared with the existing 855; a further 41 posts could be spared later. The eventual saving in salaries alone would be in the neighbourhood of 1·5 million DM. The Ministry was represented on no less than 342 'advisory boards, special committees, working groups and other bodies', which the Commissioner considered to be excessive. The resolutions of the Bundestag on the 1958 establishment of the Ministry were mainly based upon the Commissioner's recommendations.[2]

The Federal Public Health Office (Bundesgesundheitsamt) in

[1] Ibid., pp. 111–13. [2] Report dated 19 August 1958, pp. 133–4.

Berlin requested a large increase in personnel. The Commissioner was in this case uncompromising. 'I consider', he wrote, 'that the demands for an expansion of staff and for an upgrading of the senior personnel are both unjustified.'[1]

The Bundesrat asked the Federal Commisioner to investigate the rapidly rising subsidy paid to the Institute of Applied Geodesy at Frankfurt. He found that the Institute had engaged extensively in commercial map production, which had not only proved unprofitable but was not, in his view, a necessary or proper activity for a leading scientific body. He therefore opposed the construction of a new building for it and considered that the subsidy might be reduced.[2]

The Commissioner found that the headquarters of the Ministry of Labour and Social Policy, which then administered about two-thirds of all Federal expenditures of a social nature, had too many tiny sections and he proposed a reduction from 98 to 65. During the course of the audit the Ministry took the initiative in deferring its requests for increases and upgrading.[3]

The Federal Commissioner was critical of the air-traffic control body, the Bundesanstalt für Flugsicherung. The training courses for controllers were of a far higher standard than was justified by the needs of the work. This was both costly in itself and resulted in the control staff being over-graded in comparison with comparable duties elsewhere and overpaid in relation to other trades in their own office. Meanwhile the Federal Republic had heavy expenditures for airports, the less busy of which were particularly unprofitable.[4]

In the Ministry for Family and Youth Questions, which he examined on behalf of the Budget Committee of the Bundestag, the Commissioner found weaknesses in financial control. Subsidies to private bodies under the so-called 'Federal Youth Plan' were largely regulated by advice from numerous committees. These contained many representatives of the subsidized bodies. 'Since distributors and receivers in these cases are in fact identical, the danger of a collision of interests is not to be excluded,' wrote the Commissioner. The work of internal audit was heavily in arrears. Some of the vouchers from the subsidized bodies contained serious defects, and the Commissioner proposed that in appropriate cases the Ministry should send its auditors to examine the

[1] Report dated 24 October 1959, p. 139.
[2] Ibid., pp. 139–40.
[3] Ibid., pp. 141–3.
[4] Ibid., pp. 143–4.

utilization of subsidies on the spot.[1] Thus efficiency study points back to audit, from which it has itself evolved.

Any kind of state audit must develop or collect, as best it can, a set of standards, a 'doctrine', upon which to base its work.[2] The basic ideas which are emerging from the German efficiency audit have been expressed in preambles to the Federal Commissioner's reports.

In the first place, 'the tasks of simplifying the administration and raising its efficiency must base themselves upon the knowledge and experience which accrue from the continuous audit'. The co-operation of the regular auditors makes it possible to manage with a small specialized staff.

Secondly, it is emphasized that 'publicity makes possible effective control and fruitful criticism'. This principle is fundamental for all state auditing, but it now can be extended to questions of organization in public authorities; this was once a private concern of the civil service, but Parliament and national opinion now take an interest.

The Commissioner's audit has developed a theory of ministerial structure from German official tradition and an estimate of modern needs. This owes something to the views of the former Federal Chancellor, Dr Adenauer, who told the Bundestag in 1957 that Federal ministries should be capable of clear supervision by busy ministers, and that they should not, therefore, exceed a certain size. A ministry should, according to the audit reports, be 'a suitable directive instrument', not a collecting-point for miscellaneous tasks of routine as well as regulation. The duties proper to a ministry are, it is maintained, capable of identification. The list includes such obvious matters as the preparation of legislation, co-operation with other high authorities and the distribution of public funds, and, altogether, it is not very long. All 'non-ministerial' activities should be delegated to other bodies. Thus there should, on the one hand, be decentralization.

On the other, there should be 'organizational concentration'. The intentions behind this are to tidy-up the structure of the

[1] Ibid., pp. 148–9.

[2] For example, the 'doctrines' of British state audit are mostly to be found in the volumes of the *Epitome*. (It should be added that such 'doctrines' in the various countries are very far from being comprehensive in scope, and often provide no guidance in dealing with new audit cases which come to light.)

ministry by removing an excess of organizational units (whose 'empire-building' tendencies are assumed to be endemic), and at the same time to bring the whole department more effectively under the minister's control. 'Concentration' means 'making the administrative structure more compact at all levels'. Divisions and sections should be sufficiently large to avoid the danger of over-specialization and narrowness of outlook. Hierarchies should not be too long, so that heads of divisions can maintain close personal contacts with their sections and transact business rapidly. Only the divisions should be allowed direct responsibility to the minister and the permanent head; a very few exceptions to this rule, are however, justified. One of these is the internal audit (Vorprüfungsstelle) whose work requires independence and freedom from influence.

Committees and working-groups are a phenomenon of modern ministerial activity which is, in the view of the Federal Commissioner, being carried to excess. They often survive even after their original tasks are completed, and they take up a great deal of officials' time. A 'screening' of the inventory of committees is therefore necessary.

The Commissioner, however, has himself formed a committee of the Budget Officers, Organization Officers and Directors of Establishments in the various ministries, for the exchange of experiences on questions of organization. He tries to ensure that every ministry grants them the status and facilities necessary to overcome 'antiquated habits, narrow departmental thinking, personal interests and other obstacles to reform'. An 'organization group' has been set up in the new Defence Ministry, with training from the Commissioner's own auditors, and another group is bringing O. & M. into the orderly rooms of the army itself.

If some sort of firm views about the organization of ministries have now evolved, the severe problems of legal and administrative relationships between the Federal Republic and its member states are still under study, in collaboration with academic bodies. The Federal Constitution, according to the Commissioner, is not clear enough on these matters of division of labour. Another organizational field which has posed many new questions is that of scientific research in the public service.

The efficiency audit has views on many matters of detail in official organization. For instance, heavily amended volumes of regulations are considered a menace and the auditors always ask for them to be re-drafted. It has been found generally more efficient to lease ministry canteens to concessionaires, subject to contractual protection against 'an improper search for profit', rather than to administer them directly; the concessionaire is as a rule 'a specialist with corresponding commercial and management training and experience'. After what the Commissioner called 'the long years of isolation', Germany has gone to the other extreme by sending larger and more numerous delegations than other countries, to a total of over sixty international bodies; the spirit of internationalism is welcomed in principle, but efforts are made to restrain its more costly exuberances and abuses.

The German efficiency audit is working on different, or at any rate more closely defined, subject-matter than that in France or America. It concerns itself less with the expediency of administrative policy; of what the departments actually do. It is principally an audit of 'establishments' and of 'office services'; of the internal ordering of the departments, considered from a high level. Its interest in the business transacted by any official body is mainly confined to its effects upon the office organization, whereas the French and Americans study such business activity for its own sake. What is most interesting about this German audit is that although the findings are simply recommendations, they have, because of the Commissioner's various means of asserting influence, a considerable chance of being put into effect. And even if the proposals have no practical result, their publication in the Commissioner's report brings them to the notice of interested opinion. This audit is at least a significant attempt to regulate the departments of a state openly and upon rational principles.

* * * *

Efficiency audit is in existence and flourishing in three out of the four main Western countries.[1] In the United States, where the proposition that the management of government agencies and corporations should be subjected to studies as rigorous as any employed by private business has tended to be accepted as obvious, tests of organization and efficiency have formed part of 'com-

[1] In Britain, a Civil Service efficiency committee is to be formed, under the chairmanship of Sir Philip Allen of the Treasury. Its purpose appears to be the consideration, in association with the Civil Service trade unions, of factors affecting efficiency (*The Times*, 12 April 1965). It is not clear whether this committee will examine the subject of efficiency audit.

prehensive audit' for more than a decade. In France and Germany these studies were developed as a specialized technique closely associated with, but not part of, the normal state audit. Both countries now have over fifteen years' experience and are making steady progress in the use of efficiency auditing as an external control of the administration.

The audit of efficiency is not a substitute for internal organization studies but something largely different. It examines official structure, duties and performance, sometimes in a similar way, but at all levels including the highest. At other times it goes beyond the traditional field of 'O. & M.'; it looks at a piece of administrative activity from a detached viewpoint and asks itself whether what is being done makes sense. It is not a confidential servant but a constitutional critic with a constructive mission. By the use of publicity it widens the debate upon matters which affect the careers of many thousands. It provides parliaments, governments and even civil servants themselves with access to information which is otherwise not systematically gathered by anybody. Efficiency audit can and does co-exist and co-operate effectively with departmental organization study groups, which supplement its work on their own level. But for the strongest reasons of both organization and methods, such groups cannot fill the role of an efficiency audit. The groups are internal and dependent, the audit external and independent, and these positions are forever incompatible. There is therefore no real problem of competition between O. & M. and efficiency audit, but rather one of co-ordination.

The great merit of an efficiency audit is that it opens a window upon an administrative hierarchy and its activities. It is hard to see how such an insight could be obtained in any other way. The strength of hierarchies lies in their discipline, but their corresponding weakness is that it is very difficult for them to be generators of ideas. This again is a simple consequence of organization; debate and discord about new ideas must place a strain upon the disciplinary structure. The views of a hierarchy must necessarily be those of its heads, and even Commissions of Enquiry tend to receive only this view by asking questions. The 'official view' may of course be excellent, but since it corresponds to what is actually being done it does not form a basis for fruitful debate about principles. For this an informed independent view is necessary.

This is especially important in matters concerning personnel, where the executive is subject to agreements with and pressures from trade unions and individuals. It is particularly difficult for even the best-intentioned personnel management officer to be an innovator. 'Any attempt at reform by a responsible official,' says Edouard Bonnefous, 'is a dangerous adventure in which he knows that he will be blamed for failure but he is not sure that he will be given credit for success.' The most senior officers have reached a position which allows more opportunities for innovation, 'but force of habit and the success of a favourable career generally give them a satisfied attitude'.[1]

Professor Millett in America finds the same kind of situation. 'The human-relations aspects of organization', he says, 'tend often to make for organizational inflexibility. Indeed, in terms of the social relations and expectations of any group, change entails fear of the unknown or unfamiliar. The accustomed modes of work then appear to be the best, almost the only, pattern of administrative effort.' And yet, 'whenever an administrator and his staff become convinced that everything is perfect in their particular agency, one can be fairly sure that a period of stagnation has begun to set in'.[2] In such a situation the absence of all publicity forms an incomparable protection for inertia and self-satisfaction.

Those persons who maintain that administrative bodies can safely be left to adapt themselves in a progressive way, tend to overlook the very strong influences which favour the adoption by even the most originally-minded public servants of negative rather than positive policies in organizational matters. The executive is probably *not* the best guardian of its own efficiency. It needs the stimulus of ideas from a non-responsible body which has access to all the facts. Such a body can, as in America and Germany, increase the stimulus by co-operating with committees of the legislature. At the highest it can, as in the time of M. Debré's French administration, act as the instrument of a reforming Prime Minister.[3]

[1] Bonnefous, op. cit., p. 57.

[2] Millett, *Management in the Public Service*, pp. 179, 275.

[3] 'Administrative reform is not a purely technical operation; it has, on the contrary, an essentially political aspect and requires a period of vigorous action on the part of the Government. The necessary impetus, even in the matter of administrative reform, must come from the authority situated at the highest level.'—André Molitor, Chef de Cabinet, Belgian Ministry of Education and Chairman of the Supervisory Committee of the International Institute of Administrative Sciences (in *O. & M. Bulletin*, October 1953).

Efficiency has been called 'the sole ultimate test of value in administration'.[1] And yet the word has overtones of something akin to inhumanity; it may suggest the rigid discipline of the production line and the time-and-motion study man. In the present state of the English language the word has no substitute, but in its administrative context it calls for a little explanation. What is this ultimate good which is being sought?

Those who, like the Comité Central d'Enquête,[2] talk of changing a whole state of mind are perhaps nearest to the right idea. Any kind of organization may be either dynamic or static in spirit. In an age of economic expansion the national administrative services should not be static and negative, since they influence the tone and the achievements of all other institutions. They should indeed be motors and not brakes, and to be so they must be prepared to accept a regular tune-up themselves. The mechanism is sensitive, even refractory; an expert second opinion on how to tune it up is the best guarantee that it will be done properly. A degree of publicity for both faults and remedies is the best guarantee that it will be done at all.

But change can create its own dynamic and give rise to new enthusiasms in the minds of administrators. A habit in the public service of constructively and openly debating its own domestic problems might well contribute to the development of similar habits about technical problems of national importance. The idea that administrators should leave all such debate to politicians is scarcely any longer tenable; when all parties accept economic progress as a major objective, there is a very wide field for technical ideas in which questions of political principle do not arise. A really modern public service would be what R. H. Tawney called 'mentally adventurous'.

The possible effects of such a fundamental change of spirit form an exciting subject for conjecture. It might enable civil servants to meet three needs which are not yet widely recognized as essential to good government, but which are predictable for the none too distant future in increasingly complex modern states.

The first of these needs will be for administrative, and indeed political, action to be based upon profound research. In the past many large acts of policy have been founded upon small stocks

[1] By Luther Gulick in *Papers on the Science of Administration*, Institute of Public Administration, New York, 1937.

[2] Quoted on p. 230 above.

of factual knowledge, imperfectly understood. It has come to be realized that governments knew less than they were believed, or believed themselves, to know. In tightly integrated and thickly populated societies, expediency and hunches will no longer suffice as a basis for decisions. The societies themselves will have to be subjected to intensive exploration and analysis; not just occasionally but continually. One type of research, which is not entirely new, will be into the relationships between the estimated cost of alternative types of projects, policies and programmes and their anticipated yields in positive results ('cost/effectiveness studies'). A refinement of this will be research which attempts to compare such alternative programmes in terms of their total economic and social consequences. Government by research has indeed already been given its initial trial, by the late President John F. Kennedy.

The second need derives from the first. Government in the future will scarcely content itself with the mere regulation of the economic processes and the provision of an adequate minimum standard of living for all (difficult though these attainments may be and revolutionary as they would have seemed to a nineteenth-century theorist of laisser-faire). It will no longer seem adequate to provide work for the masses, or to maintain them when there is no work, if they still have to live in squalid, obsolete, ugly cities, without facilities to sample the good things of life or the values which we call civilization. Government is certain to concern itself more and more with the *quality* of life; to aim at the provision of a good environment and equality of opportunity for the citizen. It will become increasingly apparent that only government can furnish these intangible assets in an adequate and systematic way. But the task for government will be hard, and its significance here is that the essential research upon which plans will have to be based cannot be confined within the disciplines of economics, however broadly conceived. The aim of research will be nothing less than a vision of the good life itself; a vision neither utopian nor narrowly moralizing, but a reasonable, attainable objective for the augmentation of human happiness.

This points to the third need. Administration, which has always been shackled to the problems of the moment, will have to think and plan a full generation ahead. Without this, life in overcrowded societies may become intolerable; the use of space on the ground, which is fated to be the scarcest resource of all, will alone demand it. Any improvement in the quality of life will depend upon it.

These three tasks, then, loom large among others in the future of administration; permanently organized research, attention to the quality of living, and the long forward-look. They will call for a wholly new spirit, a new efficiency; for nobody could maintain that the ethos of the public services developed in the Victorian era was favourable to speculative thought. The change will be great, but not impossibly so. Since 1963, the French Commissariat Général au Plan has had a '1985 working-group', specifically charged to think of the long term future. Their planning is not confined to the stark materialism of the technocrat.

They are not satisfied (says Bertrand de Jouvenel) that we should turn out ever more goods in a worsening environment, degraded by pollution, noise and ugliness; nor that we should retrieve larger fractions of time from work without conveying the culture which makes leisure enjoyable and profitable.

The practice has therefore developed of assessing new technical processes in economic terms and then considering what influences, desirable and undesirable, they will exert upon the way of life.[1] Thus civil servants have begun to meet unprecedented challenges with suitably original responses. Perhaps we should accept that intellectual adaptability has become the highest criterion of efficient administration. It is an attribute remote from a static and mechanical view of administration, a quality which has seldom hitherto been a conscious objective of the public services; but it is destined to be greatly in demand.

We have so far assumed the search for efficiency to be a positive and progressive function; and so it should be. But another view is possible. It has been suggested that the inherent characteristics

[1] Bertrand de Jouvenel in *The Spectator*, 14 February 1964, and Bernard Cazès, 'Group 1985', ibid., 26 February 1965. M. Cazès records that the '1985 working-group' recommended, 'that at the centre of each great public administration there should be a planning section, whose task would be to provide a running analysis of long-term tendencies likely to have an effect in fields which require action by the government'. There was need for 'further research into the factors and conditions of economic growth, the social tensions it creates, and the economic imbalances which hinder its progress'. (*The Times* of 20 March 1964 maintained in its editorial that the time had arrived when the utilitarian approach to planning 'should be modified with a more active concern for worthy and pleasant living'. See also Professor J. K. Galbraith, 'Economics v. the Quality of Life', *Encounter*, January 1965).

of public administration include so few natural incentives to improvement that there is a tendency always present towards an actual decline in efficiency.[1] Following this interpretation, the work of organizational study and the stimulus of its publicity can be seen as elements of defence rather than attack. By seeking to improve here and there, the efficiency auditors and O. & M. men are fighting to maintain a general average standard.

On either view, efficiency is a practical, not a visonary aspiration. Without the systematic search for it, the public service may remain a brake or its standards may actually decline. In any event, a certain amount of change is desirable for its own sake; excessive rigidity in any organization is the despair of the bolder spirits.

Efficiency audit has shown that it works; it has contributed to the productivity of administration and reduced its cost, whilst itself costing next to nothing. It has increased awareness by its reports which, almost for the first time, have held up before the public services a true image or at least an expert outsiders view of themselves. Of course the attentions of an efficiency audit may not always be uniformly welcome to an executive. But they are infinitely preferable from its point of view to the activities of 'axeing' commissions of the old type, which may otherwise be forced upon it.[2] To take the broadest view, an 'open' efficiency audit might be a kind of protective mechanism; it may reassure opinion that the public service really faces facts and has its own affairs in hand.

[1] R. M. Dawson, *The Public Service of Canada*, Oxford U.P., 1929. In lighter but not frivolous vein, Professor Northcote Parkinson describes the process of 'organizational paralysis' in his essay on 'Injelititis', which is his name for the disease of moribund institutions (*Parkinson's Law*, London, John Murray, 1958).

[2] This old expedient is by no means forgotten. The creation of a group of 'Treasury liquidators' has recently been proposed in Britain; they were to be 'hatchet-men . . . moving from department to department'. The ministry concerned was often to have 'virtually no say at all' in their decisions (*The Economist*, editorial, 27 January 1962).

CHAPTER X

The National Auditors: Their Work and Status

The members of the greater Exchequer each have their own particular functions, but they all have the common aim and duty to protect the King's interests, without injustice, according to the laws and customs of the Exchequer. This system or procedure has the authority not only of the influential personalities who direct it but also of long-established tradition. It is in fact supposed to date from the Norman Conquest, and to be modelled on the Exchequer of Normandy, although it differs in many important respects. Some people even think that it existed under the Anglo-Saxon Kings. . . .—The Dialogue of the Exchequer, by Richard, son of Nigel, Archdeacon of Ely (later, Bishop of London) and Treasurer of the Realm, c. 1179. Book I.

A CERTAIN amount has been written in Western countries about the historical, legal, constitutional and organizational bases of state audit, though by no means all of it has been published and there is a lack of synthesis. Since the Second World War a common basis of research has begun to show signs of development, concurrently with the greatest period of experiment and advance which state audit has ever experienced.

But almost nothing at all has been written about the actual desk work of state auditors themselves. It is hardly surprising that there are popular misconceptions.

One of these is the idea that the state auditor spends his time laboriously and monotonously checking vast piles of vouchers, all alike; seeking, usually in vain, for petty infringements of the regulations and arithmetical mistakes. Such work was certainly a reality in the past. The last Premier Président of the Chambre des Comptes of Paris, vainly endeavouring to save that medieval body from the reforming zeal of the French revolutionaries, told the Constituant Assembly in 1790 that his officers had 'dedicated themselves (to use the terms of ancient ordinances) to *des fonctions moult mélancolieuses*'. Only the desire to serve their fellow citizens sustained them in 'these tedious labours'.[1] No doubt there was truth as well as rhetoric in this plea.

The modern version of the *fonctions moult mélancolieuses*, the meticulous voucher audit, is familiarly known as 'tick-and-turn-over'. State audit departments in the nineteenth century were mostly required by law or expected by their governments or parliaments to check and verify the regularity of absolutely everything which appeared in the annual accounts. With the relatively modest activities of the state in those days this was at least technically possible, although there could be no guarantee that the auditors actually and conscientiously carried out these requirements.

But in the twentieth century a total audit ceased to be even a technical possibility, unless audit staffs were to be allowed to grow to a huge size. Only in America does any attempt appear to have been made to equate numbers of auditors with the growing volume of expenditures, and the result was the unwieldy General Accounting Office which excited the wrath of the first Hoover Commission. Elsewhere, the principle of the test-audit was conceded. Even the Exchequer and Audit Departments Act of 1866 gave the Comptroller and Auditor General authority to accept as adequate certain departmental checks. This, however, applied only to the accounts of the Army and the Navy, and the Treasury could if necessary direct him to conduct a full audit.[2] The amending act of 1921 formally relieved the C. & A.G. of his statutory obligation to conduct a detailed and complete audit of all accounts, although the Treasury still retained the power to request a more comprehensive examination.[3] This change in the law was, as the Treasury said in a minute in 1922, not an innovation but was rather to give statutory effect to existing practice under which in recent years 'the examination of the public accounts had tended to diverge in certain respects from the literal and inelastic provisons of the Act of 1866'.[4]

The Reichshaushaltsordnung of 1922 gave the Rechnungshof of the German Reich quite simply the authority to 'restrict the audit of accounts according to its best judgment' and to waive the submission of vouchers.[5]

[1] Quoted by P. de Mirimonde, *La Cour des Comptes*, p. 32. (Four years later the Premier Président who spoke these words was sent to the guillotine.)

[2] 1866 Act, Section 29. See also above, Chapter IV, p. 74.

[3] 1921 Act, Section 1(2), and p. 74, above.

[4] *Epitome*, vol. 1, p. 639.

[5] RHO., Section 94.

The general adoption of test-auditing coincided with the improvement of internal audit and the growing attention of the national audit bodies to matters of greater moment than mere regularity. The test-audit was needed not only to cope with mushroom growth in the size of accounts but also to give the state auditors time to think. The decline of 'tick-and-turn-over' need not be regretted; the painstaking search for minor errors included a good deal of misplaced zeal and it tended to bring state audit into disrepute. It was hardly proper to a control body at national level to concern itself on a large scale with matters which in relation to total state spending were trivial, and which in many cases had been checked already. Some of this kind of work still exists; it may be viewed as a necessary check upon the internal audit. But it has certainly long since ceased to be the main work of state audit, if indeed it ever really was.

There is another general idea of the state auditor as a verifier of columns of figures, a checker of cash and stock balances, dedicated to detailed examination and certification of the accounts. This is the auditor in his commercial role, applying the Company Acts to that Leviathan company which is the State. There is some truth in this picture; these are necessary functions. In Great Britain the auditors do not make physical checks of cash or stores in hand; in Germany, on the other hand, spot checks of cash balances may be ordered.[1] But to a large extent these also are tasks appropriate to the internal audit. The checking of additions is rapid and simple with mechanical aid. The great columns of figures must be scanned rather to ensure that they have been properly classified and that no significant sums of money are passed without seeing what they were spent on. The verification of a major account is a responsible task mainly because it ensures co-ordination between the various auditors who are engaged upon study of blocks of expenditure within it. The co-ordinator alone can recommend when the whole account may be certified correct.

But certification is simply a matter of arithmetic and regularity. It cannot preclude subsequent observations upon matters of principle; the basis of such observations may be a piece of government business which continues through several financial years and can only then be seen in perspective and understood. It may have been wasteful and extravagant without invalidating the certification that the accounts were correct, since at no point in the

[1] Under RHO., Section 97(1).

long transaction was there technical irregularity. Certification of accounts can scarcely take note of the merit of expenditures.

Yet as we have already seen, it is the examination of such merit which is to an ever-increasing degree the *raison d'être* of the state audit of accounts. By and large, the audit of regularity is not very demanding work. The discretionary audit of the merit of transactions, on the other hand, requires skill and judgment of a very high order. Almost everything of importance which nowadays reaches the level of the published reports of state audit bodies, and thus relates to their major constitutional rule, arises in the first place from observations based in some way upon 'merit' rather than upon 'regularity'.

It is therefore vital for the best success of state audit that the nature of the merit audit, the qualities which it requires, and the organizational structures most suited to it, should be assessed and understood. This is a difficult matter, upon which one can only offer suggestions.

The state auditor at his desk is assigned a block of expenditure, small in proportion to the total spent during the year but not small by any other criterion. Five, fifteen, forty, a hundred million pounds in the year, perhaps more; it may easily be more than the entire national budget of a century ago. It will probably consist of a piece or pieces of specialized expenditure corresponding to headings in the budgetary estimates; for example the purchase of ships and stores in a Naval administration, the construction of schools and universities or the pay of teaching staff in an Education ministry, the farm and market subsidies of an Agriculture department, the grant of pensions and assistance to several kinds of beneficiaries by various authorities. It might cover the salaries and allowances of the staff of a ministry, aid to under-developed countries, or the trading activities of a postal administration. It might equally be a block of receipts, from taxation, the disposal of surplus equipment, or otherwise obtained. It may be expenditure involving subsidies to, or co-operation with, local authorities, nationalized and private industry, international organizations or foreign powers. It could be one of those blocks of unexpected and miscellaneous expenditures which governments accumulate from law-suits, grants of compensation, settlement of claims and other contingencies. Or the auditor might be assigned to a block of expenditure on a regional basis, for example the spending of a military area command or a provincial hospital authority; or as in

France, to the accounts of all local paying officers in a particular region, covering transactions of great variety. Again the state auditor may be given responsibility on a subject basis within the overall account of a ministry, without reference to any clearly identified block of expenditure; for instance 'contracts for airfield construction', 'depot and store accounts', 'trading accounts' or merely 'contracts'. And he may be assigned to the accounts of state enterprises and nationalized industries, or to efficiency audit of the public services generally, in the many countries where such controls now operate.

Within his assigned field, whatever or wherever it may be, the state auditor is sovereign and alone. Only he can explore this unknown financial territory and map out what he finds there. He will not operate in the same area for ever, but whilst he is there he must familiarize himself with its every feature and with everything which is going on. He must acquire by observation and reading, a limited amount of expertise in the subject which concerns him for the time being; in the development of new weapons of war, in hospital management, in airfield engineering or motorway construction, in tax assessment, in agricultural subsidies, in the main current problems of military or foreign policy (which will have financial repercussions), and so on. He must understand the administrative and statutory relationships which govern, or limit, the activities of whichever department he is auditing; for example, the division of responsibilities between central, and regional or local authorities. Unless he acquires a little specialized knowledge of this sort, he can hardly expect to spot when things go wrong or to understand even when they do not. And he must become a genuine expert in a few administrative subjects; perhaps the most important of these are purchasing and contracting, in all their aspects, which will certainly be among the main sources of his observations in most fields of audit.

The solitude of the explorer is a particular characteristic of this work. The state auditor may theoretically be directed in his studies and searches; in practice this is scarcely possible.[1] Nobody else

[1] This kind of audit, says the Cour des Comptes, 'certainly cannot be subjected to any compulsory rules. The volume of operations to be examined, the diversity of possible observations and the considerations peculiar to the various services oblige the auditors to work out by experience the most effective methods' (*Principes et Règles Générales de Vérification*, 1960 edition, Part III, Chapter 1).

has the time to share them with him. He may be able to obtain guidance from the audit office records and advice upon specific points. For the rest, he is on his own, and if things escape his notice they will remain undiscovered. He cannot be instructed what to find, because nobody knows what is to be found except perhaps the officials of the executive who prepared the accounts, and they have no interest in the promotion of disclosures which may lead to criticisms of their department's activities.

The auditor must acquaint himself with the legislative backgrounds, basic policies and working procedures of the authorities which are accountable for his group of expenditures or receipts. He may see vouchers from time to time[1] and note their 'regularity'; but their main utility to him will be to show what the department is actually spending its money on. He will probably notice that expenditures are concentrated largely upon a limited number of continuing services, courses of action or individual contracts. It is the nature of these which must have first claim upon his attention. By the examination of departmental files and by asking questions, he will gradually obtain a picture of them and reach the point at which he feels able to judge them critically. This may not take very long; a 'fresh' auditor recently assigned to a field of expenditure is sometimes the most fruitful critic. He is still capable of surprise and has, unless he is a raw recruit, a basis of comparison fresh in his mind. Some fields of audit are, however, so specialized and technical that their essential features cannot be learned in a short time.

There are very few fixed criteria and rules for the assessment of 'merit' in public transactions. Some guidance may be available from precedents such as those set out in the Epitome of the Reports from the Committees of Public Accounts in the United Kingdom. But it is often difficult to associate a new point of criticism with the principles inherent in completely different cases in the past.

There exists, however, a vague, empirical and uncodified set of standards as to what constitutes good administrative practice.

[1] Some state auditors may in fact hardly ever see a voucher, but may base their audit upon the circulation of documents, such as contracts. In any case the essential sources of information for 'merit' auditors are almost always the departmental files. It is part of the skill of an auditor to know what sort of files to call for and what to look for when he receives them.

To some extent this is based upon documents such as the Epitome, but for the rest its foundation is unwritten common sense and it tends to be accepted in all countries. It is not impossible that the frontiers of good and bad administrative practice could, with much new research, be closely defined. But the variety of cases which may arise is unlimited, and in the present state of jurisprudence it is perfectly possible for a shrewd and thoughtful auditor to raise quite original criticisms and create new precedents.

This points to a second special characteristic of this work; just as the man working alone upon the accounts must direct his own researches, so also must he make his own assessments of what he finds. His criticisms may be rather obvious. It is patently not good administrative practice to loan public funds to private bodies or persons without security, and the point is emphasized when the borrower fails to repay. It is clearly not good practice to maintain manufacturing accounts for a factory in a way which gives a completely false impression of the cost and efficiency of production, even though the reason may be that the accountant does not know his job properly. Most of the things recorded in Chapters VII and VIII above are recognizably much less than good administrative practice. And yet such things have happened. But in other cases the issue may be very subtle. If, for example, a government has to make extensive purchases from a trade which consists only of large numbers of individual craftsmen and if their price tenders show wide discrepancies for identical work, is it good practice for a department to suggest to the craftsmen what it considers to be a fair sort of price? If costly changes of plan seem to be desirable during the conduct of a construction contract, is it good practice to follow the expensive dictates of technical expediency or to stick to the strict terms of the contract? In all sorts of purchasing, of both goods and services, there may be conflict between technical and financial considerations, and an administative decision must be taken as to which shall be given priority. Whatever the circumstances, the auditor must look at the facts and decide whether to criticize or not, and if so upon what grounds.[1]

[1] M. de Mirimonde, of the Cour des Comptes, has this to say about the state auditor's work: 'The authority charged with *a posteriori* control must have plenty of technical skill at its disposal, because the researches which it has to conduct are difficult. . . . Often, it will be necessary to use a method similar to historical criticism. Accounts and vouchers are generally more remarkable for what they conceal than for what they state. One may have to reconstruct the whole story of transactions which were deliberately recorded

Only when he decides to raise an observation does the matter come to notice at higher level. He must not only form an opinion as to the merits of the case but must support it with a careful report and full and accurate documentation. He must open a file, and it must be historically and factually correct. Nothing is more damaging to his reputation than criticism which is based upon faulty or inadequate research, since the audited department is apt to draw a very natural satisfaction from pointing this out in reply to an official observation.

The superior officers of the auditors who open the cases must act as a 'filter' for them. They may dismiss them as trivial, or disagree with the conclusions. They may refer back to the originators for further information. They may see alternative ways of criticizing the transactions concerned. They will refer to the highest level, at which the state audit reports are produced, observations distinguished by their large scale, their novelty or their content of principle. They may occasionally suggest lines of research which they hope will be fruitful. They cannot, however, initiate the consideration of individual cases, except in the rather rare event that these come to notice from an outside source. Only the auditors working on the actual accounts are in close and constant contact with the facts and unless they personally see scope for criticism in any pieces of business these will not be brought to notice at all. It is one of the curious and inescapable characteristics of state audit that, save in exceptional cases, the initiative of practical work can only come from below.

From this the conclusion might be drawn that advantage would exist in maintaining ease of contact between the upper levels and the men who alone originate observations and are able to explain and give further information about them; in other words that 'long' hierarchies with many levels are scarcely appropriate to the work of state audit. In many 'active' administrations the problem is largely a matter of feeding directive impulses downwards; in state audit it is rather a question of feeding information

---

incompletely or piecemeal, by bringing together documents for comparison, to disclose a submerged fraud beneath a surface or regularity; one must know how to distinguish the exaggerated clauses of a contract and expose their onerous consequences; how to examine the application of laws and regulations to determine their practical disadvantages. If this work is well done . . . it will bring fruitful results. The danger to be avoided is that such a control becomes merely formal and formalist' (*La Cour des Comptes*, pp. 10–11).

upwards. But only in the Cour des Comptes, where the auditors may advise in debate and even vote upon the observations which they have personally raised, does anything by way of a specialized office structure, permitting easy contacts at all levels, exist. And even this is an accidental consequence of the judicial and collegiate nature of the audit body rather than the planned outcome of a study of its organizational requirements.

Another problem of organization is whether the audit is best conducted at a central headquarters or permanently dispersed, as in the ministries and departments of Great Britain or in regional and overseas branches of the General Accounting Office. On the one hand, dispersal permits very much closer contact with the sources of information; on the other, it attentuates the links between the researchers and the users of their findings. The former is almost certainly the more important consideration. With the growing intricacy of modern government operations, 'centralized' audit is tending to become an anachronism.[1] But the contrary consideration is nevertheless an important one, to be mitigated as far as possible. A feeling of isolation is not an incentive to good work. It may easily become a feeling of insignificance.

Besides conducting his desk researches upon departmental records, the state auditor is often a traveller. A great deal of national expenditure is incurred at what are sometimes called 'out-stations', which may be depots, regional offices, dockyards, barracks, hospitals, research establishments, prisons, airfields or a variety of other things. It is also in these places that most stores are stocked and issued and most construction projects take shape. There is no substitute for the local visit if the quality of decentralized administrative operations is to be assessed. Even if he does not use the sophisticated techniques of the efficiency auditor, the visitor is called upon to make broad judgments about the standards of cash and store accounting, contracting methods and internal controls, based upon the actual transactions which have taken place.

[1] 'The natural evolution of financial control towards more and more advanced forms should lead to the installation of permanent missions of the Cour within the organizations which are subject to its audits. Magistrates taking part as attentive and informed observers in the daily life of these bodies would penetrate much deeper than today in understanding of their mysteries' (E. Chalandon, 'Que peut la Cour des Comptes?' in *Revue de Paris*, November 1950). Nothing has yet come of this suggestion in France.

The state auditors themselves

In view of the difficulties and demands of the state auditor's duties, it is scarcely surprising that the performances of different individuals are very unequal. Nobody can blame an auditor for failing to produce observations; the explanation may always be that the account concerned offers nothing which merits criticism. The fact remains that some state auditors seem to find weaknesses in almost any account, whilst others rarely raise anything of importance from any account. The difference may be particularly noticeable when there is a change of auditors responsible for a particular block of expenditures. It is a matter of international experience that some auditors appear to possess a kind of sixth sense; in the United Kingdom this has been called 'the audit mind'. The Germans say that some of their auditors have 'a nose'; the French call it simply 'flair'. Probably some detectives and physicians have a similar attribute. The burden of productive research is everywhere borne by the limited number of persons who possess this mysterious quality. It is they who originate almost all the enquiries which end in constitutional action or at least publicity through the published reports. 'Flair' is vitally important for the test-audit; some auditors have an instinct for choosing the right subjects and documents for study. They also have a gift for analysis and comparison, without which facts and figures are often meaningless. A small staff of auditors with a flair is much more effective than a large staff without it. Obviously the state audit bodies have a real interest in finding staff likely to possess this enlarged critical sense, and in nurturing it thereafter. It is absolutely crucial for the quality of the audit and its reports.

And yet in this respect the actual practices of the various national audit institutions are of almost astonishing diversity. Whereas the four Western countries which are our central concern have some sort of common ideas about the best background and training for medical men, lawyers, engineers and even commercial accountants, there is very little sign of any common ground in the case of the profession of state auditor. Perhaps the requirements of the work have yet to be systematically assessed and disentangled from those of the 'established' professions, and until this is done the practices of recruitment in particular are liable to be based upon irrelevant historical considerations.

The facts of the staff situation are these. In the U.S.A., the

General Accounting Office appears, until the reforms carried out by Comptroller General Warren, to have had a large audit staff, 'with simple clerical skills and a familiarity with regulations'[1] but without specialization. From the time of the Government Corporation Control Act of 1945, the 'comprehensive audit' approach was adopted as an ideal and gradually introduced in practice, and a new recruitment policy was a consequence.

The General Accounting Office began to recruit graduates and qualified accountants from outside the public service. The demand was greater than the supply and the G.A.O. came under 'a good deal of criticism for sending inexperienced people around to make the evaluations demanded by the comprehensive audit'.[2] But by 1954, more than a third of the comprehensive audit staff of over 1,000 were from direct college recruitment. The G.A.O. was then conducting examinations in the universities for the position of Accountant (Comprehensive Audits) at grade GS-5 in the general classification of the American civil service. The office 'publicized through press and radio' its examination for this position, and offered higher grades from GS-7 to GS-15, designed to secure personnel with greater experience.[3] In 1955, the office had 299 Certified Public Accountants out of a total of 2,957 'accountants, auditors and investigators',[4] but recruitment was still difficult and in 1956 the G.A.O. obtained the authority of the Civil Service Commission to engage qualified college graduates for the entrance grade without a written examination. The Comptroller General reported that 'quality of personnel was being stressed'. Offers of appointments as junior auditors had been made to 104 colleges and universities, and 126 graduates accepted in June 1956. Regular contact was established with 'faculty members' in expectation that this would be 'invaluable in the recruitment of top-level college graduates'.

A training programme, which was organized in co-operation with the Civil Service Commission, was expected to facilitate more rapid advancement.[5] A recruiting programme was also in operation for 'higher grade level accountants'. A training pro-

[1] Hare, op. cit., p. 10. [2] Ibid.

[3] Annual Report, C.G. of the U.S., 1954, p. 102.

[4] Ibid., 1955, p. 1.

[5] The training consisted of an intensive three weeks' course followed by six months of 'on-the-job training'. The aim was to outline the duties, responsibilities and objectives of the G.A.O. and training included 'consideration of working problems, both theoretical and practical'.

gramme for senior personnel was planned. A general effort was being made to improve the attractiveness of the career, and the progress of every individual was being closely watched 'in order to ensure that his potential was developed to the fullest possible extent'. Some States accepted experience in the G.A.O. as counting for Certified Public Accountant examinations; the other States were being asked to do so.[1]

By 1959 the total of Certified Public Accountants had risen to 396. There were also 1,282 'noncertified accountants', and the total of 'accountants, auditors and investigators' was 2,908. 135 students from 86 colleges and universities in 34 States entered the General Accounting Office during the year. The training programme continued and it included 'seminars for supervisory and top management personnel'.[2]

The General Accounting Office has thus clearly placed itself in the hands of the accounting profession.[3] The change was initiated by Comptroller General Warren and energetically pursued by Comptroller General Campbell, who is himself a Certified Public Accountant. Signs of professionalization are abundant. In a recruiting brochure addressed to students, Mr Campbell wrote: 'The performance standards for our audits conform to those adopted by the American Institute of Accountants. Our offices . . . conduct examinations in a manner comparable to any large independent public accounting organization.' A 'complete transition to this professional concept' was a big task, but it was being undertaken as fast as the staff of experienced accountants and auditors could be increased. There is no doubt that the public accountant's qualification is now regarded as a great asset to a member of the Office; in July 1959 four out of five directors of auditing divisions were holders of it.

The Certified Public Accountants are not, however, the same group as the college graduates, although they include many of them. All men and women recruited as auditors now come from colleges and universities, and most of them have 'majored' in accounting and related subjects. Choice is by college record,

[1] Annual Report, C.G. of the U.S., 1956, pp. 4–6.

[2] Ibid., 1959, pp. 243–5.

[3] The legal side of the G.A.O.'s work is naturally separate, and for this the office recruits high-quality graduates from university law schools. In 1959 there were 508 'attorneys and employees engaged in legal and quasi-legal work', and of these 112 were doing 'work requiring bar membership'.

together with an interview. The graduates then still have to take C.P.A. examinations, and they are encouraged to do this within the General Accounting Office. The brisk general demand for such graduates not only led to a relaxation of the entrance formalities, but to a rapid system of advancement. In 1959 it was possible for a capable graduate to rise from an entrance salary of $4,980 per year in five stages to $10,000 a year within five to eight years. He then had further prospects of advancement to director with a maximum of $17,500 a year, and possibly to Assistant Comptroller General at $20,500. This compared favourably with the best channels of advancement in the American federal service, which in 1959 included only a few professional posts with salaries greater than $17,500 a year and none in excess of $22,500.[1]

Nevertheless the auditors do not always remain with the General Accounting Office. Some of them take senior posts in Government agencies, in industry[2] and in professional accounting. Mr Campbell has aimed at a policy of maximum retention of staff and he reported that the turnover in 1959 had declined. And as a result of new legislation which permitted recruitment of graduates at a higher grade (GS-7), he recorded that the new entrants showed 'a marked improvement in academic achievements'.

The United States has obviously made up its mind about the staffing of the General Accounting Office, and at least the position is clear. It may reasonably be judged that the professionalization of the Office has improved its status and corporate morale, which were patently very low in the late 'thirties and early 'forties. It may also have improved efficiency. It must certainly be a source of satisfaction to the accounting profession, which is thus installed in an influential position in the government service.

But what has happened in the United States derives apparently from the assumption that accounting qualifications are the best, and indeed the only, suitable background for a state auditor. This is a conclusion which is easily reached by a layman or a member of the profession, but it is to a considerable extent based upon unfamiliarity with the real nature of the state auditor's work. It is a conclusion which no doubt seems obvious in the United

[1] *Official Register of the United States, 1959* (U.S. Civil Service Commission).

[2] The fact that some auditors have joined the staff of government contractors does not appear to be regarded as in any way compromising or dangerous in principle.

States, in view of the name of the state audit body and its special duties which unquestionably call for the attention of professionals (prescribing of accounting principles and standards throughout the government service). But the fact remains that the studies which an auditor of the merit of transactions is called upon to make often resemble historical or other academic research, and the judgments which he has to form are about law, precedent, public policy, administrative practice and plain common sense, much more often than they involve any kind of technical considerations of accountancy other than the simplest. There is no compelling reason why state audit should be entirely conducted by qualified accountants; nor is there any strong reason for supposing that a training in accounting is best calculated to develop the essential characteristic of a state auditor, which is 'flair'. This is a very strong critical sense (dependent upon and inseparable from an ability to think deeply and systematically). A case could be made for the view that there are other less technical forms of higher education which are more likely to develop the critical faculty.[1] A state auditor should acquire at least the rudiments of accountancy, and he might occasionally benefit from the advice of a skilled accountant on some specific point. But he by no means necessarily has to be one.

That at least is the European conclusion, and the state auditors of Britain, France and Germany are not professionally qualified accountants. But if these three countries are in agreement to this negative extent, their staffing policies disagree on almost everything else.

The situation in the United Kingdom is simple. In 1920 three great general classes were created in the home civil service, based upon the Report of the Reorganization Committee of the National Whitley Council. There was to be an Administrative Class, to be concerned with 'the formation of policy, with the co-ordination and improvement of Government machinery, and with the general administration and control of the Departments of the

[1] It is significant that in the United States accountancy is regarded as a subject appropriate for university graduates. In Britain, however, the customary way of acquiring the professional qualification is still to be 'articled' in the office of a practising accountant, or in other words to serve a kind of apprenticeship, often after ceasing general education at a comparatively early age. Thus to be a member of a given profession may mean quite different things in different countries.

public service'. There was to be a Clerical Class dealing with matters of general routine. And in between these two there was to be an Executive Class, whose lower grades were to undertake 'the critical examination of particular cases of lesser importance not clearly within the scope of approved regulations or general decisions, initial investigations into matters of higher importance and the immediate direction of small blocks of business'. It was decided between the Treasury and the Exchequer and Audit Department that the work of the existing 'Examiners' fell within the definition of the duties of the new Executive Class. Part of the wording of that definition may have been arrived at with the special case of these auditors in mind. It could perhaps be argued that, having regard to the nature of the audit based upon considerations of 'regularity', which was still overwhelmingly the main occupation of the office at that time, the decision was a realistic one. It might well, however, have been more realistic to decide that the state auditors did not fit properly into any of the three classes, which were essentially designed for the work of the 'active' departments of the executive.

The decision confined the state audit service within fairly rigid career limits. It did have the virtue of establishing a generally capable[1] and coherent auditing force, based upon a fairly distinct educational and social group, with no artificial barriers to promotion between the bottom of the office and the Secretaryship next to the top. On the other hand it fixed the status and careers of the state audit staff at a level in the public service which is unquestionably and demonstrably the lowest of any major country in the Western world.[2] It made Britain the only country in which the state auditors are in the anomalous and sometimes uncomfortable position of being lower in rank than the directing grades in the departments whose financial activities they are supposed to

[1] Evidence of its capability may be seen in the fact that a discretionary audit, taking account of the merit of transactions, developed spontaneously out of the statutory audit of regularity. Such a development undoubtedly presupposed numerous individual initiatives over a prolonged period by the auditors actually working on the accounts.

There is also a tradition, which is usually borne out in practice, that auditors of the Exchequer and Audit Department give a very good account of themselves whenever they leave their own office to work elsewhere, whether as auditors or as administrators.

[2] And quite probably of any developed country whatsoever, although further analysis would be necessary to show this.

examine and criticize; the exact opposite of the position in France. What was perhaps worse, by identifying the auditors with a particular career class, the decision proclaimed their status for all the departments to see. The controllers, save for their chief, were less than the controlled.[1] Such a situation inevitably involved a danger that they would tend to confine their criticisms to matters of routine and minor importance and that the national audit body would lack the contacts and influence which it needed. In practice the high personal status of the Comptroller and Auditor General saved the independence of audit criticism as far as it concerned the government departments. The serious implications of subordinate non-professional status became most clearly apparent when the audit was needed for a new task, the control of nationalized industries.[2] The decision has, in fact, tended to restrict the audit to a traditional role.

It was recognized even in the earlier years that the national audit required very good candidates for its work, and since it was able to offer rather better promotion prospects within the Executive Class than many of the ministries and departments, a number of those with high marks in the open examinations elected to enter it. Since the Second World War, however, promotion patterns elsewhere have been relatively more favourable than formerly, and it is very doubtful whether any such advantage now exists.[3] Meanwhile, as we have seen, the nature of state audit work has been transformed, although still to a lesser degree than in most other countries.

[1] In the days of the pure 'regularity' audit it could be argued that the auditors were really only concerned with questions of an accounting nature and therefore only with the accounts branches of ministries and departments. Whatever force such an argument may then have had, the auditors are now essentially concerned with the substance of what ministries decide and do, at all levels including the highest, rather than the form in which they account for it. Many auditors nowadays, therefore, require contacts with the policy-making and technical branches, and may have little or nothing to do with the accounts branches.

[2] For the question of state audit and the British nationalized industries, see Chapter XI below.

[3] It is also almost certainly true in average peacetime years that the prospects of promotion to the Administrative Class are less than in a department with its own Administrative establishment (see Mackenzie and Grove, op. cit., p. 78). In case of such a promotion the Exchequer and Audit Department must, of course, lose its man altogether; the point has scarcely arisen in recent years, however.

No special individual qualification is required, other than success in the general Executive Class examination (or promotion from the Clerical Class, which is the source of a considerable proportion of the staff). The Executive examination corresponds to the educational level of the second year in sixth forms at grammar schools. The Clerical Class is recruited to the Civil Service at about the level of the General Certificate of Education, and persons who become auditors upon promotion from this Class are mostly transferred from different work in other departments. There is a training scheme for new entrants to the Department which includes external courses in accounting and commercial law, and internal lectures.

Like the other European state audit bodies, the Exchequer and Audit Department has expanded only very gradually in staff numbers. When the office was established by the Act of 1866, expenditure liable to audit was about £66 millions and there were 113 auditors. In 1956 there were 435 auditors but the expenditure examined was no less than some £4,500 millions.[1] In 1960 the audit staff was almost unchanged. The salary of a new entrant in that year was £440 per annum. With reasonable diligence he could expect, with two promotions, to reach a career maximum of £1,965. If he rose to be a director, the salary was £2,650. The Secretary of the Exchequer and Audit Department, holding a post of the highest responsibility, which requires performance of the duties of the Comptroller and Auditor General during a vacancy, received £3,750. The scales of pay were strictly comparable with those of the Executive Class, but the special requirements of the state audit functions had been recognized to the extent that the establishment contained an unusually large number of high ranking posts within the Class. It is unfortunate that in a stratified administration this does not take care of the problem of status and influence, which is not principally a matter of pay. Status is not always an element of traditional power or a gratification to individuals; in certain employments it is a tool of work.

It is perhaps partly the high status of magistrates of the Cour des Comptes which has permitted that body to maintain its functions with what is numerically the smallest corps of state auditors

[1] Mackenzie & Grove, op. cit., p. 307.

in any major country of the West.[1] No public servant in France is under any doubts that an auditor of the Cour is a very senior officer and this to some extent speeds and facilitates investigations. It has certainly helped the Cour to experiment in new auditing fields since the last war.

A decree of 1856 created the entry grade of *auditeur* for the magistrature, to be recruited by a special examination. This system survived for ninety years. Most of the candidates were graduates of the Paris Faculté de Droit, with a leavening from those nineteenth-century temples of learning and social prestige, the Ecole Normale Supérieure, the Ecole Polytechnique, and, under the Third Republic, the Ecole Libre des Sciences Politiques. Thus through studious discipline the wealthy bourgeoisie of Paris, often with its roots in the ancient nobility, was able to accede to honours of a kind enjoyed by the *noblesse de robe* of the eighteenth century. The list of former magistrates of the Cour is full of magnificent romantic names like Gillet de la Jacqueminière, Pellissier de Féligoude, de la Lande de Calan, Vallerand de la Fosse, and Dubut de Saint-Paul Laroche, and unlikely ones such as de l'Eglise de Ferrier de Felix, Labbé de la Mauvinière, Lempereur de Guerny, and even Le Rat de Magnitot. There were counts, viscounts, barons and marquis. There were families which furnished two, three or even four magistrates.

That system, which quite evidently was not a model of social egalitarianism, was ended by the civil service reform of 1945[2] and the consequent formation of the Ecole nationale d'Administration in 1946. Since then, the entrants to the Cour des Comptes together with the recruits of the Conseil d'Etat, the Inspection des Finances and the diplomatic services, have been among the best graduates of that school. The *administrateurs civils* of the ministries, a group founded by the reform, with the British Administrative Class in mind, are recruited from the lower-marked students of the same courses. The new system of recruitment has been described by a magistrate who entered under the old procedure as 'an auspicious attempt, and one already crowned with success,

[1] The desire to avoid 'dilution', which is common to all élites, was no doubt another factor.

At the beginning of 1961, the magistrature consisted of the Premier Président, the Procureur Général, 7 Présidents de Chambre, 53 conseillers maîtres, 132 conseillers référendaires and 33 auditeurs, a total of 227.

[2] In which Michel Debré played a leading part, see pp. 224–5 above.

to give the *grands corps* and the other major services of the State a common origin and basis of training'. 'At the same time', he adds, 'the grant of a salary to all the students of the Ecole should make it possible—and has made it possible—for the most gifted to try their luck, without reference either to fortune or to social class.'[1] There are still a few feudal names in the office list of the Cour, but not among the post-war entrants. State audit, like national administration generally, has become too serious a matter for a regime of recruitment dedicated largely to the maintenance of social privilege.

The auditeur enters at salary index 315, compared with 300 for the *administrateur civil*. The normal career expectation takes the former to index 700, as *conseiller référendaire* (*échelon spécial*), compared with 630 for the latter as *administrateur civil de classe exceptionelle*. It is also much easier for the magistrate of the Cour to attain salary index 800[2] as *conseiller maître* than for the man in the ministry to reach the same high salary (the maximum for a Director), for which he requires several promotions. The seven posts of Président de Chambre, and those of Procureur Général and Premier Président, are all attainable by the *auditeur*, and their salaries are specially graded above the general scales.[3] Thus the auditor of the Cour des Comptes, as a member of one of the historic *grands corps de l'Etat*, has substantially better career prospects, as well as prestige, than his less successful colleague from the Ecole nationale d'Administration who follows a career in a ministry. Indeed the posts of Director[4] in certain ministries are frequently filled by members of the *grands corps* on detached service.

Promotion in the Cour is regulated by law to permit the entry of a limited number of non-magistrates at higher levels. Three *conseillers référendaires* out of four are chosen among the *auditeurs*; one post in four is reserved for candidates from the services of the Finance Ministry. Similarly, a third of the vacancies for *conseillers maîtres* are reserved for outside candidates; of these half are for the higher administration of the Finance services and the other

[1] Pierre Escoube, 'Grands Corps et Grands Commis: la Cour des Comptes'. in *La Revue des Deux Mondes*, 1 October 1958.

[2] For comparison, university staffs are graded from salary indexes 225 to 800. The highest index for an ambassador is also 800.

[3] *Fonctionnaires d'Etat*: *Classement Indiciaire* (Direction de la Fonction Publique, 1957).

[4] Equivalent to Under-Secretary or Deputy Secretary in Great Britain.

half 'left to the free choice of the Government on condition that the persons concerned should be over 40 years of age and have had at least 15 years of public service'. It is the last rump of the patronage envisaged by Napoleon when he created the Cour.[1] The posts of Président de Chambre are always filled by internal promotion.

Responsible detached service in a civil service department or an international body at home or abroad, in a state enterprise or even in a private firm, is a fair expectation for entrants to the Cour, especially in their middle years. Such service must be approved by the Government. Not all magistrates receive this valuable experience, however, and it places some strain upon the limited auditing staff resources; it is probably for this reason that a policy of borrowing personnel from the services of the Ministry of Finance for audit duties was adopted recently. In 1961 there were 22 such persons. The conflict between the traditional career prerogatives of the *grand corps* and the growing demand of a developing state audit must be the cause of considerable heart-searchings.

The educational requirements for a state auditor in France are thus not differentiated from those for the senior posts in the public services as a whole, in that all must enter via the Ecole nationale, but the standard is better than the average of its graduates. Candidates are admitted to the Ecole in two groups after examination; firstly, from persons of under 27 years with a degree or equivalent qualification, and secondly from persons of not less than 24 and not more than 30 years of age with at least four years permanent, temporary or industrial employment in almost any kind of public service, including local government, education and French authorities overseas. The net is cast very wide. In practice, however, the members of the *grands corps* mainly come from the first group, since the graduate entrants tend to get higher marks and the choice of career is granted first to those at the top of the passing-out list. By this nicely contrived mechanism is the high standard of recruitment maintained, without any obvious preference for any particular educational background.[2]

[1] In most advanced career groups in the French public service a small number of 'open' posts are reserved by law. This device was perhaps originally a matter of reward for political services, but it now serves to modify the strict channels of advancement for officials in deserving cases.

[2] In fact a broadly based education in the social sciences is probably the best background for success at the E.N.A., and certainly for its entrance examination. 'The higher civil servant', says André Bertrand, Director of

Monsieur de Mirimonde, a Président de Chambre, who at well over 60 remained proud of his skill and flair as a state auditor,[1] has recorded one of the very few opinions which can be found anywhere about the requirements of this work. It is an eloquent judgment:

> In this field, more than in many others, the quality of achievement depends closely upon the merit of those who are charged with the work of examination. Audit based upon documents reminds one somewhat of those Spanish inns where the traveller finds nothing to eat but what he brings with him. In a file where a magistrate who is either a novice or lacks clairvoyance sees nothing but a heap of tiresome records without interest, an able *rapporteur* discovers either an irregularity or an actual fraud, or perhaps a question of general principle, fruitful in recoveries and economies. One must have at one's service inquiring minds, always wide-awake, equipped with broad knowledge of law, administration, finance—and even of the humanities, when an investigation has to be undertaken. If not, the voucher audit ends up as what it had become at the end of the ancien régime; mechanical drudgery, bereft of practical significance. Which amounts to saying that the future of the Cour des Comptes will depend not merely upon the powers conferred upon it, but also, and above all, upon the men called upon to use them. Thus the quality of recruitment will be the essential element in future development.[2]

Here is a viewpoint quite different from the professional dynamism of the General Accounting Office. The quality of flair is associated by M. de Mirimonde with the intrinsic civilized worth of the fully developed mind. Whether or not the education supplied by the Ecole nationale d'Administration is in harmony with this ideal, there is no reason to doubt that by teaching the theoretical functions and procedures of the public service it gives the state auditor a good basis for the assessment of actual practice.

Studies at the E.N.A., 'might be described as the social scientist in action' ('The Recruitment and Training of Higher Civil Servants in the U.K. and France', in *The Civil Service in Britain and France*, London, Hogarth Press, 1956).

[1] He told the author that he still took pleasure in going on an audit mission whenever he could, so that he could work on the accounts 'to keep his hand in'. He was still able to find plenty of observations, and considered that he had a duty to pass on his 'flair' to the rising generation.

[2] de Mirimonde, op. cit., p. 315. Compare the view of Kurt Heinig: 'In our opinion the basic essential for audit consists of a high standard of general education and knowledge' (*Das Budget*, vol. 1, p. 151).

It is far from impossible that such knowledge is more valuable for his unusual function than the acquirement of impersonal techniques, such as those of accountancy. This is not merely the traditional contest between the specialist and the man of culture; the question remains open whether if a specialized education must be chosen, accountancy is the right one. A good case could be made for several alternative disciplines; an even better case for the mingling of them.

The Germans have yet another staffing and recruitment pattern; they use one type of person to perform the audit and another type to deliberate on the results.[1] The former are members of the Senior Service (Gehobener Dienst), who enter the public service generally at the level of the school-leaving examination (Abitur) at not less than 18 years of age. They then have not less than three years preparatory service followed by an examination (the Inspektor-prüfung). The latter type of personnel are members of the Higher Service (Höherer Dienst), the directing class of the German civil service. They also have to do preparatory service for a minimum of three years and must begin this at not more than 32 years of age. Their prior qualification is by long-standing German tradition, the study of law up to the level of final university examinations (Referendar-Examen), and the preparatory service is concluded by another examination (Assessor-Examen). Members of the Senior and the Higher Service both have a further probationary period (of two and a half years and three years respectively) before they are fully qualified career officials, and an entrant to the Höherer Dienst cannot hope to attain this goal at an age of less than 30, even if everything goes smoothly.

In the earlier years after 1945, when the Federal administration was being created, very few careers were in fact able to develop smoothly in Germany. Numerous civil servants therefore have entered the service by indirect routes. Many became temporary employees and were subsequently able, if they filled the legal career requirements, to enter the permanent service after a probationary period and assessment of their qualifications by the Federal Civil Service Committee.[2] There is also detailed provision in the law which governs careers in the Federal service for

[1] Except in the case of the efficiency audit (Chapter IX above) in which both types participate.

[2] See Chapter IX above.

promotion between the Gehobener and the Höherer Dienst, as also between the other service classes.[1]

This is a brief statement of the complex and unique arrangements for recruitment into the superior grades of the German civil service.[2] The Bundesrechnungshof is not, however, staffed with direct entrants to the Federal service. It has been granted a dispensation from the general rule that all posts are to be directly filled by competition, and the Bundesrechnungshof only resorts to this when it cannot be avoided. It prefers to take over experienced civil servants from other authorities, not only of the central government and the Länder but of the law-courts and revenue departments. This transfer may result from the application of an official to the Rechnungshof, or from the recommendation by his department, or again because he has attracted the attention of a visiting audit team. The transferred civil servants are, if possible, employed to audit their own old departments. On this system of recruitment, Kurt Heinig wrote that there was a common idea that the specialized departmental knowledge of the officials was indispensable for auditing work.

> This practice (he commented) has its pros and cons. In its favour, one can be certain that such officials, if they come face to face with their former department in the role of auditors, will not be anybody's fools. Against this, the old practical and personal relationships provide grounds for excusing a lot of things which a complete 'outsider' perhaps would not tolerate.[3]

British experience certainly suggests that the 'outsider', bringing a fresh mind to bear, may be expected to note and criticize many things which the 'veteran' will take for granted. Other countries also favour the view that the best results are to be expected from the 'uninvolved' auditor with keen intelligence and a store of general experience for purposes of comparison.

The auditing sections of the Bundesrechnungshof in early 1961

[1] Bundeslaufbahnverordnung, dated 31 July 1956, Section 32. Section 39(3) of this careers code also states that 'Officials who by continuance of studies have demonstrably increased their specialized knowledge and capabilities to a substantial degree, are to be encouraged. In particular, opportunity is, as far as possible, to be given them to make use of their special knowledge in more highly graded duties and thereby to demonstrate their particular specialist qualifications.'

[2] On this general subject, see Brian Chapman, *The Profession of Government*, pp. 100–9.

[3] Heinig, op. cit., vol. 1, p. 151.

consisted of 293 officials, in addition to the 30 efficiency auditors of the President's Section and the President himself. In the whole office, taking into account the internal administrative services, there were 249 members of the Gehobener Dienst, with a superstructure of 91 members of the Höherer Dienst, including a few temporary staff of equivalent rank in both cases. But no less than 195 of the Gehobener Dienst were in the highest pay group of their class (A.12, with title of Amtsrat[1]). This is only one indication that the Bundesrechnungshof carries a staff of very high average rank. The structure and numbers of the Higher Service, culminating in the President himself, appear to correspond to those of a full scale Federal Ministry.[2] The official status of the Bundesrechnungshof is in fact that.

Despite this solid and weighty framework, the organization of the Bundesrechnungshof for the purposes of state audit appears to invite criticism. The policy of having an audit staff which cannot normally expect to reach really high rank in the office, under the direction of a senior establishment totally without experience of the principal work of the department, can scarcely do otherwise than create a schism which must be accentuated by educational and perhaps social differences. This structure is no doubt a historical survival which had perhaps some sense in the days when audit was a straightforward matter of checking regularity, but which takes no account of the development of the critical discretionary audit nor of the fact that initiative must in nearly every

[1] The approximate equivalent in the British civil service would probably be a Chief Executive Officer.

[2] In terms of the United Kingdom civil service, which for this purpose is closely comparable, the Bundesrechnungshof has:

1	Permanent Secretary (the President)
1	Deputy Secretary (Vice-President)
7	Under Secretaries (Directors = Ministerialdirigenten)
44	Assistant Secretaries (Ministerialräte)
38	Principals (Oberregierungsräte and Regierungsräte)
91	

(For purposes of comparison, the Home Office, for example, had 110 Administrative Class civil servants in 1956, the Commonwealth Relations Office 70 at home and overseas, the Treasury about 170, the Ministry of Pensions and National Insurance, 68. The Exchequer and Audit Department had one (the Comptroller and Auditor General). The numbers of such posts in all the German Federal departments except the state audit body are within the same general range as their British equivalents).

case come from below. Moreover, the experience of other national audit departments suggests strongly that effective interpretation of audit findings requires a solid practical background, which is more valuable for this purpose than a legal training, however advanced. 'Flair' is not merely a developed talent for finding new audit observations; it implies a profound understanding of the function of the auditor. The mere theorist often misses the whole point. The operational staff of a state audit department should therefore form a single coherent corps, and in fact tends to do so everywhere except in the Bundesrechnungshof. In the twentieth century the rigid stratification of public services usually creates more problems than it solves.

Stress upon legal training for the Höherer Dienst is not peculiar to the Bundesrechnungshof. The traditional supremacy of the lawyer in German administration has since the last war been a subject of warm debate in the public service generally. The 'jurists' monopoly' in the state audit body has come under criticism in the technical journal which is published for the Bundesrechnungshof.[1] It has been suggested that the lawyers' outlook is excessively formalist and resistant to change; one writer quoted Max Weber's comment that the duty of watching over existing law seemed to enlist the practicians of law in the ranks of the conservative forces. State audit, however, needs—according to articles written by accountants and economists—to be stripped of out-dated formalities and brought into line with knowledge about the general economic context.

The jurists themselves, whilst sometimes conceding that there may be room for other specialists among the state auditors, defend themselves by claiming superior administrative experience. One jurist made the point that accountants are not entirely suitable for the public service because they are 'too one-sidedly orientated towards private business'.

The case for employing economists upon state audit appears, however, to be one of substance. Why should not the financial activities of government and subordinate administration be criticized according to those modern economic criteria which are acceptable as essential to the formulation of policy? A German

[1] *Der öffentliche Haushalt* (the Public Budget), a quarterly review dedicated to the theory of financial control from the state auditors' viewpoint. Notably the articles by Ministerialrat H. Reger in Heft 5–6, 1956, by Dr R. Kopis in Heft 2–3, 1957, and by Dr H. Winckelmann in Heft 4, 1957.

contributor to the debate pointed out that the economist tended to think in terms of efficiency. He did not, for example, fully accept the formally correct view that the task of state financial management was to execute the functions laid down in law and budget with the greatest possible economy. An economist's approach would see the ultimate objective rather in the efficiency than in the economy of public administration.

These can and usually will coincide, but not necessarily so, since there are cases in which economy can even represent inefficiency. To economize means 'to avoid expenditures', whilst an efficient conduct of affairs signifies that expenditures are incurred in accordance with a sound and businesslike policy.

This nicely expresses the viewpoint of newer thinkers upon public finance and administration in many countries. The public administration, in the contributor's view, was a part of the total production process, capable of playing its part in improving general economic performance. It was necessary for the auditors to think more and more in terms of its operational efficiency and for this purpose to develop critical and comparative standards of assessment, as a substitute for the competitive standards of private firms. With the passage of time economic problems had become so difficult and complex that it would, he felt, be presumptuous and irresponsible to leave their solution chiefly to jurists.

This had, in fact, been recognized by the Federal Civil Servants' Law of 1953, which accepted studies in the economic, financial and social sciences as of value equal to jurisprudence. What was needed was the early development of career facilities and examinations on the same lines as those for jurists, and a suitable orientation of education in the universities.[1]

Thus a contest about careers can generate ideas about the purposes of a profession. It is fair to comment that legal studies in Germany have always been on a much broader basis than in countries where the career of a lawyer is directed almost solely towards action in the Courts and the provision of legal advice. Law might be called a general cultural subject. It covers, from the lawyer's viewpoint, almost the whole field of matters which may concern public administration. But if the German jurist's education is not narrow, the career traditions which he represents are.

[1] Dr Hans Winckelmann: 'Rechnungsprüfung und Juristenmonopol' in *Der öffentliche Haushalt*, Heft 4, 1957.

Kurt Heinig wrote that the effect of long periods of probation and numerous exams was that the jurists became 'sealed off from people and life, like the officer corps in conservative states'.[1]

It is now, however, clear that a breach has been made in the jurists' monopoly, although it has not yet been exploited on a large scale. The outcome of this contest is as important for the future of German society as it is for administration and audit. The jurists' monopoly is a psychological rampart of authoritarian tradition.

For the professional conduct of a state audit department, it remains an error to think that an academic or technical background, of whatever kind, can be a substitute for practical experience in the auditor's own specialized and perplexing business. On the other hand experience is not a magic formula and no amount of gazing at vouchers and documents will suffice to initiate a sluggish mind. Nor should it any longer be thought that auditing is merely an apprenticeship for the really important and dignified work of supervision. We have M. de Mirimonde's considered opinion that 'active' state audit work is a function of dignity in itself, deserving the prestige which rightfully belongs to any task of real intellectual difficulty. When this point has been established, it may become more common for auditors with flair to apply their talents directly to the work of audit until a more advanced age, and even after they have attained quite senior rank. As state audit becomes less and less negative in its approach, there will be an increasing demand for highly-skilled auditors who really audit, who can set an inspiring example to the young, and whose observations do not need to be scrutinized at four or five levels.

Although there are numerous and important differences of detail between the functions and duties of the four great national audit bodies (for example, the French, Germans and Americans make practical recommendations as well as criticisms, whilst the British auditors do not recommend), there is nevertheless a solid basis of similarity. It is very probable that a good auditor with linguistic ability could quite easily adjust himself to work in any of the four, because he would find many more familiar things than strange ones.

In view of this fundamental similarity, it is very surprising that

[1] Heinig, op. cit., vol. 1, p. 150.

there should be so much difference in ideas about careers, status, qualifications, and general educational requirements. This applies also to the age of new entrants; in Great Britain it is normally 18, in U.S.A. probably about 22, in France about 27, in Germany usually over 30. France takes persons with a degree, plus the qualification of the Ecole nationale d'Administration, the Americans take only graduates specialized in accounting for the auditing divisions, the Germans still favour jurists but are beginning to see the need for economists, and in Britain there is no specialization. It is abundantly clear that no international criteria have yet evolved; the only common ground is that state auditors must be good human material. The differences testify to the very remarkable degree of isolation which existed between the state audit bodies until recently; many of them lacked facts upon which to base a comparison, and of course they were all unable to make one within the home country. Comparisons within a common administrative tradition, for example that of the British Commonwealth, have tended to be variations upon a theme.

This is still a profession in embryo, without very clear ideas as to what it can or should do, or as to the basic requirements for doing it. A profession it is, nevertheless, taking its origins from the very ancient functions of regularity audit, but now rapidly adapting itself to the varied and specialized requirements of the big government economy. It is interesting to speculate upon the practicability of teaching state audit as a special subject, not only to give the student a broad knowledge of public administration and finance but also to expound the critical technique through case-study and thereby transmit the professional's 'flair'.

* * * *

The highest direction of the state audit bodies is a matter for separate consideration. The General Accounting Office and the Exchequer and Audit Department are purely hierarchical bodies with authority concentrated in the hands of one man. The Cour des Comptes, and to a lesser degree the Bundesrechnungshof, continue to be organized and administered in the European judicial tradition of the collegiate body, taking decisions in common. The Public Reports of the Cour des Comptes, for example, are deliberated and agreed by the *Chambre du Conseil* of the Cour, in the presence of all the Présidents and all the *conseillers maîtres*. No less than 52 persons are named at the foot of the report for

1957–8. Almost everything is achieved by debate and vote in the Chambres, which correspond to auditing divisions, and by special committees.[1] Even disciplinary measures against magistrates are decided in session of the *Chambre du Conseil.*

The collegiate procedures of the pre-war Rechnungshof des Deutschen Reiches were curtailed under the Nazi regime, because they offended against the so-called Führerprinzip, which was nothing more than a glorification of the ancient principle of hierarchy; the President's position was thereby permanently enhanced. But a residual collegiate system still survives. Decisions are personal in 'Presidential matters' and, at least in theory, collegiate in 'Audit matters'. Each Audit Division has a Senate of 5 members, which decides upon matters which are referred to it. There is also a Great Senate of 14 members, which decides cases concerning more than one Senate or matters referred to it by the President.

The President, the Vice-President, the Directors and a limited number of Ministerialräte are by law 'Members' of the Bundesrechnungshof, with the same independence as judges and irremovable status. All must be over 35 years of age and have qualified either for the office of a judge or for the Höherer Dienst of the Federal Republic or a Land; at least one-third of them must have the judicial qualification.[2] The Directors and Ministerialräte are appointed by the Federal President on the proposal of the President of the Bundesrechnungshof.[3]

The Exchequer and Audit Departments Act 1921, states merely that the Comptroller and Auditor General 'may appoint such officers and servants as he may, with the sanction of the Treasury, determine'. A clause of the 1866 Act which gave the C. & A.G. full power 'to promote, suspend, or remove any of the officers, clerks, and others employed',[4] was repealed in 1921, and nothing new was substituted. This did not, however, involve any significant change, since the Treasury had always held staff regulation powers under Section 8 of the 1866 Act.[5]

[1] 'The Premier Président does not take any important decision without previously consulting the Committee of the Présidents and the Procureur Général' (De Mirimonde, op. cit., p. 56).

[2] RHO., Section 120.

[3] RHO., Section 119.

[4] E. & A. Depts. Act, 1866, Section 9.

[5] Section 8 of the 1866 Act stated, 'The Treasury shall from time to time appoint the officers, clerks and other persons in the department of the Comptroller and Auditor General; and Her Majesty by Order in Council may from time to time regulate the numbers and salaries of the respective grades or

In practice, promotions are made by the C. & A.G. on the recommendation of a Promotion Board of senior officers; this is standard Civil Service procedure and all promotions are from within the Department.

The law is almost equally vague about staff regulation in the General Accounting Office. 'All laws relating generally to the administration of the departments and establishments shall, so far as applicable, govern the General Accounting Office,' says Section 306 of the Budget and Accounting Act of 1921; the regulations of the U.S. Civil Service Commission are therefore valid. Appointments and promotions within this framework are made by the Office of Staff Management of the G.A.O. There is nothing to prevent direct recruitment to senior posts from outside the G.A.O., and this was largely resorted to during the reorganization of the Office, until a few years ago. Internal promotions are now fairly general again, however. Advancement, as in the British, French and German audit services, is unconnected with politics.

The national chief auditors

Whether they have full statutory powers of personal decision in matters of official business, or whether they are, like the French Premier Président, in a position of *primus inter pares*, the heads of the national audit bodies are all public servants of the greatest stature and importance. The growth of state finance has given increased significance to their duties and some of them have gained considerable personal influence and even fame. Their appointments always take place at governmental level, and their office combines to a unique degree something of the status of a minister (tempered by independence and fixed tenure), with those of a permanent head of a ministry and of a judge. The chief auditor of a country holds what is everywhere a remarkable constitutional position. The very fact that state audit is at present in the midst of a period of progress and experiment means that his role is not precisely circumscribed in practice, even though it may seem to be in law. The chief auditors of several countries probably have greater freedom to interpret the nature of their functions and to innovate, than any other type of permanent officials whatsoever.

In terms of history, the doyen of these high officers of state is

---

classes into which the said officers, clerks, and others shall be divided.' (Repealed by 1921 Act.)

the Premier Président of the Cour des Comptes.[1] The medieval equivalent of his office was mentioned, if not actually created by, a decree of Philippe V in 1319; there was then a Président, or Souverain, of the Chambre des Comptes of Paris. The appointment had by the fifteenth century become that of Premier Président; it was often held by an archbishop or bishop. Save during the revolutionary years between 1791 and 1807, the office has unbroken continuity since the Middle Ages.

In its existing form, however, it is a creation of Napoleon. The law of 1807 establishing the Cour des Comptes merely stated that the members of the Cour were appointed for life by the Emperor, that the Premier Président could preside over any of the *chambres* of the Cour, that he was to take an oath to the Emperor, and that he was charged with keeping order and general surveillance. A decree of September 1807 specified that he must be over the age of 30. In practice the choice of a suitable candidate is made by the government. In the nineteenth century the post was often given to a politician; out of nine Premier Présidents before 1900, six had been ministers and the others, with one exception, had a parliamentary background. In the twentieth century the 'wastage' rate of Premier Présidents has been greater;[2] there have been no less than 14 of them since 1900. But none of these was a politician. A strong tradition of internal appointment has developed; eight out of the last eleven Premier Présidents were high officers of the Cour immediately before their nomination. All the exceptions were themselves high career officials rather than politicians. Out of the total of 23 chief auditors in France since 1807, only two were chosen among officials of the Finance Ministry (and one of the

[1] The Anglo-Norman Exchequer had an earlier origin than the French Chambres des Comptes of the Middle Ages (and in fact exerted an influence upon them). The British state audit, like the Treasury, is a descendant of the Plantagenet Exchequer, but to trace the actual line of descent would be an exercise in historical gymnastics. In fact the ancient judicial audit of the Exchequer had almost completely collapsed before 1800 and at least the parliamentary side of the present system was developed after then. It is really honest and correct to regard almost the entire existing British system of financial control, including the audit, as a creation of the nineteenth century, following upon something like anarchy in the eighteenth. A proper account of the Exchequer through the centuries is, however, one of the greatest needs of British historiography; at present the record, so fundamental for the understanding of administrative history, is only fragmentary.

[2] They now retire at about the age of 70, although nominally appointed for life.

two was a 'forced appointment' by the Vichy Government in 1940). It is an interesting difference that in Britain and Germany the chief auditors have usually been appointed from, and in effect by, the central Finance Ministry, whereas in France and the U.S.A. they have not.

The present Premier Président, M. Roger Léonard, came from outside the Cour des Comptes, with a varied background of experience. Graduate of the Faculté de Lettres and the Faculté de Droit, and of the Ecole Libre des Sciences Politiques, he became a Sub-Prefect and later a Member of the Conseil d'Etat. In 1944 he became Prefect of the Seine et Oise and from 1947 to 1954 he held the important post of Prefect of Police of the Seine. He then became Governor-General of Algeria, but left that turbulent province in 1955, before it gave way to permanent revolt and war, and has since been at the Cour des Comptes.

His duties are more surrounded by ceremony and formality than those of the heads of younger audit organizations. He is at once the head of the office and the president of a judicial corps. Since 1934, the Premier Président has had the power to organize the work of the Cour by formal order (*arrêté*). He assigns the magistrates to duties, proposes their promotions and personal honours and can address warnings to them. His influence is important in the assignment of magistrates on loan to posts outside the Cour. As head of the judicial corps, he presides over the various committees which take decisions upon important matters such as the drafting of the Public Report of the Cour, and over the *Séances solennelles*, at which the magistrates wear robes of office and members of the government attend. He signs the judicial decisions (*arrêts*) of the Cour and the *reférés* addressed to ministers. He may write to the presidents of the parliamentary Finance Commissions upon any matter to which he may decide to draw their attention. He also presides over the Central Committee of Enquiry into the Cost and Efficiency of the Public Services (Comité central d'Enquête)[1] and over the Court of Budgetary Discipline.[2] Within the highly formal framework of his duties, the Premier Président has plenty of scope for personal influence and decision.

The historical antecedent of the post of President of the German Bundesrechnungshof was that of First President (Chefpräsident) of the Prussian Oberrechnungskammer, founded in

[1] See above, Chapter IX. [2] See above, Chapter IV.

1714. After the First World War, the post of chief auditor of Prussia was held jointly with that of President of the Rechnungshof des Deutschen Reiches. Appointment to this office, and to that of Vice-president, was by the Reich President, with the counter-signature of the Minister of Finance, who presumably had considerable influence in the actual choice. The same general procedure is followed under the Bonn Republic, although the Prussian Oberrechnungskammer has ceased to exist. The President and Vice-President must, like the other Members of the Bundesrechnungshof, be over 35 and be qualified for judicial office or the higher administrative or technical service of the Republic or a Land.

There have been four Presidents since 1922. One of these, Müller (1938–45), was a member of the 'old guard' of the Nazi Party, and a frankly political appointment.[1] He was not, however, entirely without technical experience, having held several financial offices including that of Finance Minister of Hesse. He and his family are believed to have been shot by the Russians at Potsdam in 1945.

A more notable personage was his predecessor, Friedrich Ernst Saemisch (1922–38), a scion of the family of Ranke, the great historian. A student of philosophy and law, he became an official of the Treasury of the Reich (Reichsschatzamt), which later took the name of Reich Finance Ministry. In 1921, although he belonged to no political party, he became Finance Minister of Prussia. In the following year he moved to the Rechnungshof and was shortly thereafter appointed to the new office of Reichssparkommissar, which he continued to fill until its abolition in 1933. He was the creator of what was probably the world's first efficiency audit on a national level.

The first President after the Second War, Erwin Meyer (1950–7), was a typical case of a civil servant whose career had been thrown out of joint by the Hitler regime. A jurist from the university of Erlangen, he had reached the fairly responsible rank of Oberregierungsrat in the Reich Finance Ministry by 1933, but was then

[1] The possibility of political appointments still exists. As was noted in Chapter III, the President of the Bundesrechnungshof ranks as a Staatssekretär, the permanent head of a Ministry. These ministerial heads are said to be political appointees under the Bonn regime, 'and their duty is first to their party and then to their Minister' (*The Times*, 5 November 1962). The President of the Bundesrechnungshof is no doubt a rather special case, however, in view of the unusual responsibilities of his office.

transferred by the new masters of Germany to an obscure post on unspecified political grounds. He reappeared on the scene in 1946 as a senior official of the Central Financial Administration of the Soviet Zone of Occupation, but he must have found this uncongenial for by January 1947 he was a Ministerialrat in the Bavarian Finance Ministry. These were confused years of makeshifts and reconstruction, and between April 1947 and 1950, he held high rank in the emergent financial bodies which came to form the Federal Finance Ministry in Bonn.

His successor, the late Dr Guido Hertel, who died in office in 1963, was another official who obtained no promotion for the duration of the Nazi regime, but he enjoyed very rapid advancement in the Federal Ministry of Finance after his return from a Soviet prisoner-of-war camp in 1949. Before his elevation to the Bundesrechnungshof he was head of Section I (Personnel) of the Ministry, a post which probably gave him a useful background for his new duties, which as we saw in the last chapter, include the offices of Federal Commissioner for Efficiency in the Administration and Chairman of the Federal Civil Service Committee, which are held concurrently with his principal post.

The President has yet a further office, that of Chairman of the Federal Debt Committee (Bundesschuldenausschuss). This Committee, which also includes three Members of the Bundestag and three officials of the Länder, has supervision over the functions of the Federal Debt Administration, which conducts borrowing and repayment operations for the Federal Government and the Post and Railways. The Committee conducts an annual audit of the Debt Administration in which auditors from the Bundesrechnungshof may participate. This task is not, however, really central among the varied duties of the President.

Most of the Presidents of the German audit had been Finance Ministry men. The same is true of the Comptroller and Auditors General of the United Kingdom. Their great office, which was created by the Exchequer and Audit Departments Act of 1866, was then in two ways an innovation. It was, firstly, the original creation of an auditor intended to serve the legislature;[1] the first 'parliamentary officer' in the field of finance. It was in the second place an organizational novelty in that state audit had always until

[1] Though not of an audit. The Belgian Cour des Comptes was created as a legislative audit body as early as 1830.

then been regarded as a task appropriate to a board or 'college' [1] rather than to a single personage with wide discretionary powers.

The officer whose full title is the Comptroller General of the Receipt and Issue of Her Majesty's Exchequer and Auditor General of the Public Accounts is appointed with a deliberate show of formality, by letters patent under the Great Seal.[2] There is no fixed term of office, and the only limit is, by custom rather than statute, retirement at the age of 65. To be an Auditor General is the climax of a career and not a stage in advancement. This indeed is a characteristic of the chief auditor posts in all the four countries (even that of the Comptroller General of the U.S., which has a tenure limited to 15 years). It is doubtful whether any such officer in the present century has left his functions to take up another full-time post. This finality is in itself a guarantee that independence and impartiality will not be compromised, and that ambition will be centred upon making the most of the auditor's office.

There have been four Comptroller and Auditors General since the First World War. Their careers have had certain features in common; all came from leading public schools and all were at Oxford, where the emphasis of their studies was, in most cases, upon classics and the humanities. There were also notable differences. Although all four C. & A.G.s were in the Treasury at some time during their earlier careers, only Sir Gilbert Upcott (C. & A.G. from 1931 to 1946) had spent the whole time in that department. Sir Frank Tribe (1946–58), had an exceptionally wide experience in the 'specialist' ministries. He was Deputy Secretary at the Ministry of Labour and National Service from 1940 to 1942, and then successively permanent head of the Ministry of Fuel and Power until 1945, of the Ministry of Aircraft Production (1945) and of the Food Ministry (1945–6). Sir Malcolm Ramsay, a Scot

[1] The ancient idea of the 'college' for public audit, which existed in classical times, was perhaps conceived as a mutual guarantee of integrity, rather as medieval money chests had several locks, the keys of which were each confided to different officers. The collegiate structures of present-day continental state audit bodies, however, are associated with judicial organization in the ordinary courts of law, which may also be collegiate.

[2] The office of Assistant Comptroller and Auditor General was abolished by the E. & A. Depts., Act of 1921, Section 8(4). The abolition of this post and its replacement by that of Secretary were recommended to the Treasury by the C. & A.G., Sir H. J. Gibson, in response to a circular to all Departments calling for a reduction of public expenditure. (Report of the Committee on the E. & A.D. Act, 1866, Cmd. 1383, 1921, footnote.)

who was C. & A.G. from 1921 to 1931, had at one time been Private Secretary to the Earl of Balfour. The present C. & A.G., Sir Edmund Compton, was Private Secretary to the Minister of Aircraft Production in the hectic year of 1940. He was a Third Secretary at the Treasury before his appointment to the Comptrollership in 1959.

A characteristic of the Comptroller and Auditor General is his very close association with the Public Accounts Committee of the House of Commons. Other chief auditors may send reports to legislatures and representatives to their committees, but the C. & A.G. is there in person as expert witness whenever the Committee of Public Accounts is in session. He may well have briefed the Chairman of the Committee beforehand, and the debates of the P.A.C. derive their subject-matter almost entirely from his Reports.[1] But he is not only a servant of Parliament; the law subjects him on a number of matters to the instructions of the Treasury. No less than eight sections of the 1866 Act gave the Treasury specific powers of direction in matters directly affecting the audit.[2] Some of these proved to be unimportant and some of them were revised, replaced or repealed by the Act of 1921. But the provision, in Section 27 of the 1866 Act, whereby the Comptroller and Auditor General may be required by the Treasury 'to ascertain whether any expenditure included in any appropriation account is supported by the authority of the Treasury' is still of absolutely fundamental importance both for the audit and for the enforcement of Treasury control.[3] The question of Treasury authority arises in a very large number of transactions which are

[1] On the relationship between the C. & A.G. and the Public Accounts Committee, see the evidence of Sir Frank Tribe before the Select Committee on Nationalized Industries on 22/1/53, especially questions 77, 78 and 79. (H. of C. 235/1952–3). It has been said of the C. & A.G. elsewhere that: 'As a result of the audit undertaken by his staff he becomes familiar with the administrative realities reflected in the Accounts, and is thus able to guide the Committee through the mass of detailed Accounts to concentrate on a manageable number of topics which appear especially to deserve their attention' (J. S. Hines, 'Financial Control in the United Kingdom', an unpublished monograph, p. 25).

[2] E. & A.D. Act, 1866, Sections 22, 27, 29, 30, 31, 33, 40 and 44.

[3] This provision was implemented by a Treasury Minute dated 1868 (and still in force) which directed the C. & A.G. to bring to the notice of the Treasury any unauthorized excess expenditure on any subhead of a Vote, or 'any increase of establishment, of salary, or of cost of a service, or for any additional works or new services which have not been specially provided for

scarcely restricted in any way by the broad boundaries of British legislation. Already in 1876, their Lordships of the Treasury reported with satisfaction that following the 'great administrative reform' which was the Exchequer and Audit Act of 1866, they had 'with the co-operation of the Comptroller and Auditor General, been enabled to exercise far more completely than previously, the control intrusted to them by constitutional usage'.[1] The British state audit has long been celebrated as an instrument of parliamentary control; it is less well known that it is also, and was designed to be, an instrument of the financial branch of the government;[2] none of the other large Western national audits resembles it in this way. They may co-operate with their Finance Ministries but they are not bound to do so by law.

The C. & A.G.s audit is chiefly limited to the direct transactions of the central government departments and their 'out-stations', together with those of a number of quasi-governmental bodies which are audited under statute. The total number of accounts certified is very considerable; they include Appropriation Accounts, Trading Accounts, 'White Paper Accounts' covering specialized activities like the running of National Health Service hospitals, and the miscellaneous statutory accounts. Sir Frank Tribe gave the figure as 390 every year.

The Appropriation Accounts, however, include very large sums which are paid out in the form of grants, and subsequently administered by other authorities. The information available to the C. & A.G. about some of these indirect transactions is very limited and he has no powers to make even test-audits of them. For grants-in-aid to colonial territories he at least receives the audit reports of the Director General of the Oversea Audit Service.[3] For the much larger grants to local authorities he formerly

in the grants of Parliament'. The C. & A.G. was also free to report to the Treasury 'any item of expenditure which in his opinion should be subject to special Treasury authority' (*Epitome*, vol. 1, pp. 20–1). The rules have been extended since then, but this brief Minute is the principal documentary basis and origin of what has been called 'the most important form of Treasury control, the requirement of prior approval' (S. H. Beer, *Treasury Control*, pp. 25 and 36. See also R. G. Hawtrey, *The Exchequer*, pp. 36–8).

[1] *Epitome*, vol. 1, p. 58.

[2] On the subject of relations between the Treasury and the C. & A.G., see also Chapter XII, below.

[3] The Colonial Audit was at one time under the Comptroller and Auditor General, but it was decided in 1910 to form a 'Colonial Audit Department', attached to the Colonial Office (*Epitome*, vol. 1, pp. 529–30).

had access to any reports which were made by the District Auditors upon the expenditure of amounts allocated to specific purposes, such as education.[1] There was no guarantee that these reports dealt with the subjects which interested the C. & A.G. but they were at least a useful source of independent information. This source was unfortunately eliminated by the Local Government Act of 1958, which had the effect of making local authorities almost totally non-accountable to Parliament for the expenditure of grants from central government funds. The former specific grants for education, fire, local health and child care services were abolished,[2] and in lieu of these local authorities were given a General Grant, to be spent at their complete discretion.[3] In a paper submitted to the Public Accounts Committee in 1962, the Comptroller and Auditor General explained that in the circumstances it would not be possible for him to make what he called 'a value for money' report to Parliament on the expenditure on these services, except in the event that he were given, by legislation, access to the books and records of local authorities.[4]

The rate deficiency grants to poorer local authorities, under the terms of the Local Government Acts of 1948 and 1958, present another very difficult accountability problem, and Sir Frank Tribe declared in 1954 that he was not in a good position to report upon the use made of these large sums.[5]

The Budget and Accounting Act of 1921 provides for the appointment of the Comptroller General and Assistant Comptroller

[1] On the District Audit, which is the statutory regularity audit of English local government, see L. M. Helmore, *The District Auditor*, London, Macdonald and Evans, 1961. The growth of local authorities in the nineteenth century was based mainly upon local rather than central initiatives, and a separate historical tradition—of which the District Audit is a part—was formed. The French tend to regard local government as an extension of central government into the provinces; the British tendency has been to see it as a thing apart. This lack of coherence between the centre and parts, which is rather a serious matter in modern circumstances, is symbolized by the fact that relations between state audit and local government audit in Britain have been tenuous, to say the least. They should be able to help one another more than they do.

[2] Specific grants for police, highways and a few other services were retained.

[3] In 1963–4, vote provision for General Grant for England and Wales amounted to no less than £565 millions, and for Scotland £65 millions.

[4] P.A.C. 1st, 2nd and 3rd Reports, Session 1961–2, with Minutes of Evidence. Appendix 2, pp. 444–6.

[5] See Sir Frank Tribe's two monographs entitled 'Parliamentary Control

General of the United States according to the formula of 'appointment by the President with the advice and consent of the Senate', which derives from Article II, Section 2, of the Constitution. Both these officers are to hold office for fifteen years, and the Comptroller General is ineligible for reappointment.

The Comptrollers General form a different group from the European chief auditors. None of them has yet been a career official, although the present Assistant Comptroller and his predecessor were chosen within the General Accounting Office. Six of the eight Comptrollers and Assistant Comptrollers were qualified attorneys; the exceptions were the first Assistant Comptroller who was a retired General and is said to have been given almost no responsibility, and the present Comptroller General. The first head of the General Accounting Office, John R. McCarl, had been Secretary to a Senator and Executive Secretary of the Republican Congressional Campaign Committee. He became Comptroller General after advising President Harding against appointing several other candidates for the post. So determined and so effective was his opposition to the policies of the New Deal that after the completion of his full term of office in 1936 President Roosevelt declined to appoint a successor for almost three years. Fred H. Brown (1939–40), had been a State Governor and a Senator; he retired because of ill-health. Lindsay C. Warren, the reformer of the General Accounting Office, had been a State Senator of North Carolina and a member of the House of Representatives for sixteen years before he resigned his seat to take up his appointment in 1940. He had gained valuable experience as a member of the House Appropriations Committee and the Joint Committee on Government Operations. He retired on doctor's orders after thirteen years in office. Joseph Campbell, the present Comptroller General, was a professional accountant in private practice until

---

of Public Expenditure' and 'The Exchequer and Audit Department', which both stressed this point. The problem of financial control over local authority activities conducted on an agency basis for the central government and financed by grants, is a world-wide one, which does not permit full treatment here. In general, it is tending to become accepted that accountability for these large and growing grants is meaningless unless the state audit department has some access to local vouchers and records. Failing this there should at least be a really intimate working relationship with the local authority audit. Without some means of access to information, coherent public reporting is scarcely possible.

1941. He then successively served as Assistant Treasurer, Treasurer and Vice-President of Columbia University, and had the fortune to be there when General Dwight Eisenhower became the university's President. All the three previous Comptrollers had been Congressional men and in effect legislative candidates whom the Presidents had been willing to appoint to an office which Congress regarded as its own. But Mr Campbell was President Eisenhower's personal nominee, appointed in the face of a strong candidate from the House of Representatives. The procedure of Presidential appointment to this high office within the Legislative Branch is clearly not always a mere formality.

Like the Comptroller and Auditor General, the Comptroller General of the United States sits upon a lonely eminence of authority within his department. The extent of his constitutional prerogatives was shown in an unfortunate way by McCarl when he blocked New Deal expenditures on legal technicalities. The strength of his position as head of the General Accounting Office was demonstrated by the complete reorganization carried out by Comptroller General Warren, which must have been as uncomfortable as it was necessary.

Once appointed, the Comptroller General is more completely the servant of the legislature than his British colleague, although he does not have the same intimate personal contact with any single legislative committee. But in addition to his regular function of reporting to the Congress[1] and its committees he can be, and often is, charged by them with almost any kind of fact-finding activity related to finance or administration, and with the provision of expert staff to assist and advise. The Comptroller General is completely independent of the Executive Branch, except for his duties to address a report to the President if so requested, to supply information to the Bureau of the Budget on request, and to co-operate with it and with the Treasury Department in the Joint Financial Management Improvement Programme.

[1] One aspect of this reporting is the duty of making 'an expenditure analysis of each agency of the executive branch . . . including Government Corporations which, in the opinion of the Comptroller General, will enable Congress to determine whether public funds have been economically and efficiently administered and expended' (U.S. Government Organization Manual, 1957–8, p. 36).

The independence of state auditors

Something further must be said about the subject of independence. Since the time of Aristotle it has been accepted principle that state auditors should be free from direction, influence and intimidation by, and income or reward from, the authorities and persons whose affairs they are called upon to audit. In this respect they are in a position fundamentally different from internal and commercial auditors, who are paid by the organization which they are engaged to examine. These auditors protect the position of their employers by ensuring probity and regularity. But the business of state auditors is the protection of society against the selfishness and inefficiency of individuals and corporate bodies. In a parliamentary democracy society is for this purpose represented by a legislature, and the whole of the executive assumes the aspect of a corporate body. The state auditor may serve the legislature or he may stand alone; what he absolutely cannot do is to be a servant of the executive, except in minor incidentals. To do so would be to become an internal auditor and thus to accept a drastic lowering of his constitutional standing. No state auditor, or at any rate no chief state auditor, can afford to be without independence; he needs it as a judge needs it, in order to be impartial and fearless in criticism. He also needs it in order to be able to publicize his criticism in an open report.

A good deal of ingenuity has therefore been devoted to the provision of independent status. No less than twenty-five countries submitted papers in 1956 to the Brussels Congress of Supreme Audit Institutions explaining how they achieved this, or hoped to do so, since it was apparent that some of the younger countries were writing in terms of aspirations rather than working systems.

The emphasis was overwhelmingly upon the appointment of officers with irremovable status outside the executive, either in the classical tradition of a 'college' or in the person of a single high official. In many lands there is a whole group of irremovable officers and almost every country has at least one; the position in Communist countries is, however, less clear.

In many countries the executive has some influence upon the appointment of the chief auditors, though this is usually as far as its prerogatives over state audit are allowed to go. But there are a fair number of countries, including Belgium, Israel and Austria, where even appointments are made by the legislature and the executive is very thoroughly excluded from any influence at all. The exclusion is regulated in detail. In Belgium, for example, the Cour des Comptes appoints, promotes and dismisses its own staff and fixes their remuneration; all efforts to introduce general civil service regulations have been resisted by Parliament for fear that this might create an impression that the Cour depended upon the executive. In Belgium, Israel and elsewhere the office budgets and accounts of the state audit bodies are under direct legislative control, exempt from executive scrutiny; the General Accounting Office is in this category. Some countries allow such financial scrutiny but provide that if the executive makes any cuts in the amounts requested in the state audit estimates it must declare them, with full details, to Parliament; in Austria the chief auditor has the possibility of appealing to the legislature in such a case. Belgium and some other countries also have legal or even constitutional protection for the audit against any kind of executive orders or instructions. The statutes of many state audit bodies debar the principal auditors, or all of them, from political activity and in some cases from professional and commercial activities also. Belgium also excludes from membership of the Cour anyone related, even distantly, to a Minister or to an existing member of the Cour.

There is universal agreement that the state auditors must have free access to documents and records and any other sources of official information which they require; without this their constitutional function is a travesty.

France is probably the only country where the whole corps of state auditors is irremovable. The auditors of the Cour des Comptes are, at least in legal status, not officials but magistrates, that is to say high officers of judicial standing. Their independence is guaranteed by law; the founding statute of 1807 provided that the members of the Cour were to be appointed for life by the Emperor, and the general civil service statute of 1946 stated that 'Magistrates of the Cour des Comptes are and shall remain irremovable'. Their independence is also protected by provision in the Constitution for the irremovable status of all magistrates.[1] The Cour is the only French administrative body whose members have judicial status; not even the members of the Conseil d'Etat are in this category. It is a principle arising from this status that all magistrates, irrespective of their rank or seniority, have full

[1] Article 64 of the Constitution of 4 October 1958.

freedom of judgment and full personal responsibility for their reporting activities; thus their status gives the magistrates much independence vis-à-vis each other. And the Cour is not a parliamentary body; it is independent of the legislature as well as the executive. 'While', says the French paper to the Brussels Congress of 1956, 'the role of public financial auditing is to inform both Government and Parliament, it cannot be made subordinate either to one or to the other.' The great attention paid by executive, legislature, and public opinion to the Public Reports of the Cour was claimed to be 'a measure of the interest that the nation has in impartial control of the way the common heritage is being administered'. Here is the proud concept of an élite body without subordination to anyone for the conduct of its duties, and dedicated to serving the nation as a whole. Nevertheless, the Cour concedes that 'it evolved into independence with the Parliamentary type of regime'.[1]

The German paper submitted to the 1956 Congress declares that state auditors must 'obviously' be free from the influence of those whose accounts they audit; but their independence from the legislature is also considered to be justified, on the grounds that political parties might otherwise bring pressure to bear on them. The Bundesrechnungshof specified what were in its view the Five Basic Freedoms required by state audit departments:

1. Freedom from 'Instructions' (on how to conduct the audit)
2. Freedom from 'Supervision' (on staffing and administration matters, notably recruitment)
3. Freedom to submit the audit department's own budget to Parliament (to prevent 'cuts' by the executive)
4. Freedom of access to all information and records required in connection with audit.
5. Personal independence for members of the 'college' (even, professionally, against the head of the audit body).

This clearly, amounts to a high degree of general independence; most of these 'freedoms', for example, would be incompatible

[1] The anonymous author of a recent monograph entitled 'The Cours des Comptes and the Control of Public Finance in France and foreign countries' compares 'nominal' with 'genuine' independence and makes the valid point that: 'If the theoretical independence of a high audit control body depends upon the position in the State which the constitution or the law assigns to it, its real independence is to some extent tied to the autonomy of its internal administration and particularly to the methods of staff recruitment and promotion' (*Statistiques et Etudes Financières*, No. 136, April 1960).

with the present position of the British state audit in relation to the executive. The Bundesrechnungshof is fairly well satisfied with its own situation. Its collegiate members possess judicial independence in accordance with a provision made in the Federal Constitution of 23 May 1949.[1] The Founding Statute of the Bundesrechnungshof, dated 27 November 1950, describes it as a 'Supreme Federal Authority (i.e. of Federal Ministry status) independent of the Federal Government, subject only to the law'. This means in practice that it is not bound by any instructions from the executive concerning the conduct of its duties; it also means that the Bundesrechnungshof has its own departmental appropriation under a separate heading in the Federal budget. The President audits his own department's accounts and submits them directly to Parliament. The transfer, retirement, removal from office and discipline of the members with judicial status are regulated in accordance with the rules for judges of the Federal High Courts. Thus independence from the executive is carefully protected by law and the Bundesrechnungshof 'in practice is also independent of Parliament though such independence is not explicitly laid down in the law'. But in accordance with long-standing practice the state audit reports still have to be transmitted to Parliament indirectly through the Finance Ministry, and this minor servitude is resented, even though it has worked smoothly.

In both of the great English-speaking countries the essential element of independence is the personal irremovability of the chief auditor. The Exchequer and Audit Departments Act, 1866, provided that the Comptroller and Auditor General should hold his office 'during good behaviour', subject however to removal by the Queen, on an address from the two Houses of Parliament. He was not to hold any other Crown office, nor to be in either the House of Commons or the House of Lords. His salary, like that of a judge, was charged upon the Consolidated Fund, and thereby guaranteed from year to year without vote of Parliament.[2]

The Budget and Accounting Act of 1921 set up a fairly comparable set of rules for the Comptroller General and Assistant Comptroller General of the United States. Either of them may be removed from office at any time by joint resolution of Congress,

[1] Grundgesetz für die Bundesrepublik Deutschland, Article 114(2).

[2] The amount of the C. & A.G.'s salary (in principle equated with that of a Permanent Secretary) is regulated by statute from time to time. The E. and A.D.Act, 1957, fixed it at £6,000.

but only if they are judged by Congress to be 'permanently incapacitated . . . or inefficient, or guilty of neglect of duty, or of malfeasance in office, or of any felony or conduct involving moral turpitude, and for no other cause and in no other manner except by impeachment'.[1] Under American constitutional doctrine the power of removal from office has been taken as belonging to the President, by inference from his appointing authority, although the Constitution says nothing about removal. Provision for removal by Congress was therefore highly unusual, and in 1920 President Wilson vetoed the whole Act because he believed that this limitation of the Presidential prerogative was unconstitutional. It was only signed a year later by President Harding.

The amounts of the salaries of the chief auditors of both Great Britain and the United States are fixed by law. There is no comparable provision, nor protected status, for their subordinate staffs, but in practice they do enjoy a certain amount of independence as representatives of their irremovable department heads. The Budget and Accounting Act specifies that all official acts performed by designated servants of the Comptroller General 'shall have the same force and effect as though performed by the Comptroller General in person'.

The same American Act also makes the most complete provision for access by the Comptroller General and any of his duly authorized staff to almost any kind of information or records whatsoever within the audited departments. The statutes of the Exchequer and Audit Department are not clear about this; the 1866 Act stated merely that the Comptroller and Auditor General should have 'free access, at all convenient times, to the books of account and other documents relating to the accounts' of departments. It has since then been made quite plain by the Public Accounts Committee and the Treasury that departments are to supply information as requested by the C. & A.G.

The matter of access to information and records[2] is absolutely

[1] 1921 Act, Section 303.

[2] Documents concerning a few types of very special expenditure, notably for secret service purposes, form accepted exceptions. The idea that only information and records directly related to finance need be made available is not, however, tenable, because no clear line can be drawn separating supposed 'financial' material. In the twentieth century it is very hard to think of any administrative activity divorced from finance. In any case a state auditor may use a good deal of apparently 'non-financial' background information to build up a case of clear financial importance.

basic and fundamental to all state audit; if executive departments are ever allowed to withhold or delay it on a plea of policy or interest, then the auditors might as well assume that arbitrariness has become the rule for the conduct of government, and accordingly shut up their shop.

It is of course a tacitly accepted condition of free access to information that the auditors will use it with proper discretion. They will avoid publicizing observations whose significance is *solely* political (whilst always having the courage to expose mistakes and weaknesses whose primary importance is administrative and financial but which may also look embarrassing politically). They will, above all, strictly maintain the many military and other state secrets about which they have knowledge.[1]

Thus, broadly, we have a picture of a new international profession in course of development. Or rather, of an extremely old profession in course of renewal and reinvigoration. The reaction to big government has been more rapid in some countries than in others, but it must come in all countries with a modern economy if the state audit is to respond to its opportunities, or even to retain a degree of usefulness. The old routines of regularity control need not, given a properly organized liaison between state and internal audit, consist of more than a modest test check by the former. And it may be guessed that the even older techniques of judicial audit are no longer in close touch with reality. On the other hand the limitless complexities of financial and administrative activity in modern government departments and state enterprises are in urgent need of intensive study, so that errors and weaknesses may be brought to light and lessons learned from

[1] Perhaps the most vital secret of all time was the atomic bomb project in the U.S.A. during the last war. The $2,191 millions of public money spent on it before the end of 1946 were obtained in devious and unorthodox ways, without regular budgeting procedures. Although information was withheld from everyone as far as possible, the General Accounting Office was made aware of what was going on from the very early days. In April 1946, the Comptroller General testified to the Senate Special Committee on Atomic Energy as follows: 'We have audited or are auditing, every penny expended on this project. We audited on the spot, and kept it current, and I may say it has been a remarkably clean expenditure . . . from the very beginning he (General Groves, in charge of the whole atomic project) has insisted upon a full audit and a full accountability to the General Accounting Office . . .' (Leslie R. Groves, *Now it can be told. The Story of the Manhattan Project*, London, André Deutsch, 1963, pp. 360–1).

them. State audit is passing from the form to the substance of public expenditures, its main objective from regularity to efficiency. There is very little international agreement as to what arrangements are most suitable for the conduct of this work, except that independence and free access to information are absolute necessities. Without these basic assets a state audit would be blind, deaf and dumb; but even with them it may still have no influence unless it is staffed with great care and wisdom and unless its findings are brought to widespread notice and considered by the authorities which matter. The effective operation of a modern state audit is a sophisticated constitutional achievement and it poses very subtle problems of administrative organization, concerning which every example and every private speculation is to be welcomed.

CHAPTER XI

Public Accountability and the Nationalized Industries

'The effect of violent animosities between parties has always been an indifference to the general welfare and honour of the State'—Lord Macaulay, *Essay on Hallam's Constitutional History*

THE position of new public enterprises in the midst of national economies which remain overwhelmingly 'capitalist' in spirit and legal form, and sometimes under the rule of governments opposed to their very existence on principle, has in it many elements of anomaly, embarrassment and contradiction. The administrative consequences of the nationalization movement remain largely unresolved. The marriage of state and industry in Western countries is not yet a happy one.

The problem of how national enterprises should be regulated and controlled is a study in conflicting motives. In the first place there is a very strong tradition of secrecy in private commercial administration. This is claimed to be necessary in order to confound one's competitors (although secrecy is also maintained by monopolist firms, who have no competitors) and the term 'flexibility' is used so frequently as to become a watchword. Flexibility in management is said to be the great benefit accruing from an absence of public control. It has been observed in France that the administrators of state enterprises characteristically try to behave as much like private directors as possible; this is a token of the strength of the older traditions. There is, moreover, a continuing belief among many politicians and members of the public that conventional business procedures are necessary for efficiency and commercial success. Demands for independence from public control, voiced by managements of state enterprises, are therefore always liable to find support from a steady current of sympathetic opinion.

Freedom from public control, however, means the right to work in close secrecy, and this thought may give even the sympathizer pause. For it goes against a much older and even more profoundly rooted idea, which is that persons given charge of any asset belonging to the public should account to the public for the use made of it rather than act as though it were their own. As a French civil servant sharply reminds us, 'The administrators of a nationalized enterprise are not holding a fief, they are managing public property.'[1]

Far from being weakened with time, the idea of public accountability has in some ways become stronger in recent times. The political parties which have favoured nationalization as a matter of social principle have always justified it largely on the grounds that it would bring powerful economic forces within the scope of public accountability, with all the changes of fundamental motive on the part of the management which that was expected to imply.[2]

The idea has also been increasingly expressed that some sort of public accountability for firms still in private ownership, especially large commercial monopolies, is desirable in the general interest.[3]

Some of the great parties which disapproved of nationalization in principle took the view that the least to be expected of state corporations was that they should be properly subordinated to the political powers through financial accountability; this was a common opinion in the United States. And Parliaments elsewhere thought of accountability as something which they were entitled

[1] Bernard Chenot, *Les Entreprises Nationalisées*, Paris, Presses Universitaires de France, 2nd edn., 1959, p. 124.

[2] In 1933 Mr Herbert Morrison wrote: 'We are seeking a combination of public ownership, public accountability and business management for public ends' (in '*Socialization and Transport*').

A recent example may also be cited. Mr Harold Wilson, then chairman of the Labour Party, in a speech to a Co-operative conference in London, said that the State should have the right to make private monopolies 'accountable to the nation, by public ownership or other appropriate means' (*The Observer*, 28 January 1962).

[3] For example an editorial in *The Observer* of 18 February 1962: '. . . both shareholders and the general public have a right to far more detailed information on the activity of giant industrial concerns than they are at present given. . . . The shareholder would become much more of an influence for national efficiency than he is able to be at present; and in sectors where effective monopoly was unavoidable the Government would be able to spot when something went wrong at a much earlier date.' Mr C. D. Foster, Fellow of Jesus College, Oxford, has proposed that to combat 'sloth, ignorance and nepotism' in private industry, companies should be obliged to publish fuller and more frequent accounts and, more remarkably, to have an annual efficiency audit (carried out by outside consultants reporting to the shareholders) in addition to the normal financial audit. *The Daily Telegraph*, 13 April 1964.

to demand, especially since they were called upon to approve grants and loans to nationalized corporations, and at times also to cover their losses.

Finally, there were widespread doubts as to whether state enterprises would in fact operate more efficiently in secret; sometimes accountability was thought to be an essential factor making for effective management. In the case of state monopolies, accountability was seen as a sort of counterpart for the absence of competition. Secrecy could perhaps be a blanket covering maladministration, overcharging and lack of energy. Professor W. A. Robson has observed that when controls come up for discussion, 'the more conservative the industry, the more its spokesmen talk about "stifling initiative"!'[1]

If the influences in favour of accountability were stronger than those making for secrecy, there was a further complicating factor. This arose from the political debate about the principle of nationalization itself. So embittered did this debate sometimes become that it was feared, and not without reason, that information about state enterprises would be exploited to provide arguments for and against their very existence. Thus the traditional Parliamentary controls, which were often capable of impartiality in judging matters arising in government departments, became suspect of partiality in dealing with nationalized enterprises. Secrecy therefore became an element of political tactics in questions of the public corporations, without reference to its desirability or otherwise for the efficient conduct of the corporations themselves.

This fear of publicity for political reasons was sensed more keenly by the parties of the left, anxious to avoid the release of matter which might be used to discredit their own creations. Thus a left-wing deputy in the French National Assembly, Pierre Meunier, campaigned in 1947 to weaken as far as possible the controls to be imposed upon nationalized enterprises.[2] In Great

[1] William A. Robson, *Nationalised Industry and Public Ownership*, London. Allen and Unwin, 2nd edn., 1962, p. 204.

[2] Serge Allain, 'La Commission de Vérification des Comptes des Entreprises Publiques'. Thesis presented at the Institut d'Etudes Politiques, May 1951, pp. 7–9. M. Allain describes M. Meunier as 'apparenté communiste', or 'fellow traveller'. His real motive, says Allain, 'was that the nationalized industries, as the conquest of the parties of the left, should remain under their exclusive control'.

Britain, the nationalization acts passed by the Labour Government of 1945–51 made no provision for a parliamentary audit, such as had for generations been imposed upon government departments, nor for any public audit whatever. There was to be no submission to Parliament of budgetary estimates, for approval or even for information. The same government also declined to accept the idea of a Select Committee of the House of Commons to deal with the public corporations. It was one of the ironies of the situation that precisely the parties which had always argued in favour of nationalization as a means of attaining public accountability did least to implement such accountability in practice. For the mere act of nationalization does not make an enterprise accountable, either to the political powers or to public opinion; effective accountability depends upon the creation of machinery and procedures for fact-finding. The submission of annual reports and professionally audited accounts does not amount to accountability. Ministries have always presented their own accounts and reports, but they have been considered to be accountable, not through these bare documents but through the political responsibility of their Ministers and through state audit. It is of the very essence of accountability that the persons or bodies held accountable should not be able to dictate which aspects of their business will be examined; the initiative must be held by those to whom they are accountable.

Accountability of the executive to Parliament for the normal activities of government is realized through questions raised by members of the legislature, through various kinds of debates and committee hearings, and through the reports of the state auditors. There were plenty of reasons why these tried and trusted expedients could not be applied in exactly the same way to state enterprises.

The various Ministers concerned were not themselves directly in charge of the nationalized industries, but merely held general powers of supervision. For them to be answerable in the legislature they had first to obtain information from third parties in the public corporations. A kind of sub-accountability was necessary between the managements and the Ministers, who became spokesmen for matters not within their own departmental control. Ministers had rarely been placed in such an uncomfortable position before, and this was an element which, together with doubts about the repercussions of disclosures, led to a particular reticence in dealing with questions about state industries. There has been a feeling in more than one country that the procedure of obtaining information about these industries through the Ministers was much less satisfactory than in the case of traditional matters of government. It was apparent that the Ministers did not themselves know all about the industries. Indeed they did not claim to do so; in the United Kingdom, for example, they disclaimed all responsibility for what were called 'matters of day-to-day management' (a category which is extremely hard to define).

This restricted flow of information is a logical consequence of the nature of the public corporations, since, as Professor Robson has pointed out, they are 'a device for running nationalized industries in a way which is divorced from ministerial responsibility to Parliament in the traditional sense'.[1] Full political responsibility was in fact never intended, and to obtain it a conversion of the state corporations into something like ordinary government departments would probably be necessary.

In view of the admitted defects in direct political accountability, it might have been thought that state audit had, as the alternative source of inside information for legislatures and the public, a particularly important role to play in control of state industries. The need certainly exists, but other difficulties have been encountered in dealing with it.

It was not clear what kind of audit should be applied. The question of a 'regularity' control of a detailed kind was the easiest to solve; it was everywhere felt, with good reason, that such a thing would be inappropriate. It might possibly have added to overheads by necessitating the maintenance of additional records, and it was feared that it would involve the regulation of administration within the tight limits associated in the popular mind with 'Treasury control'. It would have meant a real curtailment of the desired commercial flexibility. And a budgetary audit on behalf of the legislature was pointless unless the legislature was the body which approved the corporations' budget estimates. This was rarely the case.

There remained, however, a large number of matters of normal administration which state audit might usefully have been required to study and report upon for the guidance of the legislature

[1] W. A. Robson, op. cit., p. 176.

and even of the Ministers themselves. These included such things as the quality of internal accounting and financial control, purchasing and contracting methods, cases of waste and extravagance, and especially the conduct of large capital investment programmes, which were often very largely financed by public subsidies and loans. These investments required very careful and skilled management, technical as well as financial, if they were not to be wasted upon ill-planned or unremunerative projects. Matters affecting the profitability of the enterprises were also perfectly capable of study; for example, whether they appeared to be employing more persons than the work demanded—a situation by no means difficult to envisage in modern times. Independent information and opinions about their commercial operations could have been required and obtained. A comprehensive fact-finding service by disinterested professional experts without any executive powers had been strongly advocated by Sidney and Beatrice Webb as early as 1920.[1] The establishment of an efficiency audit commission, to assess the working of public corporations and make suggestions for improvements, had been proposed by W. A. Robson in 1937.[2]

These were some of the possibilities. It also became clear that public opinion regarded efficiency as the chief criterion by which state enterprises should be judged. But in the event even Mr Herbert Morrison's proposal of a common efficiency unit to provide a private consultant service for nationalized boards was successfully resisted by the board chairmen.[3] And the nature of the existing state audit bodies, which had been created for a different purpose, was a complicating factor. They were nevertheless able, in all Western countries except Great Britain, to make some contribution to this difficult problem of control. Professor Robson has expressed the view that the public accountability of the British nationalized industries compares very favourably with that of publicly owned industries in any other country with which he is acquainted.[4] This confidence is at present shared by the govern-

[1] In *A Constitution for the Socialist Commonwealth of Great Britain.*

[2] Robson, op. cit., p. 203. (The adoption of Professor Robson's proposal for an audit commission was advocated in a pamphlet, 'Concerns of State', published by the Bow Group in 1961. It was considered that the commission should be responsible to the Select Committee on Nationalized Industries.)

[3] Ibid., pp. 204–5.

[4] Ibid., p. 211. In addition to accountability through replies to Parliamentary questions, Professor Robson mentions a number of other potential

ment.[1] The British corporations are, however, unique in escaping any kind of constitutional control through audit, and it is therefore extremely doubtful whether a favourable comparison with the accountability of public enterprises elsewhere can stand the test of a close examination of the facts. The grounds for such doubts will be made clearer in what follows.[2]

Accountability in the various countries is deeply influenced by the nature of their state enterprises. These may be classified into three main kinds: firstly, organizations created and built up for purposes of practical policy; secondly, existing industries taken over by the state for reasons of political doctrine or economic necessity; thirdly, a number of 'historical accidents'.

There has been no 'doctrinal' nationalization of existing companies in the United States or Germany. This does not mean that they have had no debate for and against state enterprise, but the existence of very large industries in Britain and France which were nationalized in the name of a political ideal has added a further dimension to their national arguments about first principles.

The Government Corporations of the U.S.A.

Except for two national banks chartered soon after the War of Independence, there were no state enterprises in the United States until the twentieth century. But in 1904 a precedent was set by the acquisition of the Panama Railroad Company from a private corporation. During the First World War, Congress established a number of public bodies, including the War Finance Corporation, the Emergency Fleet Corporation, the U.S. Grain Corporation and the U.S. Housing Corporation. Liquidation

---

sources of information; notably the annual reports of the boards, consumer councils, replies by the corporations to M.P.s' direct enquiries, and various committee investigations.

[1] On 2 April 1963, Mr A. Roberts, M.P. asked the Chancellor of the Exchequer if he would introduce legislation to provide more accountability to the House of Commons by the nationalized industries. Replying for the Chancellor, Mr Barber said, 'No, Sir. The Government are satisfied that present arrangements provide sufficient accountability' (*Hansard*, 2 April 1963; Oral answers, col. 234).

[2] The subject is surveyed factually in *The Accountability of Public Corporations*, published by the Administrative Staff College, 1955. This draws attention on p. 44 to the 'important differences' between the public corporations established before 1946 and the nationalized industries created thereafter, 'which are responsible for the greater sense of the need for increased Parliamentary control'.

followed rapidly upon the end of the war, but the expedient was beginning to be respectable. A number of Federal Land Banks created in 1916 were continued in operation under the aegis of the Farm Credit Administration; the provision of assistance to agriculture has from that time been a major function of public corporations in America. The Inland Waterways Corporation (1924) was the only important new foundation of the prosperous twenties, but in the great depression which followed, a wave of new creations for the first time established federal enterprise firmly and substantially within the American economy.

The principal purpose of the corporations created in the 'thirties was nothing less than to restore an impetus to the economy as a whole. Some of the new foundations were therefore largely financial in purpose. The greatest of these was the Reconstruction Finance Corporation (1932–53). The Federal Deposit Insurance Corporation (June 1933), the Commodity Credit Corporation (October 1933) and the Export-Import Bank (February 1934) were major creations of the New Deal. So also was the most remarkable of all American government corporations, the Tennessee Valley Administration (T.V.A.), of May 1933, which was charged to carry out a huge capital works programme in an underdeveloped region of the country.

A wide and almost indiscriminate use of the device of the government corporation continued throughout the 'thirties, although always for the development of new activities rather than the expropriation of old ones. It was applied to price-support policies, public works, unemployment relief, low-cost housing and much more.

The national war effort in the Second World War was extensively confided to government corporations under the financial direction of the Reconstruction Finance Corporation. These included the Defense Plant Corporation (1940–5), which by the end of the war owned some 2,100 factories; the Defense Supplies Corporation (responsible for provision of 'strategic materials'); the Rubber Reserve Company (with about 50 synthetic rubber plants); the Rubber Development Corporation (whose main purpose was to obtain wild rubber from Brazil), and the Metals Reserve Company. War risk insurance was entrusted to a War Damage Corporation, and the U.S. Commercial Company made 'preventive purchases' of raw materials in world markets, to keep them from falling into enemy hands. The R.F.C. and its subsidiary corporations during the war formed an industrial and financial complex on an immense scale. Government corporations were the biggest of big business. In March 1945, 58 of the corporations held combined assets worth almost $30 thousand millions.[1]

During the time of the Roosevelt administration the luxuriant development of government corporations was accompanied by a public debate about their control. In 1933, the new President was concerned mainly to obtain quick results in an atmosphere of economic crisis, and his desire seems to have been to make the corporations as independent as possible. He urged Congress in April 1933 to create the T.V.A. as 'a corporation clothed with the power of government but possessed of the flexibility and initiative of a private enterprise'. The earliest corporations of that period were created by Act of Congress, but some other important ones were established by simple Executive Order.[2]

The corporations of the New Deal and the Second World War were endowed with very considerable autonomy. They were granted an initial capital appropriation, with freedom to retain any income arising from their investments; they were thus relieved of the necessity of obtaining annual appropriations from Congress. Most of them could sue and be sued in their own name. The T.V.A. was permitted to establish its own personnel system. The corporations were not clearly subordinated to Federal Departments, and were thus only tenuously linked with the executive.

Such administrative separatism could scarcely escape criticism. Congress felt that the corporations were being used to promote policies without legislative authority or budgetary appropriation. Private enterprise feared competition from the government. Moreover, the corporations' transactions were almost entirely exempt from the scrutiny of the General Accounting Office, so that Congress had no control through the machinery of state audit.[3] Even the President must have had doubts about the position; his Committee on Administrative Management in 1937 declared that the corporations' independence had made his task more burdensome.

The situation was gradually brought under control. Already in

[1] Paul Haensel, 'Le Financement de la seconde guerre mondiale aux Etats-Unis,' *Annales de Finances Publiques*, Nos. VI-VII, pp. 37–9.

[2] Among those created by Executive Order were the Commodity Credit Corporation and the Export-Import Bank.

[3] J. D. Millett, *Government and Public Administration*, pp. 104–5.

1935 some corporations had been required to submit their budgets for administrative expenses to the Bureau of the Budget. By 1940 all posts in corporations, with the exception of the T.V.A., had been brought under the civil service system.[1] After 1939, most of the corporations were subjected to the supervisory authority of a federal department or agency, again with the notable exception of the T.V.A. In 1941, Congress set up a Joint Committee on Reduction of Non-Essential Expenditures, which became a channel for criticism of the corporations.

The decisive outcome was a very important piece of legislation, the Government Corporation Control Act of December 1945. In the opinion of an authority on the subject, this Act was 'one of the most significant developments in the art of public administration. With it the government corporation can be said to have come of age in the United States.'[2]

The Act reserved exclusively to Congress the power of creating government corporations. But its essential importance was that at last it established a happy formula for financial control of the corporations; this was the combination of a 'business-type budget' with a 'commercial' type of state audit. Each corporation was to present an annual budget on business lines, together with a plan of operations, through the Bureau of the Budget to the President and Congress. The budgets were to be 'considered' by Congress, but this did not imply a strict regime of annual appropriations. Finally, the corporations were to be audited by the General Accounting Office 'in accordance with the principles and procedures applicable to commercial corporate transactions'.

This provision was interpreted on very thorough lines and broad principles, for it gave rise to the 'comprehensive audit' methods of the General Accounting Office. And the duties imposed upon the Comptroller General by the Government Corporation Control Act, which included reporting upon the corporations' transactions and commenting upon their irregularities, led to the first recruitment of certified public accountants for the General Accounting Office.

[1] Except the most senior posts, which were mostly filled by the traditional procedure of appointment by the President with the advice and consent of the Senate.

[2] Harold Seidman, 'The Theory of the Autonomous Government Corporation: a critical Appraisal', *Public Administration Review*, Spring, 1952.

The Act fulfilled the declared intention of Congress to bring government corporations and their operations under annual scrutiny and provide for their financial control; the Bureau of the Budget and the General Accounting Office became congressional agents for these purposes. It was a major operation of constitutional and administrative integration, and at the same time a compromise which made allowance for 'flexibility' by forbearing to impose detailed legislative control of appropriations. Compromise was implied in the denial of the Comptroller General's traditional right to withhold approval of individual payments. The corporations also won a battle by obtaining a provision requiring that audits should take place at their offices, rather than at the G.A.O. in Washington.

After a period of teething troubles, when the corporations complained of inexperienced audit staff and the auditors deplored the condition in which they had found some corporations' accounts,[1] the new audit and indeed the Act generally, have worked satisfactorily. The Hoover Commission of 1949—apparently without result—recommended that the Control Act, although not the legal status of a government corporation, should be applied to no less an institution than the U.S. Post Office Department, which claims to be the largest business unit in the world. It was the opinion of the second Hoover Commission that:

> The net effect of bringing an agency under the Government Corporation Control Act is greatly to simplify budgeting, accounting, personnel management, and the use of revolving funds. Moreover, the use of the corporate form generally brings about a much more flexible organization, provides more checks and balances upon management, and ensures an effective audit by the Comptroller General.[2]

The Commission therefore recommended that a number of government credit agencies[3] should be made subject to the Act, which was felt to provide the right kind of statutory foundation for a commercial type of administration.

[1] Comptroller General Warren informed Congress that a satisfactory audit of the R.F.C. and its subsidiaries and associated companies was not possible for 1945, owing to the deficiencies of the accounts (Haensel, op. cit.).

[2] MacNeil and Metz, *The Hoover Report 1953–55*, p. 136 (Mr MacNeil was editor-in-chief to the Commission and Mr Metz was head of its research staff).

[3] The Small Business Administration, the Rural Electrification Administration, the Housing and Home Finance Agency and the Veterans' Life Insurance Programme.

In the early 'thirties there had been widespread and uncritical enthusiasm for the use of government corporations. This was followed by considerable disillusionment when the consequence appeared to be a chaotic dispersal of authority and responsibility. The Government Corporation Control Act represented a reaction in favour of governmental unity. At the same time, its passing signified congressional approval of the government corporation as a useful type of organization for certain kinds of business, subject henceforth to a strict legislative control of new creations. There were to be no more foundations by Executive Order. On the operating level a balance was also found and it has been said of this that, 'the heart of the compromise is the business-type budget and the commercial-type audit'.[1]

Although the Comptroller General was denied powers of disallowance, the success of the compromise was not founded upon the lightness or superficiality of his audit. On the contrary, the 'comprehensive audit' was very much wider in scope and outlook, if less voluminous and detailed, than the earlier auditing procedures of the General Accounting Office. As time passed and the comprehensive audit was gradually generalized, the type of questions raised with the corporations scarcely differed from those taken up with ordinary Federal agencies, though in addition consideration was given to the 'fairness' of the corporations' financial statements.[2] There was the same general concern for all aspects of management efficiency.

A good example of the impact of the General Accounting Office upon government corporations is furnished by the case of the oldest of them, the Panama Canal Company, formerly the Panama Railroad Company, which maintains and operates not only the famous canal but also a shipping line, a railway and many public services in the Canal Zone. The auditors first of all brought to light the sale of a dredger, in discreditable circumstances, for $415,600; the vessel had been resold by the purchaser within three months for $1,200,000. They then devoted their attention to matters of operating efficiency; as a result of their recomendations the Company was able to reduce its Washington and New York staffs by more than 100, with a saving of half a million dollars

[1] Leonard D. White, *Introduction to the Study of Public Administration*, New York, Macmillan, 4th edn., 1955, p. 136.

[2] Annual Report, C.G. of the U.S., 1952, p. 21.

annually. Another recommendation resulted in a housing programme for the Canal Zone, estimated to cost $80 millions, being cut by half, with a further estimated saving in maintenance costs of $1,500,000 a year; the recommendation was based upon the retention of existing housing and a reduction of the proposed scale of new accommodation and facilities. The Company also raised its stevedoring rates, which had been found barely to cover labour costs, so as to increase revenue by about $275,000 a year. A simplification of sales procedures in Company retail stores was expected to save a further $250,000 annually.[1]

This was not all. An Act of Congress in 1954 reflected the views of the G.A.O. in a provision that employees of the Panama Canal Company should be required to pay for medical and hospital treatment. A further Act in 1955 directed that no funds available to the Department of Defense were to be used in future for hospitals in the Canal Zone; this was because the G.A.O. had reported that such hospitals, costing nearly $2 millions annually, were duplicating the facilities of the Canal Company and the Canal Zone Government. The Company took the initiative in 1954 of reducing its housing programme by a further $7 millions.

The Comptroller General in 1951 had submitted to the Company far-reaching proposals for a reassessment of staff requirements, for a policy of going out to contract for construction work rather than using direct labour,[2] and for the adoption of 'many newly developed methods and techniques to improve the operation of many activities'. 'Little or no action was taken until the present Governor was appointed,' recorded the Comptroller. But the new Governor with a fresh staff 'adopted these recommendations generally in their economy and retrenchment programme'. The resulting economy in personnel costs amounted to nearly $6 millions annually.[3]

The auditors were helping to bring twentieth-century standards of administration to the old Canal Company. On a recommendation of the Comptroller General a Joint Logistical Committee, with representatives of the armed forces and the Company, was

[1] Annual Report, C.G. of the U.S., 1953, pp. 19–20 and p. 52.

[2] It seems that a general rule may be inferred from cost investigations recorded by state audit in many countries, that it is more costly for public authorities to have major construction projects carried out by their own staffs than by contractors. Like other general rules, however, it has exceptions.

[3] Annual Report, C.G. of the U.S., 1954, pp. 27–8.

appointed to investigate duplicate facilities in the Canal Zone. As a result, the Company began to obtain its oil from the Navy, 'thus making storage facilities available for rental to commercial companies'. It was able to share an Army cold storage warehouse and save a planned expenditure of $800,000 for the rehabilitation of its own. But the G.A.O. called this only 'minor progress'.

In November 1954 the Company refunded $10 millions of capital as a result of action by the Bureau of the Budget, which 'followed an audit recommendation to the Congress that the Company be required to make a payment into the Treasury in view of its large cash holdings at the time'. It also paid $2,165,000 as additional interest, following a reclassification of its capital assets, and would pay an additional $800,000 per year thereafter. 'Obsolete, slow-moving and excess stocks' were reduced by $3 millions. The G.A.O. also recommended to Congress that 'a specific plan for liquidating the investment of the United States Government in the Panama Canal Company be incorporated into the basic legislation' and that 'the formula for establishing toll rates be amended to include the recovery of losses sustained by the Company in the operation of business activities'.[1]

The auditors continued to make comprehensive audits of the Company annually. The Canal Zone Hospitals were unified under the Canal Zone Government. The auditors co-operated in a valuation of the Company's assets and sent a review of the valuation report to the Bureau of the Budget. Combining of facilities between the Company and the Armed Forces continued; for example in rubbish disposal, bakeries and fire-fighting services. Consolidation of the last of these was alone expected to save not much less than $2 millions annually. The auditors also obtained provisions to the effect that other Government agencies would be required to reimburse the Canal organization for any services rendered. The Company's regulations for home leave with free travel were amended and its internal audit service reorganized to provide 'a vast improvement of internal control'.[2]

Thus the activities of the G.A.O. resulted in nothing less than a major overhaul of the Panama Canal Company and even of the Canal Zone administration as a whole. This was perhaps exceptional, since the Zone seems previously to have been a sort of administrative backwater. Some of the newer corporations were found to have much better management, and the G.A.O. even

[1] Annual Report, C.G. of the U.S., 1955, pp. 56–8. [2] Ibid., 1956, pp. 87–90.

reported to Congress upon the St Lawrence Seaway Development Corporation that the auditors had noted no significant weaknesses in the administration of its activities.[1] But this was even more exceptional, and from year to year the Comptroller General's reports record many useful recommendations arising from audits of such great corporations as the T.V.A. and the Commodity Credit Corporation.

It becomes increasingly difficult with each report to find any differentiation between the audit of corporations and that of government departments and agencies; it seems as though the G.A.O. has for practical purposes almost ceased to distinguish between them, although they continue to be audited under different Acts of Congress and there is presumably still some difference between the forms of their accounts. There is no sign of any American dissatisfaction arising from the fact that state enterprises are subjected to a thorough and forward-looking public audit; on the contrary, their control is believed to have proved a success and a solution to what was at one time a menacing administrative problem.[2] There is an element of paradox in the fact that the United States, which is traditionally the country most firmly opposed to public enterprise, appears to be one of the very few countries which has so successfully integrated nationally-owned corporations into its administration that their control has ceased to be a major public issue.

British nationalized industries: a continuing crisis of accountability

At one time there was a superficial similarity between the events in Great Britain and those which had already taken place across

[1] Ibid., 1959, p. 74.

[2] Note for example this striking comment: '. . . now that the Government Corporation Control Act of 1945 is in operation and the Bureau of the Budget and the Corporation Audits Division of the General Accounting Office exercise so much authority over the budgeting and expending of funds, the public accountability of government corporations from the financial standpoint is at least as satisfactory as that of the major departments and establishments' (Marshall E. Dimock, 'Government Corporations: a Focus on Policy and Administration', *American Political Science Review*, December 1949).

It is rare to find an administrative measure so widely commended as the U.S. Corporation Control Act. The good order which it introduced is contrasted with the previous situation when 'the only alternative to applying regulations devised for traditional governmental activities was often to apply no controls at all'. (Seidman, op. cit.). It must be added that control in the United Kingdom still appears to be at that stage of development.

the Atlantic. The Labour Government was a great creator of national corporations, as President Roosevelt had been, and it similarly endowed them with a large measure of freedom from accountability to the legislature. On the other hand, it gave the ministers—that is to say the government in power—a very considerable degree of control over them. This was bound to be disturbing to the parties of the opposition, and it might have been reasonable to expect that a reversal of electoral fortunes and a change of government would be followed by the passing of regulating legislation on the lines of the Corporation Control Act of 1945 in the U.S.A. But this was not to be.

Apart from a few ancient bodies, such as the Trinity House, whose brethren had watched over sea-marks since Tudor times, Britain began the twentieth century almost as free of state enterprise as the United States. With the exception of the General Post Office the first major public body with an express commercial purpose was the Port of London Authority, set up by statute in 1908. The First World War produced nothing of more than ephemeral importance, but several major corporations were founded between the wars.[1] All these corporations, save the B.B.C., were established by Acts of Parliament, which gave them a very large measure of autonomy, with only a modest degree of ministerial supervision. There was no provision requiring any sort of state audit. The remoteness of these bodies from public accountability was equal to that of Mr Roosevelt's earlier government corporations.

The problem of control became much more acute when the nationalizations after 1945[2] absorbed an increasingly important

[1] Electricity Commission (1919); Central Electricity Board (1926); British Broadcasting Corporation (Royal Charter, 1927); London Passenger Transport Board (1933); British Overseas Airways Corporation (1939).

[2] The following were the major nationalizations of the Labour Government of 1945–51:

1946: The Bank of England (Bank of England Act, 1946); National Coal Board (N.C.B.) (Coal Industry Nationalization Act, 1946); The Air Corporations (B.O.A.C. & B.E.A.) (Civil Aviation Act, 1946); New Town Development Corporations (New Towns Act, 1946); Hospitals (not within the framework of a public corporation) (National Health Service Act, 1946).

1947: Railways, inland waterways, long-distance road haulage; placed, together with the existing London Passenger Transport Board, under a new British Transport Commission (B.T.C.) (Transport Act, 1947); Central

sector of the whole economy. Despite limited de-nationalizations afterwards, the transfers to state ownership effected by the government of Mr Attlee were by far the greatest in British history. Public funds were deeply involved; Sir Frank Tribe, then Comptroller and Auditor General, drew the attention of the Select Committee on Nationalized Industries in 1953 to the fact that the total of Treasury-guaranteed loans to the great public corporations already amounted to some £2,500 millions, a figure which was approaching the order of magnitude of the Funded Debt of the Realm.[1] By 31 March 1962 the outstanding guaranteed stock totalled £3,282 millions, and there were also outstanding amounts borrowed directly from government funds to a total (for the principal nationalized industries) of a further £3,320 millions.[2] Such loans sometimes amount in practice to irrecoverable public endowments or investments, and may be used in the case of the less solvent corporations as a concealed subsidy to cover operating deficits.[3]

There is nothing intrinsically surprising in this; the need of most nationalized industries for new capital was well known, and similar things have taken place in other countries. What is surprising, and not common to other countries, is that the chief state auditor was in almost no case made responsible for audit of,

---

Electricity Generating Board (absorbed the Central Electricity Board), 12 Area Electricity Boards and 2 Scottish Electricity Boards (Electricity Act, 1947).

1948: National Gas Council and 12 Area Gas Boards (Gas Act, 1948); Colonial Development Corporation and Overseas Food Corporation (Overseas Resources Development Act, 1948).

1949: Iron and Steel Corporation of Great Britain (Iron and Steel Act, 1949).

Sequels under the Conservative Government after 1951:

1953: Most of road haulage industry de-nationalized (Transport Act, 1953); Most of iron and steel industry de-nationalized (Iron & Steel Act, 1953).

1954: Overseas Food Corporation dissolved (Overseas Resources Development Act, 1954).

[1] Select Committee on Nationalized Industries, Report, with evidence. H. of C. 235/1952–3. Questions Nos. 76, 101 and 102.

[2] 'Finance Accounts of the United Kingdom', 1961–2, pp. 32–3, 56–7. (Direct borrowing by nationalized industries was authorized by the Finance Act, 1956, and there were no further stock issues after then.)

[3] The Government White Paper on Reorganization of the Nationalized Transport Undertakings (December 1960) proposes the write-off of £400 millions from the outstanding debt of the British Transport Commission in respect of accumulated losses financed from Exchequer advances. Further write-offs of a similar kind are foreshadowed.

and reporting upon, the operations of these nationally-owned corporations, despite their very deep indebtedness to the public purse. The usual statutory requirement is that the responsible Minister is empowered to appoint private auditors and is required to lay the audited accounts of the corporations before Parliament, together with the private auditor's report thereon. Only in the case of the Colonial Development Corporation and the former Overseas Food Corporation was any kind of effective intervention by the Comptroller and Auditor General required.

The situation appears to reflect some confusion in the public mind between the functions of private audit and state audit. This is not the fault of the profession, which has been at pains to explain the limits of commercial auditing practice. The professional auditors conduct a skilled 'regularity' audit which is directed to ensuring, as required by law, that in their opinion the accounts show 'a true and fair view' of the state of affairs on the date of account. Whereas the state auditor's concept of 'regularity' is largely based upon conformity with the details of pre-established budgetary appropriations, that of the auditing firms is orientated towards the precision of the profit and loss account and the balance sheet. The fundamental idea is the prevention of fraud,[1] either within the organization or by a false presentation of the organization's position to the shareholders. The professional auditor is charged with this statutory duty, and will otherwise assist his client if asked to do so, but subject to due fulfilment of the duty, he is most anxious to maintain the best possible relations and do nothing to alienate the firm which pays his fee. This is all perfectly natural, but it differs from the task of the Comptroller and Auditor General rather as that of a firm of solicitors differs from the functions of a High Court Judge. It is not a reflection upon the qualifications of anybody; it is a question of different legal status, duties and prerogatives. A private auditing firm, however reputable, cannot be expected to undertake a constitutional function.

Commercial type accounts, such as the British nationalized cor-

[1] Mr T. B. Robson, President of the Institute of Chartered Accountants, told the 1953 Select Committee on Nationalized Industries: 'The primary purpose of an auditor is to see that things are right, to see if there is a system which is working, and which is going to prevent fraud' (H. of C. 235/1953–3, question 252). See also *The Accountability of Public Companies*, published by the Administrative Staff College, 1955.

porations are mostly required by law to submit to Parliament through their Minister, are rarely illuminating documents, except in so far as they indicate solvency or insolvency. To give a 'true and fair view' of a corporation's affairs does not imply a clear view. And the so-called report of the professional auditors upon the accounts is in fact a rather lengthy certificate.[1] It bears no relation to the long critical or explanatory commentaries which constitute the Comptroller and Auditor General's reports. It tells nothing at all about the affairs of the corporation audited, unless the auditing firm feels obliged to qualify its report. This happened in the case of the groundnut scheme of the Overseas Food Corporation, but it is very rare.

But the reasons for excluding the Comptroller and Auditor General from the realm of the nationalized industries were more than a mere lack of discrimination between Company Law audit and constitutional audit.

The Labour Government, for reasons already considered, resisted the principle of exposing the nationalized industries to state audit. In 1946, amendments were proposed during the passage of the Coal Industry Nationalization Bill to empower the Comptroller and Auditor General to examine and certify the accounts. The Government rejected the amendments on the ground that there would be a danger of interference in the routine affairs of the Coal Board, and argued that since the Public Accounts Committee was in any case entitled to send for persons, papers and records, it possessed sufficient powers without the audit. Professor Chubb has commented that, 'In view of the actual way that the Committee works and of its dependence on the Auditor General, this latter reason was unsound.' [2] The New Towns Act,

[1] The wording varies, but the basic form is fairly consistent and essentially similar to the reports of auditors on the accounts of private companies. For example, the Auditor's Report to the Minister of Aviation on British European Airways' Accounts for the year ended 31 March 1960 reads as follows: 'In our opinion the annexed balance sheet, operating and profit and loss accounts, notes and accounts of subsidiaries, give a true and fair view of the state of the Corporation's affairs at as 31st March, 1960, and of the result of its operations for the year ended on that date. We have obtained all the information and explanations which we consider necessary. In our opinion the Corporation has kept proper books of accounts and received proper branch returns, and the above-mentioned accounts are in agreement therewith.' (Signed). (H. of C. 267/1959–60, p. 93.)

[2] Chubb, op. cit., pp. 145–6.

1946, in its original form, provided for audit by the District Auditors and the C. & A.G., but the words 'professional auditor' were substituted in the House of Lords.[1]

The Public Accounts Committee at first conscientiously endeavoured to examine the nationalized industries' accounts without the help of the C. & A.G. to which they were accustomed. Various potential sources of information were tried, including the summoning in evidence of members of the nationalized boards and the professional auditors, but without reports from the Comptroller and Auditor General the P.A.C. was unable to gain a deep insight, and it has been said that 'their enquiries are of peripheral interest to any broad conception of the work of the nationalized industries'.[2] Since the principle of a Select Committee on Nationalized Industries was accepted in the 'fifties, the P.A.C. has tended to confine itself to its traditional field.

The adoption of the idea of a Select Committee has not solved the problem of a state audit, despite the fact that the first Committee, appointed in 1952 to report upon methods of obtaining information about the nationalized industries, recommended the appointment of a Standing Committee to examine them, with the aid of an officer of status roughly equivalent to that of the Comptroller and Auditor General, 'with the assistance of at least one professional accountant, and such other staff as the committee may deem useful'.[3]

The question of an officer to serve in relation to the nationalized industries as the Comptroller and Auditor General did in the case of government departments was the crucial issue arising from the idea of a Select Committee. The members appointed in 1952 recorded: 'It was clear to us that the proposed new Committee would need the assistance of a similar permanent official, to direct their attention to the important matters in the vast organizations which it is set up to consider.'[4] On this question depended whether a Select Committee was to be an effective and influential organ of control on a permanent basis, or whether it would be limited to the occasional direct investigations which were as much as it could reasonably hope to undertake without basing itself upon the findings of an external audit. This issue was fairly

[1] Sir Frank Tribe in evidence to the Select Committee on Nationalized Industries, 1953 (Question 80).

[2] W. A. Robson, op. cit., p. 194.

[3] H. of C. 235/1952–3. Report, para. 34.

[4] Ibid., Report, para. 28.

clear at the time, but it encountered new and complex motives, in addition to the old obstacle of resistance on principle to accountability through a Select Committee as still expressed by some of the witnesses examined.[1]

Difficulty arose not only over the principle of whether the Select Committee should have an auditor to advise them, but on the question of who that officer might be. Sir Frank Tribe, the C. & A.G., was himself obviously the leading candidate and the Chairman of the Select Committee asked him directly: 'Is your Department equipped, and would it desire, to audit the accounts of the nationalized industries?' He replied:

I could not possibly take it on with my present staff. It would be a very large undertaking. I have a very high regard for the qualifications of my staff, and I suppose that, if Parliament so wished, they could be trained to do it, and I could recruit people to do it, but I am certainly not in a position to do it at present.[2]

It was clear from the tone of this and other replies that Sir Frank was not in favour of undertaking the work.[3] The reason which he gave is of interest in relation to what has already been said about the United States:

. . . this whole issue was considered in America in 1945. Up to then the Government Corporations in America were not subject to government audit at all, but in 1945 Congress passed a Government Corporation Control Act which subjected the corporations to budgetary control by Congress and to annual audit by the General Accounting Office (that is the American counterpart of my Department). . . . I talked to him (the Comptroller General of the U.S.) about this a year or so ago, and what actually happened was that he had to make an enormous expansion of his organization to do this. He had to recruit from the profession. He had to set up a new organization within his department staffed entirely by professional accountants who carried on doing the same kind of work they had done before, but under his aegis. I suppose that, if Parliament in this country did decide to take such a step, I should have to do the same thing, but in this country I think it is only fair to point out that it would cause enormous dislocation in the

[1] Notably Mr Herbert Morrison (who thought that a Select Committee 'would create a rather unnerving prospect' for members of the managements of public enterprises—H. of C. 235/1952–3, Question 383) and Lord Reith (who said that a Select Committee would be 'terrifying' to the corporations —ibid., Question 611).

[2] H. of C. 235/1952–3, Question 88.

[3] This view was stated explicitly: ibid., Question 136.

profession because the audit of the accounts of the whole of the nationalized industries must represent quite a considerable part of the work of the profession.[1]

In another reply, Sir Frank added:

> ... I would have to draw hundreds of professional accountants from the profession and make them civil servants, and many of the largest firms of professional accountants in the country would find their work suddenly and greatly reduced. I should have thought it would have led to great dislocation both in the Government service and in the profession.[2]

The desire to avoid a clash of interest between public and private auditors was very understandable, but it did not solve the Select Committee's problem. Sir Frank Tribe suggested that the professional auditors 'could produce some kind of report' if they were told what Parliament wanted. In reply to another question, he added:

> I think it would probably take a few years for the professional auditors to acquire the expertise of knowing exactly what a Select Committee likes and does not like, but I cannot see any other way of doing it.[3]

The evidence of the Institute of Chartered Accountants showed that the matter of expertise was far from being the only obstacle in the way of this suggestion. There was constant emphasis on the relationship between a professional auditor and his client, which bore scarcely any similarity to that between a public department and its fully independent external auditor. In a written memorandum submitted to the Select Committee the Institute stated:

> It is above all essential that the nationalized undertakings should not be given grounds for an impression that the auditor has become a professional 'snooper' whose task it was to search out the minor administrative delinquencies which occur in every business.[4]

Sir Harold Howitt, for the Institute, said, 'The auditor, of course, is not a public informer.'[5] Mr Robson, the other witness, stressed the mental attitude of the auditor:

> If he goes about ... thinking that things are wrong, and looking for things which are wrong, then he is a snooper. ...[6]

[1] H. of C. 235/1952–3, Question 88.
[2] Ibid., Question 144.
[3] Ibid., Questions 89 and 116.
[4] Ibid., p. 23.
[5] Ibid., Question 212.
[6] Ibid., Question 252.

On this definition it may be frankly admitted that a good state auditor, like a good detective, is in the line of duty a kind of snooper. His independent status makes it possible for him to be so, and a critical spirit is essential to him. His concern tends to be for major rather than minor administrative errors. This alertness is certainly not shown by experience, however, to be incompatible with good relations between public authorities and state auditors.

The Committee reported that they were not convinced that the professional auditors could or should be asked to fulfil the role of the Comptroller and Auditor General. They also resisted the suggestion which had been made in certain answers to questions that the Committee's permanent officer should be an official of the executive, perhaps of the Treasury. They felt:

> that the permanent officer of the Committee . . . should be a servant of the House of Commons, and not of the Government or of any of the corporations, and not removable except by an address from each House of Parliament.[1]

This was a very clear appreciation of the necessity of independent status for state audit duties, and since the existing officer with this status saw difficulties in the way of assisting the Committee, the members accordingly recommended the appointment of a second one.

The Government, however, was still thinking in terms of a very limited degree of public accountability, and although it accepted the recommendation to appoint a regular committee on nationalized industries, this was given extremely narrow terms of reference. The new committee was only to have liaison officers from the Treasury and other departments and it was denied the appointment of an independent parliamentary auditor, which was the most important of its requirements.[2] In addition, many types of obvious and difficult problems, such as wages and conditions of employment, matters decided by Ministers, consumers' complaints, and questions of 'day-to-day administration', were excluded from its purview. The committee was not to appoint sub-committees nor to publish all its evidence, and its powers of enquiry were

[1] Ibid. Report, p. xi.

[2] Mr Ralph Assheton, M.P., who had been chairman of the first Select Committee, told the House of Commons that he considered the appointment of an independent officer to be the key to the whole proposal, and that a committee would not be worth much without such an officer (cited by W. A. Robson, op. cit., p. 188).

restricted.[1] It was hardly surprising in the circumstances that the members of the new Select Committee reported that their terms of reference left them 'insufficient scope to make enquiries or to obtain further information regarding the nationalized industries which would be of any real use to the House'.[2] A 'harmless' control of administration is in practice invariably a useless one.

In 1956 the Government proposed the appointment of a fresh Select Committee, which was not to be specifically debarred from the consideration of any matters, but which was given to understand that both ministerial policy and questions of day-to-day administration were outside its province. At least, all matters between these two extremes were to be open for discussion. The Opposition showed its continued doubts about public accountability by dividing the House against the proposal.

The revised Select Committee began work in 1957. It had advisory officials from the Treasury, the services of an officer comparable to the Comptroller and Auditor General having again been refused. It concentrated upon specific industries and issued reports successively upon the North of Scotland Hydro-Electric Board (1957), the National Coal Board (1958), the civil aviation corporations (1959) and upon British Railways (1960). The reports were based principally upon information obtained by direct enquiry from the nationalized boards, and not at all through independent audit. The utility of such investigations is perhaps considerable, but they do not fulfil the same function as a state audit. The Committee does not have guidance based upon inside information, as to what matters really require its attention.[3] And, to mention only one other point, state audit is a continuous or at least a frequent control, whereas the occasional Committee enquiry may in the case of each corporation be followed by immunity for many years.

The Select Committee itself was dissatisfied. The members were well aware that their lack of independent advice made their in-

[1] For the detailed restrictions placed upon the activities of the first Select Committee, see A. H. Hanson, *Parliament and Public Ownership*, p. 142.

[2] H. of C. 120/1955–6.

[3] Professor W. A. Robson expresses the view that the Select Committee 'are not and cannot be an authoritative body in their present condition'. Without specialized advice they 'will remain a group of well-intentioned laymen whose opinions are unlikely to carry great weight'. Although 'better than nothing, . . . they would be immeasurably strengthened with the reports of an Efficiency Audit Commission or the advice of a highly qualified staff' (op. cit., pp. 201–2).

vestigation inefficient, and in 1959 they made a special report on their old problem of assistance.[1] They pointed out the long duration of their unaided enquiries; thirteen months in the case of the air corporations, during which the Committee asked more than 2,500 questions and the Chairman and Boards of the industry had been 'subjected to a very long-drawn-out examination'. Various suggested means of providing help for the Committee were considered, and some of the evidence taken from witnesses was an echo of the hearings on the same subject in 1953.

Upon one point the Committee members were adamant; this was that 'any staff working for them should be and should be seen to be the servants of Parliament and not of the Executive'.[2] They therefore politely declined offers of help from the Treasury. The reason why they did not think that a Treasury officer could in the future prove to be what they needed was 'based wholly upon principle'. The Committee might conduct enquiries into the effects of Treasury decisions, and it seemed to them 'hardly likely' that a Treasury official 'would be able to speak objectively on such matters; and it would be unfair to require him to try to do so'.[3]

Another matter of principle received further clarification. The Committee heard further evidence from the same two representatives of the Institute of Chartered Accountants as had appeared before it in 1953. These witnesses again made clear their anxieties about good relations with the nationalized boards and indicated that an attempt to conduct an independent audit would endanger them. Sir Harold Howitt put the matter expressively:

> The reason why we say it might be embarrassing to get the auditor to change his hat, so to speak, and go back to the office and approach the board not qua auditor and say to them, 'I have come on behalf of a Committee of the House of Commons to look into this, that or the other point', is that I think you might queer the relationship between the statutory auditor and the board.[4]

The Committee drew the appropriate conclusion, and reported that it did not think it wise 'to impose upon the statutory auditors of the nationalized Corporations any duties other than those carried out by auditors of commercial and industrial Companies'. If they should have to criticize the Boards, 'it could not fail to prejudice the relationship between the industries and the accounting

[1] H. of C. 276/1958–9.
[2] Ibid. Report, p. v.
[3] Ibid. Report, pp. vii–viii.
[4] Ibid., Question 124.

profession.'[1] If this recommendation of the Select Committee and its decision as to the undesirability of being advised by an official of the Executive were both of a negative nature, this was nevertheless a form of progress. But very little advance was achieved on the positive side; there were serious reservations about all the proposals for providing the Committee with expert assistance, and it was evident that the members had not yet made up their minds as to how this should be done. They made no clear recommendation, but asked the House of Commons to give special consideration to their problems, with a view to the provision of some assistance.

Thus, a decade after the series of great nationalizations of basic industries came to an end, Parliamentary accountability, despite all the debates about it, remained unsecured as a permanent and effective constitutional control of the public corporations; and this primarily for lack of an independent state audit.[2] The type of audit to which the nationalized boards are subjected is scarcely different from what it was before nationalization, or what any private company undergoes; but at least its irrelevance to the constitutional

[1] H. of C. 276/1958–9, Report, p. vii.

[2] Public opinion is not unconcerned with the question of accountability. For example, an interesting short article signed John Trafford and entitled 'What really *is* going on?' appeared in the *Manchester Evening Chronicle*, 30 March 1962. The writer complained:

'We were told, before nationalization, that the inestimable benefit would be that in future these industries would belong to the people. The only indications of this are that we have to find any money that they need.

Of any say in their operation there is no sign.

Parliament appears to be helpless. M.P.s find they are unable to influence the day-to-day running of these industries.

True, there are various consultative and advisory councils on which consumers are represented, but their role appears to be that of yes-men. . . .

This state of affairs must be altered. It is easy enough for any state monopoly to make whatever profit it chooses, simply by putting up its prices, though it may be riddled with inefficiency and waste.

As things are we cannot tell what is going on. We may fancy that we are shareholders in State industries, but their balance-sheets are concealed from us. . . .

There is nothing basically wrong with nationalization except that after years of experience we still permit bureaucracy to exercise autocracy. We should challenge that rule, demand the information that will enable us to see what is going on, insist on having a voice in policy.

Until that comes about, to say that these industries are run by the nation is just foolishness.'

issue has been realized. The problem of how to cope with this situation remains. Meanwhile, the Post Office Act, 1961, in giving the Post Office increased financial autonomy, has abolished the traditional form of appropriation accounts and cash accounts, and required that only commercial accounts will be prepared in future. And despite the changeover to commercial accounting, the audit is still to be carried out on behalf of Parliament by the Comptroller and Auditor General.

France

In view of the accountability problem which remains largely unsolved in Great Britain, it is particularly interesting to turn to the events in France, with its large and closely comparable body of nationalized industry.

State industries in France have some venerable forebears, such as the *Manufactures royales* of Louis XIV and his minister, Colbert; the most famous of these were the porcelain factory at Sèvres and the Gobelins tapestry workshops. The French state has also long maintained the monopoly of manufacturing tobaccos and matches, though with a fiscal rather than a commercial objective. Until the First World War, however, there was no nationalization of a modern kind, except for the acquisition of a part of the railway network in areas where private operators were unable to make a profit. There was not even much municipal enterprise, such as was common in Britain and Germany.

During the 1914–18 war, however, the government conducted all sorts of manufacturing and commercial activities on its own behalf, and at least demonstrated that this could be done. After the recovery of Alsace from Germany the state found itself owner of two considerable mineral undertakings providing nitrate fertilizers and potash.

The Popular Front government of 1936 was the real founder of French nationalized industry. In that year it expropriated all establishments making or dealing in classified war materials.[1] This nationalization was a consequence of the widespread if sometimes misplaced popular fear and hatred of the so-called 'merchants of death', which was a feature of public opinion in Britain as well as France during the inter-war years. A recent observer has commented cynically: 'Later experience showed that various branches of industry and commerce could draw their prosperity from the

[1] Law of 11 August 1936.

common misfortune, and that (the armaments manufacturers) had no more influence over national policy than many a seigneur of banking or textiles.'[1] In 1937, the government acquired the capital of the whole railway network and formed the Société nationale des Chemins de fer français (S.N.C.F.).

The greatest outburst of the nationalizing impulse was, however, that which followed the Liberation. It began at the end of 1944, before the last German soldiers had been driven from French soil, and it lasted no longer than eighteen months, up to the middle of 1946. During this brief period the industry and commerce taken over by the French state was not inferior in volume and importance to the British Labour government's nationalizations during the succeeding three years.

In 1945 the shares of the Banque de France and of the four great deposit banks, the Crédit Lyonnais, the Banque nationale pour le Commerce et l'Industrie, the Comptoir d'escompte and the Société générale, were all acquired by the state.[2] In the following year, the shares of 34 major insurance companies, handling about half the premiums in France, were also acquired.[3] Thus banking and insurance were far more completely nationalized than in the United Kingdom.

It was scarcely necessary to nationalize the coal industry. Strikes broke out in August 1944, even before the Germans had made good their retreat from the Normandy battlefields, and in most areas the miners expelled the managements and took over the mines. The structure of the whole French coal industry was settled by a law of 17 May 1946. This created a central organization, the Charbonnages de France, with actual operations confided to separate authorities, called Houillères de bassin, in each coalfield.

The French electricity industry was transferred to the state by a law of 8 April 1946, which created the corporation of Electricité de France. The gas industry was nationalized under Gaz de France by the same law. This had the advantage of establishing a similar administrative structure in the two industries, which co-operate more than their equivalents in some other countries.

In 1945, Air-France and two other airline companies were nationalized by *ordonnance*, the state taking over their shares. The

[1] Chenot, op. cit., p. 74.

[2] Law of 2 December 1945.

[3] Law of 24 April 1946.

present Compagnie nationale Air-France, absorbing the other two companies, was not created until 1948; the law provides that at least 70 per cent of the capital must belong to the state.

The most unusual group of nationalizations in France is that in the motor and aircraft industries. Here we are largely in the province of the historical accidents. The manufacture of airframes was nationalized as a war industry by the Blum government in 1936, which confided it to several Societés nationales de Constructions aéronautiques. Somewhat illogically, the aero-engine companies were not nationalized at that time, and the state contented itself with the acquisition of some shares in them. The largest of these firms, Gnome et Rhône, was however subjected to 'punitive nationalization' in 1945, for collaboration with the enemy. The decree proclaimed the motive of 'satisfying the patriotic conscience'.[1] The Societe nationale d'Etudes et de Construction de Moteurs d'avions (S.N.E.C.M.A.) was the result. This corporation still exists, and the nationalized airframe industry, after several reorganizations, was concentrated into only two enterprises, Sud-Aviation (1957), designers and producers of the Caravelle airliner, and Nord-Aviation (1958).

The famous motor-manufacturing firm of Renault was another object of 'punitive nationalization'. A profitable enterprise before the war, Renault became so again as from 1948, and it has since demonstrated that state ownership is not necessarily incompatible with the most spectacular commercial success.

The two leading French steamship companies, the Compagnie générale transatlantique and the Compagnie des Messageries maritimes, have long had close links with the state. But their full status as nationalized corporations was only established by a law of 1948. The rest of the French merchant navy remains in private hands. This act of nationalization was two years later than the main series, and was also the last of importance in France.

The French Cour des Comptes never doubted that it had a mission to accomplish in the field of nationalized industries. As long ago as 1927, the Chemins de fer de l'Etat were exempted from parliamentary control of finance in order to achieve greater 'flexibility' under commercial accounting, and were removed from the jurisdiction of the Cour. In its subsequent report the Cour protested vehemently. It claimed to have been the first to recognize

[1] Ordonnance of 29 May 1945.

the fact that traditional public accounting was too rigid for state enterprises and should be relaxed.

But adaptation of the form of public accounting to new requirements should not prejudice the competence of the court of audit. . . . Its control is not tied either to the existence of a budget or to a particular type of accounting. . . . The Cour therefore feels bound to protest against a doctrine which would consider its control irreconcilable with any accounting system which is exempted from the traditional regulations. It feels all the more justified in maintaining this point of view since there is an inherent dissimilarity between public and private industrial enterprises, which cannot be ignored. Thus the fact is that a public enterprise has no shareholders to bear from their personal fortunes the consequences of faulty management. It cannot go bankrupt. Its deficits are ultimately covered by the taxpayers, whose representatives should be fully and regularly informed about the management of the enterprise. It is, consequently, necessary for the control over the accounts to present quite special guarantees of efficacy.[1]

The principles and the conclusion expressed in this statement are extremely sound, although it appears from the context that the Cour was then still thinking in terms of some sort of judicial audit.

When M. Mirimonde published his book on the Cour des Comptes in 1947, the question of public accountability for the nationalized industries was on the agenda again. He wrote:

One would seek in vain a valid justification for the exemption from control of most of the great enterprises recently nationalized. While it is true that the customary rules of public accounting, which were developed for the purposes of political and administrative authorities, dangerously hinder the operations of an industrial establishment, it does not follow that the control of the Cour should be excluded. In fact, when the need arises the Cour's audit assumes adaptable forms, perfectly suited to commercial management methods. . . . When it becomes public property, an establishment escapes the often rigorous control which its providers of capital—whether shareholders or bankers—imposed upon it under private enterprise. If this control is not replaced by another, it is to be feared that abuses will sooner or later arise and develop. A purely internal organ of control can always easily be reduced to silence in such a case.[2]

The Cour des Comptes was soon to have its opportunity.

The nationalization laws had made varied provision for controls

[1] Quoted by Moustapha Habib, 'La Cour des Comptes en France, en Belgique, en Italie et en Allemagne' (Thesis for the Ecole Libre des Sciences Politiques, 1932).

[2] de Mirimonde, op. cit., pp. 77–8.

over the different corporations; private auditors, special control bodies for specific industries, and, for establishments with an official *comptable*, the Cour des Comptes itself. Studies conducted in 1947 pointed to the defects and confusion of these controls, and especially to the unsatisfactory nature of the *a posteriori* control, which was felt to be the most important for industrial and commercial concerns, since it involved less interference with management than control at the budgetary planning stage. Provision had in any case been made for day-to-day ministerial control, by the appointment of two permanent liaison officials to each of the main nationalized corporations. The first of these, the Contrôleur d'Etat, represented the Minister of Finance, and the second, the Commissaire du Gouvernement, was the agent of the Minister responsible for technical supervision of the industry concerned. The need was now for a type of *a posteriori* control which would be capable of a comprehensive view of the management of the whole nationalized sector of the economy.[1] The idea of the *vue d'ensemble* is one which has a great appeal for the French administrative mind. And the demand for improved control was strengthened by the fact that most of the nationalized industries were then operating at a loss.

The result was the Commission de vérification des Comptes des Entreprises Publiques, created by a law dated 6 January 1948. Although Parliament had created two Sub-Committees for nationalized industries, the Commission de vérification, which was to become the principal organ of accountability, was not an agent of the legislature. The idea was, by making use of the magistrates of the Cour des Comptes, to create a non-political auditing body for this highly controversial work. 'From the very first it was the intention of the legislature to make the Commission into a technical organization, sheltered from political influences to the greatest possible extent.'[2] The independence of the magistrates of the Cour, arising from their irremovable status, was the decisive reason why they were chosen to provide the key personnel around whom the Commission was formed.[3]

[1] Henri Lorain, Conseiller Maître à la Cour des Comptes, 'Le Contrôle des Entreprises Publiques', Address to the Institut des Sciences Juridiques et Financières Appliquées aux Affaires (of the Paris Faculté de Droit), 15 March 1956.

[2] Allain, op. cit., p. 11.

[3] J. Le Vert, Conseiller Maître, 'La Commission de Contrôle des Comptes des Entreprises Publiques', 1960, p. 10.

The law provided for the appointment of a Président de Chambre of the Cour des Comptes to be full-time President of the new Commission, which was 'to proceed annually to the examination of the administrative accounts, balance sheets and profit and loss accounts' of specified enterprises, 'and to draw conclusions from them concerning the financial results of these enterprises'. The scope of such conclusions was somewhat clarified by the nature of the individual report on the accounts of an enterprise which the Commission was to address to the Ministers concerned; this report was to contain an opinion as to the regularity and 'sincerity' of the accounts (the 'true and fair view' of British professional auditing). It was to recommend rectifications of the accounts if necessary. Finally, and by far the most important, it was to include 'an opinion concerning the quality of the commercial and financial management of the enterprise'. This opened the way to an efficiency audit.

The Commission was also to address a general report (*rapport d'ensemble*—a title which corresponded with the desire for a *vue d'ensemble*) annually to Parliament, to the Prime Minister and to the Cour des Comptes. This report was to include, in appropriate cases, the Commission's recommendations for modifications to the structure or organization of the enterprises, and was to contain 'its opinion as to their prospects for the future'. The last requirement was a particularly difficult one, and the Commission was clearly intended to take a very broad view of its activities.

The law provided that the Commission was to be divided into sections for the work of examining accounts, and in practice there have always been four sections, specializing respectively in Power; in Transport and Communications; in Credit, Insurance and Information; and finally in Mechanical, Chemical and Miscellaneous Industries. Each section was in effect based by law upon the Cour des Comptes. It was to be presided over by a conseiller maître of the Cour and three of the five other voting members of every section were to be magistrates of the Cour with some seniority. The remaining two members were to represent the Minister of Finance. Thus the sections were deliberately, and always with the intention of fortifying the independence of the Commission, given a majority of members from the Cour. Finally, in accordance with a decree of July 1948, the President of the Commission has been given the assistance of a *rapporteur general*, whose influence is great because in compiling the general report he tends to orientate the whole activity of the Commission; he also has always been a senior magistrate of the Cour. The deliberative organization of the Commission is dominated by the Cour to the extent of eighteen members out of a total of twenty-six.

The Commission, however, includes a few members without votes. There is a permanent representative of the Commissariat Général au Plan, the national economic planning body, in each section; this is because of the importance of the problem of investment in the nationalized industries. The Commissariat is the authority responsible for co-ordinating investment. This is a case of audit as a service to planning. The other two non-voting members of each section vary according to which enterprise is under examination; the first of them is either the Contrôleur d'Etat or the Commissaire du Gouvernement attached to that enterprise. The second is a senior representative of the ministry which supervises the corporation's activities. The principle behind the participation of these two members is that the section should have up-to-date information about the policies of the management and the minister concerned in each case.

If members of the Cour des Comptes predominate among the sections, this is not the case among the *rapporteurs* who undertake audits on their behalf. Their recruitment is more varied than that of their equivalents serving the Comité central d'Enquête.[1] They come not only from the *grands corps*, the higher administration of the ministries and the various corps of control, but also from among civil service technicians, engineers of the Ponts-et-Chaussées and the mines service (who form a group which has great national prestige), state economic experts, controllers of insurance, and other specialists. Particular emphasis is placed upon the value of this technical co-operation. The Commission, like the Comité d'Enquête, lacks a permanent investigating staff; the *rapporteurs* are made available on a temporary basis. There has been some complaint from the Commission that its *rapporteurs* were too few in numbers and unable to spare enough of their time. In its most recent reports there is a rising note of stress; responsibilities are said to be increasing faster than the resources to meet them. The Commission asks for a relaxation of its statutory obligation to examine the accounts annually, at least in certain cases. It presses other authorities to lend their officials as *rapporteurs* for an adequate

[1] See above, Chapter IX, p. 223.

length of time and points out that the audit missions enrich their knowledge.[1]

These plaints notwithstanding, there has in fact been some increase in the number of *rapporteurs* available; at first it was about 70 and by 1960 it was more than 130, of whom only about twenty were members of the Cour des Comptes.[2] The Commission has, like the Comité d'Enquête, been able to point to the fact that its operations have cost the state almost nothing except out-of-pocket expenses, since hardly any permanent posts were created for it.[3] This advantage, which for a financial control institution is a psychological asset, must be weighed against the risk of superficiality, to which all part-time official bodies are exposed.

Three characteristics mark the procedure of the Commission. In the first place, it is not satisfied merely to examine the documents submitted to it by the nationalized corporations; balance sheets, profit and loss accounts, commercial accounts, annual reports of the Boards (*conseils d'administration*), development statements, and in some cases, reports of the professional auditors or the Contrôleurs d'Etat. It sends its *rapporteurs* to make an investigation on the spot. Secondly, the reports which they produce are subjected to what the French call a contradictory examination; that is to say they are freely debated with the managements of the enterprises concerned, at hearings in the appropriate sections. Thirdly, the fact that the individual reports are strictly confidential documents makes it possible to deal with matters which might gravely embarrass the managements if they became public.[4]

Communication of these secret reports to Parliament posed a delicate problem. A law of 1955 provided for a permanent liaison between the Commission and the parliamentary sub-committees on nationalized industries, and specified that the individual reports were to be made available to the sub-committees. This was by way

[1] Commission de vérification, Seventh General Report, 1960, p. 9.

[2] Le Vert, op. cit., p. 12.

[3] In 1950, the Commission had a budget of 17,394,000 frs. (say £40,000). Two-thirds of this consisted of travelling expenses, allowances, and fees for professional advice. The remainder covered the salaries and office expenses of the Commission's secretariat of 12 persons (Allain, op. cit., p. 21).

[4] An example of the sort of thing which must remain secret is given by M. Le Vert. He writes that the individual reports often contain extremely detailed information about unit production costs: 'it would be highly dangerous if private competitors were able to learn such details' (op. cit., p. 16).

of a compromise, because the sub-committees had been suggesting that they would set up their own investigating service if the secret reports were withheld from them. An anxiety about the consequences of political indiscretions remained, and a special liaison sub-committee composed of members of the parliamentary finance committees and of the sub-committees on nationalized industries was set up, to avoid disclosures which would have been unfortunate for the industries concerned.

This uneasy relationship has been modified under the Fifth Republic. Parliament is no longer entitled to maintain permanent sub-committees; this ruling was part of the so-called 'rationalization' of parliamentary procedure, which was planned by Michel Debré in 1958. The new arrangement concerning the nationalized industries is that 'the individual reports of the Commission de vérification . . . are available to those members of Parliament who are chosen to follow and assess the management of nationalized enterprises. . . . These members are, moreover, entitled to call for all official documents, of any sort whatever, which relate to the operations of the enterprises, companies or establishments subject to their control'.[1] A working procedure has been devised to give effect to these rules. A quarterly list of new individual reports on state enterprises is now sent by the Commission de vérification to the Commissions des finances of the National Assembly and the Senate. A member of either of these finance committees can request communication of any new report which he requires; a control of these documents is maintained by the Presidents of the finance committees. M. Le Vert believes that this is a satisfactory compromise between the secrecy of the individual reports and the necessity of ensuring parliamentary control.[2] There is no doubt, however, that the control of the French nationalized industries rests principally upon the Commission de vérification itself, rather than upon any parliamentary body. It is possible that but for this, political passions over nationalization would have prevented the establishment of any effective permanent machinery for accountability, as they did in Great Britain.

The procedure of working with a corps of part-time *rapporteurs* with varied skills is common to the efficiency audit of the Comité d'Enquête and to the Commission de vérification. The similarity largely ends there. The Commission's control is a permanent one,

[1] *Ordonnance* of 30 December 1958, article 164.

[2] Le Vert, op. cit., pp. 17–19. Lorain, op. cit., pp. 13–14.

not a series of special studies. The rapporteurs have to visit the nationalized enterprises annually or at least every few years, and there are scores of such enterprises. They cannot, therefore, hope to stay very long; perhaps a week or two at most. The audit teams are larger for the more important enterprises and may amount to six or seven for the very large ones. But the records of great corporations such as the S.N.C.F. must inevitably be enormous, and in general the oversight of small corporations is simpler and more effective.

The *rapporteurs* should be suitably briefed from the available documents before their audit. In the offices of each corporation they do as much work as possible on the most obvious sources: vouchers, cost analyses, minutes of the Boards, and so on. Great emphasis is placed upon discussions with directors, heads of departments and others; 'it is from this dialogue with the animators of public enterprises that the *rapporteurs* will derive the best of their observations and recommendations.'[1] This kind of an audit is bound to leave many important subjects almost untouched, at least in the case of the main corporations. It can only provide a broad view of a limited number of problems. The *rapporteur* may nevertheless cast doubts upon the orthodoxies of management policy, and his commentaries may form a valuable basis for debate in the section. In any case nothing else by way of an independent report on management is available.

When the report has been written and distributed it is discussed in the appropriate section of the Commission with the chiefs of the enterprise concerned, including in most cases, the Chairman, the Director General, sometimes various department heads, and almost always the accountant of the corporation. These debates are said to be a very important innovation. M. Le Vert, himself a *rapporteur général* of the Commission, states that it is most often from the debate that the most suitable recommendations emerge.

It is by this exchange of views that mutual understanding between the two parties is born, the Commission becoming aware of the needs and the difficulties particular to the organizations examined, whilst the directors and managers responsible for the latter can convince themselves of the merits and the impartiality of the attitudes adopted by the Commission. This debate makes it possible to avoid the frictions to which exchanges of observations in writing inevitably give rise, and

---

[1] Le Vert, op. cit., p. 14.

it is not rash to think that part of the influence . . . of the Commission is due to the persuasive action of its members during discussion of the reports. Many of the Commission's conclusions imply as much when they record the declarations of the Chairman of an enterprise undertaking to put an end to such and such a practice or to act in future in accordance with the views of the Commission.[1]

The section meets together after the heads of the enterprise have left, and decides the final wording of its individual report, a document of perhaps twenty pages or so. The Commission has no powers of decision and makes only recommendations; it can however refer officials suspected of serious irregularities to the Court of Budgetary Discipline,[2] and has done so on several occasions.

The amicable relations between the Commission and the heads of the nationalized industries, as described by M. Le Vert, must be due partly to the nature of the magistrature of the Cour des Comptes, which, as we have seen,[3] is a social élite as well as a learned one. One of the least obvious but most significant features of the general reports of the Commission is a final note, which always appears, to the effect that a number of its members, named in each case, abstained from taking part in certain deliberations. Their abstention is attributed to 'Incompatibility between their functions as voting members of the Commission and those which they exercise in the establishment under examination.' This is a remarkable thing; a substantial proportion of the Commission consists of magistrates and senior officials who are themselves part-time members of the governing bodies of nationalized industries. Out of the twenty-six voting members who approved the seventh general report, ten stood down at certain times because of their responsibilities for specific enterprises. M. Le Vert himself, the *rapporteur général*, stood down during the discussion of the S.N.C.F. It is hardly surprising that such a body should win the confidence of the various managements and appreciate their viewpoints.

The matter needs, however, to be seen in perspective. All the members of the Commission are first and foremost magistrates and civil servants of high rank. Their primary loyalties are to the Cour des Comptes and the financial services to which they owe distinguished careers. In the second place, the nationalization laws provide for representation of the state on the boards

[1] Ibid., p. 15.
[2] See Chapter IV, pp. 69–70, above.
[3] Chapter III, p. 32, above.

(conseils d'administration), and it is normal procedure to appoint members of the *grands corps* or senior officials of the ministries. This is a form of patronage which resulted from the transfer of industries to the state, and a few full-time posts as Chairman or Director General are very remunerative, even in terms of the salaries of senior magistrates and civil servants. But none of the members of the Commission hold such posts, which would, in the case of the magistrates, be recorded in the Annual List of the Cour des Comptes, and which would in any case be incompatible with the time needed for the Commission's numerous sessions. They are evidently part-time board members who presumably receive only incidental fees and expenses from the corporations. And it would be to ignore the extraordinarily secure position which members of the Cour des Comptes hold in French society, were one to imagine that they were seriously compromised by holding such posts. Again, the solidarity of the members of the Commission with the 'director class' was not strong enough to prevent them referring the director general of a nationalized corporation to the Court of Budgetary Discipline in 1957.

Nevertheless the control of the Commission de vérification is an operation which takes place mainly within the confines of a fairly homogeneous social, educational and professional élite, an 'Establishment',[1] which comprises both controllers and controlled. One is entitled to take the view that this fact tends to limit the impartiality of the Commission, or that without it the control would not have worked at all. The evidence on these points is, however, insufficient; the Commission, understandably, refrains in its reports from discussing the implications of the double role played by some of its members.

The basic conception of this body brings to mind Professor Robson's old proposal of an efficiency audit commission. Its actual achievements are, however, particularly difficult to measure, because the individual reports are almost an unknown quantity. All that is known about these reports is the procedure for dealing with them. They are forwarded, as the law requires, to the Ministers responsible in each case; copies go to the Cour des Comptes, and also to the parliamentary finance commissions on

[1] The nature of the French 'Establishment' has, since the French Revolution, differed profoundly from that of Britain. In France educational status tends to decide social status rather than the reverse.

request. There is no legal requirement for the Ministers to transmit them to the managements concerned, but this is what usually happens and the Commission is strongly in favour of the practice. The Ministers have no obligation to take any particular action, although they are not empowered to approve the accounts of the various enterprises until they have received the Commission's views about them.

The absence of strong powers for the Commission provoked a certain amount of criticism at first. The late M. Emmanuel Chalandon of the Cour des Comptes wrote as follows in 1950:

> The nationalized enterprises have been shielded from the control of the Cour, by reputation too severe, and confided to that of a *Commission de vérification* which is governmental in origin and essence (despite the fact that some magistrates of the Cour sit upon it). This Commission is thus more docile or at least more timid than the Cour. In its first report of 1949 it displayed excessive prudence; it has nevertheless greatly disappointed those who do not admit any sort of criticism at all in connection with the nationalized industries.[1]

M. Allain, commenting on this view, agreed that public enterprises were 'far from having the traditions of order, honesty and economy which are, no matter what people say, characteristic of a large number of French government departments'.[2]

There remains a current of opinion which favours the eventual incorporation of the Commission into the Cour des Comptes proper. It seems unlikely, however, that such a transfer will take place in the near future, even if the Cour were prepared to renounce the application of its customary judicial audit, which the nationalized corporations would certainly oppose on principle. The Commission is, for one thing, dependent upon its corps of *rapporteurs*, most of whom come from outside the Cour des Comptes. Perhaps even more important may be the human unwillingness to disturb an organization which has given a reasonable degree of satisfaction in difficult circumstances and whose procedures have acquired the familiarity of habits.

The Commission had by 1961 produced seven general reports. As M. Chalandon observed, they differ markedly in tone from the reports of the Cour. The note of sharp criticism is often, though not invariably, lacking. The emphasis is upon tact, and the Commission has clearly been anxious not to add fuel to the public

[1] Chalandon, op. cit.

[2] Allain, op. cit., p. 91.

debate for and against nationalization.[1] Moreover, the reports do not often contain 'scandals' arising from the detailed conduct of administration in the nationalized industries. Perhaps these are mostly confided in the individual reports, or possibly the audits are too short to bring them to light in large numbers. The general reports, in any case, do not feature them, but concentrate on the broad aspects of policy. They contain a condensed account of the activities of each corporation, and the seven reports could serve as a concise history of French nationalized industry. They point to factors which stand in the way of solvency, even when these are matters of the broadest public policy such as the state of the labour market. The fact that such considerations may be beyond the control of the board concerned does not prevent the members of the Commission from commenting upon them. On the contrary, they feel obliged to do so, since their reports are addressed first of all to the government. The general reports are a form of advice to the public powers on what to do about the nationalized industries, and in particular how to make them pay their way. They are also advice to the industries themselves.

No doubt the Commission was wise to adopt a cautious tone in view of the climate of opinion. The French state enterprises, like others elsewhere, have quite often incurred losses, and a bald account of the facts has in such cases been criticism enough. The press, which has widely echoed the reports, is perfectly able to add its own polemics.

A few major scandals of waste and extravagance have, nevertheless, been reported. Some of these have been in Africa, the international graveyard of many a hopeful development scheme. A body formed to sponsor a cellulose industry based upon colonial timber resources built a factory at Bimbresso on the Ivory Coast. It was begun as a research experiment but the scheme expanded during construction and the factory eventually cost about two milliards of francs. Production never attained as much as a third of capacity, and most of the product remained unsold, rotting in a tropical climate. The factory kept going on subsidies for a while, but in 1954 the decision was taken that it would have to close. The accounts showed an accrued trading loss of 998 millions, but the Commission described this as far less than the true figure. Attempts

[1] In its first report the Committee wrote: 'The losses recorded cannot all be attributed, *a priori*, merely to the nature of nationalized bodies and to the influence of nationalization upon management.'

to sell the factory as a working unit were a failure. The Commission expressed 'regret' that public funds had not been administered to better advantage.[1]

The first *rapporteur* who visited the Algerian mining research organization, in 1951, discovered important cases of fraud and obtained the conviction of the accountant.[2]

Two colonial fiascos were reported from French Guiana; a forestry development body which had handled over 1,300 millions of francs went into liquidation in 1959 and the absence of recent accounts left a 'regrettable incertitude about the assets and liabilities'. Another body, charged with the settlement of immigrants, received 950 millions between 1950 and its dissolution in 1959; it dealt with only 207 immigrants, and all but 70 of these left the country to seek better living conditions elsewhere.[3]

Nearer at home, the Commission was critical of two radio corporations. The Societé Financière de Radiodiffusion provided the equipment for Radio Andorra, with government backing, but owing to 'political, legal and financial problems' there was no transmission for several years.[4] The Societé Radio-Impérial was formed before the last war to operate a radio station at Tangier, but its activities came to an end in 1949. The state was the sole shareholder. The Commission found that no liquidation of the company's assets, which included land and buildings at Tangier, had taken place, and no proper closing accounts had been produced. Even the existence of much of the state's property had become uncertain. The Commission pressed for the formation of a new board of the company for the overdue winding-up operation, and expressed the view that the interests of the state had been very badly protected.[5]

In dealing with small, or even defunct enterprises, the Commission has no need to practice diplomacy, and its observations occasionally sound like those of the Cour. But these minor corporations are the least significant of the 150 or so which are on the Commission's audit list.[6] The handling of powerful and celebrated public enterprises like the S.N.C.F. and the Régie Renault

[1] Fifth Report, p. 32, and Sixth, p. 41.

[2] Third Report, p. 36.

[3] Seventh Report, p. 78.

[4] Fourth Report, p. 24, Fifth, p. 28 and Seventh, p. 56.

[5] Fourth Report, p. 24.

[6] The number varies as corporations are formed or disappear, but it has tended to increase.

is naturally a different proposition, and it is this which must decide the Commission's reputation.

Renault is not a good example of its achievements. This is because the company, under a management appointed by the state, has been almost consistently successful, in a profitable and growing industry. The Commission's reports tell a story of continual progress to the position of the third largest motor manufacturer in Europe and sixth in the world, and criticism seems to have been as difficult as advice was superfluous. There was some complaint about labour agreements which were embarrassing to less wealthy sections of the economy, and in its seventh report the Commission recorded that wage co-ordination machinery had been instituted. Another subject which appears in several reports is the distribution of profits, which has been on the basis of half to the staff and half to the state. The Commission was at first dubious about the staff bonus, which was additional to other incentives, but it was mainly interested to see that Renault allocated much more to its reserves and paid the state's share more promptly. On these points at least, it received satisfaction. In dealing with a booming and well-managed public enterprise such as Renault the main utility of the Commission is perhaps, by providing a routine of accountability, to combat the tendency of directors to think and act as though they were the owners. For instance it records with some asperity:

> As before, subsidiary companies have been created and share-capital increased without the government approval expressly required. . . . It is absolutely necessary for the company to submit to these obligations henceforward. It is properly a matter for the State, which owns the company, to fix the limitations of its activity and the means by which it must be carried on.[1]

Interventions of the Commission with the board of Renault have been infrequent. It is quite another matter when the members are confronted with a corporation which constantly shows a deficit and gives other signs of mismanagement. An example is that of the Régie autonome des transports parisiens (R.A.T.P.), which administers both the Métro and the bus services in the capital.

When the R.A.T.P. first came under examination, the book losses were small, but the Commission decided that the financial

[1] Seventh Report, p. 60.

balance was 'more apparent than real'; there were subsidies from the state and from local authorities, and the amount devoted to investment was much lower than it should have been. Organizational changes would, it was thought, be beneficial; the possibilities of economies arising from unification of bus and Métro administrations had not been exploited. Meanwhile, expansion was mainly confined to the suburban bus routes, which were the least profitable.[1]

In the next report, the Commission noted the creation of a joint technical and supply directorate for the two networks, and expressed the belief that this was in response to the previous report's recommendations about fusion. But it was not sufficient merely to place two staffs under the same authority; the number of officials should be reduced by merging their duties. The Commission had strong views about investment, which was 'in proportion neither to the size of the assets which must be maintained, nor to the role which public transport is called upon to play in the economic life of the Paris region'. A special effort was needed to overhaul the arrears of maintenance. Meanwhile, losses were increasing.[2]

By 1956 the deficit was a milliard francs a month, and the Commission examined causes. One was the rule that many of the staff could retire at 50, with an immediate pension; this was based on an arbitrary comparison with coal-face miners and seemed 'far too liberal'. The mechanization of ticket sales and checking was recommended and the Commission even suggested that the Métro might be developed to work by remote control.[3]

The government of the day reluctantly gave its approval for increases in fares. 'But,' wrote the Commission, 'for economic reasons totally extraneous to the R.A.T.P., the price of workmen's weekly seasons has been maintained at the old rate.' By thus increasing the differential between these and ordinary fares, a strong incentive was being created for fraud in a form which would be difficult to disclose and combat. There had been an effort to step up the investment rate, but the Commission criticized the 1957–61 programme submitted by the R.A.T.P. to the Commissariat général au Plan for its 'lack of breadth and boldness', and its failure to face up to 'the fundamental problems of reducing operating costs'. The Commission considered why this was and concluded that the structure of the management and the

[1] Third Report, pp. 12–14. [2] Fourth Report, pp .10–11.
[3] Fifth Report, pp. 11–12.

status of the authority which regulated fares were both wrong. The board had been composed of representatives of all the interests involved, and, with such a membership, had never been in a position to follow a vigorous policy.[1]

The government of General de Gaulle and Michel Debré was by now in power, and in the following report the Commission was able to record that the structure of the R.A.T.P. had been changed by decree, and that the new organization 'did not appear to involve the elements of weakness which characterized the old'. The Commission's prediction about the abuse of workmen's season tickets had proved correct: in 1957 the proportion of passengers using seasons was 39 per cent on the Métro and 17 per cent on the buses; by the following year the figures had risen to 50 per cent and 26 per cent respectively, and had gone on rising. As a result, receipts had actually fallen, although the number of passengers was stable. Expenditures were, however, rising rapidly. The situation had called for drastic action, especially by increasing the season ticket fares, and this had in fact been done.

Much more needed to be achieved. The R.A.T.P. should, said the Commission, have the most modern commercial accounts. The expedient of varying investment expenditures from year to year according to the state of the profit and loss account was roundly condemned, especially since the total spent was inadequate even in the better years. If subsidies were to be granted to the R.A.T.P. in future, these should be so contrived as to avoid being 'an incentive to careless management'. Concessions to the authority should be conditional upon proof that possible economies had been effected. Such economies would have to take account of personnel costs, which amounted to two-thirds of the whole. There was overweight in the senior ranks, with one supervisor for every seven employees; a special effort remained to be made in order to adjust the effectives to the requirements, especially on the administrative side.

The Commission favoured the use of more temporary and even part-time staff; it was not only less costly but provided flexibility in staff management. The existing proportion of two to three per cent was much too low, and well below the civil service figure. An increase in the extravagantly low retiring age of fifty was a notable means by which the operating accounts could be brought into balance. Economies were possible in the purchase of buses;

[1] Sixth Report, pp. 18–20.

they presupposed that the R.A.T.P. would abandon certain over-specialized technical requirements, 'which increase the cost without procuring real advantages'. The Commission proposed a whole series of potential economy measures for the new management's consideration, together with suggestions for ending the under-investment which had led to 'an evident state of stagnation'.[1]

The attitude of the Commission towards the Paris transport authority was obviously one of considerable vigour, and even of impatience. The government was never without an independent source of information about a corporation which called for ever increasing subsidy, nor without suggestions for remedying the situation. The need for genuine accountability is greatest among corporations which follow the line of least resistance, incurring a permanent deficit rather than take unpopular measures and oppose vested interests.

The S.N.C.F. has also had a long series of annual losses, but the view of the Commission has been rather different. The management of the French railways has followed a policy of bold and costly investment, and the Commission has been careful to point to its technical achievements whilst deploring the losses which have accrued nevertheless. The question of these losses, which the Commission described as 'the most important of the problems which face the nationalized industries',[2] has received constant attention. A great many potential sources of economy have been given publicity; the need for a new regulation of competing forms of transport; a corrupt method of calculating overtime pay (abandoned at the Commission's request); exaggerated free travel concessions for railway staff, extended even to their parents, parents-in-law and grandparents; interruptions of major capital works for reasons of immediate financial embarrassment.[3] The Commission proposed that the railways should be permitted to vary freight

[1] Seventh Report, pp. 36–8. [2] Second Report, p. 29.

[3] Ibid., pp. 31–2. (The last of these reasons for financial embarrassment is not unknown to British Railways. There has, for example, been at least one major hold-up in the great electrification scheme of the London Midland Region, between Euston and Lancashire. But in the absence of public accountability it is not possible to do more than speculate as to the large expenditures which may have been incurred unproductively whilst work was stopped. It is not possible to hold up major capital works without compensating those who are under contract to carry them out.)

tariffs in certain cases, as a means of competing with road transport, and concessions of this kind were made by the government. Rolling-stock workshops were too numerous and heavily overstaffed.[1] The number of perquisites and bonuses granted to railwaymen led the Commission to speak of an 'unfortunate tendency for the personnel of the S.N.C.F. to obtain the advantages of both public and private enterprise'. Economies were possible through increased standardization of the 420,000 types of store items, rationalization of purchasing and reduction of stocks.[2] A full survey of the land and buildings owned by the railways ought to be made, and the redundant property disposed of. Competition between nationalized airlines and the S.N.C.F. for traffic over relatively short distances would be 'particularly irrational'.[3] In conformity with the Commission's suggestions, the S.N.C.F. disposed of part of its fleet of coastal colliers.[4]

Electrification, amounting to 6,320 kilometres at the end of 1958, was the 'trump card' of the re-equipment programme, and the Commission cited with approval the economies which had resulted on busy lines. The average operating cost of a steam engine in 1958 was 509 francs per kilometre; for diesels it varied between 250 and 355 francs; electric locomotives cost only from 174 to 314 francs.

Other notable achievements of the S.N.C.F. are mentioned in the reports. Railway staffs were reduced by a full 100,000 persons in a decade, despite considerable increases in traffic.[5] When the volume of traffic had already achieved record proportions in 1951, the Commission wrote that this 'demonstrated that the railway is not an out-of-date form of transport, and that it only has to adapt itself to new working conditions';[6] a conclusion which was an encouragement in itself. A comparison with foreign railways proved 'not unfavourable to the French railway organization'; in every technical field there had been a remarkable advance.[7] The S.N.C.F. had 'an esprit de corps of high quality' and had played 'a role of the first rank in economic expansion'. Twice as much freight tonnage was carried in 350,000 trucks in 1957 as had required 455,000 in 1938; there were only 16,600 passenger coaches compared with 50,300 and 9,200 locomotives as

[1] Third Report, pp. 20–1.
[2] Fourth Report, p. 16.
[3] Fifth Report, pp. 21–2.
[4] Sixth Report, p. 29.
[5] Seventh Report, p. 32.
[6] Third Report, p. 18.
[7] Fifth Report, pp. 21–2.

against nearly 17,000. On one line 85 electric engines had replaced 324 steam locomotives.[1] For an equivalent expenditure on power the yield in distance units had risen from 650 in 1938 to 1,750 in 1959. More than 13,000 kilometres of branch lines, or thirty per cent of the whole network, had been closed to passenger traffic as an economy measure.

But despite increased productivity and retrenchment, personnel costs had risen so rapidly that the problem of financial balance remained serious, and the need for subsidies substantial. All of which indicated to the Commission 'the necessity for co-ordination between the different forms of transport, both in operations and in investments'. The basic railway policies of technical progress, economy and increased productivity should be maintained.[2]

The Commission has developed its own 'doctrine',[3] which is set out in conclusions at the end of each general report. Firstly, there is stress upon the standard of accounting and its conformity with the 'general accounting plan', which is supervised by the Conseil national de la comptabilité. The nationalized enterprises are expected to maintain a system of cost accounts well suited to their individual requirements and adequate for the analytical study of costs. Systems of internal budgetary control and standard costing are encouraged. The Commission's work in advancing accounting methods is claimed to have been very effective. There has been proper emphasis upon the perennial problem of depreciation, which can, if inadequately solved, so easily create a false impression of the financial success of a corporation.[4] One aspect of this problem is the need for realistic and up-to-date valuation of assets, which is seldom a simple matter but especially difficult in periods of inflation.

The Commission is certainly upon firm and proven ground in stressing the vital importance of detailed preliminary studies in the conduct of capital programmes. It has, says M. Le Vert, 'never concealed the consequences of investment projects which went wrong, and has duly emphasized the inadequacy of technical planning, profitability studies, or cost estimates'.[5] The question of

[1] Sixth Report, p. 31.

[2] Seventh Report, p. 35.

[3] The Commission's own word.

[4] See, for example, the case of British Overseas Airways Corporation, in Chapter XIII, below, pp. 412–13.

[5] Le Vert, op. cit., p. 21.

whether investments will be remunerative recurs constantly; the Commission predicted that a dry-dock under construction by the Bordeaux port authority would not pay its way. The 'France-Cables' company was advised not to construct a new cable-layer until the prospects of chartering foreign and domestic vessels had been exhaustively examined.[1] There was a prophetic note of pessimism about the construction of the transatlantic liner *France*, 'destined to enter service at a moment when competition from the air will place maritime transport on the North Atlantic in a difficult position'.[2]

Questions of personnel are among the most delicate handled by the Commission. But where the financial balance of a corporation is compromised by restrictive practices or unrealistic labour agreements, it says so; and on occasion it has complained of excessive remuneration for the management.

> It is the Commission's duty . . . to stress abnormal or abusive differences between the remuneration of comparable categories of staff in two enterprises, to draw attention to abuses which sometimes arise in payment of the higher grades, to report distortions of the hierarchy,[3] and finally to denounce the too general custom of granting permanent status to all the employees in service, without retaining an indispensable reserve of auxiliary and contractual personnel.[4]

Another matter which interests the Commission is the relationship between the various nationalized bodies. Sometimes acute conflicts have arisen, and the Commission has tried to mediate. An example was a long dispute about the coal price which the electricity authority was to pay to Charbonnages de France; the S.N.C.F. similarly contested the price of its electricity supplies. After ten years of trying, it proved possible to persuade Electricité and Gaz de France to allow single employees of one or other to take domestic meter readings for both, at least in the Paris region; an important economy and a convenience to consumers. A joint invoicing and payment system for gas and electricity also operates.

Relations between the corporations and the state are another matter for consideration. On the one hand the Commission may bring the need for urgent investments to the notice of the government. On the other, it will press the corporations to make pay-

[1] Sixth Report, p. 27.

[2] Ibid., p. 23 (date July 1958).

[3] I.e. when the proportion of supervisory grades becomes excessive.

[4] Le Vert, op. cit., p. 21.

ments to the state when they are in a position to provide a yield from capital invested. The Commission obtained a reduction of the charges made by nationalized banks for credit supplied without risk to nationalized enterprises.

Many draft laws and regulations for the improvement of administration in the nationalized corporations have been submitted to the Ministers responsible. It is not clear how many of these drafts have been accepted and put into force. The Commission considered and rejected the idea of a general statute applicable to all the public enterprises alike. But from the beginning it opposed the appointment of members to the boards according to the principle of the tripartite representation of interests, with equal membership for the state, the workers and the consumers. The Commission secured a modification of most of the boards in 1953 and 1954, by the introduction of 'personalities chosen for their industrial, commercial or financial competence'. However, if we are to believe M. Bernard Chenot, the nationalized industries are increasingly dominated by the technicians of the *direction générale*, and the boards have in any case little real power.[1]

The Commission has fairly orthodox views about the proper extent of ministerial powers of supervision. The Minister should retain the exclusive right to approve acts of great importance of a type which may be expected to commit the corporation in the future; notably long-term production and investment programmes, acquisition of shares, long-term borrowing, labour agreements outside a national pattern, and (in the case of a monopoly service), the general framework of prices. On the other hand, the managements should be allowed discretion in almost all other matters, including their own operating budgets.[2] Of more interest is the Commission's conception of the place of the nationalized industries in the general economy. It has drawn attention to corporations which might be disposed of or dissolved; for example, companies formed to operate mines in countries which had subsequently turned Communist; and publicity, press and cinema organizations whose only reason for being in public ownership was that they were adopted by the German occupation authorities in the last war, and which were in any case largely unprofitable. There is an idea discernible in the Commission's reports that public ownership should in some way be associated with the public interest. It is also an instrument by which the state, through

[1] Chenot, op. cit., pp. 106–11.

[2] Le Vert, op. cit., pp. 19–23.

control of investments and prices and in various other ways, can help to orientate the whole economy. Thus in 1959 the rapid approval of investment programmes and the grant of increased loans to some major corporations made a real contribution to the ending of a period of recession.[1]

A balanced view of the Commission's activity might be that it has so far been very successful in a few fields, such as the improvement of accounting methods, and merely useful in the others. It would be wrong to see it either as a powerful Inquisition or as a major policy-making body. It furnishes impartial advice based upon ascertained facts. It provides a channel of accountability, which is to say communication, between the state and the industries which it owns, and a source of information for the nation, which at least in French theory is the sovereign of both. It has brought to notice the uncomfortable facts behind the trading deficits. One may fairly judge that the administration of French public enterprises would on the whole be more difficult without it.

In some ways a characteristically French institution, the Commission nevertheless establishes certain facts which are of international interest. It shows, firstly, that an efficiency audit of state enterprises is both feasible and useful. Secondly, it offers guidance as to method; it emphasizes the importance of basing everything upon an independent on-the-spot investigation, carried out by technicians as well as auditors, and of evolving criticism through a process of debate with management. Thirdly, it demonstrates that a sound alternative to control through Parliament can be devised when the acrimony of party opinion is such as to incapacitate the legislature for such work and the only other possibility may be no control at all. Altogether, it shows the value of improvisation when traditional arrangements for accountability and audit fail to meet new and specialized requirements; it seems that even secrecy has its uses in exceptional cases.

Germany: State shareholdings in industry

The German solution to the same general problem is less remarkable, for two main reasons. Firstly, the system of accountability for state enterprises, like most German state audit procedures, was

[1] Seventh Report, p. 86. (It may be noted that the standard of the Commission's general reports is rising. The seventh report is distinctly more profound than its predecessors.)

worked out after the First World War, whereas the American and French methods date from the aftermath of the recent war. Administratively, the German Federal Republic remains the stepchild of the Weimar Republic. In the second place, Germany in fact has very little nationalized industry in the full sense of the term.

This second consideration is curious, because the Reich of the Hohenzollerns was a notable pioneer of municipal public enterprise. That this did not lead to the development of major nationally-owned enterprises was due to historical influences rather than to the absence of a political party which favoured nationalization.

The modern history of German economic policy owes a good deal to the ideas of Bismarck. These were derived mainly from three men. From Friedrich List, he acquired the concept of a dynamic national productive impulse, developing through the uncontrolled mechanisms of a liberal economy but behind protective tariff walls. A generous-minded Prussian landowner, Rodbertus, however, pointed out in a book published in 1837 that economic liberalism did not make possible the payment of fair wages to working men, and he developed the theory of a general social interest which was not merely the sum of individual interests. He went so far as to question the revered principle of freedom in labour contracts. From Rodbertus, Bismarck and his Reich drew the conclusion that the state should play a regulating role in the economy, not merely for the protection of the workers but in the interests of the national impulse to raise productive power. The Socialist Lassalle brought home to Bismarck with greater emphasis the existence of a growing proletariat which would become a revolutionary force if exposed without protection to the law of supply and demand. It took many years for Bismarck to evolve a social policy, but when he did so in the eighteen-eighties it took the form of a state paternalism based upon the ideas of Rodbertus and Lassalle, and always with the growth of productivity as the central objective, as first indicated by List. The tradition of a dynamic economy based upon social justice has remained very strong in Germany, however imperfectly achieved, and it has canalized forces which in other countries were concentrated upon a demand for nationalization. It has ultimately, under the Federal Republic, produced a controlled capitalism which is respectable in the eyes of public opinion.

But events might have turned another way. The decisive year

was 1919, when the national assembly of Weimar was dominated by the Social Democratic Party, whose theoretical allegiance was to Marxism of a non-violent kind. This was the moment when large scale nationalization might have taken place. The Constitution of the German Reich, approved in August 1919 by the Weimar assembly, contained a chapter upon economic life.[1] Article 156 provided that the Reich could expropriate, with compensation, private enterprises 'suitable for socialization'. But this merely expressed one possibility among others, and the remainder of the chapter was heavily paternalist in tone. Everyone was to be protected against everything; it was a delicate framework of interests and aspirations rather than a programme of action.

In 1920, in the first elections for the new Reichstag, the Social Democrats lost almost half their votes and were always a minority party thereafter. They occasionally participated in coalition governments, but the dominance necessary for a nationalizing programme was never regained. Nationalization was at one time a possible objective for the Nazi party; a group on the left-wing, headed by the brothers Strasser, took the word 'socialist' in the party's title seriously. But Hitler had contempt for economic questions, believing that they could be settled by the exercise of power, irrespective of the ownership of industry. And after the bloodbath of 30 June 1934, Hitler was undisputed master of his own party, as well as of Germany. After the Second World War, the old Social Democratic Party failed to win an election, for reasons which probably had more to do with questions of foreign policy than of industrial ownership.

For all these reasons, of doctrine and of accident, Germany has no important nationalized industry in the strict sense of the term, except for the railways. In the nineteenth century this fact would not have provoked remark; in the twentieth it is very unusual. Germany does, however, have something else; a considerable body of 'mixed enterprise'. In other words, the state, the Länder and the municipalities all hold blocks of shares in companies whose legal status is that of private enterprise.[2]

'Mixed' undertakings in the cities were the principal form of municipal enterprise before the First World War, providing pub-

[1] The text is reproduced in Blachy and Oatman, op. cit., pp. 673–6.

[2] In France the term *société d'économie mixte* is commonly applied to such companies. (For Britain, where the idea has never been popular, see W. A. Robson, op. cit., p. 26.)

lic transport, electricity and many other public services. Before 1914, some of the great Länder had begun to participate in mixed enterprises. The 1914 war introduced this economic form to the central government. In the directed war economy, of which Walther Rathenau was the chief planner, mixed corporations were created to provide scarce raw materials and develop the cinema and other media of information. Most of the new companies survived under the control of the Reich after the war was over.

During the economic crises between the Armistice and the advent of Hitler to power, the state took over and retained possession of large shareholdings in many kinds of enterprises. By 1933, the state in this way dominated three-quarters of the electricity generating companies and a similar proportion of sea and river transport and shipyards. A smaller but still considerable share of coal mining, of iron and steel production, and of the great chemical industry, was also in the hands of companies whose majority shareholders were the state or the Länder. The legal form remained always that of the private commercial firm, and in most cases public authority maintained its influence only by being represented on the various boards (Verwaltungsräte or Aufsichtsräte). A further measure of control was, however, achieved through the formation of large holding companies (Dachgesellschaften, literally 'roofing companies'), themselves also commercial in form, which administered public investments in groups of mining and manufacturing undertakings.[1] The executive had its members on all the boards, but legislative control was almost non-existent.[2]

Economic expansion under the Third Reich was aimed

[1] At the present time a large proportion of the companies in which the Federal Government owns an interest are organized under a few major holding companies of which the most important are: AG. für Berg- und Hüttenbetriebe (a complex of steelworks—formerly the Hermann Göring Werke and Reichswerke at Salzgitter—also coal and by-products. Capital 426 million DM., wholly owned by the Federal Republic); Vereinigte Industrie Unternehmungen AG. (Viag.) (holding company for electrical generating companies and industrial users of electricity, e.g. for aluminium and chemicals. Capital 200 million DM., wholly owned); Vereinigte Elektrizitäts und Bergwerks AG. (Veba) (interests in the Ruhr. Capital 450 millions, wholly owned).

[2] M. Carmille, 'L'Economie mixte en Allemagne', *Annales de Finances Publiques*, No. IV.

specifically at rearmament, and the heavy industries were accordingly developed, with state capital in some cases, under a Four Year Plan of which Hermann Göring was at least the figurehead.

Thus the industrial shareholdings of the Federal Republic are not a coherent collection; they do not represent the results of deliberate decisions to place particular activities under state ownership on grounds of principle. They are a miscellaneous residue. They include such survivals from the policies of Rathenau and Göring, developed originally under the sign of Mars, as happened to be west of the Iron Curtain. There are descendants of companies which were taken under the public wing during the great economic blizzard of the Weimar epoch. There are accidental acquisitions, such as the Volkswagen motor company, a Hitlerite enterprise which outlived the Führer, and the collieries of the Saar, which were taken over from French nationalized administration only a few years ago when the Saar basin elected to rejoin the Vaterland. There are, however, some companies which were formed to execute specific public policies, such as the development and operation of civil airports. Finally, there is the single example of genuine nationalization, carried out under the terms of the Weimar Constitution of 1919. The railways, many of which had been owned by Prussia, Bavaria, Saxony and other member states of the Reich, became national property in 1920,[1] and in 1924 took the form of an independent national administration with the title of Deutsche Reichsbahn. The western remnant of the pre-war railway system, with 56 per cent of the total mileage, now constitutes the Deutsche Bundesbahn.[2]

The diverse nature of the so-called Federal undertakings (Bundesunternehmen) is shown by their contributions to national production. In 1959 they mined 36·3 per cent of all iron ore, 26·6 per cent of hard coal and 9 per cent of lignite. They produced 14·8 per cent of the total output of coke, 6 per cent of petroleum, 72 per cent of aluminium, 6 per cent of pig iron and 5 per cent of crude steel. Their contribution to the chemical industry amounted to 20·4 per cent of primary nitrogen. They built 20·8 per cent of the total tonnage of seagoing ships, and generated 16·7 per cent of the electricity. Through the single agency of Volkswagen, they

[1] The Weimar Constitution provided specifically for railway nationalization in Articles 89 to 95.

[2] Adolf Sarter, Theodor Kittel and Hans Kolb, *Was jeder von der Deutschen Bundesbahn wissen muss*, Frankfurt am Main, 1959.

made 44·6 per cent of all the motor cars. The Federal undertakings employed a total of 297,000 workers.[1]

Administration of the Federal companies, through representatives appointed to the various boards, is entrusted to a Minister for Federal Economic Property (Bundesminister für wirtschaftlichen Besitz des Bundes). The policy of the Adenauer government was during the last few years one of denationalization (Privatisierung), by the sale of shares under conditions of preference for persons in low income groups. In 1959, the Preussag corporation shares were sold as a first experiment, the success of which led to the much bigger operation of de-nationalizing Volkswagen in 1961. The Federal Republic, which formerly held all the shares in that powerful corporation, now owns only twenty per cent. The Land of Lower Saxony holds a further twenty per cent, and the remainder has been sold in small lots, the proceeds being devoted to technical research.

The Federal shareholdings in industry are all subjected to an oversight by state audit; by the Bundesrechnungshof and by the audit departments of such Länder as also own shares. This audit is useful and positive in its results, but the legal rules under which it is conducted are devious and complicated. They must, in all cases except that of the Federal Railways, take into account the fact that the companies have full private legal status; thus, for example, if there are private shareholders, the state cannot claim special privileges. The companies have to be subjected to a commercial audit under the Company Law (Aktiengesetz). The professional auditor for this task is chosen by the Federal Minister responsible for the industry concerned, together with the President of the Bundesrechnungshof, and this auditor's general instructions are also prepared by them jointly.[2] The law requires the responsible Minister himself to make an annual review of the activity of the Federal Republic as a shareholder in each company, after he receives the usual documents and accounts, together with the reports of the directors and the professional auditor upon them. The Minister sends all the documents and reports to the Bundesrechnungshof with his own comments. The state audit body then

[1] Report of the Minister for Federal Economic Property, in *Deutsche Politik, 1960*, p. 543, Bonn, Presse- und Informationsamt der Bundesregierung. The figures quoted do not include production of companies controlled by the Länder or by local governments.

[2] RHO., Sections 48(2) and 110a.

conducts its own audit, mainly on the basis of all the material forwarded to it, but with power to require further investigations by the professional auditor if necessary. In certain cases, the Bundesrechnungshof may itself audit the books and records of the company. The law requires the audit to be conducted 'on commercial lines'.[1] A special report by the Bundesrechnungshof upon the audit of Federal undertakings is to be submitted, through the Finance Minister, to Parliament, at the same time as the ordinary audit reports.[2] This special report is published.

The state auditors thus receive the accounts and documents after they have been examined by a professional auditor and by a Ministry; theirs is a super-audit, directed to ensuring that the undertakings have been well administered by the Minister's representatives. To some extent this is simply a question of the competence of the actual representatives as shown by events, but it is also in certain cases a question of whether they have been receiving good and comprehensive directives from the Ministry. The external audit is therefore a check upon the Ministry as well as the management.

The Bundesrechnungshof, like the Commission de vérification in France, has developed its own 'doctrine' about the administration of the state's commercial interests. But whereas the Commission has evolved a 'code of policy', the doctrine of the Bundesrechnungshof is better described as a 'code of discipline'. The principles of the code are dispersed among the reports of the Bundesrechnungshof, but they can be assembled into something like a system.

In the first place, the Federal Republic is directly represented in companies only by its members on the board, and state influence can only make itself felt through this channel. It is therefore very important that the channel be kept open.

A number of practical conclusions follow from this. The Federal Republic must be adequately represented, to the extent that the laws permit, by members with suitable qualifications. The Bundesrechnungshof does what it can to ensure this. For example, it obtained agreement to its proposal that in certain major companies the Finance Minister should appoint his own representative in addition to those of the Ministers responsible for

[1] RHO., Sections 48(2)2, 111, 112 and 113.
[2] RHO., Section 107 (3)2 and 108.

the particular industries. It has requested state representation on important committees appointed by boards, and upon the boards of subsidiary companies.[1]

The board, when properly constituted, has a duty to supervise the full-time management, in which the state is not directly represented. Such supervision is by no means automatic, and the Bundesrechnungshof offers advice on how to make it effective. Managements habitually take advantage of the laxity of their boards to extend their own prerogatives, and the boards must therefore maintain a disciplined effort to assert themselves. They must meet regularly and keep fully detailed minutes; the inadequacy of board minutes is complained of in a number of cases where the Bundesrechnungshof has irregularities to report. The board must not let itself be kept in the dark; it must demand the prompt rendering of accounts by the management, which must also submit reports on the conduct of business at regular intervals. It is particularly important that the management be required to submit full details and plans of investment projects, especially for buildings, to their board; and if such plans are changed they should again report to the board immediately. The state auditors mention in their reports to Parliament numerous cases where heavy overspending on capital works occurred without the knowledge of the boards concerned. Boards might well reserve to themselves the exclusive right to decide on such matters as borrowing, investment and the placing of large contracts; in any case the limits of their discretion and that of the management should be clearly recorded in writing. Special payments to personnel must be fully recorded in the accounts and should not be excessive, and loans to staff members require board authority by law. The board will be wise to establish its own internal audit.

The responsible Ministry should, in its turn, keep control of its members on the board and carry out its Minister's annual review properly; in the opinion of the Bundesrechnungshof, no official who represents the state on the board or at the company's annual general meeting should take part in the review. The Bundesrechnungshof also reported that two Ministers themselves resigned from membership of boards after it had raised observations.[2]

A limit is to be set upon the powers of board chairmen. They

[1] Report on (Audit of) Undertakings, dated 31 October 1955, pp. 12–21.

[2] Report on Undertakings, dated 24 October 1959, p. 64.

may not be granted discretion by the boards to exercise powers which are reserved by company law to the boards themselves. Boards should also see to it that proper competitive procedures for tendering and contracting are observed. Company law is extensive and detailed in Germany, and many of the principles proposed by the Bundesrechnungshof have a legal basis.

A second general consideration upon which audit doctrine is based is that of the Federal government's own policy towards state enterprises. The principles laid down under the old Reich were that state participation in an enterprise was only admissible if an important state interest was involved, if the objective could not be attained in another way, and if the use of public funds was not disadvantageous.[1] Such old rules of public interest would be very difficult to apply to the miscellaneous post-war holdings of the Federal Republic, although they remain nominally valid. Of much more practical importance is the view of the Federal Chancellor and former Minister for Economic Affairs, Professor Ludwig Erhard, a celebrated advocate and practitioner of liberal economics. His representative told a sub-committee of the Bundestag that the existence of Federally-owned enterprises was only compatible with the fundamental principle of free competition when, among other things, their dividend policy corresponded with that of private enterprise.[2]

The Federal Republic is thus unashamedly in business. The public service aspect of many nationalized industries in other countries is absent. The Federal undertakings are in any case mostly ordinary productive industries rather than public utilities; they do not do things for the Republic which in themselves suggest a clear state interest. They have been looked upon by the Adenauer and Erhard governments as black sheep strayed from the fold of private enterprise.

With the views of the government in mind, the Bundesrechnungshof has taken a close interest in the distribution of profits. The amounts paid to the Federal treasury began to rise steadily as from 1954, but the state auditors were not satisfied. The total interest paid was said to be low in relation both to the investment involved and to the earning capacity of some of the companies. The reasons given for this by the companies were dismissed as no longer of much consequence. The Audit Committee of the

[1] Wirtschaftsbestimmungen für die Reichsbehörden, Section 60.

[2] Report on Undertakings, dated 4 July 1957, p. 62.

Bundestag requested the government to ensure that in future the distribution of profits by Federal undertakings would be commensurate to their trading position.[1]

In this commercial climate of opinion, an unprofitable enterprise cannot expect a long life. As from early in 1953 the Bundesrechnungshof made observations to the Minister for Economic Affairs about the continued operation, which had been justified 'on grounds of social policy', of a worked-out copper mine at Sontra in Hesse. In September 1954 the Bundesrechnungshof pointed out that the deficit for five years amounted to 35 million DM., and it suggested that further subsidy would be justifiable only for the purpose of dealing with the social consequences of closing the mine. A decision on these lines was taken by the government and the company early in 1955.[2]

A third general proposition for the audit of Federal undertakings is that honesty and reasonable standards of efficiency are to be expected from managements. These might seem, to persons in countries where the secrecy of company affairs is very rarely penetrated, to be matters which take care of themselves. It is by no means so, at least among the German Federal undertakings whose frailties are exposed in the reports of the Bundesrechnungshof (which however leave the companies in most cases unnamed).

For example, a company formed to provide housing for civil servants made a small loss in 1956 and a very large one (4·5 million Deutschmarks) in 1957. The resulting investigations brought to light a complex tissue of fraud, which resulted in the dismissal of two Managing Directors and three Secretaries, followed by the institution of criminal proceedings against a number of persons. For several years the Bundesrechnungshof had complained of the late rendering of accounts and had pressed the board to request written reports from the management. When such a report was finally received in 1956 it was found to cover only very limited subjects. The state auditors had also protested against the practice of obtaining board approval for purchases of land after they had been made rather than beforehand. There had been no internal audit. The Bundesrechnungshof considered that supervision by the responsible Ministry ought to have been adequate to detect the frauds at an earlier date.[3]

[1] Ibid., dated 24 October 1959, p. 56.
[2] Ibid., dated 31 October 1955, pp. 60–3.
[3] Ibid., dated 24 October 1959, pp. 61–3.

There were cases of sheer carelessness. A film company leased a building for use as a studio and then discovered that it could not be heated and was therefore unusable for a considerable part of the year.[1] A company granted loans of 5 million DM. on inadequate security and lost about 4 millions of them as a result. Another company made the same mistake and suffered 'serious losses'.[2] A further company neglected to maintain accounts of internal operations and as a result failed until too late to recognize unfavourable tendencies in certain departments and was forced into liquidation.[3]

The conduct of business by an airport company gave rise to many observations. The board's control of affairs was inadequate. Sums authorized for investment were heavily over-spent. Most building contracts were placed privately. No admission charge was made for airport sightseers; this was an unjustified loss of revenue, said the report. Hospitality expenses were 'excessively generous'.[4]

Abuses in the remuneration of personnel are frequently reported. These take various forms. A managing director was granted a loan to buy a house, but in fact loaned most of the amount to a third party.[5] Excess costs were incurred on houses built for members of certain managements, and one board approved the construction of such a house without setting a limit on the cost.[6] Some officials of an airport company received lump-sum payments for use of their private cars, without reference to actual journeys.[7] A company itself bore the income tax upon payments to a member of its management.[8]

The Bundesrechnungshof claims to maintain 'a certain reserve' regarding salaries and fees paid to directors and managers. It has nevertheless raised observations when the total amounts appeared to be excessive, and the responsible Ministers have in general responded by establishing limitations. There was criticism of the payment of 'holiday allowances' and 'Christmas money' to directors.[9] In the case of one company, it was concluded that all emoluments were high in comparison with other companies.[10]

[1] Report on Undertakings, dated 4 July 1957, p. 57.

[2] Ibid., p. 59.

[3] Ibid., p. 62.

[4] Ibid., dated 24 October 1959, pp. 56–7.

[5] Ibid., dated 31 October 1955, p. 72.

[6] Ibid., p. 67.

[7] Ibid., dated 24 October 1959, p. 58.

[8] Ibid., p. 64.

[9] Ibid., dated 4 July 1957, p. 60.

[10] Ibid., dated 24 October 1959, p. 64.

The same minor inefficiencies arose in the Federal companies as are regularly encountered in government departments the world over; for example, arrears of book-keeping, delays in invoicing with losses as a result, issues of stores without vouchers, inadequate canteen accounting, and cash held by the book-keeper.[1] Lowest tenders were rejected without reason.[2] Above all, the observation recurs that, 'During the audit of investment projects it repeatedly appeared that technical plans were inadequate and therefore had to be amended later,' with large cost increases in consequence. It was essential, said the Bundesrechnungshof, for companies to estimate the cost of their own projects, so as to be able to form an opinion as to the fairness of tendered prices.[3]

It is clear from these reports that there is no particular difficulty about evolving standards as a basis for an efficiency audit of commercial companies, at least as far as their administration is concerned. It is refreshingly obvious also that a commercial form of management is not a magical protection against either dishonesty or common 'bureaucratic' inefficiency.

The German Federal Railways (Bundesbahn) are unique among German state-owned undertakings. They are operated by a staff with the full status of Federal civil servants. The Bundesbahn is not, however, a branch of the administration directly regulated by a Minister. It has a limited degree of autonomy in management and finance. There is an annual budget, which requires the approval of the Ministers of Transport and Finance, though not that of Parliament, which is merely informed. The budget is, however, understood to be merely a programme and not a strictly binding document. In the same way, financial 'discharge' after the end of the year is required, but from the Federal government and not the Parliament.

The management of the Bundesbahn is required by law to conduct business upon commercial principles and meet expenditures from internal resources, whilst at the same time protecting the interests of the national economy as a whole. Such broad objectives were attainable when the German railways, which have a longstanding tradition of efficiency, retained something like a transport monopoly. In the 'twenties, the railway system was able to pay a substantial contribution towards German reparations from

[1] Ibid., dated 31 October 1955, pp. 75–6.

[2] Ibid., dated 24 October 1959, p. 60.

[3] Ibid., dated 4 July 1957, p. 57.

its profits.[1] Until the last war it was a source of income to the state. But in the hard post-war world of competitive forms of transport, with huge bills for war damage to meet, the Bundesbahn has been hard pressed financially. In 1958, accrued losses of 1,972 million DM. were written off with government authority,[2] and annual deficits were running at about five to six hundred millions. The situation thereafter improved rapidly, until, in 1960 and 1961, losses were relatively insignificant. For a great railway system to make a profit in modern conditions seems, however, to verge upon the miraculous, and the Bundesbahn was not destined to abolish its annual deficits. In 1962 labour costs rose, and so did the loss figure; it was expected to be substantial again in 1963. The actual deficits have been as follows:[3]

	million DM
1958	576·76
1959	356·77
1960	13·52
1961	29·81
1962	110·2

The auditing arrangements for the Bundesbahn are quite different from those which apply to the Federal shareholdings in commercial undertakings. They are based upon an influential internal audit service, and upon the Bundesrechnungshof. The internal audit is charged with a comprehensive examination of the whole accounting and commercial activity of the railways. It is not limited to questions of 'regularity' but must take standards of economy and efficiency into consideration. The internal auditors must see that all the many regulations are followed, but they are also charged to look into practical questions, such as 'whether new sources of income can be opened up'. They are to submit an annual report to the Federal Finance and Transport Ministers at the same time as the annual accounts, balance sheet and report of

[1] The Treaty of Versailles made the German railways a guarantee for reparations, and by a law dated 30 August 1924 they were in fact mortgaged in the sum of 10 milliard Reichsmarks. In practice this meant that the railways paid 660 million RM. annually as reparations, in the form of principal and interest on the mortgage (Sarter-Kittel-Kalb, op. cit., p. 8). This was the largest single source of reparations under the Dawes Plan (Heinig, op. cit., vol. 2. p. 129).

[2] Roughly £165 millions. Sarter-Kittel-Kalb, op. cit., p. 51.

[3] I am grateful to officers of the Bundesrechnungshof for this information.

the Bundesbahn. For its duties, the internal audit service is officially declared to be independent and exempt from instructions from the government, from any minister, or from the Bundesbahn management itself. The internal auditors are experienced railway officials, who were selected for the task because they had shown 'energy, reliability, impartiality and mature judgment', together with a thorough knowledge of the whole service.

The Bundesrechnungshof is 'super-auditor' of the Bundesbahn. The chief internal auditor is appointed on the nomination of the Transport Minister, acting in agreement with the President of the Bundesrechnungshof. The state auditors can demand information from the internal audit, and can take part in audits or organize their own. They can prescribe principles of audit, with the particular objective of bringing procedures into line with usage in the government service. The Bundesrechnungshof submits its own report on the annual railway accounts, but this, rather curiously, goes to the same two ministers as the report of the internal audit. The Federal government decides on the annual 'discharge' of the management on the basis of all the documents.[1] These, finally, go to Parliament, which, according to railway law must 'discharge' the government for its 'state supervision' (Staatsaufsicht) of the Bundesbahn.

The Bundesrechnungshof employs only a handful of auditors upon Bundesbahn affairs, compared with nearly two hundred officials in the internal audit. But the super-audit is able to concern itself with matters of broad policy, such as railway electrification, transport law, abandonment of unprofitable lines, and the sponsorship of subsidiary companies (which operate station restaurants, travel agencies, sleeping cars, etc.). Some of these questions are rather delicate to handle for the internal auditors, who are after all railway employees, despite their nominal independence. The idea behind the superimposed audit by the Bundesrechnungshof (which itself employs senior civil servants from the railway service) is that the fully independent authority can raise matters and make criticisms 'even when it hurts'.

The Indian solution

In the United States and France, the work of auditing public enterprises is entrusted almost wholly to state audit, in its very

[1] Rechnungsprüfungsordnung für die Deutsche Bundesbahn, dated 16 November 1957, passim.

different national manifestations. But in Germany most of the detailed audit is done internally, either by professional accountants or by officials. It is interesting to see that such a situation does not prevent the useful participation of state audit. The principle of a super-audit has also been adopted by the Republic of India, where, says the former chief auditor of that country:

> by the new Companies Act of 1956, all government companies . . . come under the overriding audit control of the Comptroller and Auditor General. Though the normal provision is to entrust the audit to public auditors, they have to be appointed in consultation with him. They have to work under his general direction and in accordance with any instructions he chooses to issue. He also conducts a supplementary test audit. In other words, though the form may be different, the contents of such audit do not differ in substance from the audit of departmental expenditure. The annual reports of the enterprises, together with the financial statements and the observations of the Comptroller and Auditor General, are placed before the House and subsequently examined by the Public Accounts Committee with the assistance of the Comptroller and Auditor General. This examination is detailed and comprehensive.[1]

Here we have a solution which makes it possible for the Indian C. & A.G. to report to Parliament upon the internal affairs of nationalized industries without having to undertake the whole audit or to clash with the vested interest of those who do so.

The various national arrangements for rendering public enterprises accountable through state audit are exceptionally diverse, and some are as subtle as the problem is difficult. But may anyone seriously doubt any longer that a competent efficiency audit can make a really important contribution to parliamentary, public, ministerial and even managerial understanding of nationalized industries?

Genuine accountability adds a whole dimension to the idea of nationalization. Indeed, a case might be made for saying that, from the point of view of the general public, nationalization without it appears almost devoid of practical significance. A nationalized corporation may be more than merely the old crew in new uniforms, but without the saving grace of public accountability it is often depressingly apt to look, and behave, like it.

[1] Asok Chanda, op. cit., pp. 77–8.

CHAPTER XII

State Audit and the Constitution

> 'The officials of the Rechnungshof of the German Reich are appointed, retired and dismissed by me. . . . For special cases I reserve the right of personal decision. . . .'—Decree of the Führer and Reich Chancellor, Adolf Hitler, signed at Berchtesgaden, 23 November 1938

THE common image of state audit, like that of financial control in general, comes down to us from the age of the classical budget. It is, as we saw in the early chapters, the image of an organization dedicated solely to the enforcement of financial regularity in administration, on behalf of the planning authorities of the financial control cycle and the sovereign legislature in particular.

But as we have seen in subsequent chapters this is an inadequate view, even of those state audit bodies which were established in the classical era, and all the more so for those which were not. The relationship between state audit and the constitution admits of more nuances than we have so far shown. Moreover, although it has been stressed that state audit exists under all types of government, very little has hitherto been said about the forms which it has taken under modern dictatorships. For a broader view, therefore, we need some sort of classification of the relations between state audit and the state itself. For such a classification the most convenient basis is that of the allegiance or orientation of each audit body towards the executive and the elected assembly in its country. We shall thus have 'legislative' and 'executive' types of state audit, together with some others which are intermediate or neutral. In countries with dictatorial and hierarchical regimes, all state audit, like everything else, is ultimately 'executive' in alignment, but this primary fact is compatible with a variety and subtlety of administrative relationships.

The classification may begin with a group of national audit bodies which are exclusively 'legislative' in allegiance. They conduct their audit strictly on behalf of the representative assembly.

In the most extreme cases, such as Belgium, Austria and Israel, the chief auditors are chosen by the legislature. In these countries the law protects the activities and the departmental finances of state audit against any form of ministerial interference. This is independence of the executive in its most complete form. It is not, however, independence of the legislature, and the quality of audit work may depend upon legislative understanding of the auditors' role. In Israel and Austria this seems to be an enlightened modern view, but the Belgian Parliament tends to see its Cour des Comptes in the outdated context of the age of classical finance. It is presumably more difficult for older institutions, such as those of Belgium, to think in up-to-date terms.

The General Accounting Office is a legislative audit in a less extreme form. Since the Reorganization Act of 1945, it has been classed officially as 'a part of the legislative branch of the government'. It is the only public department attached to that branch which is broadly concerned with administration; the others are bodies with technical functions.[1] On the other hand, the appointment of Mr Campbell as Comptroller General by President Eisenhower against congressional opposition proved that this high post may sometimes be in the gift of the executive, the 'advice and consent of the Senate' notwithstanding. The General Accounting Office also retains a few functions, such as the settlement of claims and the rendering of legal decisions, which were handed down to it from the days before 1921 when it was part of an executive department. It has, in addition, the duty to collaborate with the Bureau of Budget by furnishing information on request. The Bureau is the executive authority for the planning side of the American budget cycle, the whole machinery of which dates from 1921.

Essentially, however, reality coincides with constitutional theory. The General Accounting Office audits for and reports to the Congress, draws its own funds directly from it, and provides it with a variety of personal services.

Communication between the American audit body and the Congress is not through a single channel at one season of the year, like that between the Comptroller and Auditor General and the

[1] The *U.S. Government Organisation Manual* lists only the Architect of the Capitol, the United States Botanic Garden, the Government Printing Office and the Library of Congress as parts of the Legislative Branch, in addition to the G.A.O. and the Congress itself.

House of Commons. It consists rather of a mass of separate reports, messages and personal relationships, passing through a variety of channels whenever Congress is in session. The links between the American legislature and the G.A.O.[1] are of some intimacy. According to one student of the subject the increasing tendency is for financial control to be seen from a legislative point of view in terms of accountability rather than of the planning phase.

It would appear (he says) that Congress is moving from its constitutional mandate to authorize appropriations, which affords it only a very general and ineffective form of control over the spending process, to a much more precise form of financial control with the assistance of the controlling and reporting activities of the office of the Comptroller General.[2]

The constitutional position of state audit in Britain is different, despite the fact that the Comptroller and Auditor General is a servant of Parliament with great personal independence.[3] The difference is due principally to the fact that the Treasury looms very much larger within the British constitution than does the Bureau of the Budget in that of the United States. It is almost unquestionably the most powerful single government department in any Western country. Moreover, its relationship with the state audit body was defined in the age of classical finance when, as we saw in the opening chapters, the planning side of financial control was in the ascendant and accountability was equated with mere enforcement.

To understand the constitutional position in Britain it is necessary to differentiate between the Comptroller and Auditor General's reporting powers and his authority over the practical work of audit as conducted by his staff. The C. & A.G. has absolute discretion to report to Parliament as he sees fit. His personal relationship with the Public Accounts Committee is probably still the closest and most effective of its kind in the

[1] One Congressman described the G.A.O. as the right arm of Congress. (Quoted in Annual R., C.G. of the U.S., 1953, p. iii.)

[2] Hare, op. cit., p. 19.

[3] In 1954 Sir Frank Tribe told the London and District Society of Chartered Accountants: 'I should make it clear that I am the servant of the legislature and not of the executive; so please do not address me 'care of the Treasury' for nothing can be more unconstitutional' (*The Accountant*, 23 January 1954).

world. If this were the whole of the matter, the British national audit would fall easily into the 'legislative' group.

A look at the Exchequer and Audit Departments Acts of 1866 and 1921 will show that there is another very important side to the question, which exercises a profound influence upon the C. & A.G.'s audit as a whole. The decline of the ancient Exchequer resulted in an increase of Treasury influence over state audit in Britain. The Commissioners for Auditing the Public Accounts were almost purely an 'executive' audit body with a very subordinate role. This tradition was carried over as part of the amalgam created by the 1866 Act. To suggest that this Act established a legislative type of audit would be a gross over-simplification. What it actually did set up was *an audit on behalf of both the legislature and the executive, under the detailed direction of the latter*.

As we have already noted, the Acts of 1866 and 1921 provide for enforcement by the auditors of Treasury control over government departments through the procedure of prior approval.[1] As a working arrangement this is perfectly satisfactory.

There is, however, much less to be said for some other old rules which have come down to us in the statutes. One of these provides that decisions as to who shall prepare and render accounts for audit are in the discretion of the executive,[2] and not of the Comptroller and Auditor General. The same thing applies to the form of the accounts rendered by departments to the C. & A.G.[3] Again, the numbers and the status of the auditors are controlled by the

[1] Audit of expenditures from the point of view of Treasury authority is covered by Section 27 of the 1866 Act and Section 1(3) of the 1921 Act. The auditor sees a vast amount of correspondence between the ministries and the Treasury. He also sees something which the Treasury does not see, namely the departmental records and deliberations which form the background to the correspondence, and he can therefore ensure that the department under audit has presented its facts to the Treasury with reasonable exactitude. (As petitioners for funds or authority, the departments are inevitably under a temptation to overstate their case.)

[2] '. . . the Treasury shall determine by what departments . . . accounts shall be prepared and rendered to the Comptroller and Auditor General.' (E. & A.D. Act, 1866, Section 22. This refers to appropriation accounts. Under Section 3(1) of the 1921 Act, the Treasury has discretion re the audit of accounts other than appropriation accounts.)

[3] 'A plan of account books and accounts, adapted to the requirements of each service, shall be designed under the superintendence of the Treasury; and the Treasury may prescribe the manner in which each department of the public service shall keep its accounts' (1866 Act, Section 23 and 1921 Act, Section 9(1)).

executive through its authority to regulate recruitment and salaries.[1]

At least in legal form, powers of executive direction could scarcely appear more complete, and they are incomparably more so than in any other major Western country. It is arguable that the real situation of state audit in Britain remains that of a subordinate body influenced in various practical ways by the executive, with the addition of the independent reporting powers of the Comptroller and Auditor General. And even this high officer is subject to executive authority for the broad strategic direction of the audit upon which his reporting is based. It is the executive which defines the limits of his audit and the form of accounts upon which it must be based. Not all the powers vested in the Treasury are, however, as important as they seem; they are subject to the imperatives of statute (notably that there must be appropriation accounts for money voted in supply), and they may have on occasion to take note of the views of the Public Accounts Committee.

This situation has nevertheless had consequences. There has seemingly been a tendency to make subject to audit only the accounts of bodies which are under formal Treasury control, since the enforcement of this is naturally a matter of prime concern to the Treasury. There is, however, no practical reason why state audit should not examine and draw useful conclusions from the accounts of bodies which spend public moneys under other systems of regulation, or indeed without any system at all. On the contrary, the very absence of financial control on the planning side tends greatly to increase the need for a measure of control through accountability. But, whether by coincidence or not, the fact is that more types of expenditure (and in particular those of nationalized industries, of universities and of local authorities under government grants and loans) escape from constitutional audit in the United Kingdom than in any of the other powers of the West. As a rule in Britain there is either full financial control in both the phases of planning and of accountability, or there is none at all. The survival of the classical tradition, under which accountability was merely required to enforce the decisions of planning, seems unmistakable.

[1] Treasury sanction for recruitment is required by Section 8(1) of the 1921 Act, and salaries are to be determined by the Treasury under Section 8(2) of the same Act.

Again, most other countries have made statutory provision giving the auditors at least advisory powers over the form of departmental accounts, on the grounds that they are, after all, the main 'users' of them and that regard should therefore be had to what may help them in their work. In the United States, the Comptroller General is the principal authority for the standards of accounting throughout the Federal Government.[1]

It is finally, an indisputable fact, as we recorded in a former chapter, that the status of the national audit staff in Britain is lower in relation to the administration itself than in any other comparable country. It is also the only example of an audit body in a Western country which is formally subordinated to the executive by statute for the fundamental regulation of staffing. These two facts can scarcely be without some connection. This, at any rate, is the view of an anonymous French commentator, who writes that,

> in England . . . the audit body remains subject to the indirect control of the Ministry of Finance . . . which questions the level of its effectives and the scale of their remuneration, and can as a result limit its means of action.[2]

The need for and even the expediency of most of the powers of executive direction which were ratified in 1866—and which were exceptionally strong even by the standards of that period—is open to serious doubt a century later. The principle of executive control over a body which is not part of the executive is in itself a constitutional anomaly, and all the more so because the function of state audit is to assess the conduct of financial administration by the executive. It is of course precisely because they wished to ensure that executive departments should not be able to weaken their own critics that many countries have legislated to protect state audit. This is exactly the same problem as the ancient one of protecting the judiciary.

Meanwhile, as we have noted, the law to some extent limits

[1] See Chapter IX, pp. 217–19, above.

[2] 'Les Cours des Comptes et le contrôle des finances en France et à l'étranger', *Statistiques et Études Financières*, April 1960. (On the subject of status, it may be said that when state audit was concerned solely with 'regularity', it was largely a mere check on the book-keeping, an audit of the accounts department. An audit of merit and efficiency, however, is an audit of 'policy' at a much higher level. If the auditor engaged upon it is himself of humble rank, he may feel inhibited from asking questions, because his opposite numbers in the audited department are of much higher rank.)

the Comptroller and Auditor General's powers over his own field of action. The element of independence in British state audit is nevertheless vested in him personally. His department is almost wholly lacking in the elements of a corporate independence. It has no built-in statutory defences. The choice of the person to be C. & A.G. is therefore crucial. In the absence of a strong Comptroller and Auditor General, British state audit would be a docile watchdog indeed. Since this is an executive appointment, the possibilities open to an administration or a government which wished to 'muzzle' the audit body, without the need for any change in the existing law, are evident. Fortunately nothing seems less likely at the moment, but such a situation is by no means inconceivable.

Where must the British state audit appear in the constitutional classification? It cannot be described as a 'legislative' audit in the full sense. In the 1866 Act, the words 'Parliament' or 'House of Commons' are mentioned 28 times, but 'the Treasury' appears 68 times.[1] In the 1921 Act the balance is even, both being mentioned 20 times. The audit system may best be described as a hybrid form, intermediate between a 'legislative' and an 'executive' type and with elements of both.

The situation in France and Germany is that the state audit bodies stand aloof from both legislature and executive. The Comptroller and Auditor General is the servant of both. The Cour des Comptes and the Bundesrechnungshof in principle serve neither, although in practice they co-operate with both. In terms of statute and of tradition theirs is an autonomous type of audit.

The reason is not hard to seek. They were both creations of an executive, but an executive which has long ceased to exist. The Exchequer and Audit Department, the General Accounting Office, the audits in the Low Countries, in Italy, in Scandinavia, in the U.S.S.R. and elsewhere, are all operating under constitutional regimes at least fairly similar to those which created them. Not so the Cour des Comptes of Napoleon, nor the German audit which was founded by the first Prussian monarch in the early eighteenth century. These bodies are survivors living in constitutional surroundings which have completely changed; they have

[1] This is in the text of the 1866 Act as reproduced in *Epitome*, vol. 1, pp. 779–88. Sections 16 and 17, which were repealed in the nineteenth century, are omitted.

outlived many executives and many legislatures and therefore have a veneration for neither. They have had to make new working arrangements as the political relationships around them changed and changed again. They were born to the royal executive tradition, but as the separation of powers became more real in their countries they were able to break away from the domination of the executive. This did not, however, necessarily imply a close new connection with the legislature.

The position in France in 1807 has been expressed by the Cour des Comptes as follows:

In an authoritarian state, the organs charged with the control of public finance are merely the instruments of a sound administration; agents of order and unity, they remain entirely subordinated to the executive power which created them and before which they answer for their actions. This was the Napoleonic conception.[1]

The constitutional history of the Cour des Comptes from that time has been largely one of attempts to co-operate efficiently with the legislatures. Formal arrangements for routine control duties on behalf of Parliament were accepted within a generation after Waterloo. But there progress halted, and no relationship with the legislature on lines comparable to those in either Great Britain or the United States has ever matured. A visiting magistrate from the Cour was impressed by what he saw of the Comptroller General's constitutional relationships, and on his return from Washington he lectured his colleagues about this:

If I have gone to great lengths to emphasize the assistance furnished by the G.A.O. to Congressional committees and to the Bureau of the Budget, this is because the absence of liaison which, in practice and despite the Constitution, subsists in France between the organization charged with the control of voted funds and those who prepare and pass the budget, is both illogical and gravely prejudicial to the public financies. The links which join the Congress to the G.A.O. obviously strengthen the latter's authority over the administration.[2]

The law and constitution of the Fourth Republic made provisions which seemed to aim at the development of an audit conducted specifically on behalf of the legislature. But despite occasional direct contacts with the Finance Committees, the

[1] Papers presented by the Cour des Comptes to the Havana Congress of Audit Departments, 1953, Chapter XII, p. 1.

[2] Senechal, op. cit.

parliamentary relations of the Cour have changed little beyond the point that they had reached in the nineteenth century. Its Public Reports are not addressed solely to Parliament. It does not work through a parliamentary committee but in a variety of other ways; by direct action with ministries and *comptables*, through the machinery of the Commission de vérification and the Comité central d'enquête, and through the Public Report.

In the years following the Liberation, as we have observed elsewhere, the French national audit body made important advances into the fields of administrative efficiency, nationalized industry and social security. These were mainly based upon statutes passed in the National Assembly. The Cour was aware of what it owed to such support, and in 1953 it described itself as, 'the permanent auxiliary of the representative assemblies, as well as of the Government', but it hastened to add that it remained completely independent of both.[1] If the magistrates of the Cour des Comptes are aware of any instinctive solidarity it is presumably, as members of a *grand corps*, with the executive. The constitution and proceedings of the Commission de vérification suggest the existence of such an attitude and the survival of a fundamental distrust of the legislature.[2] The Cour has shown no signs of wishing to become a parliamentary organ. In any case the record of Parliament under the Fourth Republic was hardly such as to inspire the confidence of a cautious judicial body, conscious of its own traditions.

Under the Bismarckian Reich, German state audit acted on behalf of both the Emperor and the Reichstag, and reported separately to each. The Weimar Constitution of 1919 specifically established legislative control of finance,[3] and the budget law of 1922 put this principle into detailed effect. The Rechnungshof des Deutschen Reiches then had to face the prospect of adapting itself to working with a Reichstag which intended to enforce its financial prerogatives by means of active Budget and Audit Committees. The legal relationship between state audit and the popular

[1] Papers presented by the Cour des Comptes to the Havana Congress of Audit Departments, 1953, Chapter XII, p. 6.

[2] This distrust manifested itself over the question of transmission to Parliament of the secret reports of the Commission de vérification on individual nationalized enterprises. See above, Chapter XI, pp. 338–9.

[3] Articles 85 and 86 of the Constitution.

assembly remained undefined; the Reichshaushaltsordnung merely said that the Rechnungshof was independent of the Reich government and subject only to the law.[1]

There seems, however, to have been an effort by the Reichstag and its financial committees to convert the Rechnungshof into an ally against the official forces of the executive, which were fundamentally hostile to the republic, full of nostalgia for the old Imperial Germany, and resentful of a control which in the prevailing economic circumstances was probably hard to bear. Indeed, financial chaos was such that the German budget had little meaning until about 1926. Thereafter, for a few years, the 1922 law began to work and the Rechnungshof learned to co-operate with the Reichstag. It was closer to the legislature than ever before. The budget cycle based upon legislative control came into force in Germany for the first time. But only for a very few years; the great depression at the turn of the decade threw the finances once more out of balance. After Hitler came to power in 1933, the National Socialist members attended the Reichstag and its Committees wearing holstered revolvers. One of them, Reinhardt, was made Chairman of the Budget Committee and proceeded to 'adjourn' business indefinitely. Shortly afterwards he became Permanent Secretary in the Ministry of Finance.[2]

The history of state audit under the Third Reich has been misunderstood. The story has somehow become current that Hitler dismissed the chief auditor of Germany immediately after his seizure of power, in order to suppress possible criticism.[3] This account has, however, no historical foundation.[4] What happened was much less simple.

There was no such thing as a National Socialist Constitution in the Third Reich. The constitution of Weimar and its budgetary law remained nominally in force. Parts of them were, however,

[1] RHO., Section 118.

[2] Heinig, op. cit., vol. 1, pp. 122, 259, 521 and 526.

[3] This story appears in 'Parliamentary Control of Public Expenditure' by Sir Frank Tribe (1954), in *Aspects of Audit Control* (p. 29) by Asok Chanda, Comptroller and Auditor General of India (1960), and in 'Control of Public Expenditure' by Sir Edmund Compton (1960).

[4] Although the post of Reichssparkommissar, previously held by the President of the Rechnungshof, was suppressed by a law dated 13 December 1933. This is possibly the origin of the story. This law, however, actually strengthened the position of the President within the Rechnungshof.

suspended or amended by law. The remainder was distorted and abused in actual practice. The Nazis began with the proposition that many of Germany's ills were the fault of that 'talking-shop', the Reichstag, and they took pride in the contravention of parliamentary principles.

Hitler was appointed Reich Chancellor on 30 January 1933. His dictatorship was formally established on 24 March, when an Enabling Act (called, by a superb exercise of the art of political euphemism, the Law to relieve the Emergency of People and Reich)[1] was forced through a terrorized Reichstag. This gave the government powers to make and execute laws without consent of parliament, and from that date the statutes of Germany began with the simple preamble: 'The Reich government has decided to make the following law. . . .' Thus was founded a regime under which there was no salvation save through obedience, and which elevated every 'Führer-decision' to the force of law.

The first assault of Nazi legislation in 1933 was directed against the Reichstag itself. A law of 14 July proscribed all political parties except the National Socialists, under the threat of imprisonment for up to three years, or unspecified 'higher penalties'.

With the popular assembly effectively eliminated, attention was given to the budgetary system. The decisive enactment was the Second Amendment of the Reichshaushaltsordnung, dated 13 December 1933. This brought all constitutional control of finance through accountability to an end. The wording is inoffensive. As long as the Enabling Act remains in force, it says, the observations of the Rechnungshof on the budgetary accounts will be brought to the attention of the second chamber, the Reichsrat (the Reichstag is not mentioned at all). 'Discharge' will be granted by the Reich government after discussion of the observations in the Reichsrat. A formal procedure is laid down for the government to deliberate upon the act of 'discharge', with the President of the Rechnungshof as its adviser.

The cynicism of these legalistic formulae is exposed by the sequel. The Reichsrat itself was abolished two months later,[2]

[1] Gesetz zur Behebung der Not von Volk und Reich. During the debate on this crucial law the Reichstag (then sitting in an opera-house, since its own building had recently been gutted in the famous fire) was surrounded by crowds shouting, 'The law, or else bloodshed!'

[2] Gesetz über die Aufhebung des Reichsrats, dated 14 February 1934.

although the Enabling Act had safeguarded its existence. As for the new discharge procedure, this in effect meant that the government was to discharge itself. It was accountable only to itself. The government did not in fact take its self-critical role seriously; no grant of 'discharge' for any financial year as from 1933 was ever recorded.[1]

The whole constitutional basis of accountability was thus destroyed. The Rechnungshof was reduced in practice to a simple 'executive' role. Yet curiously enough it was apparently well satisfied with the law of 1933. In accordance with the 'Führer-principle', this exalted the position of the President in his Rechnungshof and broke up the old collegiate procedures; it also created the Presidential Section of the Rechnungshof, to which the surviving duties of the Sparkommissar were transferred. The consequences of the undermining of the budget were not obvious until later. When a member of the Cour des Comptes visited the Rechnungshof in 1935 he found that many of its staff were 'more attached to the legal texts than the facts, and to the theoretical construction of the system rather than its practical working'.[2]

In one sense the Rechnungshof had never been so prosperous. It was absorbing the audit bodies of the various Länder as they lost their budgetary autonomy. The law of 13 December 1933 empowered the Länder to introduce the Reichshaushaltsordnung and thus merge their financial procedures with those of the Reich. Prussia, then dominated by Göring, did so immediately. The Law concerning the Reconstruction of the Reich, dated 30 January 1934, abolished the financial sovereignty of the Länder and obliged them to submit their budget to the Reich Finance Minister for approval. The Law concerning the Budgeting, Accounting and Audit of the Länder (Fourth Amendment of the Reichshaushaltsordnung), of 17 June 1936, finally standardized the regulation of public finance throughout the Reich. The Reichshaushaltsordnung was made obligatory for the budgetary systems

[1] Heinig, op. cit., vol. 1, pp. 34, 132 and 507. Heinig quotes a report by the President of the Rechnungshof in 1944 which confirms that there had been no 'discharges' as required by the 1933 law.

[2] de Forbin, 'La Cour des Comptes Allemande d'après la loi du 13 Décembre 1933,' *Annales de Finances Publiques*, No. II. (The author seems himself to have been blind to the facts of the German situation in 1935, and the article is not a helpful one.)

of the Länder, and responsibility for their audit was transferred to the Rechnungshof des Deutschen Reiches.[1]

In practice this meant that the most important Rechnungshöfe of the Länder now became branch offices (Aussenabteilungen) of the national audit body. They were located at Hamburg, Munich, Dresden and Karlsruhe. In August 1939, the former Rechnungshof of the Austrian Republic became a new Viennese branch of the Reich audit. Finally, in January 1942, the expansion of the Reich frontiers by war was recognized by the establishment of new audit branches in the east at Posen (Poznan)[2] and in the west at Metz. Thus did the Rechnungshof of the German Reich gain in size from the centralizing internal policies, and even from the aggressions, of Adolf Hitler.

Moreover, in 1933 the Nazi government had confirmed the independence of the Rechnungshof.[3] As late as 1937 the judicial independence of its members was again acknowledged in the new Civil Servants' Law.[4]

Far from being dismantled at the first blow by the Führer and Reich Chancellor, the German national audit body appears on a superficial view to have done very well indeed out of the Nazi regime. It is an uncomfortable fact of life that centralized official bodies of almost every kind have a tendency to expand and be satisfied under dynamic and ruthless autocracies. The phenomenon is not confined to the armed forces and the police.

In fact, however, the gains of the German Rechnungshof were illusory. It was an excellent example of a body losing the substance of power whilst gaining the trappings. The destruction of the Weimar budgetary procedures based upon the separation of powers reduced it to a modest and even humiliating role. In theory, it should have been possible to maintain a healthy financial control based solely upon the executive. 'It would be wrong', wrote a Nazi academic, 'to take budgetary law mainly for a

[1] The budgetary systems of the local authorities had already been standardized by the Deutsche Gemeindeordnung of 30 January 1935.

[2] The area around Posen was annexed to the Reich under the name of the Reichsgau Wartheland. Alsace-Lorraine was re-annexed. The General-gouvernement of Poland, the 'colonial' regime in the unannexed area, had its own Rechnungshof.

[3] Law dated 13 December 1933, Article I, Section 118. The Secretary of the Reich Chancellery also wrote to the President of the Rechnungshof in the same sense, on 8 December 1933 (Heinig, op. cit., vol. 1, p. 236).

[4] Heinig, op. cit., vol. 1, p. 126.

creation of parliamentary democracy. The Reich budget comes from Prussian law, which originated in the time of absolute monarchy.'[1]

Despite this theorizing, effective control broke down. The unification of budgetary procedures in Reich and Länder was only one side of the picture. Within a few years there was not one Reich budget but at least two. The Nazi Party became a state within the state, in a financial as well as a political sense. There was a party Treasury (Reichsschatzamt) and a Treasurer (Reichsschatzmeister), duplicating the status and functions of the Reich Finance Ministry and its Minister. The Party had various private sources of revenue; subscriptions from its members and from affiliated organizations, 'Winter help' contributions, income from collections, Party events and lotteries, sale of licences to make and retail Party uniforms, etc.; probably also confiscations. It also received subsidies from the public purse. The uses of all these funds are suggested by Heinig:

> An omnipotent party engages in the most multifarious business, from holiday camps to cremations, from private concentration camps to private executioners, and from powerful newspaper concerns to gigantic rubbish-depots full of party badges, pictures of the Leader, drums, etc.[2]

There was also a vast new administrative machine to be paid for: the Propaganda Ministry, the Labour Front, the Storm Troops (S.A.), the Winter Help Organization, the security forces (S.S.), the peasant organization (Reichsnährstandsorganisation), and many more bodies.

The Reichsschatzmeister, the 'Finance Minister of the Party', was a holder of full powers (Generalbevollmächtigter) from the Führer and independent of the Reich Finance Minister. He was accountable to nobody but his Führer, and certainly not to the Rechnungshof des Deutschen Reiches. The Party possessed internal sovereignty, exempt from the attentions of the national authorities, with its own code of law, its own administration and its own jurisdiction.[3] It also possessed its own audit body, the Reichsrevisionsamt, with headquarters in Munich and branches in every 'Gau'. This was naturally not a 'constitutional' audit institution but an element of the Party administration, directly responsible to the Reichsschatzmeister.

[1] Wilhelm Gerloff, *Die öffentliche Finanzwirtschaft*, 1942.

[2] Heinig, op. cit., vol. 1, p. 99.

[3] Ibid., p. 133.

The Nazi auditors took over increasing functions from the older audit body. Until the war the Rechnungshof remained responsible for the audit of Reich funds even when expended directly upon Party organizations, though not when paid as subsidies to the Party as a whole. For example the Reich auditors would check the pay of SS guards for concentration camps if it came from the national budget, but all internal expenditures for the camps were from Party funds and exempt from their audit.[1] In June 1934 the national auditors were warned to keep out of affairs which mainly involved Party moneys. On occasion it could be hazardous to raise observations; when criticisms were made about contracts for the Party's enormous new buildings at Nuremberg, Hitler heard of this and threatened drastic action against the auditor concerned.[2]

In April 1941, an agreement between the National Socialist President of the Rechnungshof, Müller, and the Reichsschatzmeister, brought about what Heinig called 'the utter capitulation of the highest German audit authority before the power of the totalitarian Party'.[3] The agreement stated that funds which were granted either from Reich to Party administrative bodies or vice versa would be subject to detailed examination only by the audit body of the recipient. This meant that all expenditures by Party authorities, even of Reich funds, were subject only to the Reichsrevisionsamt;[4] there was in practice no 'vice versa'. For the remaining years of the war—and of the Nazi Reich—some 26 organizations of the Party, from the Gestapo, the Waffen-SS and the Hitler Youth to the National Socialist professional associations and the 'Day of German Art', were forbidden territory for the state auditors.[5] The Party must have received invoices for many unnatural and sinister purchases, but such documents were never seen outside the circle of its own officials.

The degradation of the Rechnungshof did not, however, consist

[1] I am indebted for this and other facts to Herr Haaser, a Rechnungshof President in retirement, who kindly received me at his home near Frankfurt in March 1961.

[2] President Haaser ('drastic action' implied a concentration camp, said Herr Haaser).

[3] Heinig, op. cit., vol. 1, p. 135.

[4] As an element of Party discipline, the Reichsrevisionsamt was not negligible. According to President Haaser, there were cases of Party members being shot as a result of audit findings.

[5] Heinig, op. cit., vol. 1, pp. 134–6.

only in its gradual displacement by the auditors of the Party. It lost influence even within its own field of responsibility, the Reich budget. After 1933, its reports, together with the budgets themselves, were 'for official use only' and not available to the public. Lacking a basis in parliamentary support or public opinion, the reports were not much used, even officially. They were supposed, after 1933, to be presented to a Committee of Permanent Secretaries (Staatssekretär), which was to transmit them, after consideration of their contents, to the Finance Minister and the government. But it seems that this Committee never met.[1] At the top level at any rate, the work of the Rechnungshof, became, in the words of President Haaser, 'alles Papier'.

The aims of the government were irrelevant to the objective of the national audit, sound financial management of the state. Party funds escaped all but 'internal' control. A good deal of the pre-war armament programme was also financed in an unconventional way. Between 1934 and 1937, 12 milliard Reichsmarks out of a total rearmament expenditure of 30·9 milliards were paid in the form of a sort of industrial barter vouchers (a scheme devised by Hjalmar Schacht, President of the Reichsbank, and given the code name 'Mefowechsel') rather than directly in cash from public funds.[2]

Lacking the impulsions of constitutional machinery, public opinion or government concern, the Ministries (though not the subordinate authorities) paid little attention to audit observations. The Rechnungshof uncovered 'scandals' involving heads of the Nazi party, but was unable to do much about them.[3] Control at the top depended, in finance as in everything else, upon the Führer. The Nazi President of the Rechnungshof, Müller, told his staff that the concept of a constitutional control was obsolete because there was no longer a parliament exercising control over the government. The Rechnungshof now derived its mandate directly from the Führer as 'Holder of Sovereign Rights of Control'; it was 'more a Führer-authority than a Reich authority'.[4]

[1] President Haaser.

[2] Schwerin von Krosigk, *Es Geschah in Deutschland*, pp. 187–8. Tübingen and Stuttgart, Rainer Wunderlich Verlag Hermann Levins, 1951. (Lutz, Graf Schwerin von Krosigk was Reich Finance Minister throughout the whole twelve years of the Hitler regime. It was symbolic of his lack of influence—and of the low priority of financial control as an interest of government policy—that he remained a relatively minor figure to the end.)

[3] Heinig quotes examples, op. cit., vol. 1, pp. 126–8. [4] Ibid., p. 131.

But the Führer's contempt for matters of finance was total;[1] there was therefore no real direction or control.

The budget lacked prestige and binding force. The Rechnungshof, even where it still had the right to audit, had little to achieve by doing so. The Reich audit body had lost its whole constitutional framework of action, its entire *raison d'être* save on the lowest level of activity. A post-war Federal Finance Minister summed-up what happened as follows:

> In a state such as the Hitler-state, to which the idea of a limitation or control of personal power, the idea of the separation of powers, was necessarily foreign by nature, the Rechnungshof was also something of a stranger. It was not suppressed, which ... might perhaps have caused too much scandal. It was left to atrophy quietly; it could do its work, but this was disregarded and it did not influence the state or the government in any way.[2]

President Haaser, who was a participant in the actual events, concluded that:

> The experiences of the Potsdam Rechnungshof in the time of the Third Reich showed incontestably that even a state audit body which is still in good working order fails of its object if no Parliament stands behind it and the public hears nothing of its efforts and aspirations.[3]

This opinion must be quoted with certain reservations. It should not be taken to mean that effective audit work cannot be carried out on behalf of any totalitarian government. Not all absolute regimes work on the same principles as Hitler's, under which the predominant economic aim was to create the capital equipment needed for conquest. In such a state, with such a ruler, financial control was a trivial consideration. National wealth would, in the Führer's view, be attained through power rather than by prudent administration. As we shall see, state audit can play a more positive role in dictatorially governed countries than

[1] 'After the destruction of popular rights and institutions there was only one authority which could grant "discharge" and that was the Führer himself. He did not consider it necessary to render account to the German people; what interest', asks Heinig, 'could he have in "discharging" himself?' (ibid., p. 132).

[2] Speech by Federal Finance Minister Fritz Schäffer at the inauguration of the new Bundesrechnungshof building in Frankfurt, 19 February 1954.

[3] President Haaser, 'Die Rechnungshöfe und ihre Beziehungen zu Executive und Legislative', *Der öffentliche Haushalt*, Heft 2–3, 1954.

did the German Rechnungshof under the Reich which was to last a thousand years.

Such a role must, however, be different from that of the Western type of state audit, which, in its best manifestations, draws dignity, strength and influence from its constitutional independence. This in its turn derives from the separation of powers. The essential distinguishing characteristic of Western state audit is its prerogative of free and public criticism. Such a thing is incompatible with dictatorship, as the experience of the Rechnungshof showed. The type of audit which is most at home under totalitarian rule is rather the disciplinary instrument, working in secret, like the Reichsrevisionsamt of the Nazi party.

The case of the Rechnungshof shows that when the effective separation of powers in a state is broken down, the status of its surviving elements, even though still nominally respected, becomes irresistibly debased. Domination of France by the Führer had similar consequences for French financial control institutions. The Cour des Comptes observed after the war that the authorities of the Vichy Government had frequently violated the budgetary rules. Control had been paralysed. The French budgets from 1940 to the Liberation were similar in external form to earlier ones, but like those of the Third Reich they had lost their binding force and had become simple administrative documents.

> The authority which had prepared them was now in the last analysis the same as the one which had to carry them out and control that they were carried out properly. Moreover the Cour, although it still retained the right to denounce irregularities and protest against abuses, could address itself only to the precise groups who had committed them.[1]

The plight of the Cour was strikingly similar to that of the German Rechnungshof. The fundamental problem in a totalitarian state is that, whereas a Western type budget commits the government, 'dictatorship binds itself to nothing'.[2] In such circumstances the possibility of an effective control through accountability (except on the level of subordinate discipline, which is a simpler problem) must depend upon the degree of cynicism of the government itself. Under Hitler, and also under Vichy, this was very great, and in such cases:

> The basic requirements for genuine control, namely the statutory obligation of the voted budget and of budgetary law in general, are lacking.

[1] C. des C., Rapport, 1940–45, p. 7. [2] Heinig, op. cit., vol. 1, p. 240.

The duty to respect the legal budget turns into a compulsion to accept every infringement as an intentional act . . . The expenditures are nothing but executive remittances. The state audit organization sinks to the level of a purely administrative body with specialized duties. It may be 'Budget criminal police', uncovering misappropriations and negligence, or 'Budget regularity police', regulating the traffic in the government accounts; but it no longer has any will of its own.[1]

Under a cynical dictatorship, therefore, the financial control cycle tends to break down in both the planning phase (the decisions of which may be arbitrarily reversed or ignored), and the accountability phase (the findings of which are likely to be without influence.) Arbitrary finance is a necessary consequence of arbitrary rule. There is not even much security against irregularity, let alone against waste, extravagance and inefficiency, if perpetrated or condoned at high levels.

It would be a mistake, however, to generalize for all authoritarian states from the case of Nazi Germany.[2] There are signs that countries with planned economies have come to stress the validity of the budget as an instrument for the execution of the state economic plans. This may be a guarantee based upon expediency rather than upon constitutional practice, but it may nevertheless be quite effective as far as 'regularity' is concerned. The budget in these countries, which has lost its legislative anchorage, may have found a new one in the Plan. We shall see below that state audit and 'state control' organizations in Communist countries play a much more constructive role than that of the Potsdam Rechnungshof under Hitler.

In all its essentials, the post-war financial control system of the German Federal Republic has been a return to the best arrangements achieved by the Weimar regime. The Bundesrechnungshof addresses all its reports to the Bundestag, and the fact that it still has to forward them through the Finance Minister (who transmits them without comment or alteration) seems to be merely a symbolic survival of past subjection. The Budget and Audit Committees of the elected assembly have been revived, and the audit body sends representatives to their sessions. The work of the Bundesrechnungshof is much more closely integrated with parliamentary control than that of the French Cour des Comptes.

[1] Ibid., p. 42.

[2] As Kurt Heinig, himself a refugee from the Nazis, tended to do.

The Audit Committee of the Bundestag is composed of Abgeordneten (M.P.s) among whom *rapporteurs*[1] (Berichterstatter) are chosen to present the accounts of the ministries, each if possible a specialist in the affairs of the ministry whose accounts he presents. The report of the Bundesrechnungshof is considered by the Committee in the presence of senior officials of the ministries—although it is only occasionally that a Permanent Head (State Secretary) appears in person to speak for his ministry. The Ministers themselves can be summoned, but this is rare indeed. The Bundesrechnungshof is normally represented by a Ministerialrat (whose British equivalent would be an Assistant Secretary). The Audit Committee presents its report to the Budget Committee, which is senior to it. The latter in turn reports to the Plenum of the Bundestag, which is responsible for granting discharge to the government for the financial year concerned.[2] There is some resemblance between this procedure and that of the Public Accounts Committee at Westminster, with the notable exception that in the Bonn committees neither the ministries nor the state audit body are represented at the highest level. It should also be recalled that the Bundesrechnungshof is not solely concerned with the consideration of accounts by the Audit Committee but is also represented in the Budget Committee during the debating of estimates. Its influence is thus felt in the early as well as the late stages of the financial control cycle.

The Bundesrechnungshof, despite its work with the committees in Bonn, is not really a 'legislative' audit. Like the Cour des Comptes, it prefers the status of constitutional autonomy. The official doctrine is expressed as follows:

The supreme audit body is not subordinated to the legislative organs (Bundestag and Bundesrat), and its financial control activities cannot be

---

[1] The *rapporteur* system, which is a very important operational characteristic of continental administration, simply means that almost any formal meeting of a committee, a board, etc. is opened with a report from, and usually read aloud by, a student of or an expert in the matter to be debated. In committee work it is normal for *rapporteurs* to be chosen in advance from among the members, to study and present particular items on the agenda. This has the advantage of tending to turn committee members into persons with at least some title to be called specialists, each with his own subject, about which he has learned a good deal whilst preparing reports.

[2] I am indebted to Dr Dressler of the Bundesrechnungshof for the substance of this note upon the Bundestag committees.

classed among the functions of the legislative power. Nor is it to be listed among the law-courts, although its members have the same independence as judges and take decisions upon judicial principles. The Bundesrechnungshof is not entrusted with a jurisdiction. Its relations with the executive are characterized by its independence of the Federal government and its status of equivalence with a Federal ministry. . . . It is to some extent a connecting link between executive and legislature. Although independent of each, its activity concerns both of them. . . .[1]

It is this kind of constitutional aloofness, shared by the Cour des Comptes with the Bundesrechnungshof and some other notable state audit institutions, which has lent support to the idea that national audit is the 'fourth power' in the state, separate from the traditional three, legislative, executive and judiciary.

The full case for this view need not be argued here, but it is a piece of constitutional logic familiar in Europe and elsewhere. The German Federal Finance Minister in 1954, for example, took the matter for granted:

As an institution, the Bundesrechnungshof is part of the idea of the Constitutional state (Rechtsstaat). In the separation of state powers it stands as a fourth power by the side of the legislative, the executive and the judges. It has to perform advisory and supervisory duties *vis-à-vis* these three powers, in the general interest of the state.[2]

The case of Nazi Germany was not really typical of absolutist rule, because its deliberate intention and policy was always war. A comparable collapse of financial control is not, therefore, to be expected in all countries ruled by dictatorships. These are, in any case, widely varied in nature. There is, of course a vast difference between the traditionalist and clerical regimes of Iberia and the 'dictatorships of the proletariat' in Europe and Asia. There is even a fair amount of administrative variety within the latter group.

An example of state audit under a conservative dictatorship is the Tribunal de Contas of Portugal, founded in 1849. Its predecessor, the Casa dos Contas do Reino, dated from the Portuguese golden age in the sixteenth century, 'the age of the great discoveries'. The Tribunal was reorganized under decrees made

[1] Übersicht über die Aufgaben und die Stellung des Bundesrechnungshofes (August 1958), pp. 6–7.

[2] Fritz Schäffer, Speech at the Bundesrechnungshof, Frankfurt, 19 February 1954.

in 1930 and 1933 by Dr Antonio de Oliveira Salazar, now the veteran dictator of Portugal.

The members of the Tribunal are nominated by the Minister of Finance and enjoy irremovable status. Their function is, however, strictly limited to a control of regularity. The Tribunal has, in its own words, 'No other objective in controlling the Government's financial transactions but to ascertain their legality and to check that they have been properly accounted for.'

The Tribunal's description of its place in the constitution is a delicately euphemistic account of the realities of Portuguese political life:

> The powers of the Court of Accounts issue from the Executive and, as a result, this collegiate body cannot, in contrast to the procedure in a number of countries, act as the agent of Parliament for the control of the Government's conduct of finance. All the less can it do so because under the existing Constitution the legislative function is not exclusively within the competence of the National Assembly.[1]

The Tribunal is neither directly nor indirectly responsible to the Assembly. In fact, both the audit organization and the representative body share the same humiliated powerlessness. The Assembly goes through the motions of voting the budget, but the resulting text is then 'co-ordinated' by the Minister of Finance and 'approved' by the Council of Ministers, presided by the Chief of State.[2] This is executive rather than legislative control of the budget. The reports of the Tribunal 'are not intended for purposes of constitutional control'. The audit body and the Assembly 'exercise their control within the limits fixed by the general structure of the State'. The limits are evidently narrow; they are those of what has become an extremely conservative regime. There is probably less for state audit to do under this kind of government than any other in a civilized country. The merit of expenditures can scarcely be discussed. Finance is the private resource of the executive. Even the promotion of efficiency may not be a major interest. The prime objectives of policy are stability and continuity. State audit can assist by a control of regularity. But such is its most

[1] Paper submitted by the Portuguese delegation to the Brussels Congress of Supreme Audit Institutions, 1956.

[2] Artur Aguedo de Oliveira, President of the Tribunal, *Le contrôle exercé par le Tribunal de Contas et l'Assembleia Nacional du Portugal sur les Comptes Généraux de l'Etat*, Lisbon, Imprensa Nacional, 1957.

modest role, and under such circumstances it may tend to become a 'decorative' institution and a fount of sinecures.

In Communist countries the audit may perhaps be described as 'executive'; but we must remember that the legislature has no separate existence. Such constitutional distinctions are rejected on theoretical grounds. The Communist budget forms part—the predominant part—of the general economic Plan, so far as it concerns a particular year. By checking the execution of the budget, the auditors are enforcing the Plan. The budget, moreover, covers not merely administration and defence, as in the West, but production also. Almost every aspect of public finance, both central and local, may appear in the single budget of the state.[1]

Communist countries usually concentrate their national audit, or at least the more conventional part of it, within the structure of a ministry. For example, the Audit Authority (Verwaltung Finanzrevision) of the 'German Democratic Republic' is a special division of the Ministry of Finance. It is reinforced by 'Audit Groups' in each ministry and 'Audit Inspectorates' which control the local government bodies; both are subject to instructions from the central Audit Authority. A decree of 1952, which established the audit system, stressed that a mere routine check of cash balances and regularity was not enough. A thorough-going periodical audit of all governmental bodies and public enterprises was 'one of the principal methods by which the State should be managed'.

One of the auditors' tasks is to explain the meaning and the object of the laws, regulations and decisions of the government to the authorities whom they visit, and even, when necessary, to the general public. They are, in fact, to be propagandists as well as controllers.

They are also to be disciplinarians. They have power to take summary action upon the discovery of irregularities. In East Germany they can issue binding instructions for the rectification of errors, they can cause accounts to be blocked, and impose or recommend fines.

The most important function of the auditors is, however,

[1] In the U.S.S.R. there are also budgets for the 'autonomous' Republics and local authorities, but these are in principle kept under close central control. (See R. W. Davies, *The Development of the Soviet Budgetary System*, Chapter X, Cambridge, 1958.)

almost certainly that of analysing the execution of the budget. The intention is to acquire information about new developments or to calculate new norms which may be used for the establishment of future Plans. The auditors are also expected to deal very thoroughly with the execution of all the specialized plans, covering such matters as investments, profit-earnings and staff establishments, which regulate the detail of economic life.[1]

The Finanzrevision in Eastern Germany, like the Tribunal de Contas in Portugal, controls a budget which is voted by an almost powerless assembly. The People's Chamber (Volkskammer) is, according to the constitution of 1949, 'the supreme organ of state power', in a republic where popular sovereignty is specifically acknowledged. The Volkskammer is to vote the annual budget law, and the Finance Minister is to lay the audited accounts before it, in order to obtain 'discharge' of the government's responsibility under the budget.[2] Nothing could be more correct in democratic theory.

The reality is strangely similar to that in Portugal.[3] According to the State budget law (Staatshaushaltsordnung), the Volkskammer is to pass the budget but not to debate it and this, we are told by a former official of the Finance Ministry in East Berlin, is 'a significant differentiation in the administrative practice of the Soviet occupation zone'. Debate on the budget is the exclusive prerogative of the Council of Ministers and its Presidium. The right of discharging the government belongs to the Volkskammer only on paper. In fact the Parliament is not allowed to see the audit reports of the Finanzrevision, which is not a legislative body and is not independent, and therefore it lacks the information necessary as a basis for the act of discharge. Moreover, the budgets themselves are not made public, and in any case 'a large part of the expenditures for political and military purposes appear under titles and headings which are intended to mislead'.[4]

[1] Dr R. Kopis, 'Das staatliche Haushaltswesen in der D.D.R.', *Der öffentliche Haushalt*, Heft 2–3, 1956.

[2] Constitution of the German Democratic Republic, dated 7 October 1949, Articles 3, 50, 81, 88, 121 and 122.

[3] No doubt 'realities' in Eastern Germany are backed up by more ruthless penalties than are normal in Portugal.

[4] Hellmut Meier, 'Staatliches Haushaltswesen in der D.D.R.', *Der öffentliche Haushalt*, Heft 5–6, 1956. (In his comments upon this article, Dr Kopis expressed the view that in fact the functions of the Volkskammer were not quite as negative as Meier had indicated.)

The audit in East Germany is a fair reflection of Soviet orthodoxy. The Ministry of Finance in the U.S.S.R. maintains a similar auditing service which has the especial duty of examining the accounts of state enterprises, 'noting particularly any failures to earn the expected profits or, where applicable, to pay the planned amount of turnover tax'.[1] The functions of the Audit Control Section of what was then called the People's Commissariat of Finance were laid down in detail by a decree of May 1938. These amounted to a thorough control of 'regularity' based upon full powers of access to documents and information, in all Union, Republic and local authorities, industrial and other public enterprises, state insurance bodies and banks. The work of internal audit within departments was to be supervised; so also was that of the accountants of public enterprises, who had been declared by law to be independent of their managements. It was recommended policy that 'specially typical cases' uncovered by the auditors should be published in the press.[2]

The auditors from the Ministries of Finance represent only one of the varied controls to which public authorities and national enterprises are subjected in Communist countries. The most characteristic of these is 'state control'. The East German Republic for example, has a 'Central Commission for State Control', formed in 1953. This is described as 'an independent organ attached to the Minister President's office'; there are nine members whose conditions of discipline suggest a special interpretation of the word 'independent'.[3] The Chairman is a member of the Council of Ministers and adviser to the Presidium. The Commission employs a force of controllers who must be 'politically and morally beyond criticism'. Their task is the control of all public bodies which receive funds from the state, with special reference to their execution of the budget, the economic plan and government decisions. They examine the efficiency of the various administrations and can make recommendations; in important cases these are submitted by the Commission to the Presidium.[4]

This kind of control, based upon a corps of inspectors with wide but loosely-defined powers, in some ways recalls the original

[1] Alec Nove, *The Soviet Economy*, London, Allen & Unwin, 1961, pp. 91–2.

[2] Heinig, op. cit., vol. 1., p. 92.

[3] They can be removed from office by the Minister President and, with the agreement of the Council of Ministers, prosecuted for failures in their duties.

[4] Kopis, op. cit.

(and now obsolescent) concept of the French Inspection des Finances. It goes far beyond the functions of the French inspectorate, however, and may concern itself with matters which have no obvious connection with finance. The teams sent out by State Control bodies amount to an itinerant audit of conformity and efficiency, very broadly understood; the inspectors may, for example, include engineers, architects, economists and other specialists, to ensure that the word efficient has a comprehensive meaning. The former Polish Ministry of State Control listed the following tasks:

Control of execution of the budget, laws, decrees and government decisions.

Control of the implementation of plans by state enterprises, departments and institutions, with regard paid to quality and economy as well as quantity.

Control of the organization and efficiency of the state apparatus.

Analysis of the implementation of the budget.

Control by following-up 'complaints and grievances of the people and . . . critical articles in the press and on the radio'.[1]

The potentialities of such a control system for the support of despotism are not hard to conjecture. The German refugee official, Hellmut Meier, describes State Control in East Germany as a form of political and economic rather than budgetary control, and 'an auxiliary of the state security service'.[2] Such it certainly was in the early days of the Soviet Union. In 1920 a People's Commissariat of Workers' and Peasants' Inspection was created, under the authority of Stalin. It became a body of exceptional importance, directed against political offenders as well as against 'bureaucracy' and inefficiency. In 1923, as the result of a proposal made by Lenin just before he died, the People's Commissariat was united with the Control Commission of the Communist Party. Thus the authorities responsible for administrative-financial control and for political supervision were combined, forming 'a fearful weapon of terrorism'.[3] In 1934, the People's Commissariat was replaced by a Commission for Soviet Control, separated from but still working in close collaboration with the Commission of Party Control.

[1] Paper submitted by the Ministry of State Control of the Polish People's Republic to the Brussels Congress of Supreme Audit Institutions, 1956.

[2] Meier, op. cit.

[3] Heinig, op. cit., vol. 1, p. 86.

In the 'thirties there continued to be numerous complaints that financial control was inadequate. In 1931 Stalin stated that the principle of profitability had been undermined, that invoices were no longer submitted and that proper balances between income and expenditure were not calculated. Various cases came to light in which state enterprises had concealed their total receipt figures in order to escape turnover tax. In 1939, Molotov was still expressing concern that managers were not aware of an obligation to avoid incurring losses.[1]

The result of continued dissatisfaction was a decree of the Presidium of the Supreme Soviet, dated 6 September 1940, creating a new and nominally independent control authority, the People's Commissariat of State Control. The first article of the decree directed the Commissariat to establish the strictest control over accounting for public funds and property, and over expenditures. Its foundation was also declared to be for the purpose of creating a genuine check upon the execution of government decisions. The Commissariat was endowed with powers to impose punishments 'up to dismissal' upon officials and to give binding instructions. It was intended 'to play a great pedagogical and disciplinary role by teaching public enterprise to adhere to Soviet decisions'.[2] According to Pravda, 'nine tenths of all abuses in the Soviet Union had their origin in the previous lack of rational control'. Examples of these 'abuses' were given. Cost calculations for new installations had repeatedly been exaggerated, whilst audits often disclosed great stocks of unused materials. Some authorities had not followed the production plan or had even faked their output figure in order to be able to boast about exceptional productivity.

In the autumn of 1946, the State Control body, which by then was called the Ministry of State Control, published details of a campaign which it was waging against 'abuses' committed by party members and managements of factories and collective farms. A number of officials of state enterprises and institutions, including some of the highest rank, had been charged and punished. The Ministry had itself pronounced fines of up to 7,500 roubles and had decreed a number of dismissals. These were, however, only the relatively minor cases. Others came within the criminal code, and those found guilty had been condemned to as

[1] Ibid., p. 93.

[2] *Pravda*, 7 January 1941, quoted by Heinig, op. cit., vol. 1, p. 95.

much as ten years' imprisonment. Some of them had announced false production figures in order to gain bonuses. Others had misused budgetary funds. Still others were guilty of bribery, for example during the allocation of official living quarters. Another type of punishment was to mention individual enterprises and persons by name in the press if they had maintained inefficient and 'un-Russian' working methods. A particularly important case came to light in a great textile concern in Moscow, and this revealed the ultimate scope of discipline through State Control. All the heads of the concern were found to be implicated in the theft of a hundred thousand metres of woollen cloth over a period of several years. A number of senior officials were sent to prison for up to ten years. The Chairman was given two years for 'criminal negligence'. The Vice-Chairman and the Managing Director were condemned to death and shot.[1]

As a reminder that the Ministry for State Control was not the only auditing and inspecting authority in the Soviet Union, the Finance Ministry announced that it had carried out no less than 211,400 audits in 1946—compared with 153,200 in 1945. These included 32,500 'audits of finance and efficiency' in state enterprises. Serious violations of financial discipline and cases of illegal and wasteful use of state funds had come to light. Reports had been sent to the Councils of Ministers of the Soviet Union and the autonomous republics, to local authorities, and to the law-courts.

The Communist Party itself contained institutions which duplicated the Ministry for State Control and the Audit Control Section of the Finance Ministry. The first of these was the Commission of Party Control, whose functions, as defined in 1939, were:

a. To ascertain how decisions of the Party Executive (Central Committee) were carried out by Party organizations and by Soviet and economic institutions.
b. To find out how the local Party organizations functioned.
c. To maintain a register of all Party members, and
d. To call to account persons guilty of violating the Party's programme, statutes or discipline.

---

[1] Heinig, op. cit., vol. 1, p. 96. (Capital punishment of officials for dishonesty has recently been resumed in the U.S.S.R. In July 1962, *Izvestia* reported that four textile industry officials from the Central Asian republic of Kirghizia had been sentenced by the Soviet Supreme Court to be shot for large-scale misappropriation of State property, currency speculation and bribery.—*The Guardian*, 23 July 1962.)

There was, secondly, a Central Audit Commission with fifty members, whose duties were to conduct:

a. A financial audit of the Party Executive and subordinate institutions.
b. An efficiency audit of the secretariat of the Party Executive and central Party organizations.[1]

Over and above this array of full-time inquisitional bodies, there is, in addition, a Soviet tradition founded by Lenin, of 'popular' control, working especially through direct inspection by workers and peasants and through complaints against 'bureaucracy'.[2]

> We have here (says Heinig) a method of canalizing and making use of the discontent of the people and of individuals, which also allows them to let off steam. All dictators place exceptional emphasis on the idea that the 'misunderstood person' should have an office to which he can unburden his heart, at least in writing.

In Lenin's Russia popular control amounted to 'a deliberate mobilization of the toiling masses against the state administration'. It was, essentially, 'an instrument of terrorist rule'.[3]

Looking at the whole picture, Heinig observed a constant change of emphasis in audit and control. During the lifetime of Lenin the purpose was above all one of politics and power. Later it became more a matter of economics and administrative efficiency, without entirely losing its original objectives. There was some tendency towards familiar organizational forms, such as internal audit. In general, it was and remained true that audit in the Soviet Union served more comprehensive purposes than anywhere else in the world.[4]

The old Ministry of State Control is now the Committee of Soviet Control, an all-Union body which reports to the Council of Ministers. It still employs inspection teams with full rights of access to information and full powers of interrogation. Its general mandate is to seek breaches of regulations and instructions of all kinds.[5] The essential idea of state control has always been to provide administrative machinery for supervising the execution of the government's decisions. There is also, however, a mandate for the promotion of efficiency and for the collection of factual

[1] Heinig, op. cit., vol. 1, pp. 99–100.
[2] A Central Bureau for Complaints was formed as early as May 1919.
[3] Heinig, op. cit., vol. 1, pp. 103–7. [4] Ibid., p. 97.
[5] Nove, op. cit., pp. 91–2.

and statistical information as a basis for policy-formation by the government.

In addition to state control and audit, the banks in Communist countries are also organs of control. This is equally true of the State Bank in Russia, the Deutsche Notenbank in Eastern Germany and the National Bank of Yugoslavia. The last of these administers the budget funds and must check the vouching and legality of all receipts and payments, like a French *comptable*.[1] In East Germany also, the bank will make no payment which would result in an excess over the total approved in the budget. In the U.S.S.R.,

> the inspecting and checking role of the State Bank *vis-à-vis* enterprises arises from the fact that all the funds of the enterprises must be kept in the bank, and that it is the only source of short-term credits. The local branch of the bank has the duty of scrutinizing all payments and cheques to see that they conform to the plan and to the various regulations (e.g. relating to prices, wages, etc.) . . . The bank assumes a more detailed tutelage over enterprises which find themselves in financial difficulties.[2]

In a Communist country, therefore, the civil servant or business manager finds himself face to face with the state every time he pays funds into 'his' bank, or draws a cheque. He works within a double and triple framework of official controls, and to these must be added the most important one of all, the Communist Party itself. This has an administrative bureaucracy of its own, which duplicates the public service in almost all its branches and levels.[3] The party official is often more influential than his opposite number in the 'regular' administration. In any case, the Party maintains control through a monopoly of the right to admit others to office, a universal patronage. All significant appointments require at least the approval of a party committee, and the national party machinery (in Russia, the cadres department of the Central Committee) controls entry to senior posts. Officials may be chosen from a list prepared by the party, and are therefore frequently party men themselves. Knowledge of these realities, in the words of Nove, 'inevitably affects the behaviour patterns of all state or economic officials'.[4] One feels sure that this is no

[1] Yugoslav delegation's paper to the Brussels Audit Congress, 1956.

[2] Nove, op. cit., p. 92.

[3] There is even a party branch, sometimes with full-time officials, in each Russian factory.

[4] Nove, op. cit., p. 94.

exaggeration. Not only is the power of patronage one of the strongest of all powers; in modern totalitarian states it is reinforced by the twentieth-century device of the duplicate party administration.[1] And if, despite the surveillance of the party, an official or a manager feels tempted towards a 'flexible' interpretation of plans and instructions, he will still have to escape the attentions of the banks, the state control inspectorate and the state auditors. When a Western official, in public service or nationalized industry, raises a voice against the idea of even a mild financial control on behalf of Parliament, he might first compare his situation with that of his professional confreres in countries where the red flag flies.[2]

In such lands the role of state audit and state control can scarcely be called constitutional in a Western sense. They are merely specialized adjuncts of the administration, not public checks upon the financial activities of the government. On the contrary, their basic function is to impose upon subordinate formations the fullest obedience for central directives. But one Communist country with a longer memory than the majority of them has made an effort to restore something of the constitutional basis of its national audit. After the upheavals of 1956, Poland experienced a curious and moving renaissance of democracy and national feeling. There was a new policy of administrative decentralization, greater independence for state enterprises, the abandonment of compulsion in farm collectivization, and a democratization of public life.

In the budgetary field the role of the Sejm (Parliament) and the People's Councils increased to a fundamental extent, and this found expression in a new budgetary code, passed by the Sejm in July 1958. In procedure there was a return to the principle of the open, published national budget. . . . In the sphere of State Control, it was decided after long discussions to revert from the Ministry of State Control to the Supreme Court of Control, which is an organ of the Sejm. (December 1957).[3]

---

[1] 'A sign by which all dictatorship may be recognized is the existence of a double apparatus in the state administration' (Heinig, op. cit., vol. 1, p. 98).

[2] 'The mass of accountability to which Soviet administrative bodies are subject is amazing' (P. Haensel, *The Public Finance of the Union of Soviet Socialist Republics*, 1938).

[3] Leo Kurowski and Richard Szawlowski, 'Das Finanzsystem und der Staatshaushalt Polens', *Handbuch der Finanzwissenschaft*, vol. 3, p. 565 (Tübingen, J. C. B. Mohr, 1958).

The Supreme Court of Control is a most interesting attempt by a government of 'moderate' Communists to regain the advantages which liberal democracies obtain from the fact that their budgetary and audit controls are a constitutional check upon the executive. The Court, whose President is appointed and revoked directly by the Sejm, supervises the whole state administration and all public enterprises, in accordance with broad criteria (regularity, efficiency and general expediency).

The recently created Polish Supreme Court of Control (write Kurowski and Szawlowski, with some pride) is subordinated to Parliament and is thus unique among the State Control organs of the Socialist Countries. Except in Poland, budgetary control is everywhere the function of agencies of the government (Ministries or Commissions of Control). There are other financial control bodies in Poland besides the Court of Control, notably the audit and control inspectorates of the Finance Ministry and the internal audit bodies. The Supreme Court of Control is charged with the co-ordination of their activities and may direct them to undertake specific missions. Special auditing commissions have been created since 1957 to make an annual examination of the accounts of state enterprises.[1]

The conversion of the Ministry of State Control into a Court dependent upon Parliament seems to be an attempt to create a kind of 'legislative' Cour des Comptes, though with far wider powers than are normal in the West. Whether such a body could possibly attain in a Communist country the independence necessary for a constitutional role is another question. Its dependence upon the Sejm can scarcely mean very much unless that body itself is in some degree genuinely separate from the executive. This would amount to a real separation of powers under a dictatorship of the proletariat, which is a contradiction in terms. If there is dictatorship the separation must be a façade. But an alternative is possible; the dictatorship itself may be the façade.

What, in fact, are the benefits which Poland was seeking when it established the Supreme Court of Control? The question involves some comparison of state audit under the separation of powers with its equivalent as part of the hierarchical state.

As employed in Communist countries, state audit of the 'executive' type enjoys certain advantages. It clearly has everything that it needs by way of powers of access to the records of

[1] *Handbuch der Finanzwissenschaft*, vol. 3, p. 569.

all kinds of authorities and public enterprises. Its functions are not restricted by narrow concepts of regularity, but extend to questions of efficiency. Above all, it is able to make a real contribution to the financial control cycle through the mechanism of the Plan. The state auditor is a fully-fledged partner in the business of developing new Plans and budgets, through his analysis of what happened under the old ones. The fact of being part of the executive may be a help to state audit for this purpose. One of the reasons why the financial control cycle in Western countries is often imperfect is almost certainly the remoteness of the authorities responsible for accountability from those charged with planning. State audit bodies should be advisors to as well as critics of the executive. Where no separation of powers exists, it is probably easier for them to be the former.

On the other hand, the independent status of state audit in countries with a separation of powers remains an invaluable asset for performance of the auditors' critical role.[1] A case for the 'legislative' type of state audit was developed eloquently by Kurt Heinig, although his views were those of a partisan—a Social Democratic member of the Reichstag and a refugee from the Nazis—and on occasion his generalizations from German experience are inadequate for an understanding of conditions elsewhere.

In Heinig we have democracy defended in an unusual way—on the basis of the machinery of national finance. The open, public budget, he says, is evidence that the people have a say in their own financial fate.[2] But 'figures should be verified, not trusted'. Not only is the budget a device essential to rational administration, but its control by parliament and audit helps to draw back the veils from 'the anxiously guarded professional mystery of government'.[3] The control of regularity is necessary for 'the general hygiene of the budget', but audit and budgetary control are,

> on a considerably higher plane, not one of mere material values. They influence the general quality of both administration and the national

[1] For this purpose the concentration of state audit within a finance ministry is the least happy of solutions. An independent critic must have an independent status. Even in Communist countries it is perhaps only possible to leave the auditors within the finance ministries because many of the critical duties of Western state audit are performed by 'state control', which is nowhere subordinated to a ministry. (State Control authorities doubtless enjoy considerable independence *vis-à-vis* the administrative departments, though not, of course *vis-à-vis* the government.)

[2] Heinig, op. cit., vol. 1, p. 2.

[3] Ibid., p. 42.

conduct of finance, and in particular they give reality to political responsibility.[1]

Questions of finance are questions of power, and from the openness and quality of accountability and control the political fate of a state 'can be read, as if from a barometer'.[2] Heinig contrasts constitutional methods with the alternative of tyranny:

> Dictatorship is poles apart from the constitutional control of finance. If political criticism were permissible it would be a limitation of that power which monopolizes decision. Critical discussion and study of financial administration, its expenditures and receipts, its monetary and credit policies, are equally intolerable to it—or else it is no longer dictatorship. Of course, orderly book-keeping and accountancy are possible under a dictator. Absolutism often insists that revenue be precisely recorded and that the spending authorities keep proper books. Absolute rulers have usually maintained a close check upon their officials. Such control involves no obligation of accountability towards a third party, no duty to submit to an assessment of policies and the success thereof, nor to answer for the object and results of expenditures; it is useless for these purposes. Usurping power is able to count, but it refuses to render account to anyone else.[3]

The budget which is completely under an uncontrolled executive is exposed to all kinds of abuse. It has no real defences against the underground influences of 'the courtiers, the clique, the gang, the lobby clientele, the notables and the favourites. This can be studied from current history.'[4] With Heinig we are seldom far from the edges of the Nazi jungle.

An independent audit, according to Heinig, is 'an essential element of the constitutional and democratic form of the state'.[5] And since the executive is the accountable power, the natural ally of state audit is the legislature.[6] Their collaboration should be as vigorous as possible. 'An audit institution without a legislative echo . . . quickly loses its influence.'[7]

Heinig's views amount to a rather conservative advocacy of the classical budget system, although they must be seen against the background of German administrative history. In Germany

[1] Heinig, op. cit. vol. 1, p. 153.
[2] Ibid., p. 32.
[3] Ibid., p. 37.
[4] Ibid., p. 240.
[5] Ibid., p. 124.
[6] Lecture to the Hochschule für Politik, Berlin, 4 May 1954.
[7] *Das Budget*, vol. 1, p. 83.

the classical system is almost a recent innovation. His opinions do not make any new contribution to the solution of the post-war crisis of accountability, with its specialized problems such as the control of nationalized industries. The solution of some of these very difficult new problems has in fact had to be sought in detachment from the partisanships of the legislature. The audit of French public enterprises by the Commission de vérification is a notable example of a new kind of financial control in a democracy, which is not 'legislative' and which nevertheless offers very worthwhile constitutional guarantees. It would be unfortunate if the impression were given that no independent control of administration is possible otherwise than by Parliament; the independent judiciary is, after all, an ancient form of constitutional control outside the legislature.[1] Modern problems of accountability require an open-minded approach; in some special cases the legislature may not be a practicable channel for accountability and attempts to make it so can lead to complete frustration. The essential democratic interest is that the constitutional and financial security which comes from detailed accountability should exist in some form. As the whole recent experience of the Cour des Comptes shows, an independent audit can make a reasonable job of protecting the public interest even from a position of constitutional autonomy. On the other hand, there exist 'legislative' audit bodies which are dull and unenterprising watchdogs. Attachment to a legislature is not an automatic formula for effective audit; the legislators' ideas concerning the state auditors' functions may be out-of-date.

A strong community of interests between legislatures and state audit may nevertheless exist, as the experience of the English-speaking countries in particular shows. The auditors can provide strong support for legislative power, by holding the administration accountable in detail and providing all kinds of information about what is going on within the governmental machine. Conversely, legislatures can protect the independence and foster the prestige of state audit bodies. Developments in the United States suggest that a close alliance between elected assemblies and state

[1] State audit is itself an older institution than parliaments, a fact which is apt to be forgotten in Britain, where (exceptionally among European countries) historical continuity with the medieval audit body has been almost completely lost, and where (again exceptionally) the legislative assembly has such continuity.

audit, conceived in twentieth rather than nineteenth century terms, may become an important contribution to the restoration of administrative coherence in the age of big government. It may help to solve the crisis of accountability.

The one broad generalization which emerges from the present chapter is, however, that state audit does not *by its fundamental nature* belong necessarily to either legislature or executive. It is a flexible instrument which can and does serve the body politic and the public in a variety of ways. It is not the predestined duty of state audit to serve one particular element in the constitution exclusively but rather to make the best total contribution of which it is capable towards the overall process of government. What constitutes this contribution, and how it may be achieved, are questions of expediency.

Whatever may be the constitutional status of national auditors, their relations with the departments of the executive which they are called upon to audit remain a matter for our consideration.

Face to face with a public authority the auditor has ambivalent motives. On the one hand he is charged with the duties of a controller and is conscious of a relationship of confrontation. He takes legitimate pride in the skill with which he detects and criticizes. He learns from experience that his 'opponents' in the executive do not always put all their cards on the table and that he must be prepared to expose unsound reasoning, spurious excuses and even plain falsehoods. The 'battle of wits' is joined now and then, with results that may be exhilarating and stimulating to both participants. A mild and healthy feeling of antagonism is a spur to vigorous audit and sometimes to vigorous administrative activity also. There is an old view that an auditor's function is merely to threaten with his presence; that control is a façade rather than a serious business anyway, and that what is really desired of the audit (it is never said by whom) is the passive compliance of the rubber-stamp man. This is a dismal heresy; the state auditors should be few but active, not numerous and complaisant. Tonics are composed of strong drugs in small quantities. State audit bodies should not therefore boast overmuch of the excellence of their relations with the executive; it might be concluded that these had become an end in themselves.

On the other hand, executive and audit have to live together and for the latter to incur the former's serious and prolonged displeasure (unless in a very good cause) would be very misplaced strategy. Fortunately the correctives of mutual professional esteem and a sense of humour make it much easier than might be supposed for energetic state auditors to remain on good terms with the officials whose activities they examine. The problem of personal relationships is scarcely a serious one; the state auditor has his job to do and he will not create bad feeling by doing it well. The rare auditor who actually does so is probably a boorish fellow who would antagonize in any circumstances. And some administrative authorities actually welcome the audit as a source of thorough and objective management analysis; an audit which can provide this is more likely to be welcomed than a bumbling 'tick-and-turn-over' group of the old type. Senior administrators all too rarely have time to conduct research into the minutiae and motives of their own duties, and some of them are glad of a talk with the auditors, who have the time. Thus, in general, relationships with the executive are best when the calibre of the auditors is known to be high.

State audit is always in practice to some extent the executive's co-worker, whatever its nominal position in the constitution. For only the executive can ultimately take positive action about matters which come to notice in the course of audit. The legislature, unless it is able to initiate its own legislation to deal with such matters, can only investigate, protest, denounce and recommend; the executive remains the doing part of the constitution. Here lies a basis for co-operation; state audit can help to show it what to do, as well as (more traditionally) what not to do.

Audit observations of the sort which reach the annual reports are often a guide to future action as well as a correction or criticism of what was done before. Budgets are plans, and everyone who makes plans should be anxious to learn how they turned out, especially when he has to make more of them. Budgets are state plans in the financial field, and economic plans of the twentieth century sort might equally be described as budgets in the field of physical production. State audit certainly has a big future role to play as examiner of execution of economic plans, or at least collector of information about them. The auditors in Communist countries already treat the plan as Western auditors have long treated the budget; that is as the yardstick by which to judge actual performance. The service to economic planning has begun in Western countries; in France the activities of the Commissariat

Général au Plan are to some extent based upon the suggestions of the efficiency audit, and it makes use of information about the nationalized industries which comes to light through the Commission de vérification. Executive departments have a long tradition of self-sufficiency, but this is seldom either realistic or adequate in modern circumstances.[1] In some countries the findings from accountability have never been harnessed to serve the planners. But they might well be; and experience is a scarce resource, which can be wasted like any other.

[1] See the comments of Professor Ely Devons on Treasury Control, in *Essays in Economics*, pp. 86–102, London, Allen & Unwin, 1961.

CHAPTER XIII

Some Conclusions

> Between government in the nineteenth century and the government of contemporary societies, the difference is as great as that between the craft of the bone-setter and the technique of modern surgery. . . . The increasingly technical character of political and financial problems poses the fundamental problem of adapting democratic methods to modern needs.
>
> —Maurice Duverger, *Les Finances Publiques*

> The fact is that Parliament and the public are becoming increasingly exasperated by their lack of information from the impregnable fortresses of Whitehall. Unless Parliament can forge some new instrument to inform itself, its control over expenditure, in spite of all the heroic battles of the past, will become increasingly unreal.
>
> —Anthony Sampson, *The Observer*, 19 April 1964

A CONCLUDING chapter is a hazard for both reader and writer. For the reader, because he may be sorely tempted to read this chapter alone, in the hope that it will tell him everything of importance which has gone before; as though an academic study were the same sort of thing as the report of a committee appointed to make practical recommendations upon a specific problem. A hazard also for the writer because, foreseeing the temptation to which his reader will be exposed, he may produce a final chapter which summarizes the rest of his book, and might at a pinch serve as a substitute for it.

That is not, however, the purpose of the present chapter, the scope of which is governed by its title. We shall suggest *some* general conclusions, particularly those which seem to have a topical interest for British public administration. There are other conclusions to be read on or between the lines of the earlier chapters, which will not be reproduced here. Some of them apply to countries other than Britain; it would be presumption on the writer's part to infer much more from their national circumstances, and this chapter does not attempt to do so. Its aspiration is frankly to profit from foreign experience for the benefit of British procedures and institutions. As for the evidence for our conclusions, that is also to be found in previous chapters[1] and may only be outlined or even omitted altogether in the present one. The general facts and theories in our early chapters have scarcely an echo here. Which is to warn that this concluding chapter cannot stand alone. It is a collection of observations on some of the most important questions which have already been discussed, and no more than that.

The approach to this chapter would be much simpler if the general picture which we have already obtained of the various national arrangements for public accountability and state audit were a static one. It would then be possible to present the achievements in this special field of administrative action as the conclusion of a history of progress. It is true that some ingenious innovations of the nineteenth century, such as the relationship between the Comptroller and Auditor General and the Public Accounts Committee, have proved their value with time. It is true also that the development of standards of audit criticism based upon the intrinsic merits of transactions, rather than their mere conformity with regulations, reflects very great credit upon the pioneering work of recent decades. There has been substantial progress and we have endeavoured not to underestimate it. But the problems of financial administration which beset the modern state have grown in size and complexity at a greater rate. There are barriers against public accountability which have not been broken down, and there are those who would even build new barriers. The development of new techniques in state auditing presents both challenges and opportunities which have not yet been taken up. If anything emerges with certainty from our overall picture it is that we are dealing with a situation which is *not* static.

We must, therefore, acknowledge this fact and look tentatively towards the future. The major Western countries have all been confronted with problems which are basically similar, and their varied solutions and expedients constitute the best guide available

[1] In addition, the earlier chapters record certain practical foreign ideas on administrative subjects which do not relate directly to accountability or audit, but which may be of interest to people in this country. (For instance, we noted that Germany was engaged upon an 'attic-clearance' of unwanted old laws; and that in Paris one now pays a combined gas and electricity bill, based upon a single reading of both meters, at either the electricity or the gas office.)

to us. It is customary in the comparative study of methods and institutions to point out that what works successfully in one country would not necessarily do so in another. There is of course some truth in this, but after all, a purely technical invention is likely to function properly in any country, and in the field of administration many new ideas are no more than technical devices. Some, however, have political or constitutional implications, and it is these which require special caution on the part of the country which imports them. In matters of public administration a nation should be receptive of foreign example, although wary; it should seek to learn from its rivals, as a commercial firm learns from its competitors, and partly for similar reasons.

So, against the background of the combined experience of the countries which we have examined, we can now ask ourselves some fundamental questions.

What is the modern need for public accountability?

Nothing has been more characteristic of the twentieth century than the growth of public administrative services and state-sponsored enterprises upon a scale without precedent in all previous history. The public itself, and its elected representatives, need reassurance that these services and enterprises are under control and have not become laws unto themselves. Often little is known about their financial activities, and their own reports are inevitably documents of self-justification rather than confession. There tends to be a deep if unexpressed conflict over the issue of secrecy between the private interests of those in charge and the public interest. The plain truth is that administrators who are able to work in full secrecy have more power than those who are duly answerable for their actions. Secrecy increases power and diminishes responsibility, and a crisis of accountability arises when secrecy is allowed to prevail over an accountable status upheld by law.

The traditional and obvious way, indeed perhaps almost the only way, in which such a situation can be remedied is through the creation or extension of statutory accountability. It has been our view that the most effective form of public accountability is through the medium of an independent state audit, which alone can bring to light and publish the unvarnished truth from the original sources in the records of the organization concerned. Such an audit is not the answer to all ills, but where it is carried out under the protection of statute by conscientious and well chosen state auditors, the public has a reasonable guarantee that serious waste, inefficiency or financial abuse will be disclosed. This is probably the citizen's best defence against the misuse (using the word in its broadest sense) of money taken from his pocket. It is also a valuable if sometimes neglected source of information for those who govern, in both executive and legislature, and for those whose collective views sometimes control those who govern, the general public.

This, rather than the limited nineteenth century objective of 'regularity' in public administration, is the essence of the modern case for public accountability. Without it, the status of those who expend or invest public funds ceases to be that of responsible custodians and inevitably becomes comparable to that of company directors, or even private owners. That such a situation should be allowed to exist at all might seem improbable, if not intolerable. Yet it does exist, and on a wide scale.

The battle of 'regularity', in the advanced countries, has been won these many years. The captured positions must of course be held, but so decisive was the victory that only light covering forces are needed. These must be maintained in perpetuity, but the shock troops of public accountability should set their sights upon new objectives elsewhere.

How does public accountability in Great Britain compare at present with that in other Western countries?

This is a question upon which the evidence seems perfectly clear, at least as far as the *scope*, or *coverage*, of accountability is concerned. The details recorded in earlier chapters strongly support the conclusion that there is *less* public accountability in the United Kingdom than in France, the United States or Federal Germany; and not merely slightly less but very considerably less.

This conclusion may at first sight seem surprising, and it is as well to recall its basis. In France, America and Germany, all state-owned enterprises are subject to some type of independent state audit which publishes critical and sometimes penetrating reports. In Great Britain, the nationalized industries are exempt from anything of the kind. As we noted with some dismay in Chapter XI, the obsession of the political parties with theoretical dogma for and against the principle of nationalization has been instrumental in preventing the solution of this problem, which should be purely a matter of practical administration. The experience of France shows that such a solution is possible, even against a similar background of divided political opinion.

In Britain, accountability to Parliament for the increasingly large sums from central taxation which are confided for various purposes to local authorities is minimal, and the Local Government Act of 1958[1] made matters much worse; whereas in the other countries, or at any rate in France and Germany, such moneys can be followed with relative ease by the national audit bodies, right up to the point of expenditure, and reported upon if necessary. In the United Kingdom again, the universities, which were naturally not subject to public accountability when they were self-supporting, appear determined to retain their immunity now that they are indebted to the state for ever-growing financial support.[2] This is a unique situation. A contemporary authority has rightly discerned a 'mania for secrecy' in British institutions, which 'seriously impedes the possibility of effective *a posteriori* control'.[3]

In Britain, public accountability is ample in some places where national funds are spent (mainly the ministries), and non-existent in others. The proportion of annual expenditures for which no effective accountability exists is large and probably still increasing.

[1] See Chapter X, pp. 294–5, above.

[2] The recent report of the Robbins Committee on Higher Education places great emphasis on the maintenance of the universities' existing immunities, and even recommends that these should later be extended to Colleges of Advanced Technology and Colleges of Education. The only explanation given for this attitude is the familiar one that it protects academic freedom. The present writer appreciates the importance of such freedom, but in his view there is no logical connection between it and an enlightened public accountability. For state auditors to interfere in the academic direction of universities would be as far outside their terms of reference as it would be for them to intervene in the medical direction of hospitals (which, under the National Health Service, *are* subject to public accountability). The Committee state: 'We yield to no one in our condemnation of extravagance in the use of public money and the absence of proper accounting . . .' They would, however, deny the taxpayer his only constitutional safeguard against these and other evils, and this for an annual public expenditure which, on their own computation, will increase from £206 millions in 1962–3 to £742 millions in 1980–1. The Committee, moreover, itself criticizes defects in the administration of certain universities. (Cmnd. 2154, October 1963, paras 612, 725–32 and 752–6.)

[3] Brian Chapman, *British Government Observed*, p. 44. London, Allen & Unwin, 1963.

The position of those who spend public money without having to explain their actions, or even to announce them in any detail, might be likened to that of the lords of those 'liberties and franchises' of the Middle Ages, within which the King's Writ did not run.

It is unfortunately probable that public accountability is most necessary precisely where it does not exist. The recent financial history of British Overseas Airways Corporation, which enjoys the same exemption from accountability to Parliament as the rest of the nationalized industries, seems to furnish a case in point. In the year 1961–2 the Corporation made a loss of £14 millions on operations and at the same time wrote down the book values of its aircraft fleet by no less than £33 millions, bringing its accumulated deficit up to a total of £64 millions. The management criticized the political directives which it had been obliged to follow, as a result of which it had purchased aircraft which were not commercially competitive and sponsored unprofitable airlines overseas. It became clear, however, that the accounting of B.O.A.C. had also been at fault. The Select Committee on Nationalized Industries had noted more than three years previously that the Corporation was not setting aside enough for depreciation by comparison with its competitors. After the publication of the 1961–2 accounts, it was alleged in the House of Lords that B.O.A.C. had attempted in their 1958–9 Report to write down the values of their D.C.7c aircraft, but had been prevented from doing so by the Minister then responsible.[1]

B.O.A.C. were criticized in the technical press on the question of depreciation and also for ordering too many aircraft and failing to disclose enough information in their annual reports about their accrued loss of £14 millions on associated companies.[2] It was said that:

> . . . there can be no excuse for the manner in which the shareholders—Britain's taxpayers—have suddenly been presented with a £33m. bill for obsolete aircraft . . . should not stewardship of public capital have called for franker warning of the immense reckoning that the management must have known was to come? Instead, over the past few years B.O.A.C. have seemed to construe their results to appear better than

[1] Speech by Lord Shackleton, *Hansard*, H. of L., 13 December 1962, cols. 819–20.

[2] *Flight International*, 18 October 1962, Article by the Air Transport editor, pp. 624–5.

they have in fact been. . . . Two other big charges, namely interest on capital and the losses of associated companies, have been presented in a way which has blurred the complete B.O.A.C. financial picture.[1]

It is extremely unlikely that such a situation, whatever its rights and wrongs, could have developed as it did if the Corporation had been answerable to some form of state audit body which could have reported to Parliament, and which, seeing the ominous financial portents, would presumably have done so.

In a debate in the House of Commons on 6 November 1962, the Minister of Aviation said:

> What I cannot accept so easily is that the depreciation in the value of the Corporation's aircraft fleet has only been fully revealed this year. This is not a situation which has come upon us in a night. It has been building up for two or three years past; and in any business efficient management must call for a clear understanding and a clear presentation of the balance sheet.

The Minister then announced that in the previous July he had commissioned a private professional accountant to enquire into B.O.A.C's financial affairs.[2] The subsequent report of this accountant was treated as confidential to the Minister and was not published; it was followed by the unexplained resignations of some members of the board of B.O.A.C. If the known facts pointed to the need for public accountability, the remedy chosen by the Minister did not provide it.[3] But the essential point is that if proper accountability had existed throughout, the crisis might well have been mitigated or even avoided altogether.

This is not the only case which could be cited as concrete evidence that public accountability for the administrators of public funds or investments is an essential for the health of the body politic, the absence of which can on occasions be positively

[1] Ibid., 11 October 1962. Editorial, p. 581.

[2] *Hansard*, 6 November 1962, cols. 814 and 819.

[3] An article, 'Publish and be Damned', *Economist*, 18 May 1963, contained an attack on the Minister for refusing to publish the accountant's report on B.O.A.C. The Minister was said to be following 'two false ideas: first that no embarrassing facts should be published about a £162½ million public investment that is losing money at the fairly consistent rate of £14 million a year; that secondly even if such facts existed, no reputable accountant would draw attention to them if he thought his report was for public eyes. What do the Comptroller and Auditor General and the Public Accounts Committee think about this proposition?'

dangerous. It is some comfort to observe that in the experience of others (for example, the United States after the Government Corporation Control Act of 1945) the extension of accountability is perfectly feasible without the disasters which seem to be envisaged by those who resist it. If the resisters include the Boards of nationalized industries, they might reflect upon the measure of protection which public accountability might give them against the possibility of subjection to improper pressures by Ministers. State audit is not the servant of any Minister, and it might bring the financial consequences of such pressures to public notice.

When we compare accountability in Western countries for its *quality*, or *depth of penetration*, the evidence is rather less than in the case of its *scope*, or *coverage*. A similar sort of comparative picture nevertheless tends to emerge. The question at issue is not the skill of the state auditors but how far they are permitted to go in their investigations; whether, in fact, they are able to consider the elusive but vital problems of administrative efficiency. Such an audit may still be to some extent experimental, but it is an exciting and progressive experiment, whether its studies are based on the organization of work in individual departments or on the conduct of specific administrative operations by all the departments concerned. In America, France and Western Germany the principle of a high-level audit of administrative efficiency has been admitted, put into practice, and encouraged. In the United Kingdom it has not.

Thus, if we admit that effective public accountability, with both wide coverage and deep penetration, is desirable in the general interest, then Great Britain is lagging behind. Each country must strike its own balance of accountability, to provide the safeguards which contemporary opinion considers necessary without impairing the fulfilment of their appointed functions by the accountable organizations. There is no natural or permanent point of balance; the factors which should control the choice are constantly changing, and the choice itself should therefore be revised from time to time. It could scarcely be expected that a balance of accountability which was struck a century ago would be appropriate to the present day. It is time for Britain to redress the balance by reassessing the safeguards of accountability and spreading them over the great organizations which now spend money provided by Parliament, whether by direct appropriation, by grants, or in the form of investments in public enterprise.

Where a new balance should be struck is a large question, but one significant consideration may be put forward here. Newly created bodies, with unprecedented responsibilities, cannot be expected to conform closely to traditional routines and regulations, but this by no means implies (as it has sometimes been taken to imply) that they should therefore be totally exempted from the attentions of the state auditors. What is needed is an impartial audit survey of the activities of such bodies, on the principle that a single page of independent criticism and commentary is often worth more than a hundred pages of self-justification by the management. It may go straight to the most vital problems, whereas the interested person may seek to avoid reference to them altogether. But there is no compelling reason why legislation to establish such a survey would also have to impose all the servitudes of classical Gladstonian finance. The two things are not inseparable, and in suitable cases they should be separated, as they were for the audit of government corporations in the U.S.A. The need is not for uniformity of regulation over the whole varied field of state expenditures, but for comprehensibility, communication and, most of all, for information.

What are the potential new functions and attributes of a state audit body?

The traditional 'regularity' audit, concerned with the *minutiae* of accounts, was the lowest common denominator. All the older audit departments started from that level, and most of them have by their own efforts achieved a discretionary audit, which means that they now can take a critical interest in the major financial activities of governments. The newer audit bodies were founded by statute at about this improved level. Some audit departments, both old and new, have advanced beyond that level and have begun to learn the difficult but increasingly important profession of the efficiency auditor. And in countries which have established a constitutional audit of nationalized corporations and industries, considerable use has been made of the unique skills and experience of the 'regular' state audit staff, even when (as in France) a new auditing body has been created for the purpose.

These are the broad main lines of development. Our main purpose here, however, is to recollect some other useful, if less radical, innovations which we have noted in earlier chapters; all at least worthy of consideration.

Many state audit bodies are charged not merely to criticize, but also, when appropriate, to make recommendations for the rectification of whatever has been subjected to criticism. This may have the effect of increasing the auditors' understanding of the practical problems of administration. It certainly has on occasion drawn attention to the need for reforms, notably in the field of legislation. The detailed examination of the financial consequences of laws and regulations is an extremely valuable function of state audit, provided that there is a rational willingness on the part of governments to amend statutes which have been shown to be defective in operation.

Another thing which the national auditors can do is to advise upon the financial estimates of government departments during their consideration by Finance Ministry or committee of the legislature. This idea, as a regular rather than occasional procedure, comes from Germany. It is likely to augment the prestige of the auditors and add weight to their observations; it may also help to ensure that their detailed first-hand knowledge of ministerial finance is used to the best advantage.

Another conception of state audit service comes from the United States. The General Accounting Office is, in one aspect of its total function, a permanent financial fact-finding bureau, at the disposal of Congressional committees and of individual Senators and Congressmen (who make thousands of enquiries each year). The G.A.O. would have been well able to undertake the sort of investigation which the British Minister of Aviation commissioned from a professional accountant in the B.O.A.C. case. Thus the American legislative branch inclines towards self-sufficiency in financial and accounting skills, and American legislators perhaps tend in consequence to be better informed than their European colleagues about matters affecting the public purse.

In a less immediate way, we are aware that state audit in Communist countries renders yet other services to government. The auditors' duties cover not only financial performance but physical production; they verify that state enterprises have actually fulfilled their norms and collect statistical information upon which norms for future production may be based. In principle, there is no reason why state auditors should not think and criticize in economic as well as financial terms. They could, for example, draw attention in their reports to administrative policies which appear to be in contradiction to accepted economic doctrine; this could be done within either free or planned economies, although the doctrines would be different.[1] The association of the state auditor with the economist is potentially an important development for the future, but this is still perhaps a rather distant future, except in the Communist world, where it already exists.

A practical arrangement which provides a useful model for the present is the simple yet effective element in West German statutes which co-ordinates the activities of the provincial government auditors and the internal auditors of ministries and public enterprises (notably the railways) on the one hand, and those of the state audit body, the Bundesrechnungshof, on the other. This central authority, with its constitutional reporting responsibilities, can call for information from the other audit bodies or request them to look into specific matters, and conduct joint investigations with them if desired; though only when central government funds are concerned. In an era when enormous sums from central taxation are everywhere entrusted to decentralized authorities, an auditing network such as the German one seems both reasonable and necessary. Without one, it is inevitably difficult or impossible to find out what happens to grants for decentralized expenditure. A co-operative pattern of audit, with a statutory basis, has therefore everything to commend it.

This is by no means a comprehensive list of the ideas which can be gleaned from the varied laws and procedures of national audit bodies. Many more are recorded in earlier chapters. For example, in Chapter X we drew attention to a selection of devices embedded in the legislation of several countries for the protection of the independence of their state auditors against even the most subtle pressures which might otherwise be applied by the executive. These deserve careful consideration.

The most remarkable and valuable innovations of all are those which have made it possible for the French, the Americans and the Germans to get to grips with the formidable problems of providing a constitutional audit for nationalized industries and an efficiency audit for government departments. For instance, the

[1] As a possible example, economists everywhere have condemned 'stop-go' financial policies in recent years. The detailed financial and administrative consequences of such policies could be a concern of state audit, even in countries with liberal economies. The auditor could also assist the economist interested in 'cost/effectiveness studies' as a guide to social policy, or the statistician. So long as he remains remote from the executive decision-making process, the auditor can indulge in a variety of fact-finding activities without prejudicing his independence.

Cour des Comptes, chameleon-like, transformed itself into the Commission de vérification des comptes des Entreprises Publiques[1] for the first purpose, and the Comité Central d'Enquête sur le cout et le rendement des services publics[2] for the second. These were not mere changes of name but adaptations of organization, staffing and procedure which made possible what would otherwise have been impossible. The Government Corporation Control Act, 1945,[3] in the U.S.A., was a happy solution of an intractable problem; how to harmonize the numerous and powerful corporations created during the New Deal and the Second World War with the federal administrative structure. A vital element in the solution was the establishment of an external audit of the corporations by the General Accounting Office. For the purposes of efficiency audit, the chief state auditor of Western Germany, the President of the Bundesrechnungshof, assumes a separate role, that of Federal Commissioner for Efficiency in the Administration,[4] with different staff and working methods. We observe once more that where traditional methods and institutions are scarcely appropriate for an unprecedented task, there may be a happy compromise between the creation of entirely new and costly bodies and a decision to treat the task as impracticable and do nothing whatever. The solution may be found in an ingenious adaptation of what already exists.

This is not the place for a full account of how these countries have adapted their institutions. The story is a long one, and the essentials of it have been told in Chapters IX and XI.

What are the desirable qualifications and qualities of state auditors?

The answers to this question suggest that a good deal of hard thinking about these matters remains to be done in more than one country.

The subject of qualifications is a difficult one. We found that there was no common pattern. The General Accounting Office now recruits only college graduates of good calibre who have 'majored' in accounting; it then encourages them to qualify as Certified Public Accountants. The European tradition, on the other hand, does not accept the dominance of the qualified accountant, whose training is considered, rightly or wrongly, to be rooted firmly in commercial requirements and largely irrelevant

[1] See Chapter XI, pp. 335–54.
[2] See Chapter IX, pp. 221–38.
[3] See Chapter XI, pp. 314–19.
[4] See Chapter IX, pp. 238–51.

to the different problems of government. The Bundesrechnungshof recruits graduate jurists, some of whom are qualified as judges, for its directing grades; for the actual work of audit it 'imports' fairly senior staff from the ministries and uses them as far as possible to examine the accounts of their parent departments. The French Cour des Comptes appoints some of the most successful graduates of the Ecole Nationale d'Administration, with a status markedly higher than that of the senior grades in the ministries. In the United Kingdom, the Exchequer and Audit Department has not hitherto sought to recruit either professional men or graduates. It accepts allocations of staff either from the open Executive Class examinations for the civil service as a whole, or by promotion from the general ranks of the Clerical Class, without preference for any educational qualifications in particular.

The career status of the national auditors is naturally related to recruitment standards. The General Accounting Office offers careers which are comparable to the best in the great executive branch departments. The Bundesrechnungshof maintains an establishment which is fixed by law on the same general levels as that of a ministry, and it employs about 90 persons in the highest class of the German civil service. The 'magistrates' who comprise the audit staff of the Cour des Comptes are a *grand corps*, which means in British parlance that their status and career-prospects are 'super-Administrative Class'. These three audit bodies are therefore in accord, to the extent that the careers which they provide are at least as good as those offered in the top grades of the ministries, and in the French case better. This is sometimes thought of as a matter of principle; the controllers should, for reasons of efficiency as well as logic, be at least the equivalents in rank of those whose policies they examine and criticize. Britain forms an exception. The Exchequer and Audit Department contains no members of the highest category of the civil service, the Administrative Class, except the Comptroller and Auditor General (who is appointed from outside the audit department).

It remains to add a note about personal qualities. This must be a general assessment, applicable to all. It is as impossible as it would be invidious to say who has the best state auditors. And the qualities desirable in an auditor have changed greatly since the days of the 'tick-and-turn-over' audit, the simple check against regulations.

The modern state auditor should have a taste for patient,

thorough and imaginative study, because that is a major part of what he will have to undertake. If he is assigned to cover a major project (a pension scheme, the construction of an airfield, the design and development of a new warship, aircraft or tank, an international agreement involving finance, or whatever else it might be), he must seek to find fault with the actions of the responsible department. That is his duty. To perform it effectively, he must pursue his investigations until he almost literally knows more about the matter than the officials who supervise it in the ministry concerned. How else can he detect error and build up a case to prove it? He cannot afford to overlook anything; if he does he may raise an observation which lacks foundation. His documentation of a case must be comprehensive. The best state audit work of this kind is probably not inferior in intellectual difficulty to any other administrative work whatsoever. Its stamp and method are those of scholarly research. A major audit observation such as the so-called 'Ferranti case' of 1964 may, with its repercussions, be of nothing less than national importance. Such cases by no means disclose themselves. They have to be assiduously sought out, and there is no formula for finding them and following them up except the personal brilliance and initiative of the auditors directly concerned at the source.[1]

The state auditor therefore requires a keen and active mind. He must be a man of parts, with an extensive general knowledge, since he will be confronted with many different varieties of administrative activity. If his particular educational or professional specialization is an important consideration, it is definitely subordinate to that.

He will, rightly, receive no powers of direction over the rest of the administration. If his status is adequate, his circle of contacts in the audited department will include the best informed people, and his enquiries will be speedier and more effective in consequence. As for respect and influence, these he must himself earn, by tact and understanding as well as by critical zeal. The state auditor should have sense of mission and a feeling for the public

[1] For the 'Ferranti case' see Chapter VIII, p. 177. During a debate on this case in the House of Commons on 30 July 1964, the Chancellor of the Exchequer, Mr Maudling, described the discovery of the original audit observation as 'a very ingenious and effective piece of work'. Mr Harold Wilson called it 'a particular and very welcome success . . . due to the *ex post facto* vigilance of a small number of public servants . . .' (*Hansard*, 30 July 1964, cols. 1804 and 1859).

interest, but he must also learn to appreciate the administrator's point of view.

The presence of such lively auditors, always in modest numbers and with no powers except the right of access to information, will prove a stimulus to rather than a drag upon the departments which they audit. They will ensure that the established values and *idées fixes* of administration are occasionally queried and criticized independently. They will try to avoid criticism which is merely petty or hampering or wise-after-the-event, and will concentrate upon genuine weaknesses of policy or system. It may be that when state audit has deservedly acquired a new popular 'image', the psychological resistance to public accountability will gradually melt away.

A Royal Commission on public accountability?

The year 1966 will be the centenary of the original Exchequer and Audit Departments Act, which remains the cornerstone of the British system of public accounting and audit. This will, in accordance with a sort of undeclared tradition, provide an appropriate occasion for a review of the changed situation in which the Act still operates. As we have seen, a crisis of public accountability has arisen in recent decades and remains unsolved; some of its component problems are even becoming more acute. As we have also seen, there is scope and example for a modernization of the state audit service, which would leave its foundations wholly intact. Our evidence seems to indicate that the need for a broad and thorough review is very real.

The Exchequer and Audit Department achieved its half-century in 1916, and in 1920, when the administrative distractions of the First World War were at an end, a Committee on the E. & A.D. Act, 1866, was appointed. Mr F. D. Acland, M.P., was its Chairman, and one of the other two members was the Comptroller and Auditor General. The Committee recommended[1] various amendments of the 1866 Act, to bring the law into line with recent practice in such matters as test-auditing and the audit of trading accounts, store accounts and accounts of revenue receipts. The outcome of these recommendations was the E. & A.D. Act, 1921. But the Committee did not go beyond the consideration of audit as then actually practised, and it declined to suggest any radical

[1] Report of the Committee appointed to consider the provisions of the Exchequer and Audit Departments Act, 1866 (Cmd. 1383), 1921.

change.[1] Britain has not, in fact, produced any real statutory innovations in the field of accountability and audit since 1866. There has been no counterpart to the American legislation of 1921, 1945 and 1950, nor to the remarkable French laws and decrees of 1946—8.

There is scope on the occasion of the forthcoming centenary for further amending legislation to bring the state auditors' terms of reference up to the level of actual current practice, as was done in 1921. The statutory standard of audit is still one of 'regularity' only, although this limitation has in fact been left far behind for at least a quarter of a century. But there is a far greater need for a profound survey of the whole field of public accountability and audit in the United Kingdom, for which a Royal Commission or other broadly qualified body would seem to be appropriate.

There is a great deal for such a Commission to discuss, as we have already seen. The country urgently needs a coherent pattern of public accountability. Parliament needs a restorative for its dignity as sovereign in matters of finance.[2] The executive needs to know more about what is achieved with the money it disburses. The public has a growing interest in the efficient use of taxation. The state auditors need a directive for the future rather than a new law which merely accepts the present. The prime task for the members of a Commission would be to consider the conspicuous *lacunae* in public accountability, and above all to propose a solution for the stubborn problem of the nationalized industries, rendering them at last properly accountable to the state which provides their capital and bears their losses. The examples of France and the U.S.A. at least show that this is not an impossibility. There are other conspicuous gaps in accountability which need to be bridged, and a Commission might wish to consider whether a general principle of 'no subsidy without accountability' should be proclaimed as a fundamental tenet of public administration. This principle, as a kind of taxpayers' basic right, seems to have won tacit acceptance already, everywhere except in these islands. It

[1] Cmd. 1383, 1921, para. 3.

[2] 'Improvement is certainly needed. For as one looks back at the uncounted millions which Governments (always with the best of motives) have squandered since the war it is not difficult to lay the blame at the feet of the House of Commons. The charge against it is that it has clung to old procedural forms which no longer grip the matters they were designed to control.' (Andrew Hill and Anthony Whichelow: *What's Wrong with Parliament?*, p. 28, Penguin Books, 1964).

would be much more than a mere slogan; a shield against crises of accountability in the future.

As a question of comparable interest, though perhaps of rather less immediacy, a Commission might choose to discuss the pros and cons of a high-level efficiency audit[1] and the bases upon which such a thing could be organized.

A revision of the Exchequer and Audit Departments Acts, taking into account both work and personnel, would automatically be on the agenda. The members of a Commission could compare the tasks facing a modern state audit body with the far simpler assignment of a century ago, and then consider whether this is now one of those under-endowed public services to which attention has been drawn by Edouard Bonnefous.[2] Two specific points can be added. Firstly, it seems outside the limits of probability that a Commission would feel the need to change the well-tried prerogatives of the Comptroller and Auditor General, except perhaps to strengthen them. In the second place, a Commission might do well to consider the title of the Exchequer and Audit Department. After nearly a century, this is still mystifying to the uninitiated, and experienced auditors can testify that these include some people within the public service itself. A title such as National Audit Department or State Audit Office would be far more comprehensible, and would thus be a practical asset to auditors 'in the field,' relieving them of the need to explain who and what they are. The well-known title of the C. & A.G. need not be compromised by such a change; indeed the name, 'Office of the Comptroller and Auditor General' might be the best solution to this problem.

* * * *

The time is long past when it was sufficient to conclude that British administrative institutions were the best in the world, merely because they were British. They were designed in and for the classic age of parliamentary finance, and it may be that in the

[1] For an examination of the concept of an efficiency audit, see Chapter IX above.

[2] See Chapter IX, p. 197, above.

classic period the value judgment was justified. The feeling of superiority in any case existed; it was at once a source of satisfaction and a barrier to further change. We may recall Professor Millett's dictum that a consciousness of perfection within administrative bodies usually coincides with a period of stagnation.[1]

To have the best public service in the world is nevertheless a high and legitimate aspiration. It is, however, no longer possible for serious students to believe that it can be more than an aspiration in the absence of a spirit of progress and adaptation. We are told by Professor Chapman that, 'the institutions of British Government have been signally unsuccessful in keeping pace with the modern world',[2] and this view is widely shared by other academic observers. Our own conclusions about public accountability appear to support it.

The truth may be that the best civil administration in the world is no longer the one which most nearly approaches to certain theoretical ideals, but the one which, in a rapidly changing era, is most sensitive to change and most ready to adapt itself to it. We pay willing lip-service to the principle of experiment in the physical sciences, but we have in practice rejected it for the administrative sciences. It is fitting to end this book with a plea for a new spirit of experiment in the field of public administration and finance. Administration has, with some reason, been called 'the key to English historical development'.[3] A period of change for the public services seems in any case inevitable; it is better that the main impulse should come from the inside.

Experiment implies an atmosphere open to new ideas and constructive debate. It is difficult to think of anything which could do more to generate administrative ideas and debate than the establishment of an efficiency audit on the highest level. The extension of accountability to the nationalized industries would also be an exciting experiment, and many things would eventually become known about this vital sector of national life which are at present unknown. It must not be pretended that we know precisely how best to achieve these objectives in the British context. We should be prepared for a certain amount of trial and error. But foreign example, even if often imperfect, gives us some assurance that solutions are attainable.

[1] Chapter IX, p. 253, above.

[2] Chapman, *British Government Observed*, p. 7.

[3] Paul Johnson, in the *New Statesman*, 1 November 1963, p. 619.

For nearly a century the state auditors of the United Kingdom have rendered good and faithful service, bringing order and regularity (if not yet always efficiency) into the financial activities of the ministries. There is now much more for them to do, but until the law so directs they cannot do it, and those responsible for financial policy might now do well to take note of the fact that they could be at least as imaginatively and comprehensively served by their auditors as the boards of the most progressive firms may now expect to be, and as some foreign governments evidently are. This does not depend upon the creation of big 'empires'; the state auditors can feel a legitimate pride in the fact that few if any other branches of the public services have so effectively resisted the dictates of Parkinson's law. This is a field that depends upon quality rather than numbers.

Each recent century in English history has produced its administrative revolution. The seventeenth century curbed the Royal Prerogative and excluded the Episcopate and the Judiciary from the administrative machine. The achievement of the eighteenth century, associated with Edmund Burke and the Economical Reform movement, was to reduce gross corruption amongst office holders, together with its associated inefficiencies. The nineteenth century introduced professionalization, through a standard recruitment procedure for civil servants. It also established the 'classical' system of financial control and accounting, geared to the authorization of expenditures by Parliament.

The twentieth century has not yet made its mark, despite the arrival of 'big government'. The machine of state administration is still, in its essentials, classical Gladstonian. But those who keep an ear to the ground can now detect the rumbles of approaching change.[1] We predicted in Chapter IX that change will bring with it some new and exciting tasks for civil servants. There will be changes in structure and recruitment, required both by social evolution and to fit a new conception of the administrator's role; perhaps also as a complement to reforms in parliamentary procedures. Our basic concern here has been to ensure that when the time for change is really ripe (and that may not be long now), the importance of public accountability to administration as a whole is not overlooked. We have pictured it as a factor which, when properly understood, makes for efficiency rather than reduces it.

[1] '. . . there is, everywhere, a widespread feeling that it is time for our institutions to reform themselves', Hill and Whichelow, op. cit., p. 95.

But accountability is also a purifying element; a constant reminder that government and administration are not activities intended solely for the benefit of those who practise them—a simple fact, but one which, Heaven knows, it is easy to forget.

Index